Ronald O. Moore
-1 June 1977-

W9-BKT-946

The rise of the entrepreneur

J. W. GOUGH

EMERITUS FELLOW OF ORIEL COLLEGE, OXFORD

The rise of the entrepreneur

B. T. BATSFORD LTD | LONDON

B. T. Batsford Ltd, 4 Fitzhardinge St, London W1
Printed in Great Britain by Willmer Bros Ltd, Birkenhead
and bound by William Brendon & Son Ltd, Tiptree
Set in 10/12pt Linotype Pilgrim
Copyright © J. W. Gough 1969
First published in 1969
7134 1357 3

BY THE SAME AUTHOR

The Mines of Mendip, Clarendon Press, 1930; 2nd ed., David & Charles, 1967
The Superlative Prodigall: a Life of Thomas Bushell, Arrowsmith, 1932
The Social Contract, Clarendon Press, 1936; 2nd ed., 1957
John Locke's Political Philosophy, Clarendon Press, 1950; corrected re-issue, 1956
Fundamental Law in English Constitutional History, Clarendon Press, 1950; corrected reissue, 1961
Sir Hugh Myddelton, Entrepreneur and Engineer, Clarendon Press, 1964

EDITED BY J. W. GOUGH

Mendip Mines and Forest Bounds, Somerset Record Society, 1931
John Locke, Second Treatise of Government and a Letter concerning Toleration, Blackwell's Political Texts, 1946; 3rd ed., 1966
(with R. Klibansky), *John Locke, Epistola de Tolerantia: a Letter on Toleration*, Clarendon Press, 1968

Contents

4 | Iron and steel

5 | Copper and brass

6 | Tin and lead

7 | Gold and silver, and three notable entrepreneurs

12 | Draining the fens

13 | Land and water

Conclusion

Preface

The title of this book was suggested by the publishers, and before writing it I had first of all to decide who the entrepreneurs who rose were, and also why and when they rose. I tried to work out an answer to these questions in the opening chapter, and came to the conclusion that I should be concerned in the remainder of the book with the economic expansion which took place in England between about the middle of the sixteenth and the middle of the seventeenth century. Apart from developments in the old-established cloth industry, and some changes and improvements in transport and the use of land, much of my attention would be concentrated on the growth of the extractive industries and the introduction of some new manufacturing processes. There are monographs and articles in periodicals on all these topics, and I have drawn on them freely. I give references to my sources of information in the notes at the end of the book, and it did not seem necessary to compile a bibliography as well, as this would not serve the purpose of a guide to further reading, but would simply be an alphabetical rearrangement of the titles already mentioned in the notes.

In a few cases (e.g. in Chapter 7) I have treated my subjects biographically, but with most of them it seemed best to set an account of their activities within a description of the industries in which they were engaged, and the division into chapters is arranged accordingly. The entrepreneurs included in each chapter are, of course, only a selection from among a much larger possible number, and in so far as the deciding factor was the accessibility of information, the choice of examples may to some extent be arbitrary, but I hope I have not omitted any really outstanding figures.

I am only concerned with the rise of the entrepreneur in England

and Wales, though I also refer occasionally to Scotland and Ireland. At the opening of my period Britain was industrially backward in comparison with countries such as Flanders or southern Germany, and the rise of the entrepreneur in Britain cannot really be isolated from that of his counterpart abroad. But though entrepreneurs were playing an important part in the economic development of other parts of Europe, these must lie outside the scope of this book, except (and it is an important exception) in so far as foreign immigrants, some coming as refugees, some in response to invitation, some with an eye to money-making, were the means by which new industries, or new processes in old industries, were introduced into England. For a recent discussion of the role of the entrepreneur in a European setting I would refer the reader to the opening essay in Professor H. R. Trevor-Roper's *Religion, the Reformation, and Social Change* (Macmillan, 1967). Finally, I am glad to record my gratitude to Sir George Clark, who over a period of some months read my successive chapters in typescript, and made a number of helpful criticisms and suggestions for their improvement.

J.W.G.

Oxford

| The making of the entrepreneur

As the initiators and directors of production, entrepreneurs have played a leading part in the economic life of Britain for over 400 years; but it is only comparatively recently that they have been known by that name. The *Oxford English Dictionary*, of which the volume for the letter E was published in 1897, defined 'Entrepreneur' simply as 'The director or manager of a public musical institution: one who "gets up" entertainments, especially musical performances'. Not until its *Supplement* appeared in 1933 did the dictionary recognize that the word had a place in the business as well as in the entertainment world, and could also mean 'one who undertakes an enterprise: especially a contractor ... acting as intermediary between capital and labour'. There was indeed a considerable time-lag between the use of the word in this economic sense and its recognition in the dictionary, for the first quotation given in the *Supplement* is from F. A. Walker's *Brief Text-Book of Political Economy*, published as long ago as 1885, 12 years before the appearance of the original edition of the dictionary itself.

Here we read that the control and direction of capital and labour are so difficult that 'a distinct class is called into being, in all industrially advanced communities, to undertake that function. This class is known as the employing class, or, to adopt a word from the French, the *entrepreneur* class'.[1] Six years later another writer, R. T. Ely, still felt that he must explain why he found it necessary to import a French word. 'The one who manages business for himself was formerly called an undertaker or adventurer, but the first word has been appropriated by one small class of business men and the latter has acquired a new meaning, carrying with it implications of rashness and even dishonesty. We have consequently been obliged to resort to the French language for a word to designate

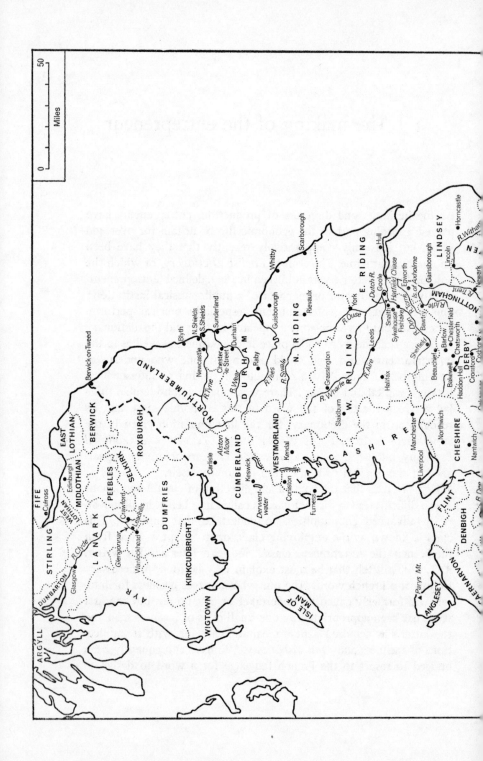

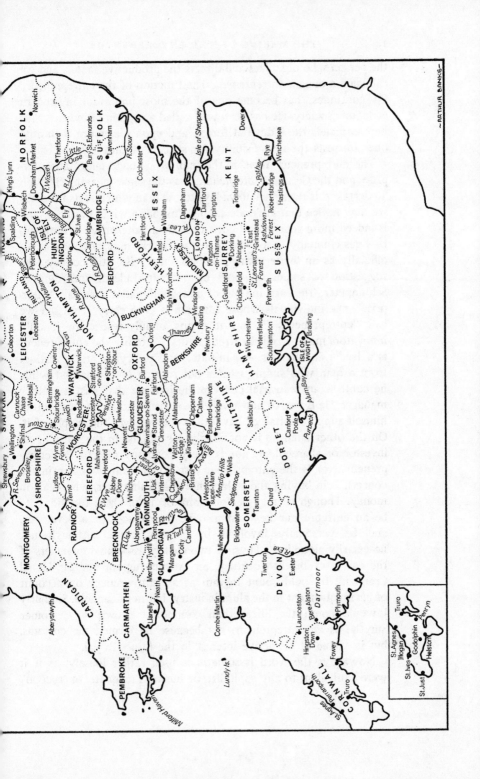

the person who organizes and directs the productive factor, and we call such a one an *entrepreneur*. The function of the entrepreneur,' Ely continues, 'has become one of the most important in modern economic society. He has been well called a captain of industry, for he commands the industrial forces, and upon him more than any-one else rests the responsibility for success or failure.'[2]

The entrepreneur, then, is the man who 'undertakes' an enter-prise, and the German *Unternehmer* has the same meaning. Though 'undertaker' is restricted nowadays to the man who directs funerals, we may notice that an 'undertaking' still has a wider meaning, and is indeed more general and colourless than 'enterprise'. A national-ized gas company or a municipal waterworks may now be known officially as an 'undertaking', but an 'enterprise' still conveys the suggestion of something bold or difficult. Indeed, according to Schumpeter, 'the carrying out of new combinations we call "enter-prise"; the individuals whose function it is to carry them out we call "entrepreneurs"'[3]; but it seems unduly restrictive if only innovators may be called entrepreneurs. Certainly the entrepreneur is a leader in business—an initiator and policymaker, as distinct from a man who simply carries out routine functions. But while he controls an industrial concern, he is more than just a factory manager. He is not, or not simply, a salaried official: he must either himself supply capital, or have some control over the supply of it. On the other hand he is not simply a capitalist in the sense of an investor or shareholder, nor is every company director an entre-preneur. Nor is the entrepreneur just a merchant, whose primary concern is in buying and selling, nor just a financier, who deals in money. Though he may perform any or all of these functions, to be an entrepreneur he must also be a producer or a developer, and be personally involved in his enterprise, although not necessarily alone in it. Thus, of two closely associated financiers of the early seventeenth century, Sir Arthur Ingram and Sir Lionel Cranfield, I would count Ingram as an entrepreneur on account of his involvement in the alum industry, but not Cranfield. Similarly I would count the Elizabethan commonly known as Customer Smythe as an entrepreneur, not because he farmed the customs, but in virtue of his active interest in the Mines Royal.

Nowadays the word is sometimes used rather loosely, as if it were equivalent to any capitalist, or business magnate, or 'tycoon'.

In their preface to the collection of essays entitled *The Entrepreneur*,[4] Professors Postan and Habakkuk described their subject as
'commercial and industrial undertakings considered mainly from
the point of view of the men who initiated or directed them'. This
seems rather too wide a definition, at any rate for the purposes of
this book. It would be hard to say precisely when commercial
undertakings had their beginning, unless one simply adopted
a Marxist interpretation of history and used that to pinpoint the
transition from a 'feudal' to a 'bourgeois' economy. It will be more
practicable to confine our attention, or at any rate our main attention, to industrial enterprise rather than include commercial enterprise in general, and with this more restricted meaning of the word,
what falls within and what outside our subject will be reasonably
plain. The period which Professor Trevor-Roper has called
'Tawney's century'[5]—the century between the Dissolution of the
Monasteries and the Great Rebellion, roughly from 1540 to 1640—
has been adopted in recent years by a number of historians, who
have recognized in it a crucial period of economic growth in
England, and we too shall find it appropriate in setting bounds to
our search for the rise of the entrepreneur.

A word frequently used in that age to denote the type of man
we are concerned with was 'projector'. In the persons of Ben
Jonson's Meercraft[6] and his like the word acquired a bad sense,
but the projector was not necessarily a villain, and in conveying
the sense of a man with a 'project' to carry out, it often corresponded with what is now meant by an entrepreneur. Undoubtedly
we could find some men in an earlier age who might be described
as entrepreneurs, some sectors of trade or industry already organized with a structure in which entrepreneurship could develop. But
generally speaking, these were exceptional rather than usual, and
if not exactly rare, they could scarcely be regarded as normal or
common. Between about 1540 and 1640, however, there was a
striking expansion both of trade, domestic and foreign, and of
industry, including the development of a variety of new manufac-
tures and processes, which were very largely the creation of projectors or entrepreneurs.

The significance of this expansion has been a matter of
controversy. Professor J. U. Nef saw it as an Industrial Revolution
more truly deserving to be so called than the more famous develop-

ments in industry in the late eighteenth and early nineteenth centuries.[7] This is an exaggeration, and it has been suggested that one reason why so much has been written about this period is that the kind of records sought by economic historians become more prolific in the sixteenth century, and create a misleading impression of expansion.[8] There may be something to this point, but it must also be true that new activities give rise to new records. Be that as it may, even when the most is made of technological development and industrial expansion in this period, the fact remains that only a small proportion of the whole employed population was affected by it, and this must throw doubt on the appropriateness of applying the term 'Industrial Revolution' to the sixteenth century.

On the other hand we may notice one feature which the sixteenth century had in common with the eighteenth. This was the harnessing of mechanical power, water power in the sixteenth, steam in the eighteenth century. Of course the use of water power in the sixteenth century was not new in the same way as the invention of the steam engine. There were water mills in the Middle Ages, bellows and hammers worked by water-wheels before the end of the fifteenth century; but in the sixteenth century water power began to be used more efficiently and extensively than before. Overshot water-wheels, illustrated in Agricola's *De Re Metallica*, published in 1556, were in use in Germany before they became known in England, and marked a considerable technological advance. At the same time they were more expensive to instal than the older undershot wheels, because they necessitated dams and artificial channels for the water. These wheels were widely used, not only for bellows and hammers at blast furnaces and ironworks, but also to work pumps for draining mines, stamps for crushing ores, and a variety of other mechanical devices. All these developments involved capital outlay on a larger scale than in the past, and called for the activity of entrepreneurs.

This use of water power undoubtedly helped to make the sixteenth century an age of striking industrial advance, though it is questionable whether it can be called one of revolution. More recently, indeed, Professor Nef seems to have withdrawn his claim for the revolutionary character of the innovations in sixteenth-century industry, and has suggested that more important than the introduction of technical inventions was a movement towards mass production—'a concentration of industrial enterprise upon the production of cheap commodities in large quantities'.[9] E. J. Hobsbawm made the same point in stressing the importance of a change from 'production for the maximum profit per unit sale' to 'production for the greatest aggregate profit—large profits, but not necessarily large profits per sale'. Hobsbawm also suggested that if the term 'Industrial Revolution' was to be used of any country in the early modern period, it could be applied, more appropriately than to sixteenth-century England, to Germany in the years 1450 to 1520, which saw the invention of 'the printing-press, effective fire-arms, watches, and the remarkable advance in mining and metallurgy summarized in Agricola's De Re Metallica.'[10] George Unwin indeed actually inquired why there was no industrial revolution in England in the sixteenth and seventeenth centuries, and found the answer in 'the feverish delusions of speculation and the selfish greed of monopoly', by which 'the triumph of honest enterprise was overshadowed'.[11] We shall come to monopolies shortly.

The Oxford Dictionary Supplement gave as one of the meanings of entrepreneur 'a contractor acting as intermediary between capital and labour', adding that he might be either an individual or a corporation. In view of the quotations given in support of this definition we cannot deny that the word is so used nowadays. Nevertheless, although the Elizabethans invented joint-stock companies, one doubts whether the activities of corporations were what was typical of entrepreneurship in that age (or for that matter in the eighteenth and early nineteenth centuries), or whether the entrepreneur was an intermediary. More characteristically, it seems, the entrepreneur was the individual whose energy, and willingness to assume risks and responsibilities, enabled an enterprise to be launched. It was in this way that the entrepreneur was the typical leader of the Industrial Revolution. He might indeed work in partnership with others, or found and organize a company or corporation, but it was he personally who dominated it; to his energy and expertise, if it was successful, it owed its success. Men like John D. Rockefeller, Henry Ford or W. R. Morris (Lord Nuffield), span the century down to our own time; but now, according to Professor J. K. Galbraith, the development of the huge modern industrial corporation spells the demise of the pioneering

B

entrepreneur.[12] 'The central event of the Industrial Revolution', it has been well said, 'was the novel handling of resources by individuals', and if this was true of the eighteenth century, it was equally true of the sixteenth. Here lies the role of the entrepreneur. 'He is the starter of enterprises, the man who puts new firms and industries upon their feet. His function is to shoulder the risks and uncertainty which attach to using economic resources in a new way.' But 'industries and firms cannot always be new. At some point or other, the organizer of the new concern must hand over . . . to the administrator and manager. This is perhaps a sign that the Industrial Revolution in that industry is past.'[13]

It may also be a valuable clue to the role of the entrepreneur. To emphasize thus the individual's share in making history may appear to be taking sides in the stale old controversy about the respective importance of men and movements. Of course the Industrial Revolution, whether we are thinking of the sixteenth and seventeenth, or of the eighteenth and nineteenth centuries, was not the only age in which potential entrepreneurs were born; but it was only under suitable conditions that their special talents could find expression. Very likely, in an age when conditions were favourable, if there had been no Henry Ford, someone else would have made cheap motor-cars. But not, surely, quite in the way Henry Ford did; and in an earlier century not even Henry Ford could have made them. Nobody but Napoleon could have done exactly what Napoleon did, nor would Napoleon's career have been what it was had he lived in a different age. So if we ask why the sixteenth century saw the rise of projectors or entrepreneurs, the answer must surely be found in the conditions that made that century favourable to economic expansion.

When production was carried on on a relatively small scale, for limited markets, with little or no division of labour, and only the simplest, if any, machinery; when a craftsman, working with only hand tools, made the whole of an article, there was little room for the entrepreneur. But when power-driven machinery was introduced, when a considerable number of workers were assembled in a factory or a mine, when the processes of manufacture became more complex and more divided, when the products must be distributed for sale over distant markets, then the entrepreneur was needed and found his opportunity. To this extent, at least, technology was an essential aspect of the position. The entrepreneur had not only to manage his factory or mine, in the sense of allocating work and enforcing discipline among his labourers; he might indeed hire a paid manager to do this for him. He must also have some technical knowledge, and be able to plan and control the whole process of production, adapting it when necessary to changing needs and conditions. He might be—in early times perhaps he often was—the actual inventor of a new process, but he need not himself be a technician if he could exploit the inventiveness of others. He must, of course, have capital at his command, because without it his undertaking could not even be begun. Above all he must be able to make decisions and take responsibility: not only to organize production but to decide 'what shall be made, after what patterns, in what quantities, at what times; to whom the product shall be sold, at what prices, and on what terms of payment'.[14] Here is where the personal genius of the entrepreneur makes itself felt. There are thousands of men who can obey instructions and carry out a plan, but only he could have devised it. Without his assistants and subordinates his plan would indeed be stillborn. But they for their part 'would have been wholly helpless and amazed in the presence of the exigencies, the difficulties, the dangers, which only arouse the spirit of the master, stimulate his faculties, and afford him the keenest zest of enjoyment'.[15]

If personal enterprise and personal involvement are of the essence of entrepreneurship, this, in part at any rate, is because it is his own fortune, his own capital, that the entrepreneur places at risk. To call him an 'intermediary' between capital and labour suggests the salaried official, the modern 'personnel manager', rather than the genuine entrepreneur. Of course the capital he stakes need not, probably will not, be all his own. He will have partners, or fellow 'adventurers', as they would be called in Tudor times, if he has inaugurated a joint-stock company; indeed, part of his entrepreneurship may be to induce others to participate in his enterprise. But the archetypal entrepreneur is not only the man of initiative, but the man who 'runs his own show'.

In the sixteenth and seventeenth centuries the usual method by which he sought to do this was by securing a grant of monopoly rights. Patents of monopoly (of manufacture to begin with: monopoly of selling was a later feature) were first introduced into

England from Italy about the middle of the sixteenth century, and at first, no doubt, were intended to encourage genuine inventors.[16] Projectors were eager to develop some new process or invention, the government was anxious to promote new industries, or the introduction from abroad of processes new to England, especially when, as in the case of the mining and metallurgical industries, or the manufacture of gunpowder, it was hoped that they would not only bring economic benefits but also enable the nation to become its own producer of vital military supplies. Often a clause in the patent for a process introduced from abroad bound the patentee to employ a number of English subjects and teach them to operate it. During the first decade or so of the Elizabethan period the patents granted could be justified on these lines, but the system was readily open to abuse, abuses soon began to creep in, and became more and more prevalent.[17] Applicants for patent rights regularly claimed that, by their inventiveness and skill, some process or device had been, or would be, not only initiated, but 'brought to perfection'. These visions of finality were chimerical, and this form of claim could easily be applied to trifling modifications of existing processes, especially before the law required precise and detailed specification. This opened the way for the extension of monopolies to industries which were not new, or which had no proper claim to protection from foreign competition. In an age of personal monarchy, influence at Court was inevitably an important factor in securing the grant of privileges of any kind, and unscrupulous courtiers and their capitalist hangers-on soon found in monopoly a convenient way of enriching themselves. Further, since in return for granting a patent of monopoly the Crown demanded a royalty or rent, there was an obvious temptation for needy monarchs to regard monopolies as a means not only of satisfying greedy courtiers but also of increasing their own revenues. Since the result was that prices rose without any improvement, but rather a deterioration, in the quality of the article produced, monopolies naturally aroused public complaints.

By the end of Elizabeth's reign the whole system was becoming so notorious an abuse, in the hands of courtiers and others, many of whom were mere speculators and swindlers, that it provoked determined opposition in Parliament. Though the Queen promised redress and withdrew some of the monopolies, abuses soon returned.[18] James indeed deliberately encouraged monopolists because, in Unwin's words, 'his intellectual curiosity and versatility made him take delight in any project because it was a project, and he had no judgment to discern a good project from a bad one', so that it was 'with something like a childish pleasure that James threw himself and his kingdom into the arms of the projectors'.[19] Attacks on the system were renewed, and led to the passing of the Monopolies Act of 1624, which embodied the main principle of our modern patent law, namely that monopoly might only be granted, for a limited term of years, when a new process, or a substantial improvement of an existing process, had either been invented or introduced from abroad.

In Charles I's reign numerous patents were granted on this basis, but there was still room for abuse. It was still possible to turn established industries into monopolies under the plea of introducing technical improvements, but the chief ground for complaint was the continual increase in monopolies granted to companies or corporations. Modern company law was not available then, and to float a company a charter of incorporation was required. Grants of special industrial privileges had been made to companies or partnerships since Elizabethan times, and in practice there came to be no significant difference between a charter and a patent of monopoly. Thus the company of Westminster Soapboilers, which aroused such hostility during the years of Charles's personal government, began as a group of patentees incorporated to exploit what was supposed to be a new invention; but they soon claimed the power to regulate all soapmaking, and acquired a virtual monopoly of making soap. These abuses in the system of monopolies came under fire once more when the Long Parliament met. Whether in the long run the system had done more to help or hinder industrial and commercial activity is hard to say. At first, certainly, it provided opportunities for potential entrepreneurs, when special protection of new processes might be justified. But that is not to say that it guaranteed success, and, later, the great privileged corporations undoubtedly tended to stagnate, aiming simply at keeping up prices rather than expansion or development.

According to F. A. Walker, whose work was quoted above, 'industrially advanced communities' necessitate a 'distinct class' of entrepreneurs. 'Class' is another word to which economists and

sociologists have given a technical meaning, and it is questionable
whether, even in the nineteenth century, which Walker presumably had in mind, entrepreneurs formed a class in that sense, distinct from capitalists in general, or employers, or indeed the whole
'bourgeoisie' of the Marxists. Even if we accepted the contentious
proposition that an English 'bourgeois revolution' occurred in the
seventeenth century, or were prepared to classify some of the
gentry as 'bourgeoisie' or 'middle class', it would be highly questionable whether the rising entrepreneurs of that age themselves constituted a class, or indeed whether they all belonged to the same class.
Professor Lawrence Stone in fact has argued to the contrary, and
shown that some of the leading entrepreneurs were members of the
nobility, desperately anxious to make money in order to maintain
their expensive style of living. 'In the Elizabethan period', he writes,
'the most active entrepreneur in the country was not some busy
merchant or thrusting member of the new gentry, but a peer of
ancient stock, George Talbot, ninth [?sixth] earl of Shrewsbury.'
Numerous other peers were doing likewise, and Stone claims that
'in this period the peerage fulfilled a role that no other class, neither
the gentry nor the merchants, were able or willing to rival'. He is
speaking here of the titled aristocracy, and emphasizes the point
that their significance was 'more qualitative than quantitative', in
that what was most important in their contribution was their initiative and willingness to risk their capital rather than the actual
amount of capital they risked. Quantitatively the peerage may not
have controlled more than 10 or 20 per cent of mining and metallurgy, for example; but, he continues, in these 'the bulk of the
production, at any rate after the very early years, was in the hands
of the upper gentry class'.[20] Sociologically, however, there is no
significant class division between the peerage and the upper gentry.
Both alike belong essentially to a landowning upper class, and the
conclusion would therefore seem to be that our first entrepreneurs
did not themselves form a class; rather, that entrepreneurship was
one of the outlets for the restless energy of the upper class.

Should we then, if we seek the origins of the entrepreneur, try
to answer the question why it was the upper class which then had
restless energy to expend, as well as the question why it was expended on industrial enterprises? Considering the prevailing
inequality of opportunity—the generally accepted notions about

'degree' and the due subordination of the ordinary masses to their betters—it would hardly be surprising if many entrepreneurs sprang from the upper ranks of society. There is indeed evidence that a number of yeomen—the landowning class immediately below the nobility and gentry—also participated in industrial activities. Cheshire yeomen, for example, had interests in the salt works in that county; we hear of a Devon yeoman named Philip Jule who controlled a tin works near Plympton, and yeomen had shares in other tin works in Devon and Cornwall. Another Devon yeoman was a stavemaker, supplying thousands of staves for beer and cider barrels, while elsewhere yeomen were concerned in paper mills, glass works, alum digging, and quarries. Numerous yeomen had interests in the Sussex iron industry, sometimes in conjunction with agriculture, and the same is true of the clothing and the coal industries. Sometimes, as notably in Sussex, yeomen so enriched themselves by their industrial activities that they were able to rise into the gentry class above them.[21] There was indeed no hard and fast line or barrier between any of the landowning classes and, as Sir Thomas Smith remarked, gentlemen were 'made good cheap in England'. But at the bottom of the social scale came what he called 'the fourth class, which do not rule', ordinary men, 'yea, merchants or retailers which have no free land'. These 'have no voice nor authority in our commonwealth, and no account is made of them, but only to be ruled'.[22] Some of them no doubt achieved wealth, and with it gentility, but it required exceptional energy, and good fortune, for members of this class to become entrepreneurs.

Why, then, did the ruling classes turn to entrepreneurship? Not all did so: some turned to politics, or to hunting and sport, or indeed to both, as they have always done. In the Middle Ages many would have engaged in war, feudal or otherwise, but under Tudor rule this outlet for their energy was no longer so readily available. The answer must be, surely, that in the Tudor and early Stuart period there were (apart from the question of monopolies) tempting opportunities and prospects for entrepreneurs. Karl Marx saw the essence of capitalism in the concentration of ownership of the means of production in the hands of a relatively small class, with the consequent depression of the large property-less class into a body of wage-earners, whose labour was treated as a marketable commodity, which they were obliged to sell because they had no other means of livelihood. Marx was undoubtedly justified in emphasizing the importance of the wage system as the characteristic feature of capitalist production, whether in the more fully developed form of the wage relationship between employer and hired labourers in a factory, or in the less mature form of the so-called 'domestic' or 'putting-out' system, where work was done at home, but the materials, and sometimes the tools, were owned by a capitalist entrepreneur. Working for wages was indeed nothing new, but the division which thus opened between capital and labour was widened by the breakdown of the medieval gilds. This breakdown occurred partly because the gilds were essentially local organizations, and exercised only partial supervision over local industries. Craft gilds were geared to regulate the processes and conditions of production, but not as a rule the purchase of raw materials or the marketing of finished products, and they lacked the means of dealing with the problems that arose when an industry catered not only for a local but for a national or an international market.

Traditionally a gild could only exercise jurisdiction within the town to which it belonged, and the gilds were in effect the means by which industry and trade were controlled by local authorities. Old industries sometimes evaded this control by migrating to the country outside municipal boundaries, and when the central government wished to foster a new industry, the antiquated and restrictive system of municipal regulation was obviously unsuitable. The breakdown of the gild system has sometimes been represented as a struggle by private enterprise to be liberated from old-fashioned shackles, but the element of freedom should not be exaggerated. On the contrary, as we have seen, early entrepreneurs generally wanted to be protected by monopoly rights. These developments did not all take place suddenly, nor everywhere at the same time. Early forerunners of capitalist production can be found in the Middle Ages; gilds were still in existence in the seventeenth century and even later, and some new gilds were formed. But the trend was all in favour of private enterprise, of promoting rather than regulating manufacture, so that the gildsman ultimately disappeared, and it was the capitalist entrepreneur who became the dominant figure in the new economic order.[23]

To record and analyse historical events, however, does not answer the question why they occurred, and all sorts of reasons have been put forward to explain the upsurge of entrepreneurial activity in the early modern period. Werner Sombart attributed it to an attitude of mind, and stressed the influence of the capitalist 'spirit' (*Geist*)—a combination of a calculating faculty with the qualities of restlessness, persistence and perseverance. These characteristics, he thought, were possessed to an outstanding degree by the Jews, though he admitted that they occurred under every kind of regime and every religion, including Christianity, Catholic as well as Protestant.[24] He insisted that capitalism was created by outstanding individuals, and did not grow impersonally or collectively. Mere thrift and frugality were not enough to make a man an entrepreneur; he must have drive and enterprise as well, and be willing to take risks. This is no doubt true, but to describe all these qualities as a capitalist spirit is no explanation of why it took effect at a particular time. Bold and calculating acquisitiveness was no new feature of humanity; there was plenty of it in the Middle Ages, and in the ancient world, and even if it became more prevalent in the early modern age, this might have been not the cause but the effect of capitalist activity. In fact, the mere urge to make large profits will not produce an industrial revolution without the appropriate social and technical conditions for capitalist production.[25]

Is the explanation, then, that whereas in the Middle Ages the Catholic Church frowned on acquisitiveness, after the Reformation Protestant leaders encouraged it? This was the famous thesis of Max Weber, followed by Ernst Troeltsch and in a modified form by R. H. Tawney; but few historians nowadays would be satisfied with a crude identification of Protestantism with a capitalist 'ethic'. The capitalist ethic seems indistinguishable from the ordinary and perennial desire for gain, which flourished in some Catholic countries (notably in the merchant cities of medieval Italy) just as much as in Calvinist Holland or Puritan England. Nor did Protestantism necessarily ensure commercial advance and Catholicism commercial stagnation: Presbyterian Scotland was economically poor and backward in the seventeenth century. It is certainly true that some Puritan teachers laid stress on the virtues of thrift and industriousness, which made for success in business; and some importance must be ascribed to changes in the current attitude to usury. In this matter, however, it is important not to make mistakes in dating, and to regard as causative what only became prominent in later years. The early reformers, including Calvin himself, repeated the medieval Church's condemnation of usury, and it was from the later seventeenth rather than the middle sixteenth century that Tawney drew most of his examples of Protestant encomiums of the capitalist virtues. But though it may be hard to say exactly what the connection was, this is not to ignore or deny the existence of any connection between Protestantism and the rise of capitalism, or to regard the connection as purely fortuitous. Whatever it was, however, we cannot treat it as one of simple cause and effect. A capitalist economy and capitalist entrepreneurs already existed to some degree before the Reformation, and Professor Dickens suggests that a safe conclusion would be 'to suppose that throughout the economic field the English Reformation did little more than accentuate trends of theory and practice already operative at its outset and by no means dependent upon its support.'[26]

This is certainly true of official attitudes to usury, apart from the emphasis of religious teachers on the virtuousness of thrift and hard work. In the Middle Ages the taking of usury was prohibited by law as well as being condemned by the Church, but it would seem that for some time business practice was less and less affected by the doctrines laid down by theological practitioners. The preamble to an Act of Parliament passed in 1545 stated that existing laws against usury were of no effect, and the Act proceeded to allow creditors to charge interest of not more than 10 per cent. In 1552 this Act was repealed and the old prohibition of usury was reinstated, but the law was changed again by an Act of 1571, which made 10 per cent interest legal once more. This limit was retained on paper for centuries, but in practice it was evaded, and the chief effect, if indeed it was not the real purpose, of Tudor legislation was to enable the government to borrow at an artificially low rate of interest. In time even the Catholic Church dropped its condemnation of interest, but the business world did not need the stimulus of theological approval, and certainly did not wait for it.

Most probably the origins of capitalism are to be sought in a complex network of causes which cannot be disentangled and isolated with any precision. One indirect, and indeed almost accidental, by-product of the Reformation, which some historians have seen as an important factor in the situation in England, was the Dissolution of the Monasteries and the subsequent secularization of monastic lands. We need not subscribe to the old-fashioned view which contrasted the benevolence of monastic landlords with the rapacity of their lay successors. Ecclesiastical estates before the Reformation were often managed, and commercially exploited, by lay stewards; but there is evidence, at any rate in certain localities, such as the Durham coalfield, or the ironworks opened by the Sidneys on the site of the Cistercian abbey at Robertsbridge in Sussex, that change of ownership was the signal for the exploitation of resources hitherto neglected. Professor Nef argued that the new lay owners of monastic property, individuals with heirs to succeed them, had stronger personal incentives to make money and amass capital than the monks, who 'thought and behaved as members of ecclesiastical institutions'. The new proprietors, he thinks, were 'far more disposed to take financial risks, and were more prepared either to invest heavily on their own account in industrial enterprises, or to grant leases on terms likely to attract wealthy economic adventurers—city men and others'.[27] There is no doubt some truth in this, but corporate property-owners can be as ready as private persons to make money—witness the management of their estates by Oxford and Cambridge colleges, or by the Church Commissioners.

Another phenomenon, which has become a controversial topic in recent years, and which has been seen as an important cause of the expansion of industry in the sixteenth century, was the so-called price revolution, due, it used to be said, to the influx of silver and gold from the mines of Spanish America. While prices rose— to about five times their previous level in the course of a century— wages lagged behind, and the capitalist employer enjoyed for a time an enormous advantage.[28] This thesis, however, has been challenged at several points, among them the chronological correlation between the levels of prices and the statistics for importation of bullion. As far as England is concerned, it has been suggested that debasement of the coinage and the increase in population, especially the growth of London and the development of the hitherto backward north and west, were more important factors than an inflation of the quantity of precious metals in circulation. The population of London certainly rose at a phenomenal rate in this period. At the beginning of the sixteenth century London had about 50,000 inhabitants; a century later this figure had risen to some

200,000, and went on rising, and so created the expanding demand necessary to sustain industrial development. It has also been argued that the rise in prices was not accompanied by a decline in real wages, or at any rate not by such a marked decline as had been supposed, so that labour in England was not so cheap after all. On the other hand the prevalence of vagabondage points to the existence of surplus labour in the Tudor period, even if the growth of industries may later have helped to take up the slack. The conclusion would appear to be, not indeed that the price revolution failed to stimulate industry—most historians seem to agree that it had a powerful influence—but that its importance in a complex situation must not be exaggerated.[29]

Increased government expenditure, a more rapid circulation of currency, easier facilities for credit, an increase in the use of bills of exchange—all these are factors, as well as the activation of the market in land by the sales of monastic and episcopal estates, which may have combined, along with monetary inflation, to stimulate economic expansion. And even if rising prices did not spell low real wages, there was another way in which they cannot have failed to assist potential entrepreneurs. Any inflationary trend favours borrowers at the expense of creditors, and this fact, especially in conjunction with expanding markets, must have been a powerful incentive to industrial enterprise. It is also clear that development had a snowball effect. The adoption of coal not only as a domestic fuel but also for industrial purposes, in the production of salt, for example, or in glass-making or soap-boiling, in great part due to exhaustion of timber supplies and consequent restrictions on its use for fuel, not only stimulated the growth of these industries but in turn led to increases in the demand for and the production of coal.

Sombart suggested that war was an important factor encouraging economic progress. War, he argued, was economically constructive as well as destructive. The cost of supplying armies and navies with weapons, food, clothing, ships of war, and other supplies, led to the development of large-scale enterprises in finance, commerce and industry, because it was necessary to assemble capital in large units. There is an element of truth in this. It is obviously true of the armament industries themselves, and expansion of these, and growth in the size of armies, will in turn stimulate activity in numerous other ancillary trades not directly concerned in the manufacture of armaments. It is also true that some of the new industries fostered by the Elizabethan government were armament industries; but many, if not most, of the technical inventions of this period were developed to meet the needs not of war but of peace, while a comparison of industrial progress in England with the comparative lack of development in France, at a time when France was torn by the wars of religion, suggests that England was fortunate in its immunity from war. Indeed, some of England's new industries were developed by refugees, driven from war-torn countries like France and the southern Netherlands.[30] England owed this immunity partly to its insular position, but largely to firm government under the Tudor monarchy. It also benefited, in comparison with other European countries, from the absence of internal customs barriers, so that it was the largest free trade area then in existence.

Dr Rowse has suggested that an important element in the economic expansion of the Elizabethan age, equally important as the monetary factor, certainly more important than the military, was another by-product of insularity, 'the aggressive nationalism of the time—of which no people had a larger share than the English —which drove men to break into preserves of trade hitherto monopolized by others, to open up new routes and markets in the outer world'. This undoubtedly seems an apt description of Elizabethan England but, as with Sombart's 'spirit of capitalism', it is hard to say how far nationalism was a cause and how far rather a symptom of entrepreneurship. Dr Rowse also thinks that the adoption of the joint-stock technique was more important than the new mechanical inventions of the time. Surely we must agree, for shortage of capital had been a marked weakness of medieval and early Tudor trade.[31]

Joint-stock companies were first started under Elizabeth, and differed from the 'regulated companies' of the later Middle Ages in that they were not only organizations for supervising and controlling the trading operations of their individual members. They differed also from partnerships, which were simply associations between two or more individuals who pooled their resources and acted jointly under the terms of a partnership agreement. Partners shared the profits in definite proportions laid down in the articles of the agreement, but they could not transfer their shares to anyone else. A joint-stock company, on the other hand, was a legal corporation, and operated as a corporate entity. Its members held shares which could be inherited or sold; they took their profits in proportion to the number of shares they held, and in course of time a stock exchange came into existence in which shares could be bought and sold like marketable commodities. Although the owner of a share assumed unlimited liability, and might have to meet a series of 'calls' to pay up more capital, the joint-stock method enabled capital to be raised from city merchants and landowners who had resources they were prepared to risk. Enterprises thus became feasible on a larger scale than would have been possible if the only available capital had been that possessed by those who were to be actively engaged in them.

When Professor Nef wrote of an Industrial Revolution in the sixteenth and seventeenth centuries, he had in mind chiefly the new technological inventions and the new industries which were introduced into or started in England at that time. Whether or not these developments amounted to a revolution, it is undeniable that England, which had been what he calls an 'industrial backwater' in the later Middle Ages, in comparison with some European countries such as north Italy, south Germany and the southern Netherlands, was by the end of this period supplying many of its own needs. Obviously it could not have done so had it not possessed an abundant supply of natural products, not only corn and other foodstuffs, but also, and especially for industrial purposes, coal, iron and other minerals. Hitherto these had been relatively neglected, but now, under favourable economic and social conditions, and with the aid of new techniques—blast furnaces, refining furnaces, furnaces enabling coal instead of wood to be used for various processes, pumping machinery enabling mines to be deepened—entrepreneurs could and did begin to exploit these natural resources. We must beware, however, of exaggerating either the speed or the extent of these developments. In spite of the growth of joint-stock companies, a money-market and all the new inventions, at the outbreak of the Civil War factory production was still 'rudimentary', to use Tawney's word and, as Harrington was to emphasize in *Oceana*, English capital still consisted mainly of landed estates.[32]

Correspondingly, the wool and cloth trades, the ancient and traditional mainstays of English wealth, still outdistanced mining and all the new industries. The entrepreneur's chief sphere of activity lay among the new developments, but the wool and cloth trades also underwent changes, and were already being conducted on capitalist lines long before the close of the Middle Ages. Apart from the manufacture of coarse cloths for local use, most English wool in early times was bought for shipment abroad by alien merchants, and the first appearance of a capitalist element was in the person of the wool dealer who acted as a middleman, collecting wool from the countryside and selling it to the exporters. Some wool dealers were merchants from London or other towns, dealing in other commodities besides wool, but many lived in the wool-producing districts, like the Cotswolds, where their wealth helped to build splendid churches. John Tame, of Fairford, who died in 1500, is a well-known example of a man who not only dealt in wool but became a large landowner, breeding his own sheep, and also making cloth. As the export of raw wool declined, and more cloth was made in England, the wool merchants might become cloth merchants as well, supplying the clothiers with wool and taking manufactured cloth in exchange; many became clothiers themselves, dealing directly with the spinners and weavers who made raw wool into yarn and cloth. Some capital was necessary for this, and it was possible in this way to gain control over both the manufacture and the sale of the finished product. Some clothiers might then be reduced to a subordinate status, while others again might abandon manufacture and themselves engage in wool dealing, as happened, we gather, on a large scale in the seventeenth century, partly, perhaps, because of the depression of the cloth industry at that time.[33] In the Tudor period, however, the clothier was, and had long been, the dominant figure in the cloth trade, and he developed some of the characteristic features of the entrepreneur. Some great clothiers already existed in the Middle Ages, though they were not yet numerous; by the sixteenth century 'the whole control of the woollen industry came to be concentrated largely in the hands of capitalist manufacturers. The clothier was the pivot of industrial organization, and his position at the head and centre of the cloth trade enabled him to supervise and direct every stage of the manufacture.'[34] Before we turn to the new industries, then, let us see how the entrepreneur affected the organization and development of England's oldest manufacture.

2 | The cloth industry

The rise of the clothier, the capitalist who by operating the 'domestic' or 'putting-out' system came to dominate the cloth industry, signalized in one aspect the breakdown of the old gilds. This was a natural result of the development in England of the manufacture of finer kinds of cloth, resulting in a trend, clearly in evidence in the fourteenth century, and proceeding apace all through the fifteenth, towards a diminution in the amount of wool exported, and a corresponding increase in the amount spun and woven into cloth, for export as well as for consumption at home. In the middle of the fourteenth century exports of wool averaged 32,000 sacks a year, each sack being supposed to contain 364 pounds of wool, while the number of manufactured cloths exported amounted to only 5,000. There was already a marked change in the balance by the end of the century, when the sacks of wool exported had fallen to 19,000, while the cloths exported had risen to 37,000. By the end of the fifteenth century not only had the balance tilted further, but the whole scale of the trade had greatly expanded, and for a time it was to continue expanding even more rapidly. The export of wool had fallen to 5,000 sacks, but against this there was an increase in the number of cloths exported to 82,000. By the later years of Henry VIII's reign this number had risen to 118,000, and raw wool exported then represented only eight per cent, manufactured cloth 92 per cent of the whole wool trade.[1]

A considerable variety of cloths were made, and different parts of the country became noted for the kinds in which they specialized. Manufacture of the traditional heavy undyed broadcloth was centred in Wiltshire, Gloucestershire and Somerset, with outliers in Oxfordshire and Worcestershire. Besides these 'old draperies', various newer types of dyed cloths were made in these counties, some of high quality, such as 'medleys', red 'stammells' and others. Some cloths were coarser, others again, such as those known as 'kerseys' and 'dozens', were lighter and cheaper. Many of these varieties were the specialities of particular regions, and it is estimated that, between them, about half the whole output of woollen cloths came from the western counties. Another important cloth-making county was Suffolk, which together with parts of Norfolk and Essex accounted for another quarter of the whole. Some broad-cloth, both undyed and coloured, was made in East Anglia, but Norfolk was chiefly famous for worsted, manufactured from combed long-staple wool. This made a smoother fabric than the heavy felted broadcloth, made from short-staple wool which had been carded. Essex became the first centre of what were called the 'new draperies'—'bays', 'says', 'perpetuanas', serges, and a number of other types of cloth. These also were lighter than the 'old draperies', being made of combed wool, though sometimes short-staple wool was used for the weft. The new draperies were introduced into England early in Elizabeth's reign by refugees from religious persecution in the Netherlands. These exiles settled first at Colchester, from which they spread into Suffolk, and later all along the south coast as far as Devonshire.

Wales and the English counties bordering on it made friezes and other coarse woollens, while another cloth-making centre, becoming increasingly important, lay in the West Riding of Yorkshire and some areas to the north of it. Here dozens, kerseys and other relatively cheap varieties of cloth were made, together with some of the heavier traditional products. Lancashire, which later became the centre of the cotton trade, then made some woollen goods, and also linen. In fact, before the advent of genuine vegetable cotton, the name 'cotton' was used of the coarse, frieze-like woollen goods formerly made in this area.[2]

Some of the wool manufactured into cloth doubtless came from the backs of locally bred sheep; some, especially Spanish wool, was imported for the manufacture of certain kinds of fabric; but much was supplied by the midland counties, then mainly rural, which were surrounded on all sides, west, north, east and south, by the cloth-making districts. The continual expansion of the textile industries is usually thought of as having made a vital contribution to the wealth and prosperity of England, but this was not the attitude of

c

the landowning gentlemen who dominated the legislature of the mid-sixteenth century. Enclosure of the old open fields, and the conversion of arable land to pasture, in order to produce more wool, was widely blamed as a cause of rural unemployment and depopulation. More recent historians tell us that these complaints were misplaced and exaggerated, at any rate for the Elizabethan period. Expanding output of cloth, accompanied by a rise in wool prices, had indeed been an incentive for farmers to turn to sheep-raising in the fifteenth and early sixteenth centuries, but after the middle of the sixteenth century the situation changed radically. Until then Antwerp had been the great entrepot through which English exports had been channelled into the European continent, but the political and religious struggles in the Netherlands, culminating in the closing of the Scheldt by the Dutch, so that Antwerp was cut off from contact with the sea, disrupted for the time being the export of English cloth, until other routes became established. In 1551 'the foreign market for English cloth collapsed and wool prices tumbled', and it was a quarter of a century before they had climbed again to their mid-century level. After that they rose again, but over the whole second half of the sixteenth century wheat prices trebled, while wool prices only doubled.[3] Wool, in fact, became a less profitable commodity than corn, and if sheep were bred it was as much for their meat as for their fleeces.

Misguided though it may have been, however, there can be no mistaking the hostility of the ruling class to the expansion of the cloth trade in general, and to the activities of clothiers in particular. The preamble to an Act of Parliament passed in Edward vi's reign declared that they 'do daily more and more study to make many than to make good cloths', and that there were too many clothiers who had not served a proper apprenticeship. Parliament therefore sought to restrict entry into the industry, check its growth in country districts, and enforce traditional standards and methods of work. The Act whose preamble has just been quoted laid down standards and rules for making cloth which, it declared, were 'to remain firm and perfect, notwithstanding any suggestions hereafter to be made by any clothier or clothmaker to the contrary'. Another Act passed in the same year provided that no one should 'weave or make or put to weaving or making any manner of broad woollen cloth' (i.e. become a clothier and give out work to employees) until he had himself served as an apprentice to weaving for seven years. A third Act prohibited the use of the gigmill, a machine for turning the teazels used to raise the nap on cloth, which was one of the earliest of the many mechanical inventions in the history of the textile industry. Already in Henry VIII's reign places such as Norwich, Shrewsbury, York, and various other towns in the clothing counties had procured special Acts of Parliament to prohibit clothiers setting up business in the adjacent countryside, and to prevent London merchants and foreigners from dealing directly with country weavers.

Regulation and restriction of the cloth industry was carried further in Mary's reign by the two Weavers' Acts of 1555 and 1558. According to the first of these 'the weavers of the realm' complained that 'the rich and wealthy clothiers do in many ways oppress them, some by setting up and keeping in their houses divers looms, and keeping and maintaining them by journeymen and persons unskilful, to the decay of a great number of artificers which were brought up in the science of weaving, their families and household, some by ingrossing of looms into their hands and possession and letting them out at such unreasonable rents as the poor artificers are not able to maintain themselves . . . some also by giving much less wages and hire for the weaving and workmanship of cloth than in times past'. Among numerous other provisions, it was then laid down that in future clothiers were to work only in towns, or places where clothing had been carried on for 10 years. A country clothier was not to possess more than one loom, and was not to hire out looms to others, while a country weaver was not to have more than two looms. The conservative temper of the legislature at this time is also exhibited in an Act passed specially for the protection of the cloth manufacture in the Somerset towns of Bridgwater, Taunton and Chard, 'decayed by the making of cloths in villages'.

Legislation of this kind did not only strike directly at the new class of capitalist employer. The well-known Statute of Apprentices, passed early in Elizabeth's reign (1563), allowed weavers to take as apprentices only their own sons or the sons of freeholders owning land of the annual value of £3, thus hampering the clothiers by preventing the bulk of the rural population from finding employment under them. It was not only the clothiers, and the rural industry they controlled, whom Parliament thus sought to check. Legislation was also aimed at the middlemen wool dealers, notably in the Act passed in 1552, described as 'an Act to bring down the price of wool', by which only manufacturers and Merchants of the Staple were to be allowed to buy wool. Had these Acts been enforced, the cloth trade must have been stifled, but in practice it proved impossible to apply them effectively. Certain out-lying regions were exempted from the first from the statutory restrictions of the Weavers' Acts, and later this exemption was ex-tended to other areas as well. The exempted areas came to include all Wales, Cornwall, Kent, Suffolk, the six northern counties, and the clothing districts in Wiltshire, Somerset and Gloucestershire (e.g. the Stroud valley). It was in these areas that the future ex-pansion of the industry was to take place; no doubt it was because the clothing interests were already firmly entrenched there that they were able to exercise pressure on Parliament to obtain exemption.[4]

By no means all clothiers were large-scale capitalist entrepren-eurs; indeed such were exceptional. A good many clothiers became wealthy, but clothiers were drawn from various levels of society. Sometimes landowners in sheep-breeding districts took up the trade of clothier in order to find an outlet for their own wool. Sometimes merchants invested capital in this way, and we hear of a lawyer who became a clothier. Beneath the more well-to-do clothiers there were 'meaner clothiers' who were manual workers themselves, although they were at the same time employers of labour. There were also regional differences in the status and func-tions of the clothier. In the north of England most clothiers seem to have been small men, themselves engaged in manufacture, and the capitalist element still consisted chiefly of the middlemen dealers who sold them their wool and bought their cloth. In the west country, on the other hand, where the industry was more fully capitalized than in the north, the clothier counted as a gentle-man, or at any rate was often called a 'gentleman clothier'. In other words, he did not work with his hands, but supplied materials to the various workers, not only the weavers, but those who carried out the other processes through which the wool had to pass on its way to becoming cloth. Here too, however, a great diversity of elements existed side by side; there were not only large and small clothiers, but weavers who still bought their own wool and yarn and worked as independent craftsmen, while at the other end of the scale there were workers who, though they worked at home, were virtually an industrial proletariat.

In Wiltshire, we gather, well-to-do weavers were rare. Most of them 'lived from hand to mouth on the meagre wages paid by the clothier'; many did not even own their own looms, but rented them from the clothier.[5] It was, of course, common in the sixteenth and seventeenth centuries for wealthy traders or merchants to buy landed estates, partly as investments, partly as means and symbols of ascent into the class of the gentry. Apart from this there was a close integration, in Wiltshire and doubtless in neighbouring counties also, between the cloth-making industry and agriculture. There were weavers who combined work at the loom with work on the land, clothiers who also owned flocks of sheep, or practised general farming, landowners who had a fulling-mill as well as a grist-mill on their estate. In Gloucestershire the usual practice was for the clothier to give out wool to be spun and woven in the workmen's cottages; he then took the cloth to the mill, often his own property, for fulling and finishing. Sometimes the monasteries had provided fulling-mills on their property. At Cirencester, for example, Leland records that 'Mr. Blake the last abbate buildid 2. fulling milles ... that coste a 700. markes of mony. They be wonderfully necessary, by cause the toun standith all by clothing.'[6]

Notwithstanding these variations in its economic structure, cloth manufacture generally hinged upon the clothier. With his warehouse and his train of packhorses, travelling round the countryside, delivering yarn to the weavers and collecting their cloth, the clothier was obviously in a stronger position than the small independent weaver, who had to carry the cloth he had made to market and accept what price he could get for it, because he needed the money at once, to buy food, or fresh yarn to work on. But the clothier who had the means could buy wool in large amounts, perhaps a whole year's supply, at shearing-time; he could choose a favourable moment to sell, and if necessary allow credit to the merchants who exported the finished cloth, and wait for payment until they had sold it. By his control of labour and materials the clothier could thus co-ordinate all the processes of manufacture, and in a primitive fashion effect a 'vertical integration' of the industry. In face of the increasing influence of the capitalist entrepreneur, the small independent weaver was at an obvious disadvantage. Unless he had a small farm to cushion him against the effects of unemployment, he might have no option, particularly when trade was slack and prices stationary or declining, but to accept employment for wages under a clothier. The putting-out system had grown up unplanned, and from the employer's point of view it had some drawbacks. Travelling round the countryside was wasteful of time, and employees working in their own cottages might steal some of the stuff the clothier handed out for them to work on.[7] These disadvantages might be avoided if the employee came to work in the clothier's house, or in his workshop, and in spite of the clause in the Weavers' Act restricting the number of looms owned by country clothiers and weavers, we gather that this was sometimes done.[8] Production might, of course, be made even more efficient if large numbers of workers were collected in a mill, with power-driven machinery. But this was a development which did not become general until the late eighteenth and early nineteenth centuries, and in the period we are dealing with the textile industry was still, in spite of a few famous exceptions, essentially domestic.

Probably the most authentic forerunner of the factory-system was William Stumpe of Malmesbury, who lived in the middle of the sixteenth century; but earlier than this we meet the quasi-legendary figure of John Winchcombe, otherwise known as Jack of Newbury, who died about 1520, and according to Fuller was 'the most considerable Clothier (without fancy or fiction) England ever beheld'.[9] His achievements formed the subject of a doggerel poem by the Elizabethan Thomas Deloney, excerpts from which have often been quoted.[10] Jack of Newbury, we are told, got on in the world by marrying his master's widow, who left him a rich man, employing a large staff of servants. He then married one of his maids, and her father came to see his son-in-law's establishment. The poem describes his astonishment at what he saw.

> Within one roome being large and long
> There stood two hundred Loomes full strong:
> Two hundred men the truth is so
> Wrought in these Loomes all in a row.
> By every one a pretty boy
> Sate making quils with mickle ioy;

the King the only recipient of Winchcombe's liberality. We read, for example, 'how a Draper in London, who owed Jack of Newbury much money, became bankrupt, whom Jack found carrying a porter's basket on his neck'. Jack set him up again at his own cost, and the draper afterwards became an alderman of London.

Some historians have perhaps taken this poem rather too literally. According to Lipson, for example, 'the type of sixteenth-century clothier is portrayed for us in the career of John Winchcombe, and 'he was unquestionably an historical figure, though many legends have gathered round his name'.[11] Unwin was rather more cautious. He regarded 'the exploits of the famous clothier, Jack of Newbury, though founded on fact', as 'largely mythological', and Deloney's poem was 'quite obviously a fantastically embroidered tradition'. But in dedicating it to the Clothworkers' Company Deloney 'would not be likely to invent business details that were palpably absurd', for instance the story of Jack's relations with the London draper who owed him money.[12] More sceptical, Mr Peter Laslett dismisses the stories about Winchcombe as 'an interesting piece of make-believe' which Deloney invented for the diversion of the London Clothworkers. Particularly incredible, he thinks, is a piece about the King, on the occasion of his visit to Newbury, taking away some of the poor children who worked for 'fabulous Jack', making some of them royal pages, and sending others 'to the Universities, allotting to every one a gentleman's living'. In fact, 'Jack of Newbury was as much of a myth as Jack and the Beanstalk'. His establishment was not a real factory (it is true that Deloney refers to it as a 'household'), and it was absurd of historians to treat it as evidence for the existence of modern industrial conditions in the sixteenth century. 'What it does show is that the successful clothier could be idealized as a hero and his household poetically exaggerated. But it was a household still.'[13]

There is some force in this criticism; yet, though many of the details about him were imaginary, Winchcombe was not simply a fictitious character. As Lipson rightly pointed out, he really existed. 'His will is still preserved in which he bequeathed forty pounds to Newbury parish church and legacies to his servants, and his epitaph survives in Newbury church, of which he built the tower and western part.' As evidence of the reputation of his cloth, Lipson cites 'the advice of the English envoy at Antwerp to the Protector

Somerset to send over a "thousand of Winchcombe's kersies" in discharge of a debt', and he also recalls that 'even at the end of the seventeenth century Jack of Newbury was the chief figure in the pageant of the Clothworkers of London'.[14] But this is only evidence of the persistence of the legend about him.

Better substantiated by historical evidence than Jack of Newbury was William Stumpe of Malmesbury, of whom Fuller said (though he got his name wrong) that he was 'in his Age one of the most eminent Clothiers of England'.[15] Of humble origins, the Stumpe family's rise to wealth and eminence seems to have begun with William's father, who was parish clerk of North Nibley in Gloucestershire, where he 'was a weaver and at last grew up to be a cloathier'. When exactly Wiliam Stumpe came to Malmesbury, and what brought him there, is not known, but we find him established in the town some years before the Dissolution of the Monasteries. He held a number of properties under lease from the abbey, was buying land in the neighbourhood, and was reckoned to be one of the four richest inhabitants of the town. When Malmesbury Abbey surrendered to the King, in December 1539, the buildings 'deemed to be superfluous', including 'the Church, Cloister and Chapelles adjoyning, the Dormitory, Chaptrehouse, Fraytre', and various other domestic buildings, were 'committed to the custodie of William Stumpe, deputie to Sir Edward Bayntun, Knight', who was a prominent local magnate and 'chief steward of the abbey'. Stumpe's son was later to marry into his family. Stumpe doubtless realized that the surplus abbey buildings would be useful for his business, and a few years later he offered to buy them from the Crown. In November 1543 he duly became the owner of the buildings, and of some lands in the neighbourhood which had formerly belonged to the abbey; he paid for them altogether some £1,500. The townspeople were anxious that the abbey church should be spared, and a petition was sent to the King on the subject. Though the choir and transepts were lost, the nave was preserved and converted into a parish church, and it is evident from the wording of Archbishop Cranmer's licence for the purpose that Stumpe's co-operation was largely responsible for this.

Stumpe had already begun installing looms in the vacant conventual buildings, and when Leland visited Malmesbury he recorded that 'the hole logginges of thabbay be now longging to one Stumpe, an exceding riche clothier that boute them of the king. . . . This Stumpe was the chief causer and contributer to have thabbay chirch made a paroch chirch. At this present tyme every corner of the vaste houses of office that belongid to thabbay be fulle of lumbes to weve clooth yn, and this Stumpe entendith to make a stret or 2. for clothier in the bak vacant ground of the abbay that is withyn the towne waulles. There be made now every yere in the towne a 3000. clothes.'[16]

There is no evidence that Stumpe ever carried out his plan to erect a street for his workpeople, but as a mansion for himself he built the house which is still called the Abbey House, and in his household there he kept a French priest who was also a good gardener. The use of the abbey buildings as a cloth factory seems to have been profitable, for in 1546 Stumpe opened negotiations with the city authorities at Oxford, with a view to acquiring the disused buildings of Osney Abbey for the same purpose, and at the same time he approached the Dean and Chapter of Christ Church, newly made into a cathedral, for leave to use some adjacent lands and streams. He undertook to employ 2,000 skilled workmen at Osney, but this seems to have been beyond his capacity, for the scheme came to nothing. At Malmesbury, however, Stumpe's business continued to grow, and there is evidence suggesting that he sent some of the cloths woven in the town to be finished and dyed in London. As he grew wealthier he bought more land, and by the time of his death, in 1552, he had amassed estates scattered over a very wide area in both Wiltshire and Gloucestershire.

With Stumpe, as with many others, commercial success was the avenue to the fulfilment of social ambitions. He had already become one of the members for Malmesbury in the Reformation Parliament of 1529–36, and he may have represented the borough in other parliaments as well. He became a J.P. for Wiltshire in 1538, and in most years from then onwards he served as a county magistrate, for Gloucestershire as well as Wiltshire. He also acted in various other official capacities, and shortly before his death he became Sheriff of Wiltshire. While he held this office he is said to have refused to pay the Clerk of the Peace the customary fees for delivering prisoners from the county gaol, and there is other evidence suggesting that this conduct was in keeping with his character, for he was 'twice impleaded in Chancery by aggrieved copyholders whom he had evicted from manors he controlled'. He appears, in fact, in Dr Ramsay's words, to have been typical of 'the new style landlords who exploited their property as business investments'. On the other hand, giving the nave of the abbey church for parochial use showed public spirit and munificence, though no doubt it also looked well. To include a clause in a codicil to his will (dated the day of his death) forgiving various debts owing to him, among them those of 'all his weavers and tennants dwelling within the precincts of the late monastery', was no doubt conventional, but the sum he left to be distributed among 'the pore people of the town of Malmesbury', £40, was a large sum for those days. Dr Ramsay thinks 'it is perhaps not unduly fanciful to discern a touch of the *grand seigneur* in his character'; unquestionably he had the qualities of determination and imagination which are so often the mark of the successful entrepreneur. And once his personality had brought him success, the wealth and social standing he had attained themselves ensured further advancement.

Stumpe seems to have become personally acquainted with Henry VIII, and Fuller tells the story of an impromptu entertainment he provided for the King. 'King Henry the 8th', we read, 'hunting near Malmesbury in Bredon Forest, came with all his Court Train, unexpected, to dine with this Clothier. But great House-keepers are as seldom surprised with Guests as vigilant Captains with Enemies. Stumps commands his little Army of Workmen, which he fed daily in his house, to fast one Meal untill night (which they might easily doe without indangering their health), and with the same Provision gave the King and his Court Train (though not so delicious and various) most wholesome and plentiful Entertainment.'[17] This episode may be as apocryphal as the legendary feast prepared by Jack of Newbury, and we can only guess whether Stumpe owed any of his success in life to royal favour. Another measure of his success is the history of his family. By his first wife, who belonged to a junior branch of the Berkeley family, he had two sons who survived him; he had a third son by the widow of the owner of a neighbouring manor, whom Stumpe married towards the end of his life. The eldest son, James, to whom he left most of his property, and who had already been knighted before his father's death, became a prominent county magnate, M.P. for Malmesbury in 1555-6, and twice sheriff of the county. The second son, John, inherited his father's looms and business, and continued to reside in the Abbey House; he too became M.P. for Malmesbury in 1584. Sir James, who died at a comparatively early age in 1563, had married Sir Edward Baynton's daughter as his first wife; on her death he married her stepmother, Sir Edward's widow, who was a half-sister of Queen Katherine Howard. The family fortune descended to his only daughter, who married Sir Henry Knyvett, and their three daughters married the earls of Suffolk, Lincoln and Rutland. The result was that, although lack of grandsons thwarted Stumpe's hopes of founding a county family, 'in the seventeenth century the blood of the parvenu clothier was carried into the noblest families in the kingdom'.[18]

Mr Laslett queries whether Stumpe's establishment was really a factory, though the buildings he occupied 'may have been of factory size'.[19] Like Jack of Newbury, Stumpe's relations with his employees, whom he apparently housed and fed, were quasi-domestic, but whether the place they worked in can properly be called a factory seems largely a matter of definition. If a factory means a building in which work is done by power-driven machinery, then of course Stumpe's workshops were not a factory, for the looms they contained were operated by the weavers' own limbs. In any case, on the principle that one swallow does not make a summer, it would be a mistake to regard Stumpe as the inaugurator of an industrial revolution, if by that is meant a general transition to a factory system, for it seems clear that his establishment was quite exceptional, if not actually unique. We hear of an Oxfordshire clothier, Tucker of Burford, who applied for possession of some of the abbey buildings at Abingdon, of which it had been reported that the town was 'like to decay unless the people be set to work to drape cloth'. Tucker stated that he already employed 500 workers, and if he could set up spinning and carding at Abingdon he would spend 100 marks a week there in wages. This application may perhaps have been inspired by Stumpe's example, but Tucker's weavers would go on working in their homes. He wanted not to buy but to rent the abbey property, and, as it seems, to take over two fulling-mills which already existed there.[20]

Fuller records a tradition about 'Thomas Cole, commonly called *the rich Clothier of Reading*', who kept 140 menial servants in his house and gave employment to 300 poor people, 'in so much that his wains with cloth filled the *high-way* betwixt Reading and London, to the stopping of King Henry the First in his Progress'.[21] But nobody has pretended that Cole owned a factory, and in any case he lived a long time ago; some of the details in his story sound improbable, and he may have been even more legendary than Jack of Newbury. Then there was Thomas Blanket of Bristol, who with certain other burgesses is said to have 'set up instruments for weaving cloth', and employed 'weavers and other workmen' in their houses. This was in the middle of the fourteenth century, and there seems little reason for saying that he 'foreshadowed' a 'movement towards a factory system.[22] We hear of clothiers in the north of England, Hodgkins of Halifax, Byrom (or Brian) of Manchester, Cuthbert of Kendal, who are said to have owned factories, but little is known about them but their names, and they may well be as mythical as Winchcombe.[23] Dr Ramsay has sketched the careers of two Malmesbury men, Matthew Kyng and John Hedges, contemporaries of Stumpe, who were much more typical clothiers than he was. Both became wealthy and prominent in the locality, both at different times represented the borough in Parliament, both acquired landed property in the neighbourhood, and ranked as gentlemen. Kyng apparently was dishonest and unscrupulous, accused of sharp practice, and fined several times for selling defective fabrics. He was also quarrelsome and constantly engaged in lawsuits, as often about titles to property as in connection with his trade. The other, Hedges, according to Dr Ramsay, was more like the usual run of his class, 'neither a genius like Stumpe, nor—as far as evidence goes—a scoundrel like Kyng'.[24]

Prosperous clothiers like this were altogether too numerous to be named individually. Every town in the clothing counties had its family or families, some of humble origins like the Stumpes, others drawn from the smaller gentry, which attained wealth and local fame through control of the manufacture of cloth. Some clothiers, like Thomas Long of Trowbridge, or Paul Methuen of Bradford-on-Avon, founded families which never lost the status of county magnates; others after a few generations slipped back into the ranks of the peasantry. The prosperity of a town was often closely dependent on the fortunes of its clothiers: Leland tells us, for instance, that at Bath, which had 'of a long tyme syns bene continually most mayntainid by making of clothe', there were three

clothiers 'at one tyme ... by whom the town of Bath then flor-
ished. Syns the death of them it hath sumwhat decayed'. While the
cloth trade was at its height these clothiers built themselves substantial houses, like Stumpe's Abbey House at Malmesbury, or the 'fair
mansion place ... buildid thoroughly by John Tame and Edmunde
Tame' at Fairford, which 'never florishid afore the cumming of the
Tames onto it'. Another typical clothier mentioned by Leland is 'one
Horton' at Bradford-on-Avon, who 'buildid a goodly large chirch
house *ex lapide quadrato* at the est end of the chirch yard without
it,' and who also 'made divers fair houses of stone' at Trowbridge.[25]
These substantial clothiers kept staffs of servants, and their wills
show that 'they slept on the newly-introduced luxury of feather
beds, loaded their tables with tankards, goblets and other pieces of
silver plate, and kept stores of silken finery'.[26]

Here and there a clothier might attain to rather more than local
fame. Such was Peter Blundell, who was born about 1520, of 'very
mean parentage', at Tiverton, which was then noted for its kerseys.
His first employment was as an errand-boy for the carriers who
came to the town; he was 'tractable in looking after their horses,
and doing little services for them, as they gave him orders'. Being
'very provident and careful' with the small money he earned in this
way, after a time he 'bought therewith a kersey, which a carrier was
so kind as to carry to London, gratis, and to make him the advantage
of the return'. After a while he was able to buy 'kersies enough to
lade a horse and went up to London with it himself'. His diligence
and good behaviour there secured him employment in the kersey
trade, until he had made enough money to become an employer of
labour and set himself up as a manufacturer of kerseys. By the time
he died, in 1599, he had amassed a fortune of £40,000, which for
the sixteenth century was 'a vast and large estate'. He bequeathed
legacies to endow numerous benefactions, best known of which is
the school that bears his name at Tiverton; but he also left money
for all sorts of charitable purposes—to churches and hospitals in
London, to the 12 great London companies for relief of the poor,
and so on.[27]

Blundell's benefactions seem to have been exceptional in date as
well as in size. In the fifteenth and early sixteenth centuries
clothiers had often built or enlarged their local churches, left money
for masses, or founded chantries or schools. The Tames at Fair-

ford have already been mentioned, and Dr Ramsay cites several similar examples from Wiltshire. On the other side of England, the Springs of Lavenham in Suffolk were a notable example of a family whose worldly success rivalled that of the Stumpes, though none of them concentrated his work-people under one roof. The second Thomas Spring, who died in 1486 (his father had died in 1440) 'left 100 marks to be distributed among his fullers and tenters, 300 marks towards building the church tower, and 200 marks towards the repair of the roads round Lavenham. But it was the third Thomas who was the rich clothier *par excellence.*' When he died, in 1523, he left money for 1,000 masses and £200 for the completion of Lavenham church. His daughter married Aubrey de Vere, son of the Earl of Oxford; his heir became Sir John Spring, and lord of 11 manors, nine in Suffolk and two in Norfolk.[28]

After about the middle of the sixteenth century, it seems that Wiltshire clothiers ceased leaving money for church purposes—possibly in consequence of the Reformation—but they went on investing in houses, and above all in land. The established gentry tried to stop this by an Act of Parliament, passed in 1576, which made it illegal for clothiers in Wiltshire, Somerset and Gloucestershire to acquire more than 20 acres. This Act does not seem to have been enforced, but there is other evidence of stiffening resistance to the social pretensions of rising clothiers. At the Heralds' Visitation in 1565, while several clothing families were 'accepted as armigerous', a number of other clothiers, when challenged, 'disclaimed the name of gentleman', and some were 'disgraded', among them Henry Goldney of Chippenham, bearer of a name which stood for solid merchant wealth. In Elizabeth's reign administrative office and membership of the House of Commons came to be concentrated more and more in the hands of the landed gentry, and it became rare for a clothier to be elected to Parliament. John Stumpe at Malmesbury in 1584 was exceptional in that respect, and the last Wiltshire clothier to become an M.P. was John Noyes, who sat for Calne in the first Parliament of James I's reign. Dr Ramsay calls this 'a change of great significance whose cause has yet to be explored': it may perhaps be connected with the decline of the old-fashioned broadcloth industry in comparison with the new draperies and other lighter fabrics.[29]

If we move from the west country to the north of England, we

find rather different conditions. There too the industry was organized on the domestic system, but the scale of operations was smaller,
and until the Industrial Revolution brought steam power and
factory organization, wealthy capitalists were rare as cloth manufacturers. The clothiers were mostly small men who, with their
families, themselves did manual labour; they lacked the capital to
buy wool in large quantities, and therefore were dependent on
middlemen dealers to supply their needs. When they had made their
cloths they had to sell them quickly; consequently there were
numerous weekly local markets, where again it was the middleman
merchant who bought up and disposed of the independent producer's goods. It was therefore in trade rather than industry that
wealth and capital were to be found, and the famous names, like
the Mosleys or the Chethams at Manchester, were those of merchants rather than entrepreneurs. There were some more substantial
clothiers, especially in the villages near Leeds, who were also
farmers on a small scale, and 'lived in simple plenty'. There were
gardens and orchards round their houses, and they owned or rented
fields in which they kept poultry and domestic animals; they worked
themselves, but at the same time they took apprentices and
employed paid labour, journeymen and women, who prepared
the yarn and wove the pieces in their own cottages, or perhaps in
the clothier's workshop. The clothier then took the cloth to the
fulling-mill, after which he brought it home to be sheared, dressed,
and tentered before it finally went to market.

Such were the origins of a man like John Harrison (1579–1656),
who became a celebrated benefactor to the town of Leeds, building
a church (St John's, Briggate), founding almshouses and a grammar
school, and leaving endowments to maintain them, as well as devot-
ing time and energy during his life to service in municipal office.
This was the conventional road to remembrance by posterity.
Another Leeds clothier, Randall Tenche, won no local fame as a
philanthropist, but with his readiness to undertake new ventures
he seems to have had more of the characteristics of the entrepreneur.

Sir Francis Willoughby, of Wollaton Hall near Nottingham,
whom we shall meet again, conceived among his numerous interests
a scheme for making fancy cloth. In 1589, hearing of this, Tenche
suggested to Sir Francis that he should undertake the dyeing of the

wool, 'and the spinning, dyeing and working of Arres work of all sorts, which he is emboldened to do, more especially as he has found out a workman or two that will join him or be under him, who will work any work that shall be set out unto them by a painter in colours and to work the same either in woollen yarn being fine and small, or in crueles or in silk, or in silver and gold, or altogether' (crewel is a fine worsted yarn used in tapestry and embroidery). He offered to visit Wollaton, 'and Sir Francis shall draw a little carpet or cushion in what colour shall be thought fittest for the same'; before a contract was concluded Tenche would work it to Sir Francis's satisfaction. It appears that Willoughby welcomed this proposal, and was willing to pay Tenche £50 a year as well as the workman's wages of 6s. 8d. a week. Willoughby and Tenche accordingly drafted plans for weaving and dyeing this fancy cloth, but whether they were put into effect is unknown. At home in Leeds, where he lived in the Tenters (where the cloth was stretched), near the river, Tenche was churchwarden of the parish church in 1591, and is said to have been 'of some importance in the religious life' of the town. He died in 1628.[30]

Another clothier whose enterprising readiness to experiment with new processes differentiates him from the ordinary run, and makes him specially deserve the name of entrepreneur, was a man who regarded himself as 'the most industrious of the profession in the kingdom'.[31] Benedict Webb was born in 1563 of a family of clothiers in south Gloucestershire, and at the age of 16 he was apprenticed to a London linen draper, who three months later sent him abroad. For the next four or five years he spent most of his time in either Paris or Rouen, with occasional visits to Italy. While he was abroad Webb observed foreign methods of manufacture, and entered into a contract with a merchant at Exeter to have two looms made for him, sending full directions for their construction. On his return to England he established himself near Taunton, and began to put into practice the lessons he had learnt. By 1589 he was experimenting with two types of cloth, neither of them the traditional broadcloth of the south-western counties. He made not only perpetuanas but also a Spanish type of cloth, 'which he characteristically called "Webb's cloth" '. The first was a thin, light cloth, already familiar as one of the new draperies, which was being exported in large quantities; the second, a medley, or cloth of mixed

D

colours, Webb claimed to have improved by devising 'diuers and sundry cullers . . . which manner of drappery is now exseadingly increased in many parts of the kingdum'. Webb's claim is borne out by the testimony of a family which followed him in this manufacture: 'Benedict Webb . . . was the first that made Medley cloathes (before they were blew, green etc. coloured cloaths) Mr. John Ash of Freshford [near Bradford-on-Avon] was the second that made Medleys, who improved the art, and got a great estate by it tempore Caroli primi.'

After a few years Webb moved to Kingswood, near Bristol, where he inherited his father's clothing business. Here he was not only concerned in the manufacture of cloth, but like many other clothiers he had considerable landed estates to manage, and in addition various commercial interests, among which he kept up his connections with France. He rented meadow and pasture land in other parts of Gloucestershire, for stock raising by hired labour, but clothing was his main concern. By the early seventeenth century he had built up an extensive business, and had established a great reputation in the west of England. The French government prohibited the importation into France of English tenter-stretched cloths, which meant virtually all English cloths. In this crisis Webb's knowledge of the English trade with northern France enabled him to give the English government valuable advice; negotiations with France led to the withdrawal of the prohibition, and the livelihood of English merchants was preserved.

Almost immediately after his return to England Webb had begun experiments to produce 'a kind of oyle to be made of Rape seed and other smale round seedes for the use of Clothinge'. Oil is an essential factor in cloth manufacture, to replace the natural grease lost in cleaning the raw wool; according to one sixteenth-century estimate, for every cloth two gallons of oil were needed. For this purpose olive oil and other oils were imported, but at least as early as 1565 there were schemes for using home-grown rape seed oil. In that year Armigil Wade and William Herle obtained a patent for the 'manufacture of sulphur' and the extraction of oil from seeds for finishing cloth. Probably the process was not successful, for in 1571 another inventor, a draper named Giles Lambarde, secured a patent for making oil, and in the following year a Bill was drafted in Parliament to confirm this, but again apparently nothing came of

it.[32] Webb grew his crop of rape on his own land at Kingswood
and elsewhere, particularly on land in the Forest of Dean which he
leased from Sir William Throckmorton. By 1625, when the business
was flourishing, he agreed to rent 550 acres of Throckmorton's land
for growing rape; how much of his land elsewhere he used for
rape is unknown. He had begun to put up an oil-mill at Kingswood
in 1605; four years later he appointed his first oil-maker. He then
endeavoured to improve his technique, 'perficting his mills and
engines until he is come from makinge one gallon of oyle in a day
when he first began after his cominge out of France, nowe (1626)
to makinge above twenty gallons in a day at one mill'.

Expansion of the oil business seems to have been slow. Until
about 1618 it was still in an experimental stage, and it was not fully
under way till 1621. By December 1624, when he was granted a
patent for the sole use of his invention for 14 years, at an annual
rent of £5, his business had evidently reached sizeable dimensions,
but the financing of the project had involved him in increasing
difficulties. He had already spent more than £2,000 on his experiments, a very large sum for those days, but he continued to pile
up debts with unfailing confidence that he could make the project
profitable. He reckoned that the cost per 100 acres, including the
rent of the land, the labour of ploughing, harrowing, reaping, truss-
ing and winnowing the crop, making the oil, and putting it into
casks, amounted to £480. The oil produced would sell for £825,
leaving a profit of £345. Rape had other advantages, he thought.
It could be grown on dry or sandy soils, and would enrich them;
also the harvesting of it would provide employment for the poor
at a time of year when agricultural work tended to be scarce. On
the other hand, careful cultivation was necessary, particularly in
harvesting the crop, for which special tools were required.

Clothiers at first were suspicious of Webb's oil, but he persuaded
them to try it by promising to make good any damage or failure
they might suffer. By 1620 many Gloucestershire clothiers had come
to recognize its advantages and were using it exclusively, and within
a few years its use had spread through the neighbouring counties.
Giving evidence at Wotton-under-Edge in April 1626, 22 'principal clothiers' of Gloucestershire, Somerset and Wiltshire 'spoke
warmly of its excellent qualities.' Most of them agreed that previously they had never dared to use rape seed oil for their best cloths,

but they now found Webb's oil not only much more efficient but also considerably cheaper. Whereas they had formerly paid £40 a tun at London and Bristol for imported oil, they were now saving amounts which they variously estimated at from £4 to £20 a tun. Only a year after obtaining his patent, however, Webb became involved in a dispute with a Bristol soap-boiler, Richard Warner, who was infringing it. According to Webb, Warner had visited his house three or four times under the pretence of buying oil, but while 'receiving Entertainment at bedd and board' he was really observing Webb's engines and enticing his servants away. Warner then proceeded to set up a mill at Caerleon, in Monmouthshire, where he made large quantities of oil. He admitted that his intention was 'to overthrow Webb's patent', and he planned to erect another mill at Hampton, in Gloucestershire, where he was raising seeds. The case seems to have been left unconcluded, possibly because Webb abandoned his suit. We do not know what became of his industry, but it seems clear that the amount of oils imported declined between 1620 and 1640, and the use of rape seed oil was firmly established. To contemporaries Webb seemed 'full of pride and vanitie, and void of conscience and reason', but for all his arrogant self-confidence there can be no doubt that the west-country cloth industry benefited by becoming more diversified, and his rape seed venture was technically a success, even if he exaggerated its profitability.

Historians are agreed about the disastrous results for the clothing industry, up and down the country, of Sir William Cockayne's famous project, launched in 1614, to encourage the dressing and dyeing of cloth in England. Much cloth was exported in an unfinished state to the Netherlands, where it was dressed and dyed before being distributed for sale in other parts of Europe. With the export of cloth largely in the hands of the Merchant Adventurers' Company, Cockayne suggested to James I that their privileges should be withdrawn and a new company, to be called the King's Merchant Adventurers, should be founded, under his direction, with a licence to export finished cloths only. He gained the King's ear with tempting promises of increases in the royal revenue. The proposal was that clothworkers should pay the King five shillings for every cloth they dressed. With an estimated annual turnover of 80,000 cloths, the addition to the King's income would be £20,000.

Besides this, it was calculated that the increased importation of dyestuffs would add another £20,000 annually to the customs revenue, while additional sales of alum would bring in a further £7,500 a year. For Cockayne himself, no doubt, there were to be even larger profits, but the scheme was a total failure. The Dutch replied by prohibiting the importation into the Netherlands of all cloths, finished or unfinished, and in any case the new King's Merchant Adventurers were quite incapable of organizing the finishing processes in England. The immediate effect was a crisis of overproduction and unemployment in the cloth industry : clothiers went bankrupt and weavers rioted. Within two years Cockayne and the King had to admit defeat, and the old Merchant Adventurers had their privileges restored. Should we, then, count Alderman Cockayne as one of our entrepreneurs? He was a wealthy capitalist, but primarily a merchant in London, of which he became Lord Mayor in 1619; his business was selling rather than making textiles. He was indeed a 'projector', and on the face of it his project might have appeared likely to benefit English industry. But obviously it was ill-conceived, and one suspects that his real motives were jealousy of the exporting privileges of the Merchant Adventurers (he was himself a prominent member of the Eastland Company), and the hope of making a large profit for himself as a monopolist.[33]

Although Cockayne's project collapsed and was revoked, it had inflicted lasting damage. In 1621, partly because of the outbreak in Europe of the Thirty Years War, the cloth trade was still suffering from a sharp depression, which Parliament was rather helplessly trying to alleviate by legislation; and though the situation was partially relieved by increased manufacture of the various new draperies in place of broadcloth, the former prosperity was never fully restored. In this crisis the government turned for help to a man who for some years had been engaged in various schemes to relieve unemployment by spreading the manufacture of the newer kinds of cloth. We first hear of Walter Morrell in 1608, when he was engaged by the Earl of Salisbury to establish at Hatfield 'the art of clothing, weaving, spinning, carding or any such like commendable trade which the said Walter shall think good'. At the outset the scheme resembled previous attempts elsewhere to use the Poor Law organization for this purpose, but instead of being financed out of the rates it was to be subvented privately by Salisbury himself. Morrell, however, had grander ideas. He hoped that the county gentry would follow Salisbury's example and extend the scheme to cover the whole of Hertfordshire, and that other counties would then follow suit. In 1615 he sent a petition to the King, asking that the leading men in Hertfordshire might be incorporated in order to establish and regulate the manufacture of the new draperies throughout the county. After an inquiry the Privy Council gave the scheme its approval, and in 1616 the 'Master, Wardens, Assistants, and Comminaltie of the Company of Drapers in the Countie of Hertford' was duly incorporated. The company included 27 county gentry as members with Salisbury as the first Master; Bacon, who had drafted the charter, became a Warden, and Morrell held the office of Clerk. When it came to subscribing money, however, the gentry hung back, 'unless they might be secured of their principall to be repaid them howsoever the project should succeede'. They raised various objections, against which the Council's exhortations were unavailing, and for the time being the scheme had to be shelved.

Morrell had another chance in 1622, when a committee appointed to investigate the decay of the cloth trade after the collapse of Cockayne's project advised that in every county a corporation 'of the most able and sufficient' men should be set up to promote the manufacture of cloth. This was virtually Morrell's plan, and for the next three years he urged the government to put it into effect. Early in 1625 the King and Privy Council approved draft schemes for companies in seven counties, and shortly afterwards they issued orders for schemes to be prepared for 32 counties. But Morrell's hopes were to end in disappointment after all. The schemes were never completed, and though he and a relative of his returned to the charge several times in the ensuing years, and a committee of merchants in 1638 urged the adoption of the plan, the government had graver matters to attend to, and never seriously considered it again.[34]

Though the cloth industry in the middle of the seventeenth century was less prosperous than it had been in its heyday, we must not exaggerate the decline in its importance. It was still far and away England's largest and most important industry, accounting for more than three quarters of the total exports of the country; and it was to retain its pre-eminence for many years to come.

3 | Coal

Of all the developments in the economy of sixteenth- and seventeenth-century England none was more important, and none more fundamental, than the increase in the use of coal. Nowadays the coal trade is shrinking, but for many years the very existence of Britain as an industrial country depended upon it. In the Middle Ages there was practically no industrial use of coal, and in domestic grates it was burnt only within very short distances of the places where it could be gathered, from shallow pits or outcrops on the surface of the land, or on the seashore. After about the middle of the sixteenth century, however, the situation altered markedly. Supplies of timber were being used up, either directly as fuel or by conversion into charcoal, which the iron industry was demanding in increasing quantities. The Elizabethan government could not allow the forests to be denuded of the oaks required for building ships of war, and placed restrictions on the use of wood fuel, which in consequence became scarce and dearer. Coal began to be used not only for various industrial processes, such as brewing, boiling brine in salt-pans, glass-making, and later for other purposes, but also as fuel in domestic hearths and kitchens. An extensive and expanding sea-borne trade in coal developed between the Tyne and London, where in the seventeenth century the domestic use of coal became general, as it already was in places adjacent to the coalfields.

It has also been suggested by Professor Nef that the secularization of ecclesiastical lands, and the greater willingness of their new owners to grant mining leases on favourable terms, stimulated the exploitation of coalfields hitherto neglected. This certainly seems to be true of lands belonging to the bishopric of Durham, where formerly the bishops had granted only short leases, which did not encourage mining. In Elizabeth's reign long leases were granted, and it became more worthwhile for entrepreneurs to sink capital in long-term projects. Whether this kind of situation was general, however, seems to be unproved. Coal measures underlay the estates of many landowners in different parts of the country, and Nef has noticed that a high proportion of coal-bearing land had been in ecclesiastical hands.[1] Some of it was worked, albeit on a small scale, in the Middle Ages; but then the demand for coal was small. If landowners now began to exploit their resources more vigorously, it does not necessarily mean that they were more enterprising than their predecessors; they may have done so in response to rising demand. And by no means all the coal raised came from large-scale enterprises. Landowners with coal on their estates often did no more than they had done in the past, opening up one or two small, shallow workings to supply the local needs of themselves and their tenants.

Whatever the reasons, however, the expansion in output in the sixteenth century was undoubtedly remarkable. In 1564 Newcastle-on-Tyne, then the only important coal-shipping port, shipped just under 33,000 tons of coal; 70 years later the amount shipped had risen to over 450,000 tons. By 1634 the coal shipped from Sunderland, a negligible quantity at the beginning of Elizabeth's reign, had reached nearly 70,000 tons. The Tyne accounted for about half the coal trade, and the amounts shipped from other ports were much smaller, but there, too, shipments were rapidly increasing: from the Dee and the Mersey they rose in the same period from 1,000 to over 12,000 tons, while coal from South Wales multiplied nearly tenfold. The midland counties lay at first at a comparative disadvantage, owing to their distance from the sea, for overland transport was almost prohibitively expensive: it was estimated that as short a distance as three miles might add 60 per cent to the price of coal at the pithead.[2] In districts within reach of a navigable river, however, such as the south Nottinghamshire coalfield, where there was an abundance of easily accessible coal which could be shipped down the Trent, development was more rapid. Collieries in the west Midlands similarly relied on access to the Severn. The amounts of coal shipped from east-coast ports to London alone increased from about 24,000 tons in 1586 to 74,000 tons 20 years later, and it seems that the proportional rate of increase, though not of course the actual amount of coal produced, was greater in the late sixteenth century than it was even at the height of the Industrial Revolution 200 years later. The annual output of coal from the whole country in about 1540 has been estimated at under 200,000 tons; a century later it was over 1,500,000 tons, and at that date Britain is thought to have produced at least three times as much coal as the whole of the rest of Europe.[3]

This expansion was achieved partly by developing fresh coalfields, partly by sinking deeper pits when surface or shallow workings became exhausted. Deeper pits required more capital, both to open and to keep working, especially as they had to be drained and ventilated; they also employed more miners and other labourers. Here lay the need and the opportunity for the entrepreneur. There were some small coalfields, as for instance in the Forest of Dean or in Somerset, where pits were opened and worked by a mining peasantry. More often, however, landlords were the controlling personalities, and they commonly regarded the development of their mineral resources as a branch of estate management, and let the mining rights on their land on lease to professional entrepreneurs, or to more adventurous neighbours who were tempted to plunge into large-scale mining on their own account. This was a risky business, and not infrequently involved them in heavy losses. Sometimes, as happened in Nottinghamshire in the early seventeenth century, it led to over-production, as a result of which some local families were ruined. Another reason for financial difficulty was that working costs rose steeply as shafts were sunk deeper, and although a succession of inventors claimed to produce new or improved devices (the Calendars of State Papers Domestic are full of such claims) the efficiency of the pumps then available could not keep pace with the increasing depth of the mines.

In some mines drainage was effected by an 'Egyptian wheel', an endless chain with buckets, not unlike a dredger; in smaller workings a simple windlass and bucket might still be in use. The commonest mechanical apparatus used in the seventeenth century, which has been called the 'wet period' of coal-mining, was the rag-and-chain pump. This consisted of an endless chain with broader leather bindings, or sometimes bunches of rags, at intervals along it, fitting closely into a pipe, which might be anything up to some 20 feet in length. In a later improvement, called the plate-and-chain, the chain carried circular iron plates. The apparatus was worked by a handle on a wheel at the surface and, catching up a series of short columns of water, it served to drain small mines, but demanded very heavy labour from the relays of men who turned the wheel, and in deeper mines a series of these pumps was necessary. Sometimes the pumps were worked by a waterwheel, or in deep mines there might be a series of waterwheels one above the other; another device was the horse-gin, or horse-whim, in which the motive power was a large upright drum, turned like a capstan by a team of horses.[4]

In suitable terrain mines might be drained by horizontal galleries called soughs or adits, sometimes combined with mechanical pumps to lift water from lower levels. As a result of these developments the amount of capital outlay required was continually on the increase. Nef refers to instances in Elizabethan times when £100 or £200, or even less, was enough to start a coal-mine, but by the seventeenth century far more was needed. He mentions a colliery near Wigan in which in 1599 £400 had been invested, but by 1626 the amount of capital sunk there was said to be as much as £3,000, and he cites numerous other examples in the early seventeenth century, which he thinks there is no reason to regard as exceptional, where the outlay ran into several thousand pounds. These increases no doubt were partly a reflection of monetary inflation, but to a large extent they represented more expensive equipment. By the middle of the century there were pits as much as 300 or 400 feet deep, and the capital expended in the boring of these shafts, in the elaborate pumping and winding machinery they necessitated, in the buildings at the pit head, and in the huge quantities of timber props required underground, might represent an investment of as much as £10,000 or even £20,000.[5]

To raise capital on this scale was beyond the means of most people, and after the first quarter of the seventeenth century almost the only large collieries which remained one-man enterprises were those which were the property of landowners still working their own coal. Joint-stock companies did not appear in the coal industry until the very end of the century, and the predominant arrangement was for partnerships to be formed to work the mines. The partners in a mine assumed what could be extremely burdensome obligations. They not only undertook to pay their share of all the various kinds of expenditure involved in running the mine, some of them unforeseeable, in cases of accidents or explosions, for instance, or sudden flooding; besides these risks, according to Nef, 'the theoretical conception of an enterprise in which every partner had an equal voice was seldom realized in practice'. What usually happened was that one of the partners took charge, and this led to difficulties when disagreements arose, or when some of the partners defaulted in their contributions. When the partners had come to the end of their own resources, or could raise no more capital from relatives or friends, or possibly from the traders in the neighbouring town (for example, when the Beaumonts in 1616 had to give up trying to monopolize the local coal supply, one of their collieries was taken over by a group of merchants at Coventry), they usually had recourse to the city of London. Money could always be borrowed there, but on terms which might press very harshly on the borrowers.[6]

When London merchants or money-lenders supplied capital for mining, they usually required the borrowers to give what were known as 'bonds' or 'statutes staple' for at least double the amount of the loan. By these instruments the borrowers undertook to pay off the principal by instalments on specified dates, together with interest, often calculated at much more than the legal 10 per cent. If the entrepreneur was unable to meet these payments, his creditors could force him to assume liability for a much larger sum, and in the end he might become so burdened with debts that he could not hope to discharge them. The bond then took effect like a mortgage, and the creditors could seize the colliery. It was probably worth many times the amount of the original debt, which generally formed only a small part of the total amount of capital invested in the mine; indeed, sale of the coal already extracted and stacked above ground would sometimes produce enough to meet both principal and interest. When a colliery came in this way into the hands of money-lenders, they could either sell it or lease it to fresh adventurers, of whom apparently there were always plenty, or they could themselves hire labourers to get out all the coal they could without investing more capital. This was what happened, as we shall see, when in 1618 a syndicate of London financiers belonging to the Grocers' and Fishmongers' companies took over Strelley colliery in Nottinghamshire. In five years it was drowned and wrecked, but they made £9,000 out of a debt which originally was no more than £2,000.

There were other ways in which real control was apt to pass from the owners of collieries to the merchants and money-lenders who supplied additional capital. Coalowners were generally dependent on the services of middlemen and wholesale merchants, and an even greater outlay was involved in the distribution of coal than in the collieries themselves. There were carts and horses and their feed, wharves and buildings, harbours to be constructed and dredged, barges and lighters by the thousand. The coastwise transport of coal in the mid-seventeenth century employed over 1,000 sea-going hoys, each worth from £1,000 to £3,000 or more. The coal trade came to be dominated by the capitalists who controlled the ships and the London coal yards, and in order to dispose of his coal the colliery-owner had no option but to sell it to the merchants, who could form a ring and fix prices to suit themselves. These traders also could sometimes exact bonds or statutes staple of twice the value of the coal the owner undertook to sell, in case he should fail to carry out his part of the contract. As conditions in a mine might make it impossible for an owner to deliver the full quantity at the time and place specified, he then became a debtor to the middleman, who could seize the mine in case the full amount of the statute were not redeemed.[7] Mines have always been risky investments, and when such conditions prevailed it is not surprising that some people were ruined. But with good luck, and adroitness in taking advantage of favourable circumstances, there were chances of making a fortune.

One of the most successful of such entrepreneurs was Thomas Sutton, founder of the Charterhouse in London. The export of coal from the Tyne in the sixteenth century was a monopoly in the hands of those privileged freemen of Newcastle who formed the company of Hostmen.[8] Trade in Newcastle, as in many other places, was governed by the custom of 'foreign bought and foreign sold'. This meant that if a 'foreigner' (that is, anybody not a freeman of the town) brought in anything for sale, only a freeman could buy it, and if a foreigner or an inhabitant who was not a freeman wanted to buy anything, he must buy it from a freeman. In other words, one of the parties to every transaction that took place in the town must be a freeman. Freemen were further benefited by an

Act of Parliament passed in 1529 with a view to facilitating the collection of the customs due to the Crown, which provided that ships should not load or unload cargoes anywhere on the Tyne except at Newcastle. The consequence was that the owners of collieries both north and south of the river not only had to bring their coal to Newcastle for shipment, but also, instead of selling it direct to 'foreign' buyers, they were obliged to sell it to the freemen, who then resold it. In early days probably all trading freemen had the right to be 'hosts' to strangers, and so to become 'hostmen', but in course of time this privilege had become confined to a select body of the freemen, who also controlled the corporation of the borough. By the early sixteenth century the supply of coal and grindstones, the two special products of the district, was entirely in the hands of the hostmen, and there seems to have been practically no opposition to this monopoly, since they made it a practice to admit as hostmen the freemen who owned collieries. Having the sole right to sell coal at Newcastle, they were able to acquire possession of all the mines in the neighbourhood, and by the end of the century they dominated the whole trade. In 1600, in return for their guaranteeing the payment of an increased customs duty, Elizabeth I, as part of a charter to the borough, made the hostmen a corporate body, and confirmed their monopoly of exporting coal and grindstones. The royal charter not only strengthened their privileged position, which hitherto had rested only on custom, but allowed them in future to select new members of their body. As there was considerable competition to secure admission, they were able to charge fees for membership of £10, £20 and even £30.

The ambition of the Newcastle hostmen to control all the collieries along the Tyne gave Thomas Sutton his opportunity to enrich himself. Born in 1532 in Lincolnshire, he was not himself a native of Tyneside, and had been educated as a lawyer, but after service in the army at Berwick and elsewhere, in 1570 he became Surveyor of the Ordnance (that is, he was responsible for military supplies) in the north of England. Realizing the potentialities of the coal industry in those parts, he used the influence he had at Court, through the patronage of his Dudley relatives, the Earls of Leicester and Warwick, to obtain a long lease of rich coal-bearing land in the manors of Whickham and Gateshead, part of the bishopric of Durham. In February 1577, when there was a vacancy in the see,

Richard Barnes, then Bishop of Carlisle, as the price of being nominated as the new Bishop of Durham, granted a lease for 79 years.
In April 1582 this was replaced by another for 99 years, which
became known as the Grand Lease. The nominal lessee was the
Queen, who transferred the lease to the Earl of Leicester, but actually it was taken up by Sutton. The rent was only £90, so that in
effect the bishop had renounced his mineral rights for a century to
come in return for a fixed annual sum far less than the real value of
his property, while Sutton was able to profit by disposing of his
rights as lessee. Thus in 1583, the year after he obtained the Grand
Lease, he negotiated a deal whereby two of the leading Newcastle
merchants, Henry Anderson and William Selby, obtained an assignment of the lease, nominally from the Queen; but Sutton is said to
have received £12,000 in consideration for his part in the transfer.
Other merchants of Newcastle are said to have paid him at least
£5,000 in order to obtain an interest in the profits, and there can
be no doubt that Sutton himself derived a large income from the
lease while it was in his hands. The Lord Mayor of London is reported to have complained that the effect of the monopoly was that
the price of coal at Newcastle rose from 4s. to 6s. a chaldron; later
the price is said to have risen to 7s., 8s. and even 9s.[9]

Having feathered his nest, Sutton left the north (according to
legend he travelled south with two horseloads of money) and settled in London. Like other successful men of business he acquired
landed property, and he added to his fortune by marrying the
widow of John Dudley, but the bulk of his wealth came from his
part in the coal industry. He is said to have had landed estates worth
£5,000 a year, as well as other property amounting to some £60,000
—in itself a millionaire's fortune by modern standards. He was
reputed to be the richest commoner in England, and gained a great
reputation by his liberal contributions to charitable purposes,
culminating in 1611, the year of his death, in his purchase of the
Charterhouse for £13,000. He established there a hospital and a
school, which he endowed with his estates in Essex, and he was
buried in its chapel.[10]

As the coal industry developed, there grew up a class of technical mining experts, operating either independently or in the
employment of mine-owning landlords. A South Welsh yeoman
named John David Griffith, who had coal under his land at Llanelly,

wanted to know whether he was likely to make a profit if he opened a colliery. He asked advice of 'one that dealt in such business and had skill therein', and on receiving a favourable reply he instructed the expert to sink shafts and manage the work. Men like this, 'skilful and expert in the trade of getting Coales', occupied an intermediate status between the owners or adventurers who put their capital into mines, and the labouring colliers who actually worked there. Some of these men were attached to a particular enterprise and combined the functions of technician and colliery-manager; others had no permanent engagements but 'put themselves at the disposal of all adventurers who wanted advice, and of some who did not'. There were men who made it their profession to go about the country prospecting for coal and trying to persuade landlords and merchants with capital at their command to risk it in opening up new collieries. Large enterprises led to more division of labour, and we find men, often claiming to have invented or to possess the secret of some new or improved device, who set themselves up as specialists in draining mines.

A well-known example, Thomas Surtees, combined this occupation with that of a mining adventurer on his own account. His work as a drainage expert seems to have been lucrative; his engagement to pump dry the collieries belonging to several partnerships at Whickham was said to bring him in a 'clear profit' of £16 a week, a large sum for those times. He himself took 'parts' or shares in several collieries, not only at Whickham and Benwell in the Tyne area, but also at Raby in south Durham and at Lumley and Offerton on the Wear. But Surtees was at a disadvantage in not being a hostman of Newcastle. The hostmen's privileges usually compelled 'unfreemen' to sell out, unless they were nearly related to prominent hostmen; in fact Nef noticed a 'general movement' among unfree mine-owners in James I's reign to sell their colliery interests in the neighbourhood of Newcastle, and by 1638 the hostmen had made the conditions for unfree miners so unfavourable that hardly any remained. Surtees seemed to be in quite a strong position, for he married a hostman's widow and had a stepson and two sons-in-law who enjoyed the privileges of the company. But in spite of these connections Surtees was obliged to give up direct participation in Tyneside collieries. He leased his share in the Benwell mine to a hostman, Thomas Crome, and made over most of his Whickham interests to four other members of the company and the widow of a fifth, who enjoyed the right to trade in coal.

The coalfield in the Tees valley, in the southern part of the bishopric of Durham, began to be developed early in Elizabeth's reign. The principal entrepreneur there, Henry Smith by name, had acquired the mines in the lordship of Raby by 1568, and the scale of his operations soon widened. In 1587 he obtained from the bishop a lease of the mineral rights at Raby, Hargill and Grewborn, and opened a new mine at Carterhorne in the lordship of Raby. The rent he paid—£107 16s. 8d.—was rather more substantial than Sutton's rent for the Grand Lease; in 1598 his collieries were said to be bringing in a clear profit of at least £100 a year. Evidently this was an enterprise on a smaller and less profitable scale than the mines on Tyneside, but we gather that most of Smith's mines continued to produce substantial quantities of coal under the control of his successors throughout the seventeenth century.[11] Another mineowner who fared well in that region was Lord Lumley, who 'leased out some small pits' there and worked the larger ones himself. The coal produced by his mines was said to be the best in the county and sold well, some locally, some by shipment down the River Wear to the coast, and so to the London market. Later in the century Lord Lumley's heir was drawing an income of £300 a year from five pits let on lease, £600 from the pits in his park which he kept in his own hands, and £140 a year in wayleaves from other coalowners.[12]

Development of the coalfields north of the Scottish border was slower than in Northumberland and Durham, but there too rapid strides were made from about 1575 onwards, particularly at Culross on the Firth of Forth, where Sir George Bruce, who also operated salt pans, sank several thousand pounds sterling in his colliery. The workings were said to extend a mile under the Firth, and the mine had two shafts, one on the shore, the other on a small artificial island near low water mark. It was drained by an Egyptian wheel, turned by horses, with 36 buckets, of which 18 were continually ascending full of water, while the other 18 descended empty. This mine was a far more ambitious industrial undertaking than anything hitherto conceived of in Scotland, and it became 'the marvel not only of King James and his Scottish subjects but also of travellers from less backward England'. John Taylor, the self-styled 'water-

poet', who visited it in 1618 in the course of a journey on foot
from London to Braemar, reported: 'I did never see, read or heare
of any worke of man that might parallell or bear equivalent with
this unfellowed and unmatchable worke.' The King's visit a year
previously provided the occasion for one of the anecdotes that illus-
trate James's characteristic apprehensiveness. The royal party was
taken down the shaft on the land, and brought back up the shaft on
the island. By the time they had regained the surface the tide had
risen, and when the King found himself surrounded by water he
immediately suspected a plot and shouted 'Treason!'. His host reas-
sured him, and showed him 'an elegant pinnace' waiting to take the
party back to shore.[18]

In the century after about 1590 the coal industry became one
of the principal fields for the investment of capital, mainly drawn
from landowning families, supplemented by loans from town
merchants. Up and down the country there were families, like the
Lowthers in Cumberland, the Byrons and the Willoughbys in
Nottinghamshire, who owed their affluence to working the
minerals under their land. Some of the more venturesome would
seek to widen the sphere of their operations by leasing the mineral
rights under the territory of other landowners, sometimes at quite
a considerable distance from their own neighbourhood. Sometimes
court favourites ventured into coal-mining, but it needed more
capital than most of them were able or prepared to put up, and they
preferred to benefit from sinecures in which less risk was involved.
Nef concludes that the large majority of the gentlemen who financed
coal mines in counties distant from their own estates were not
'sinecure-seeking courtiers' but 'genuine adventurers'. Some of
them became so possessed by the fever of speculation that they
risked not only their own fortunes but 'every penny of borrowed
capital their credit would permit them to raise'.

Typical of the more successful of such entrepreneurs was Sir
William Gascoigne, who belonged to a prominent Yorkshire family,
and worked coal-pits on his own estate of Ravensworth in the West
Riding. He also had interests in Tyneside mines, and married the
daughter of Henry Anderson, the chief coalowner and coal merchant at Newcastle, and the leading figure among the hostmen. Together with a relative from Yorkshire, Richard Gascoigne, Sir
William then entered into parnership with two Newcastle merchants

E

and a local landlord, and proceeded to develop the collieries at Chester-le-Street. In 1589 he had been described as 'a man of great wealth'; in 1607 he apparently decided that he had gone far enough, for in that year he disposed of all his Durham property and sold his estate at Ravensworth to his wife's brother-in-law, Thomas Liddell, who was a prosperous Newcastle merchant. The property remained with his descendants, who later became Earls of Ravensworth.[14]

For the variety of his undertakings, and the scale both of his ambitions and of the financial encumbrances in which he involved himself and his family, no sixteenth-century colliery entrepreneur can compare with Sir Francis Willoughby.[15] He owned the manor of Wollaton, a mile or two west of Nottingham, and built Wollaton Hall, which stands as a monument to his wealth and ostentation. Wollaton had belonged to the Willoughby family since the thirteenth century, and coal was being dug there for local consumption in Nottingham and the neighbourhood since at least the fourteenth century. By 1493 Sir Henry Willoughby was making a clear profit of £200 a year from the five pits he worked there, and in Henry VIII's reign the annual output of coal ranged between 6,000 and 10,000 tons. In 1552 the Willoughbys constructed a sough, or adit, more than a mile long to drain their mines. This was a considerable engineering feat for the middle of the sixteenth century, involving heavy capital expenditure, but it was rewarded by a further expansion of output, which by 1598 had risen to some 20,000 tons, and went on increasing all through the following century.

Besides the money he had sunk in the mines on his own estate, Sir Francis Willoughby entered into numerous commitments further afield. By 1572 he had acquired an interest in pits belonging to the Beaumont family at Coleorton in Leicestershire, and shortly afterwards he made a proposal to buy this property. These negotiations fell through, but in 1576 he was still working collieries at Coleorton, and at Bedworth in Warwickshire, in partnership with Nicholas Beaumont. He also lent money to John Zouch, who wished to develop coal mines, iron pits, and ironworks on his estate at Codnor in south-east Derbyshire. This no doubt was a calculated risk, for when Zouch failed to meet his obligations promptly, Sir Francis was able to extract from him a lease of all these ventures for 20 years. In fact, Sir Francis's interests had already branched out into iron and other projects besides coal. About 1570 he had begun to participate in iron manufacture in the Middleton district of north Warwickshire, where he had another estate, and where in the course of the next 20 years his enterprise converted a medieval bloomery into a modern ironworks.[16] Besides this, and the works at Codnor, Willoughby also had ironworks at Duffield, a few miles north of Derby, and his accounts show that, in 15 weeks in 1591, 105 tons of pig iron were made there, 75 tons of which were converteed into 50 tons of bar iron.[17] At Codnor alone the outgoings in the 1590s came to nearly £20,000 a year, and at the same time we find him in possession of an iron furnace and forge which he rented from the Countess of Shrewsbury at Oakamoor, some 20 miles to the westward, in north Staffordshire.[18]

All these enterprises lay at considerable distances from Wollaton, yet they do not exhaust the list of Sir Francis's industrial activities. We saw in the last chapter how the Leeds clothier Randall Tenche offered to come and assist him in his project of making 'arras work' at Wollaton. This was only part of more ambitious plans to introduce the cultivation and dressing of woad and to found a dyeing industry in Nottinghamshire. A dyehouse was erected at Wollaton, and experiments went on for some 10 or 12 years in the 1580s and 1590s. The enterprise was not successful, but it is not clear whether failure was due, as Willoughby believed, to the dishonesty of his agents, or to other unavoidable causes. Glass-making was another project at Wollaton, partly to stimulate the demand for coal, and among the Middleton papers are articles of an agreement, dated 8 December 1615, between Sir Francis's successor, Sir Percival Willoughby, and Sir Robert Mansell, who then held the glass-making monopoly. It is evident, from the scale of his enterprises and his style of living, that Sir Francis's various works must have brought him in a great deal of money, or at any rate the capacity to spend it in large amounts; but in fact he had overborrowed and overspent, particularly on that 'foolish display of his wealth', as Camden called it, his extravagant mansion. His last folly was his infatuation for his second wife, whom he married towards the end of his life, and to whom, having quarrelled with his heir, he made over large parts of his property. In 1575 his estate was said to be 'very well known to both Her Majesty and the whole Counsel to be noth-

ing inferiour to the best', but when he died, in 1596, Sir Percival
Willoughby inherited, as he complained in a letter to Burghley, 'a
multitude of myseries'. He was 'leafte a poor remnaunte' of the
estate, 'charged with dyvers greate annuities ... besides other
collaterall bondes and statutes of infinite value', portions to pay to
three younger daughters, and '8,000 *li.* of principall debte at the
leaste'. To meet 'so greate a burthen' he had 'not above iiij.C.*li.*
yerely revenewe'. He was also involved in lawsuits, and when he
went to London he found himself detained by his creditors, 'a
recommended prisoner to the Fleet'.[19]

Just north of Wollaton lay the manor of Strelley. Here, and at
Bilborough close by, coal had been raised from early times by the
Strelley family, in rivalry with Wollaton. But the Strelleys had less
capital at their command than the Willoughbys, and their collieries,
further from Nottingham and the river, were less favourably placed,
so that sometimes they were dependent on the Willoughbys for
assistance. In May 1545 an agreement was drawn up between the
Willoughbys and Sir Nicholas Strelley, who, it appears, could not
get his coals 'by reason of the superfluous abundance of water', and
the Strelley mines were to be 'thyrled thoroo' into Wollaton Park.[20]
By the 1590s the Strelleys were so heavily in debt that they offered
to let their collieries on lease to Sir Francis Willoughby. But Sir
Francis himself was then in no position to take on fresh commitments, and Sir John Byron stepped in. The Byrons were a Lancashire family who some years after the Dissolution had acquired
from the Crown most of the estates of Newstead Priory, some
eight miles to the north of Strelley. There was coal at Newstead,
which Sir John may have worked himself, but according to Professor Nef the Byrons generally acted not as entrepreneurs but as
'calculating money-lenders, or as speculators who rented coal mines
or coal-bearing manors with a view to subletting them'. Sir John
Byron lent Sir Philip Strelley over £10,000, and in return Sir Philip
granted him a lease for 21 years from 16 May 1597, at the nominal
rent of £20 a year, of all the 'colemynes, delves and veines of coles'
under his Nottinghamshire manors of Strelley and Bilborough, and
several manors in Derbyshire as well. When this deal was completed Byron and Willoughby between them had a temporary title to
virtually the whole of the southern end of the great Yorkshire–
Midlands coalfield, extending over an area of some 200 square miles.

Sir John Byron did not sustain for long the risk of working all these newly-acquired mines on his own account, and in 1603 he sold the remaining 15 years of his lease of Strelley and Bilborough for £4,000. He retained his other interests, however, and later they passed to Sir John Byron the younger (the first Lord Byron), who was actively engaged in developing and adding to his mineral property, particularly in Lancashire.[21]

The purchaser of the remainder of the Strelley and Bilborough lease was Huntingdon Beaumont, a younger son of Nicholas Beaumont of Coleorton, with whom, as we have seen, Sir Francis Willoughby had entered into partnership to work the mines there. Born about 1560, Huntingdon Beaumont was a reckless adventurer of apparently limitless optimism, and his career as an entrepreneur ended in disaster. The mines at Coleorton were run by Nicholas and his eldest son Sir Henry, so that Huntingdon had to look for employment outside the family estates. He and another brother, Sir Thomas Beaumont of Stoughton, obtained possession of the Bedworth colliery in Warwickshire, in which Sir Francis Willoughby had formerly been interested, and they proceeded to buy up the mining rights in several adjacent manors.

To finance these ventures Huntingdon and his brother borrowed at least £10,000, some of it from another brother, Francis Beaumont. By 1616 they had given up these mines, and some years previously Huntingdon had been looking about for fresh opportunities. He had known Sir Francis Willoughby, and he may have seen in Sir Percival's embarrassments an opportunity to gain a footing in Nottinghamshire. His association with Sir Percival ended in litigation and hostility, but at first they seem to have been on friendly terms, though Willoughby later alleged that Beaumont had ingratiated himself by claiming 'great skill in coolemynes and greate love for many extraordinary pleasures and profitts which Sir Francis Wyllughby had done to preserve his father's house and lande to himselfe and his posterytye'. At any rate, while Sir Percival was detained in London, Huntingdon Beaumont obtained the custody of the Wollaton mines for three years from October 1601. No rent was specified, but he undertook to pay Willoughby 2s. for every rook (about 1½ tons) of coal sold. In July 1602 a new agreement for four years provided that Sir Percival was to take three-quarters of the clear gains, while Beaumont kept a quarter for himself. He also made a bargain with Sir Percival when he took over the Strelley mines, promising Sir Percival half the profits in return for his bearing half the costs.

Beaumont declared that Wollaton and Strelley had 'taken handes and become frendes'. No doubt he was hoping to establish a local monopoly, and apart from this some economies and advantages might well be secured if the pits were managed in conjunction. But Sir John Byron had driven a hard bargain. By the final agreement, dated October 1603, Huntingdon was to pay £4,000 in annual instalments of £500, and besides this he had to pay Sir Philip Strelley £200 down and £126 13s. 4d. a year for 'quiet enjoyment' of the mines. Beaumont half admitted his lack of caution. 'This bargain I think the worst I could have made', he wrote, 'and yet I hold it better a bad one than none at all.' To justify it costs would have to be kept down and sales expanded to the utmost, and Beaumont undoubtedly made great efforts to achieve these objects. He put forward a number of schemes, and tried to persuade Sir Percival to sell all his property except the manors of Wollaton and Middleton and plunge even more deeply into coal mining, but 'such appeals from a landless man of business were not likely to persuade a landowner prepared to endure the indignity of the Fleet rather than sell out'.[22]

Nevertheless, important developments were introduced, and within a couple of years Beaumont had laid down a wagonway of rails for the carriage of the coal. Similar devices were being used elsewhere in the early seventeenth century. Thus in 1606 a Shropshire mining adventurer, James Clifford, spent 200 marks (£133 3s. 4d.) on his 'very artificiall engine of timber' to carry coal to the River Severn through the demesne lands of the manor of Broseley,[23] and Beaumont himself later introduced a wagonway in the Northumberland coalfield; but the rails at Wollaton seem to be the earliest on record. They ran from Strelley across the Wollaton field, ending at the lane leading to Nottingham, and were laid down in 1605, as appears from Beaumont's statement of account to Sir Percival Willoughby for the year: 'Item the halfe of the charge of the rayles is 83 *li*. os. od.'[24] In 1609 Robert Fosbrook, a local coal merchant who acted as agent for Sir Percival, entered into an agreement to collect 3,000 rooks of coal every year for seven years 'at Wollerton lane end at the new rayles end', and the usefulness of the rails is clear from a request from Fosbrook next year 'to bring coales downe the rayles by wagen . . . for Strelley cartway is so fowle as few cariadges can passe'.[25] Coal which cost 4s. or 4s. 6d. a rook at Strelley Coalpit Field sold for 5s. or 5s. 6d. at the rails.

There were limits to the amount of coal that could be used locally, and soon there were signs of overproduction. 'We shall all in Nottinghamshire soone be cloyed with coales', Beaumont wrote to Willoughby, and he made great efforts to gain an entry for Nottinghamshire coal to the London market, and urged Sir Percival to press its sale in London. 'I cold . . . wishe that you lyinge at London', he wrote, 'wold be pleased a little more to . . . take the fittest opportunitie to doe us good bie our owne meanes. . . . Neither was there fitter time then now when the winter is so sharpe, and the provision for fewell in London so slender, when you may make a good fier in a frostie morninge before the maiestrates at Yealde [Guild] Hall or at the Lord Mares and stande bie the same fier and talke of the goodnes thereof with them. Now I say to undertake to sell them ten thousand tun a yeare at 18s. the tun and to have them received of us as we bring them wold as I thinke be a pleasinge motion unto them and a thing which we may performe, with some monie lente us for to provide boates and shippes to convey them, and the same monie again repaide them in coales to be delivered. . . .'[26]

In July 1604 an agreement was reached with John Bate, a London merchant, and Hugh Lenton, a contractor at Newark, for 7,000 loads of coal every year to be delivered at Nottingham bridge for shipment by them down the Trent, with a proviso that this quantity might be doubled if there were sufficient demand. The voyage down the river, however, involved hazards and difficulties as well as expense, and before long Bate and Lenton withdrew and sold their boats on the Trent, and at Gainsborough and Hull, to Beaumont and Willoughby. The Middleton papers contain numerous references to the boats and the difficulties they encountered, and it seems unlikely that any further serious attempts were made to ship coal to London. The boats continued to be used for trade on the river, and Fosbrook undertook to take charge of them, but there were further troubles: in 1610, for instance, we find him describing to Sir Percival how one of the boats was leaky and

'caste on Newark weare'. On another occasion Beaumont
complained that 'though Trente be almost continuallie banke full
and bootes might goe downe at pleasure, and they might have sente
downe three or foure hundred pounds worth of cooles and made
us some retorne that way, they will doe nothinge at all, not one
boote styrrethe or one boote moveth, but lay a heavie loade upon
my back, and will not put to their little finger to it to ease the
same'. In the same letter he referred to 'usurie, which biteth to the
verie boone, and the continuall charge of removing cooles to the
bridges, everie loade whereof I doe hier to be done, and pay weekelie
the same', so that he had 'much adoe for monie'.[27]

Beaumont felt sure that the London market, if he could reach it,
would cure his financial troubles and make his fortune. If he could
not establish a regular trade from Nottingham, he would turn to
the north-east and 'challenge Newcastle on its own ground'. So he
took leases of pits at Bedlington, belonging to the Bishop of Durham,
and in September 1605 he acquired, for £374 3s. 4d., the remainder
of a lease of all coal mines and salt pans in the manors of Bebside
and Cowpen, at the mouth of the River Blyth. The mines here,
which had been worked in the Middle Ages, had become derelict
by the sixteenth century, but Beaumont hoped that with his experience, and the aid of new devices, he could reopen them and make
them pay. He persuaded his nephew-in-law, the Sussex ironmaster
Sir John Ashburnham, to join him in this enterprise, and four
London merchants also agreed to contribute. Each partner was to
provide a sixth of the expenses, but the merchants afterwards
claimed that they had paid more than their share. During the next
few years over £6,000 was spent in laying down rails and other
equipment for the mines—'rare engines not then known in these
parts; as the art to boore with iron rodds to try the deepnesse and
thicknesse of the cole; rare engines to draw water out of the pits;
waggons with one horse to carry down coales . . . to the staithes,
to the river, etc.' Huntingdon's hopes were high, but back at
Nottingham Robert Fosbrook was more sceptical. 'Mr. Huntington
is to have Strelley agen', he wrote to Sir Percival Willoughby in
January 1610, 'paying 3,300 *li.* within one yeare and six moneths
next; his entrance is now. He hopeth of 1,500 *li.* gayne from Bedlington pittes this yeare . . . and 500 *li.* from Strelley . . . towardes
the payment aforesaid, butt I pray God this adage be nott trew

in this case *parturiunt montes, nascetur ridiculus mus*.'[28] The
London merchants expected a quick return on their outlay, and
when this was not forthcoming they soon refused to spend any
more of their money. In May 1612 they pulled out, but Sir John
Ashburnham could not escape. He and Beaumont bound themselves
in 17 statutes of £1,200 each to deliver to the merchants £1,050
worth of coal and salt every year for the remaining 17 years of the
lease.

Soon afterwards Beaumont had to abandon his northern adventure. 'For want of stock [i.e. capital] the said workes were quite
overthrowne', and in the often quoted words of William Gray's
history of Newcastle, 'within a few yeares, he consumed all his
money, and rode home upon his light horse'. His only hope now
lay in the pits at Strelley, and he worked them so energetically that
Francis Strelley, who had inherited the manor, complained of his
working day and night with double shifts instead of following the
local custom of a single day shift of 12 hours. The ground was
covered with great stacks of coal, although Beaumont used 'new
and extraordinary invencions and practises for the speedy and easy
conveyance away of the said cooles'. How to dispose of all the coal
produced was indeed the pressing question, which he recognized
as 'one principall part of a Coolemine', and he feared that prices
would fall. 'All we poore colliers have but one poore shift left
which is to crie downe', he wrote, 'and that overthroweth all.'
Meanwhile he conveyed his lease of Strelley to his brother Sir
Thomas on account of debts incurred in the Northumberland
venture. As Sir Thomas died in 1614 and the lease passed to his son
Sir Henry, the London merchants, possibly uncertain of their legal
position, held their hand for the time being, but next year they
accepted a bond of £4,000 undertaken by Sir Henry Beaumont
and Sir John Ashburnham jointly, by which Sir John's debt was to
be paid off by annual instalments of £260. Though Huntingdon
knew that the end must be near, he remained cheerful; Fosbrook
reported that 'Mr. Huntingdon saith the merchants will have
Strelley pits and all he hathe, yett he sent word to provide gynn
horses, and he is merrye'. When, inevitably, the debtors defaulted
on their instalments, in April 1618 the merchants seized the mine
with a clear title, and proceeded to work it for the remainder of
the lease.

Soon afterwards Huntingdon was 'clapped up' in Nottingham gaol, and after five years there his position looked desperate. In a last appeal to Chancery he complained that the merchants had not worked the mine 'orderlie as by the Art of Collierie might be done'. His lease, which was now nearing its end, had provided that all pits and soughs should be left in good order, and six pits were to be left 'open and chalderable, in good worke'. But the merchants had 'run into the Bassett [the seam near the surface, or outcropping] and left the deepe drowned, and pulled out all the coales to be gotten at an easie Chardge'. With the ruin of the mine his last hope of regaining his liberty had vanished, and he died in prison early in 1624. A pathetic letter from his widow to Sir Percival Willoughby, begging him to 'give his body, which you have long deteyned here in misery, a gentleman's buriall for a farewell',[29] suggests that Willoughby was responsible for his imprisonment—presumably as a reward for disappointing his early hopes.

Though none of them was ruined so disastrously as Huntingdon, other members of the Beaumont family lost heavily through their colliery ventures: more than one, as we have seen, had put money into Huntingdon's schemes. The mines on the family estate of Coleorton went on paying well; in 1621 Viscount Beaumont (son of Sir Henry Beaumont) was said to be making £1,000 a year from these mines, and they were still paying him over £300 in 1642. But in 1611 he had added to his commitments by acquiring from Sir Francis Anderson (whom Nef describes as 'another Midland "gentleman-adventurer" of the Byron type') the remainder of a lease of a colliery at Measham, a few miles away. This cost him £500 a year, and it turned out a disastrous venture. Thirteen years later he calculated that he had lost £4,890 at Measham, so that a large part of the profits from the mines on his own land at Coleorton were eaten up in meeting his debts.[30] Such might be the luck of the colliery entrepreneur, and herein lay the strength and the weakness of the spirit of entrepreneurship. Without its willingness to take risks, nothing would have been accomplished, but when it tempted a man already in debt, like Huntingdon Beaumont, to take even greater risks in the hope of retrieving his position, it was scarcely distinguishable from pure gambling.

4 | Iron and steel

In order to generate the heat required for smelting and casting iron, a blast furnace is needed. The heat attainable in the open hearths or forges known as bloomeries, which were used in the Middle Ages, was sufficient to extract from the ore a spongy mass of metal called a bloom, but not to melt it completely. Consequently it was not possible to make cast iron, and the only iron known was wrought iron, which could be forged and hammered into bars, tools or weapons. Small ironworks of this kind probably existed in many parts of the country, supplying local needs. The blast furnace was a closed furnace, in which the ore or ironstone was introduced at the top; the molten metal flowed out at the base and was cast into 'pigs' or (as they were usually called in the sixteenth century) 'sows'. In both bloomery and blast furnace the fuel used was charcoal: mineral coal could not be used because of the sulphur it contained.

Bloomery forges had small bellows, sometimes worked by the feet of men standing on them; in blast furnaces the draught was created by much larger bellows, generally worked by water power. The cast iron could be run into moulds and used direct in the form of castings, but for many purposes it had, after casting, to be worked in a forge to convert it into 'bar' iron (i.e. wrought iron), or to undergo other treatment, involving the absorption of more carbon, to make steel. All these processes required relatively elaborate plant and buildings, and they made possible a much greater output. A bloomery of the later Middle Ages might produce between 20 and 30 tons of wrought iron in a year, but a sixteenth-century blast furnace could turn out as much as 200 tons of cast-iron, out of which 130 to 150 tons of bar iron might be made in a forge. The new processes also involved more capital, and it is with them that the entrepreneur enters the industry.

The earliest purpose for which cast iron was used in England was the manufacture of cannon, and the traditional date for this is 1543, when cast-iron guns were being made at Buxted, on the borders of Ashdown Forest in Sussex. The exact date when the art of making cast iron in a blast furnace first became known in England is uncertain, but it seems clear that it had been introduced by iron-founders from France some years before 1543. There were several ironworks in Ashdown Forest, which was Crown property, and at one of them, at Newbridge, guns were made with cast iron barrels and detachable chambers before the end of the fifteenth century. The entrepreneur was a Southwark goldsmith named Henry Fyner, who in 1496 was commissioned by Henry VII to erect buildings and engage 'founders' and labourers in order to supply the guns required to meet the threat of war against Scotland.

Fyner seems to have supplied the capital, but the work was carried out by a succession of Frenchmen belonging to the royal artillery in the Tower of London, and it was they who possessed the technique of the new process. They occupied the works as Fyner's tenants, at an annual rent of £20. The first of them, Graunt Pierre, was there for a year or so, but he then complained that he had been arrested and lodged in chains for non-payment of a debt to Fyner. The rent seems to have been too high for profitable working, for Pauncelett Symart, who succeeded Pierre, also got into arrears with his rent, and did not manage to pay it off for 30 years. The rent was reduced to £14 13s. 4d. in 1512, when the works were taken over by Humfrey Walcott. By this time Englishmen were replacing the French ironfounders, here and at other ironworks in the neighbourhood, some of them supplying shot and other requirements, such as tyres for the wheels of gun-carriages. Meanwhile ironworks were being set up in other parts of Sussex, as for instance at Rotherfield, on land belonging to Lord Abergavenny, and the employment of some French workers suggests that there too furnaces were being introduced.

What happened at Buxted in 1543 may have been the first casting of guns by Englishmen, but it was a revival of a process already introduced, not the first introduction of a new process. Henry VIII had imported guns from the Netherlands and employed foreign gunmakers to cast bronze instead of iron guns, and the manufacture of iron gun-barrels in England seems to have been discontinued. In 1543, however, when there was a prospect of war with France, the King needed large quantities of ordnance, partly for equipping forts on the south coast, and cast iron was cheaper than bronze. Fortunately the English industry, though suffering from a setback, was still in existence. At Buxted gunshot were being cast, though not the guns themselves. This work was supervised by the rector there, William Levett, who is described as 'maker of iron-stones for the office of the ordnance in the Tower'.[1] Though a cleric, Levett was a man with experience of the management of ironworks, albeit not himself an ironmaster. For several years he had been deputy to the Receiver of the King's revenues in Sussex, including those from the ironworks on Crown land, and he acted as executor for a brother who had an ironworks in Ashdown Forest. With the assistance of the King's French founder of bronze guns, Peter Baude, who was sent down to Buxted, guns were successfully made in cast iron; moreover, the guns were cast in one piece, like bronze guns, instead of having only their barrels made of cast iron.

The manufacture of heavy siege guns needed more cast iron than the relatively small furnaces of those days could contain, and when in 1545 Levett was given an order to make 120 big guns and large quantities of gunshot, he had a double furnace built, that is, a pair of furnaces side by side in a single structure. This was a few miles south-west of East Grinstead, in the Forest of Worth, where there were ironworks belonging to Thomas Howard, Duke of Norfolk. On his attainder for high treason in 1546 his property was forfeited to the Crown,[2] and Levett was put in charge of the ironworks and iron-pits. Double furnaces were rare, and the one erected at Worth in 1547 was the first we know of in England. By 1574 there were two others in Sussex, one of them at Newbridge in Ashdown Forest. Levett died in 1554 and was succeeded by his servant Ralph Hogge, the technician who had been in charge at the ironworks. Hogge had a long career as an ironfounder, and by the time of his death in 1585 had made large quantities of guns and shot, most of which were sent to the Tower. These developments were so successful that they stimulated a great expansion in the Sussex iron industry. By the middle of the sixteenth century there were over 50 ironworks in the county, and the industry began to spread into adjacent parts of Kent and Surrey.

Almost every landed proprietor in the districts where iron ore was to be found—that is to say on the belt of Hastings sand stretching inland and north-westward from Hastings, by Ashdown Forest, Worth and St Leonard's Forest to the southern borders of Surrey—set up ironworks on his land. The typical establishment consisted of a single furnace in association with a single forge, but a few proprietors owned only a furnace, or only a forge. Here and there a larger ironworks could be found, such as the three furnaces and four forges owned by John Ashburnham.[3] But though each establishment was generally on a small scale, by the middle of Elizabeth's reign some 80 such works had been established in the Weald, and loud complaints were raised that they were destroying the woodlands, so that soon no timber would be left for building ships. A further ground for complaint was that a number of works were controlled by Catholic recusants, and that much of the iron was used for making ordnance for shipment abroad. An Act of Parliament had been passed in the first year of the Queen's reign to restrict the felling of large timber for iron-making, but it did not apply to the Weald of Sussex and Kent and some areas in Surrey.

One of the incentives for a landowner to establish an ironworks was to turn his woodlands into a source of revenue, but the consumption of charcoal by the iron industry was so heavy that supplies were rapidly used up. Professor Stone cites calculations showing that to make a load of charcoal required between two and three cords of wood, a cord being 8 x 4 x 4 feet, or 128 cubic feet. Between two and three loads of charcoal were used to make a ton of pig iron, and three loads of charcoal to make a ton of bar iron at a forge. Casting and forging together used up to 16 to 20 cords per ton of bar iron, or 2,100 to 2,500 cubic feet of wood. The average output of a furnace and a forge was between 100 and 150 tons of bar iron a year, so that together they might consume in a year some 3,000 cords, more or less, or the produce of perhaps 20,000 acres of woodland. The lease of a furnace and forge at Petworth allowed the lessees to take wood at the rate of 2,000 cords a year,

According to Straker, the historian of the Wealden iron industry, complaints against the ironworks were exaggerated. Other industries were also heavy consumers of charcoal, and in any case the main source of charcoal was not large timber but coppice-wood, which regenerates quickly, so that by proper management, and cropping only at intervals, regular supplies could be maintained. This is no doubt true, but it would seem that, in some districts at any rate, it was not till some time later that landlords learned to be provident in this respect. In the sixteenth century many used up the woodlands recklessly, provoking a crisis in the supply of fuel, and driving the industry to new areas where there were fresh woods to exploit.[4]

While the woodlands lasted, however, the iron industry flourished, and in the latter part of the sixteenth century its capacity had increased so much that, instead of importing guns, England, after supplying all its domestic needs, including guns for coastal fortresses and for the armament of warships, had a surplus for export abroad. In 1567 Queen Elizabeth had granted Ralph Hogge the sole right of exporting 'cast iron ordnance with gunstones' to foreign countries, provided they were not required to supply the needs of the artillery at home. From Hogge's complaint when his monopoly was infringed by others we gather that ordnance was being exported to Denmark, Flanders, France, Holland, Spain and Sweden. The demand for English cannon abroad continued until well into the seventeenth century, but eventually it fell off, owing to competition from iron foundries in Germany and Sweden.[5]

Several years before the casting of guns at Buxted, important developments had been started at the former Cistercian abbey of Robertsbridge, which was acquired at the Dissolution by Sir William Sidney. There is no evidence that the monks had worked the iron on their estate, or that Sidney bought it for the sake of its mineral resources, but as soon as he took possession he had a furnace and a forge built there, and a year later a second furnace was built some six miles away, at a cost of £65 16s. 9d., on a rented site at Panningridge.[6] For a few years both furnaces were used, but in 1546 the furnace at Robertsbridge was discontinued, and smelting was concentrated at Panningridge. The reason for this is not clear: possibly the stream at Robertsbridge (a tributary of the River Rother) was insufficient in a dry season; yet in 1576 the Robertsbridge furnace was rebuilt. As at Buxted, the local parson, Sir John Horrocke, vicar of Salehurst, was in charge. He was steward of Sidney's household, and drew up the first account book, covering the period from February to August 1541, when the furnace and forge were being erected at Robertsbridge. Later accounts were kept by Henry Westall, the clerk of the works. The whole cost of construction was £253 14s. 8d., of which a considerable part was for making dams and watercourses and diverting the stream. Output of bar iron at the forge, six tons in 1541, rose to 130 tons in 1542, and while the output varied considerably from year to year, the average for the next 30 years was about 115 tons per annum.

The undertaking soon showed a profit, and it seems clear that its financial success was largely due to the high degree of vertical integration attained. Even when smelting was transferred to Panningridge, where a rent of £21 a year had to be paid, and the expenses of carriage added five per cent to the cost of pig iron at the forge, operations were largely self-contained within the estate, so that considerable savings could be effected. Charcoal cost 3s. a load to buy, but was produced at Robertsbridge for 2s. 2d. a load; a sow of cast iron weighing 10 cwt, delivered at the forge, cost in labour and materials 12s. 2½d., whereas to buy one would have cost 16s. As a result a ton of wrought iron, of which the market price was £5 18s., could be made at the forge for £3 17s. 2. By the end of 1543 Sidney had realized about £1,400 from an expenditure of £1,068, and over the nine years from 1541 to 1549 his average income from the ironworks was £221 a year. Compared with the works at Newbridge, Sidney's establishment also appears to have been more efficient technically. The Panningridge furnace used 4·9 loads of charcoal and 5·9 loads of ore to make a ton of sow iron, while at Newbridge the corresponding figures were 5·7 and 7·0. To make a ton of bar iron at the Robertsbridge forge needed 33 cwt of sow iron, at Newbridge 40 cwt. On the other hand the consumption of charcoal per ton of bar iron was higher at Robertsbridge—seven loads as against five loads at Newbridge. By 1559 the yield of the Robertsbridge forge had improved, and from then on a ton of bar iron was produced from 30 cwt of sow iron. Later some of the advantages of integration seem to have been lost, for in 1562 there was a considerable reduction in the output of sow iron at Panningridge, and next year the furnace was closed down. Thereafter sow iron had to be purchased, only occasionally at less than the market price. The reason for this change is not clear. The furnace may have been defective (it required rebuttressing in 1558), or possibly supplies of ore and fuel at Panningridge were being exhausted;

possibly also a fall in the market price of sow iron may have made it worth while to abandon production and rely on purchased supplies. The bar iron (the only saleable product) was shipped down the Rother from Bodiam bridge to Rye, whence it travelled by sea to London and elsewhere.

On the death of Sir William Sidney in 1554 the property passed to his son Sir Henry, who was less able than his father had been to give personal attention to the ironworks, as he was absent for long periods on government service, as Lord President of the Council in the Marches of Wales, and Lord Deputy of Ireland. From 1555 the Panningridge furnace was let on lease,[7] though it continued to supply pig iron to Robertsbridge; after 1573 the works at Robertsbridge itself were also leased, at a rent of £200 a year, reduced to £170 in 1576, when the tenant rebuilt the furnace there. The accounts then show increases in the cost of carrying fuel, which suggest the exhaustion of supplies in the immediate neighbourhood.

While the Wealden industry was at its height, the fixed capital—furnace and forge, with their dams and ponds, buildings, hammers and tools—was provided by the landlord. Sometimes, like Sir William Sidney, he employed his own servants to work them, but more usually, like Sir Henry Sidney, he leased them, often for quite short terms, to tenants, who were required to maintain them, and hand them over in good repair at the end of the lease. There seem to have been no provisions for obsolescence or depreciation, and little incentive for progress, as improvements would benefit the landlord. The cost of reinstatement after mishaps such as the silting up of a pond or a watercourse, or its destruction by a flood, might be beyond the capacity of the tenants, who seldom had much capital, and were soon in difficulties and forced out of business when trade was bad. We gather, nevertheless, that on the whole the 'lesser gentry, yeomen and skilled tradesmen', who managed the works, made a good living from them, and became 'an important and wealthy middle class', as is evident from their 'substantial houses, equalling or surpassing the manor-houses of the same period'.[8] While supplies of wood and mineral lasted, the great landowners made substantial profits, and London merchants were ready, in this as in other industries, to lend money as an investment or speculation.

This happened when the Sidney enterprise at Robertsbridge

F

launched out into one of the earliest attempts in England to make steel.[9] In 1564 Sir Henry Sidney sent an agent over to Antwerp and engaged two 'Duchmen' (most probably Germans from the neighbourhood of Cologne) to come to England and start the manufacture of steel at Robertsbridge. Their names were John Frolycke and John Bowde (or Budde), and they arrived in March 1565; after spending a month, possibly examining the iron produced at the local furnace and inspecting possible sites for the steel forge, they returned to Germany to fetch appliances and workmen. Apparently they were not satisfied that Sussex iron was suitable for making steel, for on his second visit to England, in June 1565, Bowde and three others described as 'myners and Bergeknighten', went straight from London to Bristol, en route for South Wales. On 8 August 1565 Queen Elizabeth granted a licence to Sir Henry Sidney, Edmund Roberts of Hawkhurst, Raufe Knight and David Willard, to introduce during the ensuing 20 years 'so many strangers or alyens', up to a limit of 100, as the patentees 'shall enterteyne onelie for the searching, digginge and conveyinge of the mynes ewer and stone for the makinge of steele and iron wyer'. Roberts was a member of the Merchant Adventurers' Company, and also an iron merchant, who had purchased the iron produced at Robertsbridge since the works were started there in 1541. Willard, who had been an 'yronmaker' at Tonbridge in 1555, soon dropped out of the partnership, and Knight, receiver-general of Sir Henry's English estates, died in 1567. He was succeeded by his wife Johane (or Joan), and from 1568 Sir Henry Sidney and Joan Knight owned half the enterprise, and Edmund Roberts the other half. Sidney himself, owing to his absence, probably had only a monetary share in the concern, but it seems that his wife took an interest in metallurgy. She was the Lady Mary, daughter of John Dudley, Duke of Northumberland, who had built an iron furnace in Kent, and later she was actively interested in a scheme for transmuting iron into copper by treating it with blue vitriol.

Besides introducing foreign workmen, the partners hoped to obtain a monopoly for the manufacture of wire in England, but in this they were disappointed. Two Bills were introduced in the House of Commons, one for 'making of steel and plates for armour', the other for 'making of steel and iron wire', but in 1566 the House of Lords rejected them both. The wire monopoly, however, was granted to William Humfrey, of the Mineral and Battery Works, under whose auspices wire-works were set up at Tintern in Monmouthshire. The reason for this seems to have been political. In 1561 Humfrey had been appointed Assay-Master at the Mint, and had the ear of Burghley, who relied on him for advice on technical and metallurgical questions; whereas Sidney, through his marriage with Dudley's daughter, was the brother-in-law of the Queen's favourite, the Earl of Leicester, between whom and Burghley there was rivalry and mistrust for years. The manufacture of wire had been the principal object of the enterprise, but the partners were obliged to abandon this part of their plan and confine themselves to making steel.

Altogether over 50 German steel makers, some accompanied by their families, were brought to England. They came from the mountains of southern Westphalia, where the industry had long been established, and an interpreter had to be engaged in order to communicate with them. It seems that the 'Duchmen' were disliked in the neighbourhood of Robertsbridge, for in March 1567 the Privy Council wrote to some of the Sussex magistrates, saying that complaint had been made that 'John Sharpe, of Robertsbridge . . . naming himself a master of fence', had not only 'beaten diverse Duchemen which hath been employed in that county by the procurement of Sir Henry Sydney . . . for the making of steale, but also hath used such unfitting wordes against them as is not to be suffered'. The J.P.s were to see that 'the said Duchemen may have no further just cause of complainte'.

Steel was made in a forge by what is called the finery process. For this purpose the iron from the furnace, instead of being cast into pigs, was cast into thin flat bars called 'plats', and in December 1565, when the manufacture of steel began, 20 tons of plats were shipped from Cardiff to Rye. They came from a furnace, owned jointly by Sidney and Roberts, a few miles up the valley of the Taff, probably near Tongwynlais. The German steel workers must have decided that the haematite ore obtainable in South Wales was suitable for steel-making, and from 1565 until the end of the enterprise all the plats for Sidney's steelworks were made at his Glamorgan furnace from local ore. The first steel forge was at Boxhurst, in Kent, a few miles from Robertsbridge, but later a forge was set up in the brewhouse of the abbey. The outlay on these works was considerable, £1,960 in the first year, while Frolycke and Bowde received 2,000 'dollers' (5s.). The steel was sold in firkins, 27½ tons of plats being used to produce 57 firkins of steel. By September 1566 74 firkins of steel had been shipped to London and various other places, including Wales and Ireland.

At the outset the enterprise was highly successful, and German steel merchants immediately found themselves with unsold steel on their hands. In August 1567 their London representative reported to his headquarters in Cologne that more than 300 barrels of imported steel could not be sold, and that the English were making as good steel ('*so guett sthaell*') as the steel from Germany. The success of the home-made steel, however, was short-lived. The Merchant Adventurers displaced the Hanseatic merchants in the English market, and they imported large quantities of steel from the Baltic at a price with which a single enterprise such as Sidney's could not compete. As prices fell, so did his sales. The price, which was £7 a firkin in March 1566, had fallen to £6 by 1568, and sales declined correspondingly, from 166 firkins in 1566 to 51 firkins in 1568. In 1570–1, when the price was £5, only 18½ firkins were sold, and shortly after 1572 production ceased. Sidney had large estates and held public offices, and could stand a loss, but his partner Roberts was another example of the entrepreneur who came to grief. Besides his share in the steelworks and the iron furnace near Cardiff, Roberts also had a furnace and gun foundry at Abercarn in Monmouthshire, which he established in 1576, and which he still possessed when he died in 1581. But he lost all the money he had made in the iron trade, and was described at the time of his death as 'a poor man', owing debts of £2,700 'at the least'.

The iron industry had been established in South Wales long before the visit of the Germans. In more recent times great iron and steel works have been opened there because deposits of iron ore lie in juxtaposition to a coalfield. Sixteenth-century ironworkers were attracted to South Wales because, in addition to its outcrops of ironstone, its hills were thickly wooded and it had numerous rivers and mountain streams to turn the waterwheels, for the bellows at the furnaces and the hammers at the forges. It seems that ironworks had probably been established at Aberdare and Merthyr Tydvil in Henry VIII's reign, and the remains of early furnaces have been observed at various places lower down the Taff valley. As wood for charcoal became scarcer and dearer in Sussex, ironmasters from the Weald directed their capital and energies to the county of Glamorgan.

Anthony Morley, who belonged to a wealthy family from Glynde in Sussex, and was one of the partners in an ironfounding enterprise at Merthyr, became bankrupt in 1586 and died in the following year. The petition addressed by his widow to Sir Christopher Hatton, then Lord Chancellor, complaining of her treatment by certain local magnates, gives us a few glimpses of the state of the industry in the county at that time. According to the widow, Morley owned freehold lands of the value of £200 or £300, and held on lease woodlands worth £400 or £500. He had a furnace and a forge, which with all the associated tools, implements and materials were estimated to be worth 'at least £1,000'. He had got into debt, and some of his creditors, fearing he would become bankrupt, had preferred a bill of complaint to the previous Lord Chancellor, Sir Thomas Bromley, asserting that Morley owed them £600, and praying that a commission might issue for the sale of his lands and tenements to meet this and other debts. A commission was granted, and the whole of Morley's woods and ironworks were sold to one Thomas Menyfey. Finding they had a surplus of £500 or £600, the commissioners made Morley's widow an allowance of £40 a year for eight years, but Menyfey, who was charged with paying the annuity, had failed to do so. Trusting to the commissioners' assurances, she had left the residence attached to the ironworks, and now she and her four children were left unprovided for. Litigation followed, the outcome of which does not appear, but we may note that Menyfey, or Monyfee, belonged to a Kentish family, and another party cited in the case, William Relfe, who took a third share in the 'iron forge, furnace, and ironworks . . . late in the occupation of Anthony Morley', belonged to a Sussex family from Mayfield, and later acquired some of the Ashburnham property.[10]

The Sidney family obtained a further footing in Glamorgan through the marriage in 1584 of Robert, son of Sir Henry Sidney, to Barbara Gamage, heiress to the lord of Coity in that county, while his sister Mary married Sir Henry Herbert as his third wife, and so established a connection with the powerful family of the Earls of Pembroke. Robert Sidney later became Earl of Leicester, and his Coity marriage gave him possession of large estates, well wooded

and close to good supplies of ironstone, and he is said to have
devoted himself to the family interest in the iron industry. In Glamorgan he had a furnace near Coity castle, and other ironworks
further east in the direction of Llantrisant. He also acquired ironworks in Shropshire, at Neen Savage and Cleobury Mortimer, close to
the woods of Wyre Forest, and not far from Ludlow, where his
father Sir Henry presided over the Council in the Marches. He drew
a rent of £1,600 a year by letting these on lease to John Thornton
and John Crosse, two experienced ironmasters to whom Sidney also
entrusted the management of the new works on his Coity estate.
They were 'to build a work for melting, making and casting iron
sows, and make iron by forge and furnace or other means', to
acquire 'all iron myne and iron ore' in the manor, and also to use
the timber there for cord-wood, but the timber 'thought meet for
the provision of Coyty Castle' was to be reserved. The agreement
was for 14 years, during which period they could take wood at the
rate of 3,000 cords a year, paying 1s. 2d. a cord for it, and 'myne'
(i.e. ore) sufficient for this quantity of wood, at 2d. per load. They
were to keep the works in good repair and pay all the expenses of
cutting cordwood, digging sea-coal, and all the costs of carriage of
both wood and iron ore.[11]

The iron produced was exported to Dublin, to Somerset ports
such as Bridgwater and Minehead, and also to London. The Sidney
accounts show that their Glamorgan ironworks produced some 130
to 170 tons a year, a figure comparable with the output of their
works in Sussex. The numbers of men employed and their wages
were also similar in both counties. In the course of the seventeenth century the Coity furnace came into the hands of John
Matthew, a member of a prominent family of local ironmasters
who had works at Radyr and Pentyrch, in the valley of the Taff.[12]

In Monmouthshire ironworking began a little later than in Glamorgan, but it was in full swing by the middle of Elizabeth's reign.
The chief entrepreneur was a London Goldsmith named Richard
Hanbury, who obtained the controlling share in a lease of the
Mineral and Battery Company's wire-works at Tintern.[13] This, as
we saw above, was an enterprise first started by William Humfrey
(also a member of the Goldsmiths' Company), who was the
moving spirit in the formation of the Mineral and Battery Company.
'Battery' meant the flattening of metal ingots into plates by

hammers, and included the use of hammers for making household utensils such as kettles and pans. Wire was of vital importance for the cloth trade because it was needed for wool-cards, and owing to the inferiority of home-produced wire most of the wool-cards used in England were imported from France. The government was anxious that England should be more self-supporting, particularly in various kinds of metal-ware, and the Mineral and Battery Works had the dual objective of making brass articles and iron wire. German experts and workers were brought over to England but, as we shall see in the next chapter, various difficulties were encountered, and the works at Tintern, originally intended for brass-making, were diverted to the drawing of iron wire. This also met with obstacles at first, for the German technicians were skilled at brass-making but not at wire-drawing. It was necessary to bring over a skilled wire-drawer to train the workmen, but they were 'so dulle learners' that this took over two years.

For the wire-works to be a success it would be necessary to establish in Britain the manufacture of the specially pure iron, of high ductility and tenacity, known as osmund iron (the word appears to be of Swedish origin), and carefully selected ore was required for this. Humfrey therefore imported an expert osmund iron worker from Westphalia, and sent him to Wales, where he arrived in 1567 at an ironworks near Machen on the Rhymney River, which forms the boundary between Monmouthshire and Glamorgan. Humfrey then sent him to Sussex, to test the iron made at the forge at Robertsbridge, but apparently this was not satisfactory. Finally suitable ore was found in Monmouthshire, the best coming from near Abergavenny. Between 1568 and 1572 iron-mills, a furnace and a forge were erected at Monkswood, near Usk, on land formerly belonging to Tintern Abbey, and at last there were prospects of success for the Tintern works. The company granted a lease of the works to their secretary, Andrew Palmer (also a Goldsmith), in partnership with a certain John Wheler, but the lessees soon found they were losing money at the rate of about £3 a week. Palmer quickly decided to clear out, and sold half his interest to Richard Hanbury for £6 13s. 4d., and the other half to another Goldsmith called Eccleston. When Wheler died, in 1575, his widow sold her interest to Hanbury, and as Eccleston was only a sleeping partner, Hanbury then had virtually sole control.

The works by themselves can hardly have seemed an attractive proposition, but Hanbury had his eyes on wider possibilities. Together with the wire-works he also acquired the company's osmund iron works at Monkswood, which had been leased to Palmer and Wheler along with the wire-works at Tintern. He built a second forge there, and he also built a furnace at Trosnant, near Pontypool, on land leased from the Earl of Pembroke. At the same time he acquired extensive tracts of woodland between the valleys of the Rivers Ebbw and Usk, and he also got possession of practically all the woods within a 10-mile radius of Tintern. Being thus in control of all the supplies of charcoal and iron, he was in a position to dominate the whole industry. Unfortunately he could not resist the temptation to exploit his power dishonestly. The wire-works were entirely dependent on obtaining supplies of pure osmund iron, but an iron manufacturer could make money more easily by producing ordinary 'merchant iron', for which there was a ready sale, while at the same time, by making osmund iron scarcer, he could put up its price. The Mineral and Battery Company later complained to the Privy Council that when they granted Hanbury the tenancy of the wire-works, for which he was to pay a rent of £24 per annum, he had entered into a covenant to use the woods and ore only for the benefit of his partners and not for his own sole benefit. Instead he had made ordinary iron for sale to iron merchants at Birmingham and Bristol, and had failed to deliver good osmund iron at Tintern.

Hanbury not only incurred the disfavour of the company. He also made himself very unpopular in Monmouthshire by his wholesale felling of trees, and in May 1576 a number of local inhabitants, who had ancient customary rights to use wood for building purposes as well as fuel, staged a violent protest. Some 20 of them, 'armed with swords, bucklers, long pikes, staves, forest bills, glaves, and bows and arrows', assaulted Hanbury's woodcutters and charcoal burners in Glascoed Wood, and forced them to swear that they would not cut any more wood. They also told Hanbury's clerk of the works at Monkswood that if he was found there again he would not write to London any more with his right hand. Next year a party of local objectors met Hanbury himself on the road between Chepstow and Usk, and one of them said 'it were a good deed to give him a stripe or twain so that he should not have good liking or will to come to Monmouth to maintain ironworks and destroy our woods'. Hanbury made counter-complaints, but in 1578 proceedings were initiated against him by a common informer for breach of the statute prohibiting the use of timber trees for charcoal. A commission was appointed to investigate his 'lamentable spoyle of most goodly tymber trees' in the Usk valley, but there seems to have been considerable disagreement between the witnesses who gave evidence, and a second commission was appointed.

Possibly as a result of these threats, and the risk of heavy penalties for breach of the statute, Hanbury parted with some of his woodlands and ceased to frequent the district, but he continued to build up his ironmaking empire. He was later described as being 'at this first entrance in these actions a poor man and of small credit', but he was steadily amassing a fortune for himself. In partnership with Richard Martyn and Andrew Palmer, shareholders in the Mineral and Battery Company and fellow Goldsmiths, he took a lease of the ironworks at Machen on the Rhymney, and he also acquired the works at Abercarn which had previously belonged to Edmund Roberts. The company complained that he abused his control of timber and iron, but, as he later pointed out, the company had done nothing to ensure a supply of fuel to keep the wire-works going. That wood was available was entirely due to his efforts, and he evidently felt himself entitled to make what he could by selling iron on the market.

In 1583 fresh arrangements were made. On the expiry of Hanbury's lease the wire-works were let to Richard Martyn, in partnership with another shareholder in the company, Humphrey Michell, and Hanbury undertook to supply osmund iron at an agreed price, £11 10s. a ton. The manufacture of wire proceeded apace for a time, but before long there was fresh trouble and litigation, and once more Hanbury was accused of not abiding by his covenant. A body of prominent people in the county wrote to the Privy Council, complaining that Hanbury's iron was of poor quality, and that in consequence large numbers of workmen were being thrown out of work. He had consumed the greater part of 38,000 cords of wood, but the iron he had delivered should have required only 6,000 cords. Most of the rest of the wood he had used for making flat bars which he sold to smiths for making scythes and other tools. For 20 years he had been practising 'a very secret gainful trade', making merchant iron, and 'by his close and injurious dealings he is grown to great riches.' He should be compelled to exhibit his account-books.

The company branded him as 'a malicious adversary' to his partner Martyn, and declared that he had done the company 'many wrongs', besides breaking his contract. No entreaty, they thought, would bring him to reason and equity in these matters. He had made £3,000 by falsifying his books, and it was not true, as he pretended, that the company owed him £220 for osmund iron. On the contrary, on account of arrears of rent and other debts, he owed them £900, and he was greatly wronging them when he declared that non-payment of this £220 was the reason why he could not pay his workmen or supply the wire-works with iron. The Privy Council ordered him to supply good osmund iron, but he seems to have persisted in his fraudulent behaviour, making merchant iron for sale and supplying the wire-works with iron so hard and brittle as to be useless.

In 1597, after a commission had sat at Chepstow to take evidence from a number of witnesses about conditions in the industry, further charges were brought against Hanbury. He was now in partnership with his son-in-law, Sir Edmond Wheler (also a Goldsmith), and it appears that they were standing out for an extra £1 6s. 8d. per ton for the osmund iron. Even when they had been committed to the Fleet prison, there were complaints that they would rather obstinately remain in custody than comply with the Council's orders, although as a result the wire-works had stood idle for three months without iron, poor workmen and their families were utterly beggared, and the realm was unfurnished with wire. The Sheriff of Monmouthshire and some other local magnates were instructed to sequester Hanbury's and Wheler's property, water-courses, and woods, and to prevent them from making any more iron, or using any charcoal or iron ore, except to make osmund iron for the wireworks. In July 1598 Hanbury and Wheler agreed to pay £100 per annum for nine years, to deliver osmund iron in accordance with the orders of the court, and to refer all contentious matters to arbitration, and on their giving their bond to carry out these conditions they were set at liberty. Hanbury's story fades out at this point, though we gather that he spent the last years of his life, till his death in 1608, as a lonely man, at Datchet near Windsor. What we know of his business career illustrates the closeness of 'vertical integration' to monopoly, and how easy it was to pass from monopoly to fraud.

The wire-works eventually became a highly lucrative concern, and when fully working they were said to employ over 5,000 workpeople. Besides wool-cards, the wire produced was used for a great variety of articles, such as needles, birdcages, mousetraps, rings and rods for curtains, and chains for keys. It was distributed all over the country, and in 1607–8 a second wire-works was built further up the Wye valley, at Whitebrook, at a cost of £900. For some years the Mineral and Battery Company's lessees had a complete monopoly, and attempts to break it were suppressed. The first of these attempts had been made by a member of the company itself, Sir John Zouch, the owner of ironworks at Codnor in Derbyshire, which, as we saw in the last chapter, passed into the hands of Sir Francis Willoughby. Zouch started a wire-works at Makeney, near Duffield, in 1581, but the company was able to get it stopped. Then in 1603 a certain Thomas Stere erected a wireworks in Surrey, at Chilworth near Guildford. This was a more serious threat, because Stere bribed skilled workmen from Tintern to supply details of their methods, and succeeded in enticing some of them to come to Chilworth to work for him. Legal proceedings were taken against Stere, and in 1606 it was found that he had acted in violation of the company's patent. He had to undertake to discontinue working at Chilworth, but he must have been a skilled man himself, for the company agreed not only to purchase his tools at a reasonable price but to employ him at their own works at Tintern.[14]

The Forest of Dean, a few miles to the east of the Wye valley, had been an ironworking district for centuries, and the toughness and ductility of its iron should have fitted it well for the manufacture of wire. Humfrey heard about it from his German prospectors, and mentioned it in a letter to Cecil at the end of June 1566, but does not appear to have followed it up.[15] Mining in the Forest was in the hands of a community of 'free miners' with their own code of local laws or customs, and the old-fashioned methods of production persisted there into the seventeenth century. The principal magnate in the late sixteenth century was William Herbert, Earl of Pembroke, who held the office of Constable of St Briavel's Castle, 'with the

keeping of the deer and woods there', and it was under his direction
that the first furnaces in the Forest were erected, sometime
between 1612 and 1614. The earl was not actually the first person
to propose the introduction of modern ironworks. In June 1611
a certain Giles Bridges and others had obtained from the Crown a
licence to erect works and 'take myne oare and cynders' (cinders
being the refuse of old forges, which could profitably be resmelted
in the new furnaces), but there is no evidence that Bridges did anything to put his powers into effect.

Early next year, on 17 February 1612, his licence was superseded
by a similar licence to the earl, a man of great power and influence,
who besides his position in the Forest owned vast estates in
Monmouthshire and South Wales, and had the capital necessary to
finance new developments. At the same time he was Governor of
the Society of the Mineral and Battery Works, who owned the
wire-works at Tintern close by. Pembroke's licence included powers
to erect furnaces and forges within the Forest, to use 'all water and
water-courses . . . free and without stoppage', and to 'make so many
stancks, ponds . . . trenches, floodgates and passages for water in
any part of the Forest as he shall think fit'. He could enclose up
to 12 acres of ground for each ironworks, take timber to build and
repair the works, storehouses, houses for workmen, and other buildings, and up to 12,000 cords of wood a year for charcoal-burning,
at 4s. a cord. Four furnaces were erected, at Cannop and Parkend
in the middle of the Forest, at Lydbrook in the north, and Soudley
on its eastern border, and there were three forges, at Lydbrook,
Parkend and Soudley. In the exercise of his powers the earl or
his agents came into conflict with the local people, who wished to
carry on their ancient occupation in their accustomed fashion, and
there was rioting. Pembroke lodged a complaint, and in 1613 it was
ordered that 'out of charity and grace, and not of right', the miners
should be allowed to dig for mine, ore and cinders, but they were
to carry them only to His Majesty's ironworks. This order was to
be of temporary duration, until the miners' case had been heard
and settled, but it would seem that they were able to establish their
right to their ancient privileges, and soon afterwards (May 1615)
Pembroke assigned his grant and the works he had erected to Sir
Basil Brooke. Brooke apparently operated only two of the ironworks, at Parkend and Soudley, in partnership with Robert Chalde-

cott: the works at Cannop and Lydbrook were taken over by two other men in partnership, Richard Tomlins and George Moore.

Sir Basil Brooke's tenure of the works in the Forest of Dean is notable for his introduction of steel-making by the process known as cementation, in which the iron, with added materials, was smelted in closed pots in a reverberatory furnace. This superseded the finery process which had been used in Sidney's steel works in Sussex. After complaints about the rising price of imported steel, trade in which was in the hands of monopolists, and demands that the home production of steel should be encouraged, to make the country less dependent on foreign sources of supply, a patent to use the cementation process, which was already practised abroad, had been granted in 1614 to William Ellyott and Mathias Meysey. They succeeded in making steel, and in 1616 the importation of foreign steel was prohibited, but next year there were complaints to the Privy Council of the poor quality of the home-made steel. Scythe-makers and gun-makers said they could get no steel fit to use, and in the following year various cutlers, gun-makers, blacksmiths and locksmiths, declaring that the patentees' steel was worthless, sought permission to resume the import of foreign steel. Possibly because, being a man of considerable influence, he could more effectively defy such complaints, Ellyott and Meysey had their patent transferred to Sir Basil Brooke.

Meanwhile rivals sought to enter the field, and one of them, Dr Robert Fludd, a Fellow of the Royal College of Physicians, whose disregard of its rules caused the College some embarrassment, started work on his own account to upset Sir Basil's patent. He erected a furnace at which he employed a Frenchman named Rochier, persuaded some users of steel to certify that Brooke's steel was bad and Rochier's excellent, and offered to pay the King £5,000 for a licence to manufacture steel. In 1620 Fludd made a fresh offer: if he were granted a patent the King should have a third of the profits. The King was present at the Council meeting at which this offer was considered, and no doubt found it tempting. At any rate the Council agreed to issue a patent to Fludd and Rochier, but it seems doubtful whether the project got very far, as Rochier died a few years later, and no more is heard of it.

Brooke took the process invented by Ellyott and Meysey down to the Forest of Dean, and it was from there, apparently, that it later spread to other parts of the country. When in 1635 the grant of a new lease of the works in the Forest was being considered, Brooke claimed that it was he who had succeeded in establishing the new invention of steel-making in England. His name undoubtedly became well-known in connection with steel, and it was from his process that later improvements in steel-making were developed. Writing some years after Brooke's death, Fuller referred to him as 'the great steel-maker in this county' (i.e. Gloucestershire), but his steel was still evidently not of the highest quality. According to Fuller it served for ordinary 'knives, sithes, scissars, shears &c.; but fine edges cannot be made thereof, as lancets for letting of blood, incision knives, dissecting knives, razors, &c.'[16]

Steel-making was carried on in the Forest of Dean long after Brooke's time, and in the later seventeenth century the steel made there was regarded as the best English steel. Brooke held the works for about five years; after that there were numerous changes of ownership, though Brooke's name reappears more than once in association with different partners. Most of these changes seem to have been due to allegations that the lessees were taking more wood than they were entitled to, and according to evidence given at an enquiry about the destruction of the woods, some of the woodwards were bribed by the ironworkers. Meanwhile the industry was growing steadily, and by 1640 there were as many as 12 furnaces and 12 forges in the Forest, though probably not all of them were at work simultaneously. In that year the whole of the Crown property passed into the occupation of Sir John Winter. He was the grandson of Admiral Sir William Winter, to whom Queen Elizabeth had granted the manor of Lydney, and in 1604 his father had owned ironworks, probably bloomeries, on the estate. Winter sublet two of the furnaces and four of the forges to Sir Bainham Throckmorton, of Clearwell near St Briavel's, who had previously been a partner in some of the works, but Winter controlled the greater part of the iron production in the district. He was Queen Henrietta Maria's secretary, and in favour at Court, and took a prominent part on the royalist side in the Civil War. In the opening years of the war his control of the Forest was undisturbed, but in 1644 the parliamentarians took possession and destroyed his ironworks, and Winter had to make his escape by sea.[17]

Old-established ironworks in other areas also suffered from the

Civil War, because many landlords and ironmasters had taken the losing side. Many of the ironworks in Sussex, for example, were destroyed by the parliamentarian general, Sir William Waller, and the industry there, already hit by the consumption of its woodlands, never recovered from the disaster. In 1650 orders were given for the surviving ironworks in the Forest of Dean to be destroyed because they were consuming timber required for the Navy. During the next few years there was a considerable revival in the industry, but mainly in new areas: a number of ironworks in Cheshire, for example, were started at this time. Once more the motive was probably the desire of landowners to raise money quickly by selling the woods on their estates to ironmasters, royalists to pay the fines to compound for their 'delinquency', parliamentarian merchants who had bought forfeited estates, in case a change of fortune should deprive them of their newly gained property.[18]

Two different ways of financing ironworks in the early seventeenth century are illustrated by agreements entered into by Sir John (soon to become the first Viscount) Scudamore, of Holme Lacy in Herefordshire. By the first of these, dated 4 March 1628, he and his cousin William Scudamore combined to construct a forge on the latter's land. The cost of erection and the running expenses were to be divided equally between the partners, the necessary fuel being supplied, at 5s. a cord, from Sir John's coppice-wood. To find a profitable use for the wood was doubtless the principal object of the enterprise, and the agreement laid down that the produce of up to 21 acres might be consumed every year. The wood was to be at least 15 years old, and if more were needed it was to be bought in. The second agreement was for building a forge at Whitchurch, on the Wye. Here Lord Scudamore contracted to erect the forge or else to contribute £300 for the purpose, as well as £500 of working capital, repayable at the termination of the agreement; he was also to provide 200 tons of sow iron at £4 10s. a ton delivered at Whitchurch. Scudamore was thus to find all the capital, while the other party or parties (their identity seems to be unknown) were to be responsible for managing the forge. They undertook to buy 1,500 cords a year at 5s. a cord from Scudamore's woods, at Abbeydore and elsewhere, and to pay interest on the £500. Scudamore would thus obtain a return on his investment as well as a profitable use for his wood.[19]

The Birmingham district had long been a centre for metal-working crafts, whose products found their way to market through the agency of the ironmongers. In the sixteenth century these were not the retail tradesmen of today, but wholesale dealers in hardware, who sometimes supplied the capital and materials needed by a multitude of small producers.[20] In the course of the sixteenth century the iron industry in the Midlands, as elsewhere, changed its character under the entrepreneurship of the local landlords, who introduced blast furnaces, and proceeded to exploit the minerals and woodlands on their estates. In several ways they were in a favourable position for competing with the older industry in Sussex. With a higher rainfall they had more abundant water power, their woodlands were comparatively untouched, and they were well placed for supplying the metal-workers, nailers, cutlers and others, who plied their crafts in the neighbourhood. Of the numerous Midland landowning families who thus developed their natural resources we may take three as outstanding, typifying in different ways the wastefulness, the scale, and the enterprise of the landowning entrepreneur: the Pagets, the Talbots, Earls of Shrewsbury, and the Willoughbys.

The Pagets' headquarters were in Staffordshire, in and about Cannock Chase, where there were mines of ironstone and large areas of woodland, and the pattern of development followed the usual course. William, the first Lord Paget, the son of a Wednesbury nailer (or so his enemies alleged), rose in the royal service under Henry VIII. In 1546 he was granted the manor of Cannock by the Crown, and in 1549 was created Baron Paget of Beaudesert. There may have been primitive ironworks in Cannock Chase before it came into Paget's hands, but the earliest direct evidence appears to date from 1553, when there were three iron-mills there. It was under his son Thomas, the third Lord Paget, that modern developments began to be introduced. In the Chase he erected two furnaces and two forges, with five cottages for his workmen, and he also had a forge at Abbot's Bromley; but he was a Catholic, in 1583 he was suspected of being implicated in the Throckmorton plot to place Mary Queen of Scots on the throne, and he had to take refuge in exile. His estate was then escheated to the Crown, and in 1588 Burghley obtained a report 'towchinge the Timber and Woods in Canke wood', which showed a falling off in profits since the works had been in the hands of the Crown. The timber, according to the report, was too far from the sea or a navigable river to be of much use to the Queen, 'unlesse it be converted to Ironworks to which no doubt Lord Paget did mynde to convert it'. No doubt he did so mind; indeed he had already put his intentions into effect. He had stepped up iron production so rapidly—in the later 1570's the output of his works was 330 tons of bar iron a year—that by 1581 he was having to buy wood for fuel.

Ruin was not far off, and came when a lease of 'Canck wood' and all its trees, together with its furnaces, forges, 'all waters thereto belonging', and the cottages, was granted to Sir Fulke Greville. Greville's only interest in the estate was to make a quick profit, and an inquiry in 1595 reported that instead of cropping the woods he had devastated them. An Act of Parliament passed in Henry VIII's reign had provided that when woods were felled, in every acre 12 'standels' or young oaks should be left to grow into timber, but Greville had felled the trees indiscriminately, including some marked for the Queen's use, and he had failed to leave any 'standles or samplers according to the Statute'. Had Paget remained in possession he would probably, like other improvident landlords, have done the same. At any rate, when the estate was restored to the Paget family in 1597, for lack of woods it was impossible for them to continue the production of iron, and the industry migrated either northwards or towards Birmingham.[21]

George Talbot, sixth Earl of Shrewsbury, was one of the richest men in England, with estates covering a huge area in the west Midlands, in Herefordshire, Shropshire and Staffordshire, as well as further north in the neighbourhood of Sheffield. They were well wooded and, like other owners of woods, he wanted to make them pay. If trees could not be sold for timber, they might be made into charcoal for ironworks. The earl had sent his bailiff round to potential buyers of timber, but they would not give more than 8s. 3d. a tree, whereas the earl wanted 20s., and as the bailiff reported in 1562 writing from Whitchurch in Shropshire, 'when they understand the price they flee every man'.[22] The earl therefore decided to follow the current fashion and enter the iron industry. In 1564 a blast furnace was erected at Shifnal, with a forge and two fineries close by at Lizard, where a smithy already existed. Charcoal came from the woods in the immediate neighbourhood, the iron ore from

G

a mine at Snelshill, between Shifnal and Wellington. As production
increased the works at Lizard proved inadequate, and the earl's
steward reported that 'the workmanship of the dam, the gate [i.e.
the floodgate], the great wheel and divers other things there were
nought', and he was obliged 'to make much thereof new'. Altogether 40 men were employed, including the woodcutters, charcoal-
burners and ore diggers, as well as those at the ironworks themselves. Some of the unskilled labourers were paid only 12d. a week,
together with meat and drink, and 'if they stay at Christmas they
will get their wages. But if they go to their friends in that time, to
have no wages.'

One difficulty at Shifnal seems to have been to secure adequate
supplies of iron ore. Winter weather might bring digging to a halt,
and unless a stock had been accumulated it would be impossible to
keep the furnace in blast. The earl's manager advised him to rent
an additional iron mine in the neighbourhood, from the Earl of
Arundel; even so, the supply of ironstone, and of charcoal, might run
short for lack of oxen to carry it. In October 1574 30 steers were
sent to Shifnal from Hallamshire, but even if the number of oxen
were sufficient, it might be hard to find enough grass to feed them.

There was another centre of the iron industry in the Wye valley,
between Goodrich and Whitchurch, on the earl's Herefordshire
estates. Here too there were extensive woodlands and supplies of
ore. Iron was being made near Goodrich in old-style bloomeries in
the 1540s, with a monthly output of two tons. The work was directed by an ironmaster named Robert Sybrance, but he got into difficulties and failed to show a profit, partly through neglecting to keep
proper accounts. This did not suit the earl at all, and he appointed a
certain John Dewe to supervise. As there were debts to be paid,
Dewe proposed to seize the iron produced, but Sybrance resisted,
and it was only vi et armis that Dewe got the iron carried away.
By 1553 Symbrance was in debt again, and borrowing £20, quite
a large sum in those days, from a local clergyman. We hear no
more of Sybrance, but the production of iron went on at Goodrich,
much of it being taken up by the needs of agriculture and building
on the estate, and by the blacksmiths in the village; nailmaking also
went on in the district. In the later sixteenth century a change was
made to more modern methods of production, and a furnace there
is referred to in 1575. Early in the next century, in the time of the

seventh earl, iron was being sent by boat to Gloucester and Bristol, but in March 1604 his agent at Goodrich wrote to tell the earl that business was at a standstill owing to the plague at Bristol, where people were dying at the rate of 30 or 40 a week. He also complained that a weir on the Wye was hindering the ironworks.[28] In April 1609 it was carried away by a flood following the break-up of a severe frost; the earl was asked to supply timber to repair it, but George Moore, who was then in charge at Goodrich, advised against this, explaining that the weir had the effect of 'pounding up the water so high upon the forge that not one bar of iron could be made in twelve weeks'. Moore, who had a share in ironworks close by in the Forest of Dean, suggested that the earl might safeguard his fuel supply by acquiring timber marked for sale in the Forest, where there were enough trees to keep 'six furnaces and as many forges' going for 20 or 30 years, but there was 'no wood in Your Honour's lands that will be very fit to coal twelve or sixteen years'. It seems doubtful, however, whether the earl was able to get timber from the Forest, as the King was advised not to sell any.

A third centre of activity in the Shrewsbury empire was in the neighbourhood of Chesterfield and Sheffield. In 1578 a merchant named Robert Bainbridge owned a forge there, near Higham, but it was the earl's employees who worked at it, while the earl himself owned an iron mill near by; 10 years later there were smithies owned by the earl at Barlow. About the same time there is evidence of a blast furnace at Kimbersworth, the pig iron made there being refined at 'the hammers' at Attercliffe, and a new furnace and forge were erected at Kimbersworth in 1608. These developments were undertaken by the seventh earl, and the ironworks seem to have been highly profitable investments: in 1593 they were producing about 330 tons of bar iron, worth about £4,250. Fuel came from the earl's own woods and, leaving this out of account, expenses came to £1,550, so that there was a profit of £2,700. The sixth earl had also been advised by one of his agents to establish a steel works, in order to profit from the large and expanding demand of the Sheffield cutlery trade. Before the end of the century the steel plant he erected, the third on record in England, was making a cash profit of between £200 and £400 a year, with an annual output of 30 to 45 tons of steel.

Shrewsbury was one of the largest ironmasters in England, but iron and steel works were only part of his varied undertakings, and Professor Lawrence Stone ranks him as the most active entrepreneur of his age. His estates yielded coal and lead as well as iron; he exploited both, and helped to develop a new technique for smelting and refining his lead. Another of his industrial undertakings was a glassworks, and he also owned ships, with one of which he sponsored exploration and the opening up of new trade routes. He was also a demesne farmer on a large scale, and Bacon may well have had him in mind when he wrote in his Essay *Of Riches:* 'I knew a nobleman in England that had the greatest audits of any man in time—a great grazier, a great sheep-master, a great timber-man, a great collier, a great corn-master, a great lead-man; and so of iron, and a number of the like points of husbandry; so as the earth seemed a sea to him, in respect of the perpetual importation.'[24]

Sir Francis Willoughby, as we saw in the last chapter, acquired an interest in several ironworks in the Midlands, and developed these simultaneously with his collieries at Wollaton and elsewhere. His first move was to start an ironworks on his own estate at Middleton in north Warwickshire, but this lay at some distance from the main iron-producing areas of Staffordshire, and to begin with he needed information about local conditions and costs. On 7 December 1571 his agent at Middleton, John Tyror, reported that he had 'spoken with the yronmen about Walsall', and had heard that ironstone could be got there for 4s. the load, but carriage to Middleton would add another 3s. to the price. Tyror learned that it would be difficult to purchase 'any grownd where the stone is gotten . . . for it is dayly layed for by my Lord Paget, and hath benne longe', but Paget, it seems, could 'neyther take nor purchase, as I am credebly informyd by honest men'. Willoughby decided to proceed with his plans, although supplies of charcoal might be difficult.[25] At this date the process, as described by Tyror, was still that of an old-fashioned bloomery worked by hand; there are no indications of any mechanical power, and the blast furnace had not yet arrived. In the course of the next 20 years Willoughby's works were modernized in two stages. The first step was taken before 1577, when Nicholas Lesurde, or Lecett, 'hammer man of Montgomery, smith and tenant to the Earl of Shrewsbury', offered his services to Willoughby. He undertook 'to devyse you a hommer, and appoynt you all implements and toles thereunto belonginge', and 'be your hammer man'. Willoughby accepted this offer, and a site for a hammer worked by water power was obtained from 'Master Worley' (Wyrley, of Handsworth, who owned land and water rights in the neighbourhood); a formal agreement between Sir Francis Willoughby and 'Nicholas Lecett, hammerman', shows that Sir Francis obtained a lease for 21 years from 'Mr. Wirley', and was to pay Lecett £30 towards the cost of building the hammer. Lecett undertook to produce 60 tons of iron a year, and in 1579 the accounts show that against outgoings of about £604 'iron made at Middleton' yielded £752.

The next stage in the modernization of Willoughby's iron-works began to take shape about 1590, when estimates were obtained for the erection of a blast furnace, a forge, two fineries and a chafery, all blown by water power. There was some delay, however, before the full output of these new works could be obtained. They needed a capital outlay of £400, which Willoughby seems to have had difficulty, or at any rate was slow, in producing; another difficulty was to get the larger quantities of iron ore required for the new plant. Sir Francis's manager tried and apparently failed to get ore from a new source at Polesworth, and it was not till 8 May 1592 that the furnace was eventually put in blast. Production then went ahead, fresh sources of ironstone had to be sought, and finally in 1595 an agreement was reached for getting it from a site at Wednesbury. There was an assured market for bar iron close at hand among the Birmingham ironmongers, and no doubt this helped to make the enterprise profitable.[26]

The iron industry grew up in several areas in northern England, more than one of which was on the land, and even (like the Tintern wireworks) on the site of a monastery. Thus in Yorkshire, besides the Earl of Shrewsbury's furnaces and forge near Sheffield, the Manners family, Earls of Rutland, had a furnace and forge at Rievaulx, which in 1602 produced 160 tons of bar iron.[27] Another well-known iron-producing centre lay in the Furness region of north Lancashire. The monks of Furness Abbey had formerly mined the haematite ore on their estates, but had apparently ceased to do so some time before their house was dissolved in 1537. Seven years later William Sandys, who in partnership with John Sawrey had taken a lease of the abbey's three bloomsmithies, obtained a licence to dig for iron ore. Sandys belonged to a distinguished family, orig-

inally from St Bees in Cumberland, a branch of which had settled
in Furness in Henry IV's reign. His search for ore may have been
unsuccessful, for there is no record of any revenue from iron mines,
and neither Leland nor Camden mention iron mining in their
description of this region, but Sandys and two of his sons after
him seem to have kept the bloomsmithies at work. Then we hear
no more until early in the seventeenth century, when a certain
William Southwood applied for a lease of the iron-mining rights.
There is nothing to show whether he was more successful than
William Sandys, and he may have given up the search, for within
a few years there were other applicants for the rights 'lately leased
to a certain William Southwood'. The likelihood is that nothing
much was done in this area till the eighteenth century, but when
at last it was developed a leading part was taken by members of the
Sandys family, who had been among the earliest entrepreneurs
there.[28]

In Scotland the iron industry was being carried on in more than
one district, and early in the seventeenth century there was even
a blast furnace in a remote part of the north-west Highlands. This
was at Letterewe, on Loch Maree, and appears to have been started
in 1607 by Sir George Hay. Hay had previously been concerned
with ironworks in Perthshire, of which county he was a native, and
in which the industry had long been established: in 1598 James VI
had granted him the Carthusian priory of Perth, as well as some
church lands in the district. What took Hay to the far north-west
was his interest in a scheme for colonizing the isle of Lewis, whose
inhabitants, it seems, were divided by feuds. In 1598 a grant for this
purpose was made to a body called the 'Fife Adventurers', but their
project failed, and in 1607 a further grant was made to Sir George
Hay, in company with Lord Balmerino and Sir James Spens. They
were no more successful as colonizers of Lewis than the Fife Adventurers, but on their way to Poolewe, whence they proposed to sail
to Lewis, they passed the site of some bog-iron ironworks on Loch
Maree. Wood for fuel was abundant, and there seemed good
prospects of developing iron manufacture there into a profitable
business. Hay and his partners thereupon sold their rights in Lewis
to Lord Kintail, and obtained the Letterewe woods in part payment.
Hay was a gentleman of the bedchamber and in touch with
James VI, who wished to develop the resources of the northern

kingdom, and had engaged the services of some English iron-workers from Ulverston. Though he had failed to colonize Lewis, with the King's backing Hay established 'a colony of Englishmen' at Letterewe, and in 1608 one Farquhar McCra was selected by the Bishop of Ross to 'serve' them. They were casting cannon at the furnace, as well as making iron, and though an Act was passed in 1609 to protect the woodlands of Scotland, apparently this did not impede Hay's activities, for the making of 'great guns' went on at Letterewe 'untill the woods of it was spent'. How long they lasted seems to be uncertain: Hay became Earl of Kinnoull and died in London in 1634. The furnace may have gone on working after his death, but in any case it appears to have become disused by 1660. The produce of the ironworks was carried by boat to the end of Loch Maree, then overland for a short distance past the unnavigable rapids of the River Ewe to Poolewe, whence it was shipped by sea. Hay was the active member of the partnership, and seems to have been a versatile entrepreneur. In 1610 he was granted 'the privilege of ... glas workis within the kingdom of Scotland' as well as the 'making of yron'. His glass furnace was not on Loch Maree but in a cave at Wemyss on the coast of Fife; it did not pay, however, and was abandoned.[29]

Meanwhile in England a great iron-working empire was being built up by Richard Foley, who constructed what was probably the first slitting-mill in the Midlands. The origins of this device, which mechanized the process of cutting iron into thin strips for making nails and similar objects, are in dispute. According to Stow's *Annals* the invention was brought to England from Liège and set up in 1590 at Dartford in Kent, by a man named Geoffrey Box. Two years before this, however, a patent for a water-driven machine to slit iron into 'small barres or roddes' for making nails had been granted to Bevis Bulmer, a man of many accomplishments, whom we shall meet again. It seems possible that Box was in his employ, and that the mill at Dartford did not come from abroad but was Bulmer's invention. In 1606 Bulmer obtained another patent, for the same machine or an improvement of it, and soon afterwards transferred his patent to Clement Dawbeney, who may have taken over the mill at Dartford. Dawbeney wanted a monopoly for his products, and in 1612 he asked for a renewal of the patent with an additional clause prohibiting the import of foreign iron cut into rods; but this was opposed by the Ironmongers' Company, who were interested in maintaining imports. An inquiry was held, as a result of which Dawbeney's patent was called in, but he got it renewed in 1618. By 1629 Dawbeney was once more a petitioner. He had been at great charge and expense and had brought his machine to 'a more absolute perfection' than ever before, but his patent was being infringed by other persons. The Privy Council confirmed Dawbeney's patent, adding an injunction that no one was to make or use the machine devised by Bulmer and Dawbeney, or 'any other like engine'. In January 1630, however, Dawbeney was petitioning the Council again; although the King had lately confirmed his patent, other persons were still presuming to infringe it. His complaint was referred to the Attorney-General, but the outcome has not been traced.

The offender, however, was undoubtedly Richard Foley. Born at Dudley in 1580, he was the son of a nailer, and is said to have begun his career simply as a seller of nails, but later he acquired a forge and began making them. He did well out of his business, and moved to Stourbridge, where he built himself a house. By 1621 or 1622 he had a blast furnace at West Bromwich, and said he was spending £1,000 a year on ironstone, wood, and charcoal. In 1627 he leased some land and a mill at Kinver, on the River Stour, and about 1628 he erected his slitting-mill there. There are divergent accounts of how he discovered the process. According to one story he went to Sweden as a fiddler and learned the secret of the mechanism there; another says he played the flute and went to the Netherlands. Both stories seem improbable, but apparently Foley was the first to call the slitting-mill by that name. Before long he was involved in litigation. He maintained that his lease at Kinver included a right to dam the River Stour and other streams, and a wayleave for carts over neighbouring lands, but his landlords denied this. According to Foley his mill was of great benefit to the country, but his opponents said that on the contrary it caused great injury, and divers poor men engaged in slitting iron were put out of business. They also branded him as a monopolist, and charged him with damaging the roads by carrying heavy materials over them and failing to repair them again.[30] Apart from his part in the development of this machine, Foley used his wealth to gain a stranglehold over a large part of the iron manufacture in the Birmingham district. By 1633 he had leased at least nine furnaces and five forges, some from Lord Dudley and Lord Paget, and was blamed for buying up all the local supplies of fuel and iron. His purpose in leasing rival works, it was said, was simply to suppress them and raise prices. According to statements made in 1636, when Foley was being prosecuted by the Attorney-General, during the previous nine years he had wasted 200,000 loads of wood from timber trees for the purpose of his ironworks, and had engrossed no less than 19 furnaces and forges in several Midland counties.

Foley denied having converted timber trees into charcoal. He declared, moreover, that he had not built any new forges: he merely hired works already existing, and in any case it was no crime to convert wood into charcoal to make iron. Iron was as useful to the kingdom as wood, and he gave employment to large numbers of people. Professor Stone says that as Foley never built an ironworks himself he was not an entrepreneur. He was only a skilful financier who manipulated the production and marketing of iron to get maximum profits. But at least some of Foley's achievements were those of an entrepreneur, just as entrepreneurs may do many things that are not strictly entrepreneurial. Stone calls him 'a new phenomenon, whose appearance marks the end of the leadership of the aristocracy' in the industry of the west Midlands. At any rate he was clearly a man of energy and enterprise, and he founded a dynasty of ironmasters.[31]

The consumption of wood for charcoal, which was the subject of constant and repeated complaints, stimulated a series of inventors to try to devise a furnace in which iron could be smelted with mineral coal. A patent was granted in James I's reign to Simon Sturtevant, but it was withdrawn when his claim to have succeeded was not substantiated, and a new patent was granted to John Rovenson, but he also failed. Then Dud Dudley, son of Edward Lord Dudley and Elizabeth Tomlinson, 'a base collier's daughter', claimed that he had succeeded where all previous experimenters had failed. According to his own story, which has often been repeated, he was 'fetched' from Balliol College, Oxford, in 1619, at the age of 20, to look after a furnace and two forges belonging to his father at Pensnet Chase in Worcestershire. There was plenty of pit-coal in the neighbourhood, but wood and charcoal were scarce. Dudley altered the design of the furnace and claimed to have succeeded at the first trial in making good-quality iron with pit-coal. A second trial was also encouraging, he thereupon wrote to his father reporting his success, and in 1621 his father secured a patent for the process. Dudley declared that his iron was approved in 1623 by the London Ironmongers, but he was unable to prosecute his invention because his works were 'ruinated' by a disastrous flood, and then he was hindered by neighbouring ironmasters, who were jealous of him for making cheap iron with coal. He had to move to another site, where he encountered fresh difficulties and opposition; then, when at last he had erected an improved furnace of his own design, and found a suitable local coal, and the outlook seemed brighter, his enemies attacked him again, forcibly ejecting him and destroying the bellows of his furnace. He obtained a fresh patent in 1638, but he served as a colonel on the royalist side in the Civil War, and lost his estate. In 1651 he reappears as an entrepreneur at Bristol, with a project for establishing an ironworks there in partnership with two local men, but after £700 had been spent he quarrelled with his partners and the scheme collapsed. Later he was concerned in various other projects for smelting iron with raw coal in the Forest of Dean and at Bristol, but for one reason or another they broke down. The final blow was the disappointment of his hopes of recovering his estates at the Restoration, and he wrote his book *Mettallum Martis*, which was published in 1665, in self-justification. Dudley claimed to be a patriot whose career had been dogged with undeserved misfortune, but in fact he seems to have been litigious and boastful, and his assertions cannot be taken at their face value. He quite probably did make iron of a sort with coal, but not of merchantable quality.

A number of writers have believed Dudley's story, supposing that his process was successful because he first coked the coal, as Abraham Darby did when in 1709 he undoubtedly succeeded in making cast iron with coal, and as had been done before that when other metals were smelted with coal. But there is no evidence that Dudley did this. What he actually claimed was to have used small coal from a local seam which otherwise would have been wasted, and it has been shown, not only that to make coke with this particular coal would have been technically impossible, but also that it could not have been used raw with the kind of bellows Dudley had. Good pig iron could not be made in a blast furnace with raw coal until the hot blast was invented in 1824. Blacksmiths could, and did, use coal for heating bar iron, once made, in their forges, but if raw coal were used in a furnace with a cold blast, the sulphur in the coal would be absorbed by the iron and make it brittle, so that it could not withstand hammering. Other inaccuracies, among them the dates of his residence at Balliol, have been detected in Dudley's story, and the conclusion must be that though he may have been a persevering entrepreneur, there is no reason to believe that he was successful as an inventor.[32]

At the time of Foley's prosecution for wasting wood it was estimated that there were 'about 300' ironworks in England, and a rough, indeed partly conjectural, calculation suggests that in the century after the Reformation the output of iron increased five-fold, or even possibly more, reaching totals of between 20,000 and 43,000 tons of pig iron and between 15,000 and 33,000 tons of bar iron.[33] Towards the end of James I's reign the growth was halted, principally no doubt by exhaustion of the woodlands and the consequent rise in the price of fuel (three times that of commodities in general), which made iron manufacture less profitable. While it lasted the expansion was largely due to the entrepreneurial activity of great landlords, whose chief incentive, according to Professor Stone, was the prospect of turning their woods into money. He also suggests that after the initial excitement of launching a new enterprise had worn off, landlords tired of the responsibility of running their own works with a manager, especially when the market became more uncertain and profits smaller, and they tended to lease their works to contractors, or professional entrepreneurs like the Foleys.[34] Some landlords undoubtedly were mercenary, and many improvident, and their indifference to the prospect of coal-pits in their parks, even in front of the windows of their mansions, points to an attitude very different from that of their successors in the age of landscape gardening and the 'picturesque'. But they had the enterprise to take quick advantage of their opportunities, and the values of one age should not be judged by the standards of another. After all, from the aesthetic as well as from the humanitarian point of view, it was scarcely more admirable to do what their successors did—preserve the amenity of their private demesnes, but on their property outside allow, and profit by, the squalor of modern industrialism.

5 | Copper and brass

Though there are occasional references to copper mines in England in the Middle Ages, chiefly in the western counties, there was very little working of the metal until the reign of Elizabeth I, and the manufacture of brass (an alloy of copper and zinc) was entirely unknown. These industries were established by the enterprise of German capitalists and technicians, who came to England not as refugees but with a view to profits, and were welcomed by the English government, which wished to make the country independent of foreign sources of supply. There had been some previous attempts to interest German industrialists in English mining, but none led to any very striking results.

In 1528 Henry VIII appointed 'Joachim Hoegstre' (i.e. Höchstetter) as 'principal surveyor of all mines in England and Ireland'. He was to 'search for and work mines of gold, silver, copper, and lead in England, Wales, and Ireland ... taking up workmen and materials at the King's expense'. Höchstetter proposed to take six German experts, and 1,000 workmen, to the mines in Devonshire, and suggested building a foundry at Combe Martin, where there was a famous silver mine. On his arrival in England he seems, like many other foreigners, to have met with a hostile reception from the local inhabitants, and abandoned his appointment. His name is of interest, however, for his son Daniel later settled in England, and opened the Mines Royal company's copper mines at Keswick, and his descendants took a prominent part in English mining ventures for 100 years. For the time being, however, the mining industry was at a standstill; in 1539 it was said that the lead mines 'are now dead'.[1]

Another German named Joachim Gundelfinger was at work in Ireland, 'mining and melting' at Clonmines in county Wexford in

Edward VI's reign, but the venture did not pay. About the same time Burchard Kranich, or Cranach, was engaged in producing lead and silver, first of all in Derbyshire, later in the west of England. He introduced a furnace of a particular design, which later became a subject of dispute, but he forsook engineering for medicine, and became well known in London as Dr Burcot, who attended Queen Elizabeth when she was ill with smallpox. Another foreigner who made his first appearance in Britain about this time was a Netherlander, Cornelius de Vos, whom we shall meet again in more than one capacity.

Soon after Elizabeth's accession there were renewed calls on German technical knowledge, when Sir Thomas Gresham undertook to restore the debased coinage. Foreign assistance was needed because, while it had been easy to debase the coinage by mixing molten silver and copper together, nobody in England knew how to separate them again once they had been mixed. Shortly after this a decisive step was taken by a clergyman, Thomas Thurland, who apparently had some knowledge of Germany and was interested in mining matters.[2] Thurland, who was Master of the Savoy, restored and endowed by Henry VII as a hospital for poor men, opened negotiations with a German miner named Johann Steinberg, or Steinberger, and an indenture was drawn up by which Thurland and Steinberg were authorized to search for and open mines. We hear no more for a time; then in 1563 Daniel Höchstetter arrived in England on a prospecting visit. In June 1564 he came again with a colleague, Hans Loner, or Lohner, and 12 workmen, whom he took with him to Keswick, and there they found copper ore. Steinberg's name then drops out, to be replaced by that of Sebastian Speydell, a German engaged in the recoinage at the Mint, but his participation in the venture was also only temporary, for in October 1564 a fresh indenture transferred the right to search for metals to Thurland and Höchstetter. The grant, which was for gold, silver, copper and quicksilver, covered the counties of Yorkshire, Lancashire, Westmorland, Cumberland, Devon, Cornwall, Gloucestershire, Worcestershire, and the Principality of Wales, and on 26 May 1565 they sent a report to the Privy Council, announcing the discovery of copper ore containing silver in Cumberland.[3]

Daniel Höchstetter was a partner in a famous Augsburg firm of merchants and financiers, David Haug and Hans Langnauer. They had not originally been concerned with mines, but were dealers in draperies, silks and cloths, and they also traded in groceries and spices from the East; but they had recently taken over the control of copper mines in Hungary, and of mines in the Tyrol at which copper, silver and iron were raised. They already had business dealings with England, and were looking for a new outlet for investment and trade. On the discovery of copper ore in Cumberland, Thurland and Höchstetter asked and obtained leave to bring in 300 or 400 foreign workmen. The first batch of 30 or 40 miners arrived in July 1565, and the government encouraged the undertaking by granting exemption from various taxes, and authority to fell trees for use at the mines. Höchstetter went home to Augsburg at Christmas; when he returned to Keswick in October 1566 he found that his German workmen were as badly treated by the local inhabitants as Sidney's steelworkers in Sussex. One of them had even been murdered. The government sent instructions to the justices of Cumberland and Westmorland to protect the German workers, but Thurland seemed to be unable to maintain order, for fear of offending local people, and Höchstetter wrote to Loner saying that he hoped somebody more fit than Thurland might be appointed to take charge of the works and the workmen: somebody who should 'also ... be more paynfull in the veuinge and overseinge the expenses about the same and for the better kepinge of Reckoning thereof, and speciallye at the tyme of the meltinge, for suerlye (althoughe he wolde gladlye do well) throughe his simplicitie and lak of souche understanding as appertaynethe he dothe somtyme more hurte then good.'[4]

It was not only at Keswick that Thurland's conduct was provoking criticism. As early as 1561 he had been alienating properties belonging to the Savoy, ostensibly to raise money for the hospital, but one suspects that he intended it for his mining projects. It seems that he even pawned some of the plate of St Paul's cathedral, deposited for safe keeping at the Savoy on the occasion of a fire, and he also borrowed money from various creditors, who presently began threatening him with arrest. By November 1565 he was in the Fleet prison, but he appealed to Cecil for protection,[5] and during Höchstetter's absence in Germany in 1566 he was able to return to the mines. He had the satisfaction of witnessing the fulfilment of his ambition, the first manufacture of 'English copper', but his creditors were still a cause of anxiety, and there were more troubles in store, culminating in 1570 in complaints sent to Cecil of the 'evil husbandry, or rather spoil committed by the Master' at the Savoy. 'Truly, in our opinion, if the Master continue in office the house cannot stand long. ... If Master Thurland has deserved well of the Commonwealth (as you seem to signify by your letters), it were good that he should be recompensed *ex publico* and not *ex sanguine pauperum*.' According to the complainants, Thurland owed the hospital over £2,000, and a whole list of charges against him included not only misappropriation of the hospital's property but failure to reside as required by the statutes, maintaining his kinsfolk at the hospital, not receiving Communion, and spending time in bowling and gaming.

Thurland tried to reply to some of these charges, and Grindal, who was Visitor of the Savoy, and newly appointed Archbishop of York, at first hesitated to take action, knowing that 'Her Majesty is very favourably inclined towards the Master of the Savoy'. But in the end, he told Cecil, 'I moved her Majesty yesterday for the Savoy. ... I declared unto her Highness that the master of the Savoy had converted great sums of money to his own private use, which ought to have gone to the relief of the poor. I prayed Her Majesty that we might proceed to the removing of the Master.' The Queen replied that she 'was desirous to be informed more particularly in the matter', but on 29 July 1570 the blow fell, and Thurland was deprived of his office. A further complication arose when it appeared that he had let his rooms in the hospital to the young Earl of Oxford, a prominent figure at Court, and it looked for a moment as if Burghley thought of reinstating Thurland instead of appointing a new master. But in April 1574 Grindal told him that he had 'moved Her Majesty in it at my last being at the parliament, praying Her Majesty to remember that it was her grandfather's foundation and that it was the cause of the poor, and therefore Christ's own cause. Her Highness was then resolutely determined that Thurland should never be restored to that room any more.' This was final, and on 7 October 1574 Thurland died. Höchstetter was left as virtually managing director of the company, but for all his weaknesses Thurland had been successful as a company promoter, inducing English shareholders to risk their money in the undertaking; and his efforts to raise funds, if not pardonable, were at any rate understandable.

Meanwhile more copper ore was found at Newlands, on the western side of Derwentwater, in such quantities that the Germans called the mine there 'God's gift' (*Gottesgab*);[6] but trouble arose when the Earl of Northumberland claimed the mineral rights as owner of the land. A writ was issued against him in the Queen's name, and the judgments in what became a famous case were given in the Court of Exchequer in Hilary Term, 1568. The case against Northumberland rested on the principle that all mines of the precious metals, gold and silver, whether in the land of a subject or not, belonged by prerogative to the Crown. All the 12 judges who heard the case were unanimous in upholding this principle. Three judges held that a mine of base metal would not be royal, but would belong to the owner of the soil, unless there were enough of the precious metals in the ore for their value to exceed the value of the base metal. The other nine judges held that all mines containing gold and silver were royal, even though the value of the precious metals in them were less than the value of the base metal. All agreed that a mine producing nothing but base metal was not royal.[7]

The effect of these judgments was to leave the definition of a royal mine in some doubt, but the majority decision does not seem to have been rigorously enforced, and Sir John Pettus, Deputy-Governor of the Mines Royal company, writing in 1670, endorsed what amounted to the dissentient view. But he upheld the right of the Crown or its licensees to search for the precious metals on anyone's land, and the uncertainty of the law gave cause for anxiety to landowners in mining districts and tended to inhibit private enterprise. The position was finally clarified by legislation in 1690 and 1693, the effect of which was that mines of copper, tin, iron or lead could no longer be treated as royal even though they might yield some gold or silver, but the Crown was to have the right of pre-emption of the precious metals at fixed rates.[8]

A noticeable feature of the case against the Earl of Northumberland is that neither side submitted any evidence about the presence or the actual quantity of gold or silver in the Newlands ore. The mine never produced any gold afterwards, and the probability is that it did not in fact contain any, or at any rate not in sufficient quantity to be detectable by the methods of analysis available in Elizabethan times. It contained some silver, but the Queen's lawyers were not required to prove this. The earl acknowledged the presence of gold and silver and, like a plea of guilty, this acknowledgment lost him the case. The court simply ruled that it must be assumed that the precious metals admitted to exist had the greater value, and all the judges agreed that the mine was royal.

Once judgment had been obtained against Northumberland, and copper was actually in production, the way was clear for the adventurers to be incorporated, and on 28 May 1568 the Society of the Mines Royal received its charter. Its sister company, the Society of the Mineral and Battery Works, was incorporated at the same time, and these were the first joint-stock companies to be formed in England for industrial purposes. The capital of the Mines Royal company was divided into 24 shares, and at the outset of the venture, in 1564–5, these had already been divided among shareholders. Eleven were in the name of Daniel Höchstetter, and represented the Haug-Langnauer interest in the concern. Thomas Thurland held 2½ shares, and the English government's participation was represented by two shares held by Sir William Cecil, and two by the Earl of Leicester. Two shares were taken by Benedetto Spinola, a well-known Genoese banker resident in London, William Humfrey, the moving spirit in the Mineral and Battery Works, held 1¼ shares, another 1¼ stood in the name of Roger Wetherall, and one each were held by Edmund Thurland and Cornelius de Vos.[9]

A considerable and increasing outlay had already been incurred before the company was formally incorporated. Up to the end of 1565 the amount laid out was £2,884; in 1566 £3,927; in 1567 £5,076; in 1568 £6,722, making a total of £18,609. Most of this money was absorbed in the mines themselves and their accompanying plant, smelting-houses, smithies, and so on. When Höchstetter wrote to Loner in October 1566 he told him that he hoped the melting house would 'this nexte weeke (by gods grace) have the Roofe sett up', and building the furnaces was to be put in hand in the week following. Money was also needed for dwellings, and as much as £2,328 was spent on travel, board and lodging for the Germans.[10] As early as June 1566 each whole share had been called on for two payments, one of £100 and one of £50, and further large calls would soon be necessary. Nowadays the nominal value

H

of shares in a company is fixed, and fresh capital is raised by creating and issuing new shares. In the early Elizabethan companies, however, the number of shares was fixed, and holders were called on from time to time to make further payments. If an unexpectedly large call were made, the only way in which some shareholders could meet it might be by realizing part of their holdings, if necessary splitting them into fractions, and using the proceeds to meet the liability on the remainder. By the time the Mines Royal was incorporated, each share had been called on for £850, making a total capital of £20,400, and both Thurland and Höchstetter had reduced their holdings. Thurland disposed of one of his shares and now held 1½, Höchstetter's holding was reduced from 11 shares to 9¾, and 15 new shareholders came in, most of them taking fractional shares. Among them were men prominent in public life, such as Admiral Winter and the Earl of Pembroke, who was also a shareholder in the Mineral and Battery Works, Lord Mountjoy, whom we shall meet again as a pioneer of the alum industry, and Customer Thomas Smythe, to whom we shall return later in this chapter.

The firm of Haug and Langnauer had been hoping to develop their drapery business in England, and tried at first to sell silk, satin and other costly materials at Keswick, but they found little demand except for linen, woollen goods and sacking. They managed to sell over £400 worth of goods, partly to their own countrymen, but this did not go far to meet their outlay, nor did the sale of copper come up to expectations. Expenses, however, continued to mount. Apart from the buildings and equipment at the mines themselves, the island called Vicar's Island in Derwentwater was bought and a garden was laid out there, a bakehouse and a brewhouse were built, with a dovecot, pig-styes, a beer-cellar, a timber windmill and a thatched peat-house. Mines were opened at Grasmere and Coniston as well as Keswick, Höchstetter introduced a new method of smelting the ore, which embodied a considerable advance in metallurgical technique on anything hitherto attempted in England, and the production of copper went rapidly ahead. A number of the German workers married English wives and brought up families in Cumberland, and Höchstetter himself decided to devote his career to the copper industry in England. In July 1571 he went back to Germany to fetch his wife, five children and two maids; they reached London in November, spent the winter there, and moved to Keswick in March 1572. An inventory of the contents of his house at the time of Höchstetter's death shows that they lived very comfortably. There were 12 featherbeds and 21 rugs, besides numerous bedsteads, tables and other furniture, and quantities of plate and household utensils.

Not all the workers at the mines were German, but only the unskilled labour was English, apart from some colliers imported from the mines in Shropshire belonging to one of the shareholders, the Earl of Leicester. These were evidently in a state of bondage, and a bailiff and constable were employed to prevent them running away. The firm's accounts were kept at Keswick and made up seven times a year, at Shrovetide, Easter, Whitsun, St James's Day (25 July), Holy Cross Day (14 September), All Saints (1 November) and the end of December. They were then sent up to London, where Höchstetter's colleague, Johannes Loner, was established as the firm's agent, and it was his task to co-ordinate and balance them. Between 1567 and 1584, when smelting was begun in South Wales, the amount of copper produced in Cumberland was 10,348 cwt, an average of a little less than 610 cwt per annum. By a clause in the company's charter a one-fifteenth share went to the Queen: the amount actually delivered to her use up to 1584 was 673 cwt, leaving 9,675 cwt for sale by the company. Total income from sales over this period was about £34,000, or £2,000 a year; a small income also came from the sale of silver, of which 5,184 ounces were produced during these years. A royalty on it of 10 per cent was due to the Crown; sales brought in about £80 a year, or four per cent of the firm's total income.[11]

These sales were quite insufficient to meet wages and current expenses, let alone show a profit on the capital invested, and it soon became clear that the company was steadily losing money. Stocks of copper were piling up, and it seemed impossible to find a market for it all. Its military use must have been diminished by the substitution of cast iron for bronze guns. Apart from this, an obvious outlet would be to use it to make household utensils, brass and wire, and when the company was founded no doubt it was hoped that the Mineral and Battery Works would absorb the Mines Royal's copper in this way. Unfortunately it was a long time before this company succeeded in producing brass on a commercial scale, and during its early years it concentrated on the manufacture of iron

wire. In 1571 a suggestion was made that the shareholders in the
Mines Royal should themselves buy up the unsold copper, but this
was scarcely more than a thinly disguised demand for more capital.
It seems that the Germans agreed to accept the copper as security
for their advances of money, and the Queen herself undertook to
buy some copper; but she refused to listen to a request by one of
the German partners to be allowed to import wine duty-free, and it
is doubtful if the purchase of copper commended itself to the
English shareholders, some of whom were already in arrears with
the contributions due on their shares.

The government did not want the works to be abandoned, and
agreed to purchase £1,383 worth of copper, and even made the
company a loan of £2,500 at eight per cent, but this was not enough
to relieve the parlous state of its finances. Hans Loner left the
business in 1576, and by 1579 his principals, Haug and Langnauer,
had decided to withdraw. They probably suffered a considerable
loss in extricating themselves, but the other shareholders were in
an even less enviable position. Unless more money were forthcoming, they would lose everything they had invested, but how was
money to be raised except by further calls on their shares? Höchstetter, who had committed his career to the project, proposed two
alternatives: either the shareholders should each pay up another
£41 per share, or else the company should lease the Cumberland
mines to him personally for 15 years at a definite rent. The latter
plan was accepted, but the lease, dating from Christmas 1580, was
made out not to Höchstetter alone but to him jointly with Customer
Smythe. For the first nine months, until Michaelmas 1581, no rent
was to be paid; after that the annual rent to the company was to
be 500 marks (£333 6s. 8d.), plus a ninth part of the produce of the
mines. The lessees also undertook responsibility for the Queen's
royalty, and bound themselves to keep the principal mines in operation, to maintain a scheme for draining them, and to employ 20
labourers gathering ore.

From the company's point of view there were evident advantages in this arrangement. For 15 years the shareholders had had no
return on their capital, but the rent would now at any rate provide
some income, small though it was, while those who had no more
capital to subscribe would be freed from liability for further calls.
The granting of this lease constituted a milestone in the company's

history. Henceforward it no longer operated its own mines, but confined itself to granting leases and drawing rents, leaving the actual work of mining, with its attendant risks, to its lessees. Höchstetter himself did not long survive the new arrangement. His health had begun to fail and on 14 May 1581 he died, and was buried in the churchyard at Crosthwaite. His children at first declined to take on their father's commitments, and for the next 10 years, until his death in 1591, the management of the mines was virtually in the hands of Customer Smythe. Before describing the new developments for which he was responsible, we must return to the affairs of the Mineral and Battery Works.[12]

This company, like the Mines Royal, owed its inception to two men, one English and one German, William Humfrey and Christopher Schütz, though the formation of two separate concerns does not appear to have been the original intention. Humfrey was a Goldsmith who had been appointed Assay-Master of the Mint in July 1561, when the government was engaged in restoring the purity of the coinage. As Assay-Master Humfrey was responsible for weighing the silver as it was coined, and checking that it was of the proper standard. This brought him into contact with the German metallurgists engaged in the recoinage, and it was not long before he quarrelled with them. When copper was first found in Cumberland, Thurland sent a specimen to Cecil, who passed it on to the Mint for analysis. The Mint's report on the metal seems to have been faulty, and although Cecil's belief in Humfrey as a metallurgical expert apparently remained unshaken, the Germans conceived a low opinion of his technical ability. Disagreement then arose over the development of 'battery', the hammering of metal into plates and utensils. On the plea of shortage of wood for fuel in England, the Germans had planned to produce only raw copper in this country, and transport it to Germany for what was called 'manuring', i.e. refining and working; but they learned that the export of copper from England was prohibited by an Act of Parliament passed in 1530. The art of making brass and battery was a closely guarded secret, which the Germans were unwilling to disclose to their English partners, and when attempts were made to persuade Hans Loner to 'bring the art of battery into England' he had refused.[13]

When it became clear that the English government would not allow copper to be sent to Germany, while the Germans were unwilling for the secret of making brass and battery to be known in England, Thurland and his partners decided that they would have to concentrate on the production of copper, but Humfrey conceived a scheme to launch a separate concern for brass and battery work. His hope of securing Loner's cooperation had been disappointed, but he had found another German technician, Christopher Schütz, who he hoped would serve instead. Schütz, whose home was at Annaberg, on the northern slopes of the Erzgebirge in Saxony, was an experienced miner, but financially he was far less substantial than men like Höchstetter and Loner, who had the firm of Haug and Langnauer behind them. Humfrey, however, gave Cecil a glowing account of Schütz's talents, and asked that letters patent should be granted to Schütz and himself. 'The Allmayne Chrystopher Shuts', he told Cecil, had agreed to come to England and 'becum the Quenes maiesties subiect and to spend his lyfe in this Realme and also to fetch in such other mo as shalbe of profownde knowledge in the said woorks'. According to Humfrey, in Schütz 'this Realme shall recon such a Iewell as all germany hath not his like, by report of his master and bringer up, who is called the Lanterne of germany as touching mynerall and mettalyne affayres in all manner knowledge'. By 'the lantern of Germany' Humfrey was doubtless referring to Georgius Agricola (Georg Bauer), author of the great illustrated compendium of German mining and metallurgical techniques, *De Re Metallica*. Schütz, Humfrey assured Cecil, would 'by his Connyng erect myll or mylls ... for the plating of Iron and stele', making wire, and 'for all manner Batery and wyer woorks to be made of copper, and the Comyxed mettall with the Callamyne stone'.[14]

Humfrey sought not only a patent for these processes, but also the right to search for the 'royal' metals in the counties not covered by the grant to Thurland and Höchstetter. Since these counties, as he put it, were 'of small name for minerals', he asked for Ireland to be included as well, apparently with an eye on mines in the isle of Lambay, which lies off the Irish coast a few miles north of Dublin. There was some discussion in the Lords about mining concessions, but eventually Humfrey got what he wanted, in the form of two patents, issued on 17 September 1565. The first covered the search for metals, and also contained a clause prohibiting for 21 years the imitation or use of any of the patentees' 'tools, instruments, or engines' without written licence from Humfrey and Schütz. This clause, which later gave rise to litigation, was the only effective part of the first patent, for no use was made of the right to open 'royal' mines, in Ireland or elsewhere. The second patent granted in perpetuity the sole right to dig for calamine and use it for making latten and mixed metals, together with the right to make 'all sorts of battery wares, cast work, and wire of latten, iron and steel'.[15]

Humfrey had wire-making in mind as a second string, in case the manufacture of latten, or brass, should not succeed, but brass was his immediate objective. Before this could be made he had to find a supply of calamine for alloying with the copper. Search was set on foot in various places, but none was found, and in November Humfrey feared that calamine would have to be imported from Aachen. Early in 1566 search was resumed, and on 30 June he was at last able to report success. 'Sithence february last', he told Cecil, 'a stranger and an Englysh mann have rangyd by dyreccion to the most lekely places for the fynding of the Callamyn, and nowe, thanks be gyven to the Creator of all things, it is founde and yet un knowne to the fynders, for they have brought it by resemble of such descripcion as have bene gevin them.' It had been assayed along with calamine from Germany, and 'we cann fynde none commparable to this of England'.[16] The locality of the discovery was in Somerset, at several places on or about the western end of the Mendip Hills, and at one of these, Worle near Weston-super-mare, Humfrey and Schütz took a lease of some ground and 'set ten or twelve persons strangers and English to mine and search for calamine'.

Humfrey had originally thought of establishing brass works at Wandsworth, but when calamine was discovered in Somerset, Bristol seemed a more convenient place; coal and iron were available close by, and the Earl of Pembroke offered temporary accommodation in the castle. But they needed water-power, and about Bristol 'all the pleasant rivers' were 'set full of grist and tucking mills'. The prospectors therefore 'crossed the Severn to view the rivers of Usk and Wye in Wales'. The Wye itself was too big a river for their purposes, but they 'sought by the riverside to find some water descending from the mountains', and eventually chose a site near Tintern Abbey. There, towards the end of September,

Humfrey reported that works were being built; but technical difficulties were encountered, funds also were short, and it was not
till February 1568 that he was able to send Cecil a specimen of
the latten produced there.[17] The time then seemed ripe for
Humfrey's venture to receive its charter of incorporation, and the
Society of the Mineral and Battery Works accordingly came into
being on 28 May, simultaneously with the Mines Royal.

Its capital was nominally divided into 36 shares (as compared
with the 24 shares in the Mines Royal), but only 24 were actually
taken up, and the Mineral and Battery Works was in fact a much
smaller concern, with less than a tenth of the capital of its sister
company, though the number of its shareholders (37 are named
in the foundation charter) was greater. As in the Mines Royal,
shares had been allocated and payments made by shareholders
before the company was formally incorporated. Each share had
been called on three times (for £20 on 3 August 1566, £25 on
20 December 1567, £28 on 19 February 1568), making a total of
£73 per share, or £1,752 altogether for the 24 shares. As usual,
shares were subdivided into fractions, and several of the shareholders (Humfrey himself, for example, and persons prominent in
public affairs, such as Sir William Cecil, and the Earls of Leicester
and Pembroke) also held shares in the Mines Royal; Customer
Smythe also was a shareholder in both companies. Some of the
members of the Mineral and Battery company were country gentlemen, others were London business men, some of them Haberdashers,
but mostly Goldsmiths, possibly because Humfrey himself was a
member of the Goldsmiths' Company, whereas many of the shareholders in the Mines Royal belonged to the Mercers.

Brass had been made at Tintern, but it seems clear from subsequent events that its production was still only in an experimental
stage, and no regular commercial manufacture was established. The
processes involved required a high degree of expertise: copper and
calamine had to be mixed in certain proportions, varying with the
quality of the raw materials, and considerable skill and experience
were needed in applying the proper degree of heat. The German
workmen were not accustomed to handling English copper and
calamine, and after these early experiments the company seems to
have abandoned the attempt to produce brass. Instead, as we saw in

the last chapter, the works at Tintern were given over to the manufacture of iron wire.

This decision had unfortunate repercussions for the Mines Royal
company, whose charter did not include battery, and it was left
with unsold copper on its hands. In 1575, when it had become clear
that the Mineral and Battery company would not in fact make
brass or battery work, the Mines Royal at length obtained a licence
for battery, and began turning some of its surplus copper into
kettles and other household utensils. This was a sensible step, not
only giving employment to coppersmiths and others, but bringing
custom from a number of people in the Lake District as well as
further afield. But by this time the company was saddled with an
accumulated deficit of over £32,000, and the new development
was on too small a scale, and came too late, to save its finances.
In 1580, as we have seen, the company decided to hand over the
operation of its mines to lessees, and the Mineral and Battery Works
followed the same policy. Humfrey himself seems to have been
discouraged by the failure to establish brass-making at Tintern, and
went off to the lead mines in Derbyshire, where he died in July
1579. He became involved in disputes about a furnace and a sieve
of a particular pattern, in which he claimed exclusive rights, but
we must leave these to a later chapter.

Schütz also died in the 1570s, some time before Humfrey, and
while the production of iron wire was carried on, though not
without difficulties and setbacks, by the company's lessees at
Tintern, brass-making remained in abeyance. Then in 1582
Richard Martyn, Goldsmith and Alderman of London, who was a
shareholder, and lessee of the wire-works, offered to pay the
company £50 a year for its brass and battery rights. The company
agreed, and granted him a lease for 15 years, but included the name
of Humfrey Michell, who in the following year became his co-
lessee of the wire-works. For five years they apparently did nothing, but in 1587 the agreement was widened to include two other
names, Andrew Palmer and John Brode, both Goldsmiths. Palmer
was a shareholder and secretary of the Mineral and Battery
company, and also an employee of Martyn's at the Mint; Brode
was Palmer's son-in-law, and was evidently the member of the
group who claimed to know most about brass-making. How he
acquired his knowledge does not appear.

To meet the first year's expenses Martyn agreed to put up £3,000 as a loan at 40 per cent, but this arrangement was rescinded. Instead, Martyn and Michell laid out £1,134 16s. 11d.; while Palmer and Brode laid out the same amount. In the following year each partner's contribution was to be about £800. They proceeded to erect 'divers working houses, melting hearths, water works, furnaces and other engines with great bellows, stampers', etc., at Isleworth in Middlesex, and Brode was put in charge of the works. Unfortunately disputes broke out almost at once. Brode, who was confident that he alone had discovered the secret of making brass, was determined to force his partners out, and indeed before long Martyn and Michell withdrew from the business.

In 1590 the company granted a fresh lease for seven years, at £50 a year, to Brode and Palmer, but fresh troubles arose when in 1594 a goldsmith from Fleet Street, named William Laborer, agreed to take up a quarter share in the brass-works, which at that time seem to have been flourishing. Laborer claimed to have more experience of battery than Brode, but Brode denied this, and jealously determined to keep his own knowledge secret. He ordered the workmen to 'keep Laborer out of the melting-house by the space of 10–12 days when the greatest mystery of their work was in doing, whereof they perceived Laborer to be ignorant'. After this, matters went from bad to worse. Laborer was to have paid for his share in the business in seven instalments, but failed to meet his obligations; Brode then refused to pay the rent to the company, which replied by cancelling the lease and granting a new lease, at £400 a year, to a Dutch merchant named Abraham van Herwick and others, who erected a rival mill at Rotherhithe. Brode was also at loggerheads with the company over the supply of calamine. He had hoped to obtain possession of the calamine originally dug by Schütz's men in 1566, 30 tons of which had been transported to Tintern, but when 17 years later Brode made a journey to Tintern, he found that barely a hundredweight remained. He was told that when the company abandoned the attempt to make brass, the calamine was left lying near the abbey for a long time, and finally was used, 'together with other waste stones', to repair a fishing weir in the river. Brode then made his own arrangements with a landowner in Somerset for obtaining fresh supplies of calamine, but the company claimed that he had no right to do so except under

licence from them, and procured an order from the Privy Council
prohibiting the acquisition of calamine by Brode.[18] Brode replied
by accusing the company's agents of breaking into a building hired
by him as a store for his calamine, and stealing his property. Litigation over these and other matters dragged on for years, until
in 1605 Brode reached the end of his resources and retired from the
scene, an embittered man.

He claimed that 'by the good blessing of God he was the first
man here in England that comixed copper and calamine and
brought it to perfection viz. to abide the hammer and be beaten into
plates and raised into kettles and pans by hammers driven by water'.
He complained that the Mineral and Battery company had 'taken
the work out of the hands of Englishmen and put it into the hands
of strangers. Which strangers always endeavour to advance their
own commodities and have overthrown that work in England and
thereby the price of that metal is double it was in Queen Elizabeth's time.' Brode may have had cause to feel aggrieved, but his
jealousy and pugnacity had not helped him.[19]

In spite of the recent agitation against monopolies, in 1604 a fresh
charter from James I confirmed the privileges enjoyed by the
Mineral and Battery company, and it continued in existence as a
licensing authority. The original members were all dead, and there
were now 22 shareholders, including the Earl of Pembroke, Sir
Robert Cecil, and Sir Julius Caesar, later Chancellor of the
Exchequer. About 1630, in the hope of increasing its sale of brass
wire, it leased the calamine and brass works to James Lydsey, who
was actively engaged in the pin-making trade. Lydsey thus secured
control both of the production of wire and of the market for it.
We must reserve for another chapter the story of this enterprise, in
which Charles I himself took a hand. The Mineral and Battery
company found its position weakened, and attempts were made to
break its monopoly. A London pewterer named Peter Brocklesby
approached the company for a lease of its brass works, but though
some of the shareholders were agreeable he withdrew his application and started a works of his own. In 1632 Lydsey was trying to
get this interloper suppressed, an inquiry was set up, and Lords
Pembroke and Dorset, Governors of the company, intervened. But
Brocklesby was still at work in 1639, and when Lydsey made
another attempt to dislodge him, Brocklesby declared that he was

giving employment to English labour, whereas all Lydsey had done was to raise prices.

The company also suffered from the competition of foreign copper and brassware, which protective legislation failed to prevent, very likely because the imported goods were of better quality. In March 1635 it was said that pans, kettles, and copper wire to the value of some £40,000 were imported annually from 'Aken [i.e. Aachen] and a place called Salt-wedell [Salzwedel] in Lunenburgh'. This statement was made in support of a proposal to maintain battery work in England with imported copper and English 'calumey earth'. But there is no evidence that anything came of it.[20] By the time of the Civil War and the Commonwealth the company could no longer enforce its privileges; most of its leading shareholders were royalists, and it became easy for others to defy it. After the Restoration the two sister companies, the Mines Royal and the Mineral and Battery Works, combined forces, and made fresh efforts to resume their authority and functions, but this lies outside our chosen period.[21]

It is time to return to the work of the Mines Royal after Höchstetter's death, when Customer Smythe was its chief lessee. Thomas Smythe, the son of a yeoman clothier from Corsham in Wiltshire, had married Alice Judde, heiress of Sir Andrew Judde, at one time Lord Mayor of London, and a man of widespread business interests in the City. Smythe had been a collector of tunnage and poundage in the port of London since 1557; he also farmed the impositions on wines, and in 1570 he obtained the farm of the London import duties for six years at a rent of £17,500 a year. His organization of the customs collection was extremely efficient; he made a handsome profit, and in succeeding years he obtained a series of renewals of the customs farm, each time at a higher rent. Thus as trade expanded, the government's revenue increased, but so likewise did Smythe's income. For his fourth and last farm, which ran from 1584 to 1588, he paid the huge rent of £30,000 a year, but even so he made a profit for himself of over £16,000. Altogether his four farms brought him in some £50,000, and he could well afford to risk some money in the Mines Royal.

There are varying accounts of conditions in the Lake District mines under Smythe's control. According to one report Smythe made a profit of £3,691 in the first seven years of his tenancy, but according to a later account he incurred a capital outlay of £11,000, on which, so far from getting any return, he made a loss of £500. These figures may include his expenditure in Cornwall, where he most probably lost money, for it seems possible that the Keswick mines showed a profit for a time, though they fell off later. Smythe took a fresh lease of the mines for 10 years from 1589, and agreed to pay the company a higher rent, 650 marks (£433 6s. 8d.); presumably he would not have done this if he had been losing money. Next year, indeed, the prospects seemed bright enough to tempt Daniel Höchstetter's son Emanuel, together with Mark Steinberger, to join Smythe as partners, each side agreeing to put up £600 more capital to finance an extension of the works. But prosperity was evidently short-lived. By 1597 the Keswick mines were once more in difficulties, for which the mines at Coniston, now being exploited more vigorously than in the past, could not make up. Customer Smythe died in 1591, and his interests were inherited by his son, John, but before the end of the century any profits made in previous years were more than wiped out.

At an inquiry in 1600 it was stated that in the 36 years since the venture began £68,103 had been received from the sale of metal, and £4,500 had been paid to the Queen. On the other side, expenses totalled £104,709, and there had been a capital outlay of £27,000. The German immigrants and their families no doubt brought trade and employment to the Lake District, but the entrepreneurs, and not least the Augsburg merchants, must undoubtedly have suffered heavy losses. Höchstetter's sons kept the mines going, under lease from the company, until the Civil War, but the net result was a loss of £9,606.[22]

Although the Mines Royal company had power to open mines in a number of counties, they confined their attention at first to the Lake District, where the original discovery of copper had been made, but Customer Smythe decided to operate in a wider field. As early as 1579 Peter Edgecumbe, a Cornish landowner who had previously had mining interests in the West of England in association with the German Burchard Kranich, wrote to Burghley, offering to form a partnership to develop unworked mines in Devon and Cornwall; but Edgecumbe was not then a member of the Mines Royal company, and his offer was not taken up. Instead, in 1582, the company granted a 15-year lease of their rights in Cornwall, at a rent of £200 a year, to Thomas Dudley of London and John Weston of Neen Savage, in Shropshire.[23] In the following year they were joined by Customer Smythe who, besides his tenancy of the mines in the Lake District, had also taken a lease of the company's mining rights in Wales. The combined rental for Wales and Cornwall was £300 a year, and henceforward Smythe was the controlling member of the partnership, though he conducted the whole business without stirring from his house in Fenchurch Street.

Lead and silver mines in Cardiganshire had been worked intermittently since prehistoric times, but by the sixteenth century they were largely disused. Smythe employed a local man, named Thomas Evans, to get some of them reopened; he discovered the mine at Cwmsymlog, some miles inland from Aberystwyth, which acquired a great reputation in the next century as a rich source of silver. The success of the work Smythe organized there was reflected in a marked increase in the amount of silver sent from Wales to the Mint in the later years of the sixteenth century.[24]

Tin, for which Cornwall was famous, was subject to a special law and lay outside the ambit of the Mines Royal, but Cornish mines also produced silver-bearing copper and lead. Smythe was in touch with a group of Cornish gentry, the most active of whom was William Carnsew, of Bokelly, near St Kew, and in 1583 he sent Ulrich Frosse, the German secretary and accountant at Keswick, down to Cornwall, to take charge of operations, while Weston seems to have acted as his travelling agent.[25] Treworthy lead mine, near Perranporth on the north coast, had previously been worked by Carnsew with the assistance of Burchard Kranich, but had lain disused for 23 years. Frosse got lodgings in the parish of Cubert, close by, and set to work to get Treworthy reopened: he also sent a man named Bernard or Barnard (whether a local man or another German seems to be uncertain) to explore further afield. Bernard reported favourably on the prospects of getting copper farther down the coast, at St Agnes, Illogan, and St Just, but Frosse later complained to Carnsew that he had 'run away, like a naughty deceitful man'.[26]

Smythe kept a tight hand on the cash, doling out small sums of £50 or less at infrequent intervals, and grumbling when Frosse had spent £60 without showing any results. In Germany, Frosse explained, they were willing to spend much more money before they expected a mine to show a profit; and considering that the mines in the Lake District were costing £3,000 a year to run, the outlay in Cornwall does not seem excessive, but Smythe was hard to satisfy. Carnsew had proudly told him that the Cornish miners were as skilful as any in Europe, and had proposed holding a competition between them and the Germans at Treworthy; Smythe's reply was to grumble at the high wages expected by the German miners when local workmen could be had for less.[27] The situation at Treworthy was not encouraging. By December 1583 the miners had opened up the old workings and dug down 15 fathoms, but water then held up operations until the spring. Work was resumed in April, and a level was driven below the old workings, in order to drain them, but the ore found yielded only two ounces of silver to the hundredweight, and this would not pay. Then in August, just when what seemed a good lode of ore had been struck, water broke in so suddenly that the workmen barely escaped with their lives.[28] Frosse was in low spirits, and complained that he could not keep his workmen unless more money were forthcoming to pay them, and his sight was failing through care and lack of sleep. 'I cannot climb these dangerous cliffs myself', he wrote, 'for my sight and my head will not serve me.' Poor man, he had been accustomed to working in an accountant's office, not to being lowered on a rope down the face of Cornish cliffs.[29]

Probably he felt happier next year, when after a visit to Keswick to see his wife and family he was moved to South Wales, to take charge of a copper smelter which was to be set up at Neath. Carnsew's mother was a Stradling, from St Donat's on the coast of Glamorgan; the two families were in correspondence, and this connection may have influenced the choice of a site. Treworthy mine had been a disappointment, but the prospects of copper at Illogan were more hopeful, though the mine there did not in fact come up to expectations.[30] At St Just, however, copper was found in large quantities. Arrangements were made to ship the ore to Neath from St Ives, and the boats returned with loads of timber, needed for the mines but scarce in west Cornwall. Very good lead was found in a mine at Penrose, near Helston, and for a time the outlook for the enterprise seemed rosy. Then in 1587 work at St Just was suddenly suspended; the mine was seized, presumably to satisfy some creditors, and the miners had to be discharged. Frosse reported to Carnsew from Neath that 24 cwt of copper could be smelted there in seven hours, but work was held up for lack of a constant supply of ore. This is the last we hear of him, for Carnsew died in 1588, and the letters from Frosse, which reveal so much of the fortunes of these ventures, come to an end.

Customer Smythe himself died a few years later, and his son John was not prepared to risk any more money in the mines. Peter Edgecumbe, who in the meantime had become a shareholder in the Mines Royal company, took over his lease of the Cornish mines, but soon found himself in difficulties. In October 1594 he wrote acknowledging liability for the rent of £200 a year, but had to ask to be allowed to defer payment. Three years later the outlook seemed brighter, and he wrote to Sir Robert Cecil, Governor of the Mines Royal, seeking a renewal of his lease. Customer Smythe, he pointed out, 'had a good purse to follow the mines while he lived, but he left no successors willing to continue the great attempt'. The Cornish mines would have 'lain dead' if Edgecumbe himself had not taken them in hand. Devon and Cornwall, he wrote, had many gentlemen and others 'of good wealth and account', but he could not find anyone 'willing, much less desirous, to adventure any money with me in such a desperate and forlorn hope'. This was the voice of reason, but Edgecumbe had the invincible optimism of the genuine adventurer. The mines themselves, he declared, 'do not deserve this slander', and he cheerfully admitted that he had sunk 'at least £4,000' in them.[31] It is more than doubtful if he ever saw his money again.

he could sell his tin, the tinner must take it to one of the 'coinage'
towns, there to be stamped and taxed by Duchy or Crown officials.
As 'coinage' took place only twice (later four times) a year, in the
meantime the poor working tinner had to borrow money in order
to live, and local dealers and tin-owners would often compel him
to accept part of the loan in the form of truck.

When the lender asked why he needed the money, 'Saith the
Tynner, I will buy bread and meate for myselfe and my household,
and shooes, peticoates and such like stuffe for my wife and children.
Suddenly herein, this owner becomes a pettie chapman: I will serue
thee, saith he: hee deliuers him so much ware as shall amount to
fortie shillings, in which he cuts him halfe in halfe for the price,
and foure nobles in money, for which the poore wretch is bound
in Darbyes bonds to deliuer him two hundred waight of Tynne at
the next Coynage, which may then bee worth fiue pound or foure
at the verie least.'[2] Some tinners were reduced to working for
wages, possibly under a landlord exploiting the mineral resources
of his property, possibly under some other prosperous tinner who
had had the luck to strike it rich, and could afford to become a
master and hire labour. More often they preferred the chance of a
windfall to the security of a regular wage, and became 'tributers',
undertaking to work in return for a share in the produce of the
mine. Nominally the tributer preserved his independence, and in
a sense was himself a small entrepreneur, in that he shouldered
part of the risk of the enterprise, but his real position was subordinate as well as precarious. He borrowed money on condition that
he produced a specified quantity of tin, but if the mine failed, he
would be destitute, unless he had a smallholding to fall back upon;
and even if the mine yielded well he would find it hard to escape
dependence on credit between one coinage and the next.

Larger tin-masters too might be equally in bondage to the middlemen and dealers who bought their tin, while above them in turn
stood the great London merchants, mostly members of the Pewterers' Company.[3] Richard Carew, who had compiled his *Survey
of Cornwall* 15 or 20 years before it was published in 1602,
commented on the 'hard dealing' of these London merchants.
'When any Western Gent. or person of accompt wanteth money
to defray his expenses at London, he resorteth to one of the Tynne
Marchants of his acquaintance, to borrow some; but they shall as

soone wrest the Clubbe out of *Hercules* fist, as one pennie out of their fingers, unlesse they giue bond for euerie twentie pound so taken in lone, to deliuer a thousand pound waight of Tyn at the next Coynage, which shall be within two or three months, or at farthest within half a yeare after.'⁴ The price the merchant paid was usually very disadvantageous to the tinner. All he would get for his tin was £15 or £16 a thousandweight (1,200 lb), but the merchant would sell it for £28 or £30, and trading in tin could build up a considerable fortune. A notable example of this was the rise of the Robartes family. Originally a 'servant to a gentleman of this county, his hind', one of them settled at Truro and made £5,000 or £6,000 by trading in 'wood and fferzen'. His son carried on the business, and began lending money, 'and his debtors paid it him in tin. He, engrossing the sale of tin, grew to be worth many thousands (£300,000).' His grandson built a country mansion and paid the Duke of Buckingham £20,000 to be made a baron.⁵

There were other ways in which the organization of the tin industry had become capitalistic and weighted against the small man. By the end of the fourteenth century contemporary sources refer to the holding of shares in mines by merchants and others who were not the actual working miners, and as long ago as 1357 'Abraham the Tinner' was said to have owned two mine works and four stream works, in which he employed over 300 men, women, and children. By the end of the sixteenth century the working tinner had largely been extruded from participation in the stannary 'parliaments'; their members were nominated by the mayors and councils of the stannary towns, and mostly belonged to leading county families.⁶ Capitalism also entered the industry as the miner who dug the ore became differentiated from the 'blower' or smelter who extracted the metal from it. In the earliest days these two functions were probably performed by the same person, who having dug some ore would smelt it by kindling a fire on a rough hearth of stones. By the early Middle Ages smelting was being carried out in a furnace enclosed in a building, or blowing-house, at first a rude shack, later more substantial, and the two occupations had already become separate. At first the blower may have been a small craftsman with a status comparable with that of the free independent miner; by Elizabethan times he had become a small capitalist, smelting the tinner's ore in return for a proportion of the product. He was the owner of his blowing house, either employing labourers to perform the actual smelting, or letting out parts of the house to small blowers who worked on their own account.[7]

Though some little one-man workings remained, by the sixteenth century mining was usually too expensive to be carried out by independent individuals. As Carew explained, 'when the new found worke intiseth well with probabilitie of profit, the discouerer doth commonly associate himself with some more partners, because the charge amounteth mostly verie high for any one mans purse, except lined beyond ordinarie, to reach unto: and if the worke doe faile, many shoulders will more easily support the burthen. These partners consist either of such Tinners as worke to their owne behoofe, or of such adventurers as put in hired labourers. The hirelings', he adds, 'stand at a certaine wages, either by the day, which may be about eightpence, or for the yeare, being betweene foure and sixe pound, as their deseruing can driue the bargaine'.[8]

Landlords received a proportion, called toll-tin, usually a fifteenth, of the tin raised within their manors, and for many this constituted an important part of their income. Some were more adventurous, and risked capital by active speculation in mining enterprises. In the last chapter we met two such men, William Carnsew and Peter Edgecumbe; they were in search of lead and copper, or rather of the silver mixed with these metals, but there were others whose principal interest was in tin. Notable among these was a family which was to rise to eminence in national as well as local affairs. The ancestral home of the Godolphins was near Helston, in western Cornwall, on the slope of Godolphin Hill, where by the sixteenth century the rich deposits of tin were beginning to be worked. There was some activity here in Henry VIII's reign, under Sir William Godolphin, but in the next generation Sir Francis Godolphin made striking advances, and is credited by tradition with having taken the lead in introducing technical improvements into the industry. For this purpose, like other mining entrepreneurs, he sought foreign advice. His friend Richard Carew says that Godolphin 'entertained a *Duch* mynerall man, and taking light from his experience, but building thereon farre more profitable conclusions of his own inuention', found 'a more sauing way' of smelting, and 'made Tynne with good profit, of that refuse which the Tynners rejected as nothing worth'.[9]

This was about 1580, and the reference to improved methods of smelting has led some writers to infer that the foreign expert was the German Burchard Kranich, who had previously worked in Cornwall and constructed a new type of furnace; but he died in 1578, and there is no evidence that he had been in Cornwall since the 1560s. Possibly the man's name was Edmundus Erasmus, but his identity remains a mystery.[10] Whoever he was, it seems likely that besides improved furnaces he supervised the erection of stamps driven by water power, for breaking up the ore preparatory to smelting. These may have been the first mechanical stamps at tin-mines in Cornwall, though it is possible that Kranich may have anticipated Godolphin in using them for other metals. According to Carew, Godolphin employed some 300 persons at his works. Other owners copied his methods and made large profits, and the Queen's revenue from tin duties rose by at least £1,000 a year. Besides becoming one of the largest tin producers in Cornwall, he played a prominent part in local administration, and in organizing the defence of the country against the threat of a Spanish invasion.

In spite of these developments, by the end of the sixteenth century the tin industry was suffering from a severe depression. This was partly because the export trade now had to face competition from tin raised on the Continent, so that the price of the metal fluctuated and fell; partly too because production became more expensive as alluvial streaming was superseded by underground mining. After protracted discussions in the Privy Council, the government decided to revive the royal right of pre-emption, which had been in abeyance for a long time, and take up the whole annual output at a fixed figure. This, it was thought, would relieve the working tinners by guaranteeing them a reasonable price for a term of years. Another motive, however, was doubtless the expectation of revenue for the government, and in practice, like the other monopolies of that age, the pre-emption was generally farmed by lessees. In 1598 Lord Buckhurst and the Pewterers' Company each bid £7,000 for it, but these offers were not accepted, and in May of the following year it was proposed that the Queen should take the pre-emption into her own hands. There was disagreement, however, about the price she should pay for the tin. The price suggested was £28 a thousandweight, but the Queen was advised that she would lose money if she paid more

than £25. The question was still undecided when in October of the
same year a higher bid came from Bevis Bulmer. He offered £10,000
a year for a lease of the pre-emption, subject to modifications if
the total amount of tin were greater or less than 1,000 thousandweight, and he would pay the tinners £26 13s. 4d. a thousandweight for their tin. He also undertook to lend them £10,000 free
of interest, thus relieving them from dependence on the dealers
during the intervals between coinages. The Queen, however, wanted
a firm offer, and in the end decided to retain the pre-emption herself.

The effect was that it was exercised in her name by Sir Walter
Raleigh, as Lord Warden of the Stannaries, but as Raleigh was unwilling to pay more than £25 a thousandweight, and Bulmer meanwhile had offered £29, Raleigh was aggrieved and had difficulty
in coming to terms with the tinners. The Queen is said to have
advanced £8,000 each year she nominally held the pre-emption, and
it is not surprising to find that by 1601 the monopoly had been
placed in private hands again. James I took it over himself for a
short time at the beginning of his reign, hoping to make a profit
on resale, but finding himself burdened with a large stock of unsold
metal he soon handed the monopoly back to be farmed again.
From then until the Civil War, except for a few years, it was
managed by a syndicate whose leader was Sir Thomas Bludder. It
is doubtful if the tinners benefited in the end, because while prices
generally continued to rise, the price paid for their tin fluctuated
considerably, but did not rise correspondingly. The dealers naturally opposed the monopoly, but the tinners themselves presumably
thought it was to their advantage, for they petitioned the government that it might be continued.[11]

The history of the tin monopoly is complicated, and outside the
scope of this book, but there can be no doubt that while some of
the bigger men in the industry, owners or merchants, made money
(and some lost it too), 'the general lot of the tinners was one of
poverty and insecurity'.[12] We must remember also that while the
developments in the sixteenth century were important in their way
'as signs of industrial awakening', they were much less important
and far-reaching than the improvements and inventions introduced
in the late seventeenth and eighteenth centuries. It was these which
marked 'the great period of technical advance', sending the annual

output of tin 'by successive leaps to double the previous figures'. And after that the output was more than redoubled. In the first half of the seventeenth century production was usually between 500 and 700 tons a year, but a 100 years later it was well over 2,000 tons; there were years in the later eighteenth century when it exceeded 3,000, and in the early nineteenth century it sometimes rose above 5,000 tons.[13]

Lead had been mined in Britain at least from the time of the Roman occupation. This is shown by the pigs of lead, stamped with the names of emperors, which have been found in various parts of the country, and the probability is that this metal was being worked before the Romans arrived. Lead mining went on during the Middle Ages, and in certain areas, Alston Moor in Cumberland, the Peak district in Derbyshire, and the Mendip Hills in Somerset, systems of customary jurisdiction and law grew up, which later were codified and reduced to writing. Though less elaborate than in the Stannaries of Devon and Cornwall, this organization gave the lead miners of these areas a degree of independence, subject to their paying certain dues to the lord of the manor or to the Crown, as the case might be. Similar but more restricted rights were enjoyed by the iron miners in the Forest of Dean.

The processes of digging, cleansing and smelting lead ore were similar in many ways to those used for tin, and in early times many small mines were worked by independent adventurers, or by groups working in partnership; but here again there were instances of capitalist enterprise, where the miners were paid wages instead of working for profit at their own risk. There were occasions in the fourteenth and fifteenth centuries when some German adventurer asked leave to practise his skill in English minefields,[14] but it was not until the sixteenth and seventeenth centuries that the entrepreneur made his appearance on a significant scale. The basic reasons for this were the same as in the other mining industries: deeper pits were being sunk, mechanical methods of drainage and ventilation, as well as improved processes of dressing and smelting the ore, were being introduced, or copied, from abroad, and all this required more capital and technical expertise.

In Derbyshire, which was the most important centre of lead production in England, the miners themselves were generally poor men, owning their small mining properties, but the smelting and marketing of the metal was in the hands of a relatively wealthy class, who bought the ore from the working miners. By the sixteenth century many of the landed gentry in the mining areas were adding to their incomes by establishing smelting works with technical improvements on their estates. Some of the lead they produced was sold locally, mostly at Chesterfield, some at Derby, but much was bought by London merchants, and some was exported. The Gells of Hopton and the Babingtons of Dethick had been in the lead business in this way since the fifteenth century; by the sixteenth century the list of landowning families in the county with lead works on their estates had been greatly extended.

A prominent part in these developments was played by George Talbot, sixth Earl of Shrewsbury, whose multifarious entrepreneurship has been noticed in a previous chapter. Already the owner of vast estates in different parts of England, his marriage to Bess of Hardwick in 1568 gave him possession of her previous husbands' Derbyshire properties, at Barlow near Chesterfield, and Chatsworth. He established lead works on both of these estates, his production of the metal went rapidly ahead, and by the 1570s and 1580s he had built up what was probably the largest lead-smelting business in England. In the later 1570s he was spending over £500 a year in the purchase of ore, and the output of lead from his works rose from between 40 and 50 fothers to about 100 fothers in 1585. (A fother, or fodder, was a variable measure, usually a little less than a ton.) He had a store for his lead at Bawtry, whence it travelled by river to Hull, and so by sea to London or the continent. The production of lead was continued and expanded by his son Gilbert, the seventh earl, who succeeded to the title on his father's death in 1590, and by Sir William Cavendish, who later became the first Earl of Devonshire. By the end of the century the annual output of lead had risen to between 240 and 350 fothers, the cost of running the works ranging from £1,300 to £3,000 a year.[15] The increase in output was partly the result of the introduction of technical improvements by the sixth earl, and this brought him into contact with William Humfrey, the Assay-Master of the Mint.

Disappointed in his hopes of making brass, Humfrey gave up his interest in the wire works at Tintern in 1569, and moved to Beauchief Abbey, a few miles south of Sheffield. This had been acquired after the Dissolution by Sir Nicholas Strelley, the Nottinghamshire coal-owner, and was now occupied by his second son, also called Nicholas. Here Humfrey set up plant for treating and smelting lead ore, involving the use of the two pieces of apparatus which he claimed to be new, a sieve and a blast furnace. He also applied to Cecil, as Master of the Court of Wards, in whose hands the neighbouring manor of Calver then was, for a lease of the lead mines there, and obtained them at a rent of £12 6s. 8d. per annum.[16]

Like the ores of other metals, lead ore had to be dressed and cleaned before it could be smelted. Until mechanical stamps were introduced, it was broken up by hand with hammers, and shaken with coarse wooden sieves in 'buddles', or troughs with running water, which carried away the earthy impurities. Humfrey used a sieve with a much finer mesh of iron wire, to be used in tubs of water, thus saving the small pieces of metalliferous material which previously had been wasted. The oldest method of smelting in Derbyshire had been in rough stone structures called 'boles', with openings on one side. These were built in exposed situations, facing the prevailing wind, and could only be used when the wind blew from that direction. Apart from this disadvantage, the boles must have been extremely wasteful, as lead is volatile when the ore is smelted, and a considerable proportion of the metal is carried off in the smoke. In the Middle Ages the boles were already being supplemented by slag-hearths, in which the imperfectly smelted slag from the boles, containing quite a large residue of metal, was resmelted. These were open furnaces, not unlike blacksmiths' forges, but on a larger scale, with an artificial blast created by bellows, usually in pairs, worked by the feet of men who stood on them and put their weight on each alternately. Timber was used for fuel in the boles; the slag-hearths were generally fired with charcoal or peat, sometimes mixed with chopped wood, known as 'gads' or 'white coal'.

Humfrey did not use the old-fashioned boles at all for smelting his ore, but put it straight into the furnaces, of which he had two at Beauchief, with large bellows worked by water power, provided by the little River Sheaf. He claimed that his process saved more than half the fuel consumed in a bole, and yielded a larger output of lead: one furnace, he said, could produce three fothers of lead a week. Relying on the terms of one of the patents granted to himself and Schütz in 1565, by which the imitation or use of any of their 'tools, instruments, or engines' was prohibited, Humfrey claimed exclusive rights in his sieve and furnace, and when he found that other people in Derbyshire were operating similar processes, he accused them of infringing his patent.[17] It had long been the practice for independent workers to glean the small pieces of ore left behind in old heaps of refuse, and take them to the slag-hearths, where they could be smelted. Humfrey brought charges against these poor people, known locally as 'purchasers', and sought an injunction 'to forbid them from melting lead after his manner and sifting to get ore by means of an iron sieve, whereby the washing of old refuse of waste earth, which was long since cast away from the old work, did get an infinite quantity of good ore'.[18]

The 'purchasers' were small fry, though the threat to their means of livelihood was a serious matter and caused local concern; but Humfrey was also bold enough to challenge the Earl of Shrewsbury himself. When Shrewsbury decided to set up smelting works in Chatsworth Park, Humfrey had apparently offered to assist if the earl would become his licensee, but instead Shrewsbury brought in 11 men from the Mendip lead mines. Humfrey then wrote to him, on 12 April 1574, saying that he had been 'credibly informed that your Lordship had garnished your new melting house with furnaces and stamps like unto mine'. This, he warned the earl, was contrary to 'the Queen's Majesty's privilege granted to the Company whereof I am in countenance the very meanest and a servitor in these affairs'. He accused two of Shrewsbury's workmen of having spied on his process, and also alleged that the earl's melter had tried to entice some of his men with offers of higher wages.

Humfrey's claims had government support, probably through his influence with Burghley, and in May 1575 the Court of Exchequer sent a warning to Henry Cavendish, the Countess of Shrewsbury's son by her second husband, that his furnaces at Cromford were violating the patent. Sir John Zouch of Codnor was included in the same warning, but he seems to have ignored it, for in November he and Richard Wendesley of Calke Abbey were told that they risked a fine of £500 each for using processes 'to the hurt and hinderance' of Humfrey, and 'contrary to Her Majesty's prerogative'. It appears that the Earl of Shrewsbury came to terms with Humfrey, but a number of other landowners continued to defy him, and in February 1579 he brought an accusation against 11 of them who, he said, had erected houses for smelting lead in violation of Her Majesty's letters patent. Besides Zouch and Wendesley the list of names included that of Nicholas Strelley. Presumably he continued the production of lead at Beauchief, although Humfrey was now collaborating with Shrewsbury. Another alleged infringer was Paul Tracy at Calver.

Sir John Manners of Haddon Hall, from whom Burghley had ordered 10 fothers of good lead for the new house he was building, was also unwilling to submit to Humfrey's pretensions. On 5 January 1579 he wrote to Shrewsbury, saying that he had had an advantageous contract which he hoped to fulfil, and asking Shrewsbury to support him in continuing to use a footblast for smelting his lead, in spite of Humfrey's attempt to stop him.[19] What action Shrewsbury took does not appear, but two years later Manners's name was included in the list of defendants in a further action for infringement of the patent.

It was not that all these had installed furnaces with bellows driven by water power. Humfrey, with what may have been simply bluff, seems to have assumed that his patent covered any furnace with bellows, even of the established type worked by men's feet. In a letter to Wendesley Humfrey warned him 'in Her Majesty's name not further to melt by your footblast whereby you do imitate my melting indirectly'. He accused him of 'practising sundry ways to molest me . . . by the prosecuting of your new works', of making 'low bargains' with the Earl of Shrewsbury, and 'bringing the ore of all the county very near through your hands'.

Humfrey died in the summer of 1579, but in the meantime Zouch, Wendesley and Strelley had decided that they had better come to terms. They acknowledged that Humfrey's methods were 'more easy, beneficial and commodious, as well in respect of their own private commodity as for the weal public, in the saving of fuel', and in January 1580 they agreed with Humfrey's executors to take over his rights in return for a royalty of 5s. a fother.[20] They then tried to prevent other Derbyshire owners, including Shrewsbury himself, from using the methods in which they now claimed exclusive rights. On 27 April 1582 the earl asked his brother-in-law, Roger Manners, to take this matter up with the Lord Treasurer,

Burghley;[21] meanwhile, at the suggestion of the Mineral and Battery company, in whose name Humfrey had purported to be acting, Burghley had appointed a commission of enquiry, to establish the facts about the processes in use in the county. The commissioners met at Bakewell in the summer of 1581, and after visiting a number of mines and smelting places they embodied their findings in a report. Conceiving that this confirmed their case, the licensees then brought two actions in the Court of Exchequer, Zouch v. Manners and Zouch and others v. Tracy and others; but the defendants offered determined opposition, maintaining that Humfrey's processes had been in use long before his time, and that he was not entitled to exclusive rights over them. Witnesses were summoned from the Derbyshire and Mendip minefields; some of them gave contradictory evidence, but it is clear from their depositions that Humfrey's pretensions were greatly exaggerated.

It was soon established that Humfrey had not been the first entrepreneur to introduce new processes to Derbyshire. He had been preceded by Burchard Kranich, who had worked at Duffield in 1552–3, and had used there both a sieve and a tub, and a furnace blown by a water-wheel: with these he had produced lead at the rate of 1½ fothers in 24 hours. It also appeared that there were two kinds of furnace at the Mendip lead mines. Originally the furnace used there had been fixed, like the Derbyshire bole, but for the last 40 years this had been replaced by an improvement known as a turn-hearth, so called because it could be turned, like a windmill, to face a wind from any direction. The turn-hearths had bellows at the top, and did not depend on the force of the wind to create a draught; but they had to be turned in the right direction in order that the wind should not blow the smoke in the faces of the men working the bellows. The other hearth, called a slag-hearth, was blown by a foot-blast, and could be used for smitham (small-sized ore) as well as for resmelting slag. Somerset men employed by Shrewsbury to start his works at Chatsworth gave evidence that the hearth erected there was not copied from Humfrey's but from the Mendip hearth. Both hearths were really similar in principle, the only difference between them being that Humfrey's was blown by water power and the other by 'the treading of men'. Humfrey's hearth, in fact, was just an improved form of the existing slag-hearth.

One witness declared that Humfrey had not invented the wire sieve either. On a visit to Mendip he had seen wire sieves in use there, and was told that they were made at Bristol. He went to Bristol and bought one, took it to Derbyshire, altered it slightly, and passed it off as his own. The Mineral and Battery company charged this witness with perjury, and at a later stage in the proceedings Cornelius Avenant, their solicitor, drafted a statement declaring that, so far from Humfrey's sieve being an imitation of the Mendip sieve, the Mendip sieve was known there as a 'northern sieve', and had been 'brought out of Derbyshire' by a Mendip worker who, 'hearing of the famous new work of Humfrey's', had 'repaired there covertly', and 'for some reward given subtlely and secretly' had 'come by one of Humfrey's sieves there, and therewithall returned unto Mendip'.[22] This seems an unlikely story.

From technical details given in evidence about the construction and dimensions of the sieves and furnaces in dispute, it seems likely that Humfrey may have been responsible for some modifications in the size and material of the sieve, but there can be no doubt that some kind of sieve had been widely used before his time. It was in fact adopted in every minefield, and continued in use until well into the nineteenth century, work with it usually being done by women. The court ordered models to be made of the different furnaces, and a picture, with annotations in Burghley's handwriting, illustrating the 'old order' foot-blast, 'Burchard's furnace', and the Mendip furnace, has been reproduced in more than one book.[23] It seems that Humfrey's furnace differed both in pattern and size from Burchard's, which was a closed furnace and much larger, resembling furnaces depicted by Agricola. The 'old order' appears to be simply a bole, but with bellows at the top; the Mendip furnace (presumably the slag-hearth) was an open hearth standing inside a small building. The most important difference between Humfrey's furnace and the type of hearth already in use seems to have been that Humfrey's furnace could be used for the first smelting of the ore, and not only for previously smelted slag. The point was made that (in contrast with the boles, which depended on the wind), lead could be smelted continuously in Humfrey's furnace, and it seems in fact to have been a forerunner of what became known as an ore-hearth. This was undoubtedly an improvement on the 'old order', but Humfrey placed undue and irrelevant emphasis on the use of bellows, and, conflicting and confusing as some of the evidence is, it looks as if he had overstated his claim to exclusive rights. Nor were Zouch's relations with the Mineral and Battery company such as to qualify him to appear as a champion of their privileges, for on his own estate he had recently erected a wire-mill, which the company had had stopped.[24]

According to Coke, Humfrey's claims for the sieve were rejected on the ground of prior user at Mendip, and though the case for the furnace may have been stronger, it collapsed in 1584 when the licensees handed over the conduct of it to Humfrey's widow and son-in-law, who gave up the attempt to press it any further. Humfrey did not claim to have actually invented the washing of ore by sieve and tub, nor the use of water power to work the bellows of a furnace. Both processes were in use in Germany, and were described and illustrated by Agricola, whose pupil Humfrey's colleague Schütz had been; Agricola in fact gave details of more than one type of furnace, and Humfrey admitted that he had himself read Agricola. Nor was he the first to introduce these processes to England, for apart from Burchard Kranich's works, furnaces blown by bellows with water power were used by the German miners at Keswick. Moreover Humfrey introduced his sieve and furnace *after* receiving his patent, and one of the questions in dispute was whether letters patent would cover a subsequent invention. The upshot of the whole affair was that it helped to clarify patent law and establish the principle that 'letters patent for an invention did not secure . . . the right to hold a monopoly for a process that had already been commercially operated. The process, in fact, must be *new*.'[25]

While improved processes of dressing and smelting the ore were being introduced by enterprising landlords, many of the Derbyshire mines themselves remained in the hands of the working miners, either independently or in partnerships. But a capitalist element became increasingly present, either financing the miners by loans, or by purchase of shares or interests in mines; and by the early seventeenth century, as the mines were sunk deeper, work in them was becoming seriously hampered by the ubiquitous problem of flooding. To deal with this pumps had to be installed or, if the lie of the land allowed it, a mine could be drained by a sough, or adit. Both methods gave openings to entrepreneurs, and a new pro-

fession of 'soughers and undertakers' came into existence, in which
lead merchants and smelters often took a hand, becoming 'adventurers' who invested their money in soughs and mines. Thus when
work in the Tearsall mine near Winster was brought to a standstill
by the water in 1633, a 'skilful Ingineer' named John Bartholomew
was called in, and in return for a third of the ore raised he undertook to instal an engine (probably a chain pump worked by a
horse-whim), while the partners agreed to take the main shaft down
to a depth of 160 feet and drive levels to bring the water to the
bottom of the shaft, whence it would be pumped to the surface.
Bartholomew was to keep the pump going continuously, night
and day, 'Sabbath Dayes and Christmas dayes only excepted'; but
he was alleged to have 'absconded' without leaving a deputy, and
'once or twice left the said Engine when it hath been out of temper'.
In consequence the mine was flooded again, and £400 worth of lead
ore in prospect was lost. The miners then planned and drove an
adit, which proved much more effective, and permanently un-
watered the mine.[26]

Bartholomew, described as servant to the Earl of Dover,[27] had
previously been engaged to drain one of the largest and most famous
of the Derbyshire lead mines, the Dovegang mine near Cromford.
When water made this mine unworkable, about 1615, an adventurer named George Sayers called a meeting of the miners and
undertook to drain it in return for half the yield. Lacking enough
capital to finance the work alone, he got three others to join him
as partners, one of whom, Thomas Wright, was also part-owner of
a sough at Winster, and may be identical with a Chesterfield lead
merchant of that name. Later, when the inevitable disputes arose,
they claimed to have spent £3,000 on sinking an engine shaft
with pumps 40 fathoms deep, by which they 'laid the mine dry';
but further flooding and other mishaps prevented them producing enough lead to meet their outlay. Some years later, about 1628
or 1629, Bartholomew was engaged to drain the mine, the Earl of
Dover providing the money, and they claimed that after considerable expense there were good prospects of success, when their
possession of the mine was challenged by Sir Robert Heath. Heath
was an eminent lawyer who, as counsel or judge, took part in some
of the famous political trials and contests of Charles I's reign. In
October 1631 he had entered into partnership with the Dutch entre-

preneur Cornelius Vermuyden, well-known later for his part in draining the Fens. Vermuyden was to receive no less than two-thirds of
the profits in return for his skill in draining the mine. Just now, as
we shall see in a later chapter, he was in trouble at Hatfield Chase,
where he was faced with unexpected expenses and hostility;
whether his experience in the reclamation of flooded fields was
relevant to the problems of draining mines seems questionable,
but undoubtedly he and Heath made a formidable combination.
Vermuyden was an energetic and ambitious man, who never hesitated to undertake a fresh adventure in the hope of making money
to help pay off the debts incurred in a previous one. Besides his
partnership with Heath he took shares in other mines on his own
account, but he cannot have had much time to spare for Derbyshire: in 1633 he spent some time in prison for debt. Mining was
not his only project in the county, for he also had a scheme to
make the River Derwent navigable between Derby and its junction with the Trent, but this was not carried out until 1720.

Heath's and Vermuyden's action for possession of the Dovegang
mine was heard first in the Barmote Court, which administered the
local mining law. Sayers and the Earl of Dover and their other
partners declared that they had 'laid dry the vein' at Dovegang
three times, and 'discovered the wealth thereof, but by casualties
and the water running in upon them they could never get any
great profit' to meet their expenses. They had installed several
'engines', for the workings were 'annoyed with continual waters
in great measure'. Heath and Vermuyden, however, showed that the
mine was 'all runn in and stopt up with weeds and grasse', and the
court awarded it to them, in accordance with mining law, on the
ground that the previous owners had neglected to work it for over
a year. The Dover–Sayers partnership contested this decision, and
brought an action against Heath and Vermuyden in the Court of
Chancery to recover possession of the mine. No owner of a mine,
they argued, could lose his title to it 'for not working thereof so
long as his grove or mine is troubled with water, or in case of want
of winde'. In fact they had left pumps, chains and engines in position, and Vermuyden's servants had used them. According to the
latter, to do so was in accordance with mining custom, but it was
evidently more than John Bartholomew and his friends could
endure, and they forcibly interrupted the new occupants' 'quiet

possession'. Probably some of the disturbances at Dovegang were due, as in many other places, to resentment at the intrusion of a foreigner, but the Court of Chancery warned the parties to 'use no tumultuous course' on pain of 'a severe and exemplary punishment of the offenders', and Heath and Vermuyden eventually emerged as the victors.

But this was far from the end of the disputes about Dovegang. Among his various debts Vermuyden owed money to a fellow-countryman, Jacob Droogbroot of Middelburg. He offered to assign a third of his interest in the mine as security, but Droogbroot demanded two-thirds. Vermuyden could hardly agree to this, as he had already transferred a third to another Dutchman, Marcellus Vandurne, who had taken a share in the scheme to drain Hatfield Chase. This dispute led to a mass of litigation in the court of the Duchy of Lancaster. According to Vandurne, Vermuyden had previously defaulted in payments due to him, on more than one occasion, and he claimed that he was entitled not only to Dovegang but to other mines as well, which Vermuyden had conveyed to him. Vermuyden's son, Cornelius II, countered this claim by the contention that his father had conveyed the mines to Vandurne in trust for him during his minority. The history of these entanglements, which dragged on for years, does not concern us, but before leaving the subject we may note that when Cornelius II died, in 1693, he still held the two-thirds share in the mine which his father had had, in partnership with Sir Robert Heath, over 60 years before. The magnitude of some of the sums of money involved is also worth notice. Dovegang was held on lease from the Crown at a rent of £1,000 a year; one of the alleged debts was for £2,000 which, according to Vandurne, Vermuyden had persuaded him to lend for making a sough.[28]

Records of the mines in the Alston district appear to be scanty, but there, as in various other areas in the north of England where lead was mined, control was evidently in the hands of the local landowners. Sometimes the Crown was tempted to venture into mining, as Charles did in 1629, when he appointed commissioners to open a mine at Thieveley Pike, in north-east Lancashire. But the King's hopes that it might relieve his financial needs during the years of unparliamentary government were soon disappointed, and six years later the mine was abandoned as a failure.[29] Lead mines

K

were also opened in several districts of Yorkshire, and there, too, while some survived, others did not pay. Several of the Yorkshire mines lay in territory which previously had been monastic property. Some of them were not opened, however, until years after the Dissolution of the Monasteries, which suggests that the determining factor was the state of the lead market rather than the greater commercial enterprise of the new owners. Lord Wharton purchased the manor of Muker in Swalesdale in 1544, and later acquired half the manor of Healaugh; exactly when he opened mines there is uncertain, but mines were at work in both manors by the end of the sixteenth century. Apparently they lost money at first, and Wharton's son Philip, finding himself in debt, tried to raise his tenants' rents and abolish some of their customary rights. They resisted this, and were supported in their resistance by the court of Chancery, though Wharton was confirmed in his right to open and have access to mines wherever he chose on his land, and to take timber on the common for use in them. Later in the seventeenth century the mines there seem to have been more profitable.[30]

Further south, in Wharfedale, Bolton Abbey had had large estates, part of which came into the hands of the Earl of Cumberland, but there is no evidence of any working of the lead there until 1603, when the earl brought in some miners from Derbyshire. After some prospecting, mines were opened near Grassington, but as a money-making venture they, too, were rather disappointing at first. By 1612, when the costs of smelting and wages were £109 11s. 0d., there was a small net profit of some £86, but the profit declined in the next few years, and by 1615 had fallen to only 6s. 7d. After that there were losses, and the scale of operations was reduced. In 1616 receipts were £328 and expenditure £347; in 1617 receipts were only £296 against an expenditure of £315; in 1618 receipts fell to £315 and expenditure to £169. The earl then decided to give up operating the mines on his own account with hired labour, and for the next two years he let them to the miners to work for themselves, though as 'lord of the field' he kept the smelting plant in his own hands. The miners had to take the dressed ore there to be smelted, handing over a third of the metal to him as his dues, while he provided them with such timber as they needed.

Shortly after this mining began to show a profit again, output increased, and in 1630 the earl had a second smelting works built.

During the next few years, on an annual output of between 50 and 110 tons of lead, profits varied between some £150 and £300 a year; in 1638, when the output was about 80 tons, lead fetched about £8 15s. a ton, and the earl's takings from the sale of his dues amounted to some £213. Though Grassington was not in one of the ancient 'free mining' areas, the Derbyshire miners who went to work there, or rather the second generation of them, together with the local men who worked with them, asked for the recognition of a set of customary laws to regulate the conditions of their labour, and to settle disputes or questions of procedure among them. The earl (or his agent) agreed, and in 1642 a meeting of the miners was held, at which 20 laws were drawn up. Though their wording and arrangement were different, most of them corresponded in substance with the Derbyshire code.[31]

The financial relationship between the miners and the lord of the manor, however, was unlike what prevailed in Derbyshire. There, while the landlord generally owned the smelting works, he bought the ore brought in by the working miners: sometimes also he advanced money to finance their operations. The arrangement in Yorkshire, by which the landlord took a proportion of the lead and the miners made their living by themselves selling the remainder to lead merchants, was more like the system prevailing in the Mendip Hills. This area, a royal forest in the Middle Ages, had become divided by the sixteenth century between four principal local landlords known as 'lords royal', who owned places, called 'mineries', where the dressing and smelting of the ore was carried out, under the charge of a manorial official called the lead-reeve. The local codes of mining custom provided that the miners must take their ore to one of the mineries and there pay over a tenth of the lead produced as 'lot-lead'. This was a much smaller proportion than the third demanded at Grassington by the Earl of Cumberland, and was one of the advantages of working in an ancient 'free mining' district. Not that the Mendip landlords, one of whom was the Bishop of Bath and Wells, had any cause to complain, at any rate in the early seventeenth century, when the mines on their estates were in full production.[32]

Apart from their ownership of the washing and smelting plant at the mineries, the lords royal do not appear to have provided any capital for the industry, and it remained in the hands of the small and usually poor mining peasantry. Often the miners worked in partnerships; some were rather more prosperous and had a hired labourer or two; sometimes they borrowed money from the Bristol merchants to whom they sold most of their lead. Generally they worked with simple tools and primitive technique, excavating comparatively shallow pits or trenches until they had taken out all the accessible ore, or until they could no longer cope with the water that flowed in. Then they usually abandoned their workings and broke ground somewhere else; some turned to agricultural labour in the winter when their pits were waterlogged; some had smallholdings; for some farming was their main occupation, and they became miners only intermittently.

There were occasions, however, when an entrepreneur appeared from outside, planning to introduce more up-to-date methods of drainage, so that deeper and larger mines could be opened up. One of these, Bevis Bulmer, came about the end of the sixteenth century, another, Thomas Bushell, about the middle of the seventeenth. Both got into difficulties and met local hostility, and after a few years they moved on elsewhere. Both had long and variegated careers as engineering entrepreneurs, but their ventures in the Mendip lead mines were only brief episodes, and left little if any permanent mark on the industry there. As miners their main interest centred on the precious metals, which will be the subject of our next chapter.

7 | Gold and silver and three notable entrepreneurs

While sixteenth-century entrepreneurs were expanding the production of metals such as copper and lead, the government which encouraged them in so doing, and the foreign experts on whose assistance they often relied, were even more interested in finding the precious metals. Gold was never found in any significant quantity in England, but its discovery in Scotland aroused great excitement for a time, and tempted a number of adventurers, including James VI himself; but none of these projects had more than temporary success. Silver, on the other hand, generally found in association with lead, was much more plentiful. The Romans had extracted silver from the lead they mined in Britain, large quantities of silver were obtained from lead mines in the Middle Ages, and in the sixteenth and seventeenth centuries, when the government was often desperately short of bullion to maintain the currency, there seemed good grounds for hoping that the mines in England and Wales, as well as in Scotland, would make a significant contribution of silver to the national needs.

Gold was discovered in Scotland, at Crawford Moor in Lanarkshire, during the reign of James IV, and in 1526 a group of Germans, of whom Joachim Höchstetter was the leading member, obtained a lease of all the mines of gold, silver, and other metals in the country. Next year Höchstetter and his partners entered into a contract to coin into money all the gold and silver they should find; but their enterprise cannot have been much of a success, or at any rate not a lasting one, for in 1531 there is a reference to 'the Duchmen quhill cam here for the myndis, at their departing hamewart'.[1] Joachim Höchstetter had a similar engagement in England and, as we saw in an earlier chapter, he did not stay to fulfil this either. A few years later, miners were brought to Scotland from

Lorraine to work the mines for the King, and a goldsmith named John Mossman was put in charge of them. For a time a workable quantity of gold was found, but again the project lapsed. What had been discovered were probably pockets of alluvial gold, and when these had been exhausted work came to a standstill until another deposit was brought to light.

There was little or no mining in Mary's reign, but gold was found again during the infancy of James VI, and in sufficient quantities to attract capital from England.[2] A group of London merchants decided that the venture was worth pursuing, and in 1567 they sent Cornelius de Vos to the north with a letter of recommendation from Queen Elizabeth. De Vos was an artist from the Netherlands, commissioned by the Queen as a painter; he is also described as a 'lapidary', and was one of those immigrants who were prepared to try their hands at a variety of enterprises. He was interested in the English alum industry in its early stages, and was one of the first shareholders in the Mines Royal company. Favourably received by the Scottish government, de Vos went to Clydesdale to prospect, and there 'he gott a small taste of small gold. This was a whett stone to sharpen his knife uppon; and this naturall gold tasted so sweete as the honny, or honny combe, in his mouth.' He took some of it to Edinburgh, in search of partners, showing them the gold he had found, 'which he called the temptable gold, or alluring gold. It was in sternes, and some like unto birds' eyes and eggs: he compared it unto a woman's eye, which intiseth hir joyes into hir bosome.'[3]

Four adventurers succumbed to this temptation: the Earl of Morton, Robert Ballentine, and a 'Dutchman of Edinburgh', who had previously lived in London, named Abraham Peterson, each took 10 shares; James Reade, 'burgess of Edinburgh', took five, while de Vos and his London backers also held 10. They obtained a licence from the Regent, Murray, to work gold and silver in any part of Scotland for 19 years, paying a royalty of eight ounces out of every 100 obtained by washing, and four ounces for every 100 purified by fire. They laid out £5,000 Scots (about £400 sterling); de Vos, with the title of 'Superiour of his Majestie's Gold Mines', was 'chosen to governe and direct both artists and workmen', and for awhile the enterprise was highly successful. 'Six score' men were employed, as well as 'ladds and lasses', and within a month eight lb of gold, worth £450 sterling, had been taken to the mint at Edinburgh, apart from unspecified amounts which 'with the tolleration of the superiour' some of the workmen picked up and sold privately. The 'mines' were evidently alluvial diggings, the gold being found, not 'in solid places, but in combes and vallies, where a long time before it had laid, being washed downe since the generall deluge'.

De Vos and his English partners, one of whom was a fellow artist, Nicholas Hilliard, the famous painter of miniatures, wanted to carry off their share of the profits, but Scottish law forbade the export of bullion from Scotland except to pay for imports or the expenses of travel. From de Vos's point of view, therefore, the enterprise was scarcely worthwhile, and in 1572 he returned to London and assigned his rights to another artist, Arnold Bronkhurst, or van Bronkhorst, on condition that the proceeds should be transmitted to him and his partners in England. But the new Regent, Morton, refused any relaxation of the law restricting the export of bullion, and the assignment therefore never took effect, though Bronkhorst's title was said to be still in existence in 1592. In 1576 work at the diggings was being carried on under the direction of one of the original partners, the Dutchman Abraham Peterson, also referred to as Abraham Grey, or Grey-beard, 'for so was he called, because of his great long beard, which he could have bound about his middle'. He found gold at Wanlockhead, evidently alluvial gold again, for he never 'sought the mountains . . . for a solidd place, nor for a bedd or vaine thereof', but only 'washed and scoured in vallies and combes'. The gold must have been quite plentiful, however, for with it 'was made a very faire deepe bason', big enough to hold 'an English gallon of liquor'; this was filled to the brim with gold coins, and presented to the King of France by the Regent, who explained that both basin and coins were made of 'natural gold, gotten within this kingdom of Scotland, by a Dutchman, named Abraham Grey. And Abraham Grey was standing by, and affirmed it uppon a sollemne oath'.[4]

One or two other Scottish adventurers obtained concessions to search for gold and silver, but for some years nothing very effective was done. About 1578 an Edinburgh goldsmith named Thomas Foullis engaged Bevis Bulmer, described as an 'ingenious gentleman', to come and work at his lead mines at Leadhills and elsewhere in Lanarkshire. Bulmer had been mining in Scotland, probably for lead, some 10 or 12 years previously, but apparently without success, and soon afterwards he had returned to England. This second engagement in Scotland does not seem to have lasted much longer, for within a few years he was back in England again; but before the century was out his association with Foullis was to lead to renewed activity in the Scottish goldfields.

Bevis Bulmer, with whom we have already come in contact more than once, has no place in the *Dictionary of National Biography*, and his origins are unknown, but he was a man of great versatility, and took part in an extraordinary variety of enterprises.[5] His talents must already have been recognized by the government in 1584, when he was sent to Bristol as a commissioner to investigate a dispute about the cargo of a ship from St Malo which had been seized in reprisal for acts of piracy. This appointment probably arose from an association with Sir Julius Caesar, then a judge of the Court of Admiralty, who had schemes for erecting beacons and sea-marks to aid navigation, and for preventing piracy by exacting bonds and sureties for good behaviour from the owners of all ships sailing from English ports. Nothing apparently came of these schemes, but Bulmer's visit to Bristol led to his becoming interested in the Mendip lead mines, where the problem of flooding had become acute, particularly at a place called Broad Rake in the Chewton liberty. Bulmer acquired a mining 'pitch' there—whether on his own initiative or by invitation of local miners is not clear—and having done so he proceeded to place 'engins and instrumentes for the drawing of water' from the pit, on the understanding that the miners working in adjacent pits would share in the labour and contribute towards the expenses. As so often happened in such situations, some of the miners were not only uncooperative but actively hostile. Bulmer complained to the Privy Council, which in 1586 sent instructions to the local authorities to deal with these disorders.[6] Presumably this intervention by the central government had some effect, for Bulmer remained at work, 'a great lead-man upon Mendipp', until 1587.

In that year Adrian Gilbert, brother of the navigator Sir Humphrey Gilbert, and a 'lapidary' from London named John Poppler, found some rich silver-lead ore at Combe Martin, on the coast of north Devon, where there had been a mine for many years, though latterly it had become disused. 'Artists from sundry nations came to viewe it', but the ore was 'stobborne to melt', and they could make nothing of it. Then someone took a specimen to Bulmer. He tested it, recognized its value, and immediately rode off to Combe Martin, where he negotiated a deal with Gilbert, by which he was to take half the proceeds in return for bearing the whole cost of digging and melting. Though it lasted only a short time, this turned out an excellent bargain, and in the first two years each party made £10,000. The yield then began to decline, probably because working was held up by water, but the mine was kept open for another two years; in its last year, when the miners were 'at the deep', the proceeds were worth £1,000.[7]

It was while he was at Combe Martin that Bulmer engaged the services of Stephen Atkinson, author of *The Discoverie and Historie of the Gold Mynes in Scotland*, which has been quoted above. Atkinson was a 'finer', employed at the Mint in the Tower of London, and after work ceased at Combe Martin it seems that Bulmer himself obtained employment there, for in 1595, when Raleigh brought back some ore from his voyage to Guiana, it was assayed by 'Master Bulmer and Master Dimoke, Assay-masters.'[8] This was only one of Bulmer's diverse occupations about this time. A few years previously, in 1588, as we saw in an earlier chapter, he had obtained a patent for a machine for slitting iron into rods; presently he was to make a contribution to the water-supply of London. For some years the population had been outgrowing the available supply, and though various schemes were in the air, little had been done to put them into effect. Parts of the city near London Bridge had been supplied since 1581 with water pumped from the Thames by a water-wheel erected under one of the arches of the bridge, but much more was needed. In 1593 Bulmer obtained a licence to instal chain-pumps worked by horses at Broken Wharf, on the bank of the river not far from St Paul's, with cisterns and pipes to supply the western parts of the city. The installation was completed in 1594–5, and no doubt was a useful contribution to the needs of London. As a commercial proposition it did not pay, but Bulmer commemorated its achievement by presenting a silver cup for the use of the Lord Mayor, with his portrait and the following inscription engraved upon it:

> When water works at Brokenwharffe
>   At first erected were,
> And Bevis Bulmer by his arte
>   The water gan to rear,
> Dispersed I in earth did lye,
>   From all beginning ould
> In place called Combe where Martyn longe
>   Had hidd me in the moulde;
> I did no service in the earth,
>   Nor no man sett me free,
> Till Bulmer by his arte and skill
>   Did frame me thus to be.

He also presented a cup with a verse inscription to the Earl of Bath, Lord Lieutenant of Devonshire, both cups being made from the last cake of silver from the Combe Martin mine.[9]

Bulmer was also concerned in a number of other mining ventures in widely scattered districts, among them the mines in Ireland at which Robert Record and Gundelfinger had worked in Edward vi's reign (see below). Bulmer had the ore shipped to Combe Martin for refining, but he does not seem to have been any more successful in Ireland than his predecessors had been, and was still owing money there when he died. Even if this venture and the waterworks were unremunerative, however, other schemes were paying handsomely, and in 1599, as we saw in the last chapter, he made a bid for the tin monopoly. Meanwhile he retained his interest in the Mendip mines, where he left a deputy named 'John Hole of Hawkes' in charge. This time, in the master's absence, it was not the neighbours but his own servant who caused trouble there, for in 1605 Hole was found to be selling Bulmer's ore and pitches as if they were his own. The Privy Council intervened again on Bulmer's behalf, and Hole was convicted of misappropriating Bulmer's property, but when we lose sight of him he was still refusing to make restitution.[10]

Some years before this Bulmer had moved to Scotland. In January 1594 Thomas Foullis had obtained a 21-year lease of the mines in Lanarkshire at a rent of 1,000 marks. He invited Bulmer to join him again, and by 1597, or possibly earlier, they were working in partnership, for in that year they sent a joint complaint to the

Privy Council of Scotland that their lead had been stolen by border robbers. Bulmer, however, was after gold, not lead. He went about searching in various places, and succeeded in finding gold in quite large quantities. He diverted a watercourse for washing the gold, and at Langclough Head he built a stamping-mill 'of the kind known in Cornwall as a plash-mill', whereby he got 'small mealy gold'. He bought lands and cattle, and built himself a country house in Glengonnar, with a verse over the doorway:

> In Wanlock, Elwand and Glengonnar
> I wan my riches and my honour.[11]

Bulmer was reputed to have made a fortune of £100,000 sterling, but he was incapable of retaining his wealth; apart from being robbed by thieves who broke into his premises he entertained lavishly and was prodigal with gifts. He had a porringer made of the gold from Crawford Moor and presented it to Queen Elizabeth, who was so delighted with it that she encouraged him to ask for any lucrative appointment 'that is not already graunted, nor prejudiciall to us, or our crowne'. As Atkinson put it, Bulmer 'was made one of hir Majesties sworne servants: and this was his first stepp at Court, and from thence he learned to begg, as other courtiers doe'.[12] He proceeded to beg for the farm of an impost on sea-coal, and for £6,200 a year was granted the right to levy 5s. on every chaldron of coal exported and 1s. on every chaldron carried by water within the realm. This is said to have brought him in a profit of £1,000 a year, but there was determined resistance by the municipal authorities at Newcastle-on-Tyne, backed up by the Earl of Essex. Essex's opposition may have been aroused because his own livelihood was threatened when in 1599 Bulmer made an offer for the impost on sweet wines, then held by Essex. Though Bulmer was supported by Buckhurst, then Lord Treasurer, he did not obtain this, but by now he was evidently well-established in the circle of courtier projectors, and it was about the same time that he made his bid for the tin monopoly.

With the accession of King James the throne was occupied by a monarch with a ready ear for the schemes of projectors. Bulmer had an audience with him in the first year of his reign, and dilated on the value of the gold mines in Scotland. The King then 'devised a plot' (i.e. thought of a plan) which should at the same time provide capital for exploiting the mines and bring in revenue to the royal coffers. Bulmer was to find 24 substantial gentlemen with property worth £10,000 or an income of £500 a year; each was to subscribe £300, and in return they should be known as 'knights of the golden mynes', or 'golden knights'. Salisbury, however, opposed the idea, and to Bulmer's disappointment it was abandoned. According to Atkinson only one knight was made, Sir John Claypoole, who had already put up £500, but apparently Bulmer himself was given a knighthood, for from this time forward Atkinson refers to him as Sir Bevis Bulmer.[13]

Bulmer returned to the Scottish mines, but now a rival appeared in the field, an Englishman named George Bowes. The government may have thought that two projectors would produce twice as much gold as one, and the Privy Council allocated some rivers to Bulmer and the River Wanlock to Bowes; in other areas both might work, either separately or together. Both were to have financial assistance from the government, but Bulmer was the more favoured. In January 1604 he got £200 down and a promise of such sums in the future as he should require and the Lord Treasurer allow, but the total granted to Bowes was only £300—£100 at once and the balance later. Not surprisingly there was friction and rivalry between the two. Bowes thought himself unfairly treated, and his sense of grievance was heightened when Bulmer secured a proclamation from the Scottish Privy Council; Bowes resented this because he thought it gave the impression that he lacked government support.

Bowes engaged skilled workmen from England as well as local labour, and began operations by diverting a stream so as to tear up the ground, in the hope of finding veins of gold, but the wintry weather was against him. Work was held up by a snowdrift a quarter of a mile long; after that the workmen's tents were blown down four times by gales; there was continual rain, and Bowes himself and seven of his men were laid up with scurvy. Such were the hazards of the mining projector's life, and the results were hardly commensurate with the effort. Apparently Bowes found a small vein of gold at Wanlockhead, but if Atkinson is right in saying that he 'swore his workmen to secrecy' and did not disclose it to the King or the Council, perhaps he deserved the discrimination against him. Bulmer also put it about that Bowes's finances

were unsound, with the result that his workmen would work for
Bulmer for 5d. a day in preference to earning 6d. from Bowes, unless
Bowes would guarantee them employment for a long period. This
he could hardly do, and in fact his £300 was exhausted within a
few months. He wrote asking for more, giving details of his labours
and the difficulties he had experienced. He had intended, he said,
to make a 'plat' of the works, but could not do so because the damp
climate had spoilt his colours and instruments. But the government refused any more funds, and Bowes had to abandon his
work. He was accidentally killed on a visit to the copper mines in
Cumberland, when a ladder broke and the earth fell in on him.[14]

Bulmer was left in sole possession of the field in Lanarkshire,
but in his search for gold he does not seem to have been much
more successful than Bowes, and in 1606 he moved to what seemed
a more promising venture. A collier picked up a piece of silver ore
at Hilderstone, in West Lothian, and took it to Bulmer, who immediately saw an opportunity to be grasped. Hilderstone belonged to
the King's Advocate, Sir Thomas Hamilton, of Monkland, or Binnie,
who obtained a licence to develop the mines on his estate, in return
for a royalty of a tenth of the produce. At first Bulmer seems to
have acted as Hamilton's manager, but the yield of silver was
disappointing, and in 1607 he went back to Lanarkshire, where in
the meantime 'broken men from the border' had destroyed his
works. The King, however, hoped that the Hilderstone mine might
still be made to pay, bought it from Hamilton for £5,000, and by a
warrant dated 25 April 1608 appointed Sir Bevis Bulmer 'Master of
the Mines' for life at a yearly salary of £1,440 Scots and a daily
wage of £8 as long as he resided at the mines. Bulmer also had
£500 'of his majesty's free gift', and a debt he owed since the
time of the sea-coal farm was cancelled. The undertaking was on a
a sizeable scale, with 61 miners employed underground, besides
those who worked at the fining mills; but the yield seems to have
been variable,[15] and towards the end of 1610 Bulmer gave up his
appointment and moved to Alston Moor in Cumberland. The
silver-lead mines there had been celebrated in the past, but when
surveyed about this time they were reported to be 'nearly dead'.
Bulmer, who had run through all his money, no doubt hoped to
revive them; but though they became very prosperous again in

the eighteenth century he failed to do so, and he was in debt when he died at Alston in 1615.[16]

During his engagement at Hilderstone Bulmer went off on prospecting expeditions to other parts of Scotland, including the Highlands and the coast of Galloway. He reported the discovery of various stones and minerals, including amethysts, one of which he presented to the King, and even pearls, but none of these discoveries had any serious commercial value. It may have been at this time also, or possibly while he was at Alston Moor, that Bulmer began work at a mine at Brunghill Moor, in the parish of Slaidburn, in the West Riding of Yorkshire. He is said to have 'got good store of silver ore' there, but the owner of the land disputed his title to the mine, and he had to abandon it.[17] After Bulmer's death his servant Atkinson obtained a grant of the Lanarkshire mines, and composed his history of the gold mines in the hope of winning the King's support. He had a shrewd idea of what would appeal to James, but in spite of references to various prophecies, and the 'wonderful resemblances which many of His Majesty's gracious deeds' had with those of David and Solomon, the King remained unmoved. Probably Atkinson did not lose much, for though occasional odd bits of gold were found in later years, the chief deposits had been exhausted.

Atkinson says that Bulmer wrote an account of his mining career, called *Bulmer's Skill*, but it was never printed, and the manuscript apparently does not survive.[18] But he records Bulmer's characteristic oral comments on the qualities needed by a mining projector: 'Some cheife points that I observed from Mr. Bulmer, within these thirty yeares, &c. And he said, (1) Whosoever is a menerall man must of force be a hasserd adventurer, not greatly esteeming whether it hit, or miss soddainly, as if he were a gamester playing at dice, or such unlawful games, &c. (vizt.) Thine or mine at all, said he. (2) If once a little be adventured in seeking of meneralls or menerall stones, and thereby he happen to wyn, he must esteeme it as nothing, said he. (3) But if he hope to wynn, and throwe at all, so loose all and gett nothing, yett must he thinke he hath gott something. (4) And if a man find a rich vaine of mettle, by arte or accedent, lett him not esteeme thereof, for it is like a man stonge with a nettle; sayth he. And if he do seeke in hope to find, albeit thereby noe profitt nor principall doth come, yet must he thinke himselfe a rich man, and beleeve that he hath, or shall have, that he hath not; and if he cannot embrace the lessons he cannot be a right menerall man; sayth he. But I say [adds Atkinson himself], and beleeve it too, That when mynes, menerall or menerall stones, doe hitt in, it is the best gotten goods in the whole world. It is profitable to all parties, and doth prejudice none.'[19]

Bulmer was the model Elizabethan adventurer, the industrial counterpart of the navigators, explorers or privateers who typified that age. Nor did his gambling instincts by any means exclude shrewdness and business sense. The tenancy agreements for consumers of the water from Broken Wharf provided that the supply should be cut off if they failed to pay their rent, and gave power to enter their houses in order to make sure that they had not installed extra cocks. Tenants had also to agree to their installations being kept in repair by a plumber, and were liable to a fine of half a crown if they allowed the water to run to waste. Again, while Bulmer was at Hilderstone, earning £8 Scots a day, it is worth noticing that in the week of Christmas and the New Year he felt entitled as manager to draw £56 for himself, though the workmen were paid for only five days. But if he knew how to make money, he could not keep it. As Atkinson remarks, he had too many irons in the fire, and along with his adventurousness went an equally characteristic vanity and prodigality. 'By such synister means he was impoverished, and followed other idle veniall vices to his dying day, that were not allowable of God nor man; and so Once downe aye downe. . . .'[20]

Silver was found in a number of places at different times in the Middle Ages, particularly in the western counties.[21] Besides the mine at Combe Martin there were highly productive silver mines in other parts of Devonshire, particularly about Beer Alston, near the Cornish border. In the eighteenth and nineteenth centuries this area was intensively mined, chiefly for copper, but in the sixteenth century the more accessible ore seems to have been exhausted. When experts from Germany came to England in the hope of reopening derelict mines and making them pay again by the application of up-to-date techniques, they often turned to the west of England, but at the end of Henry VIII's reign hopes were centred on some lead mines in the south of Ireland, at Clonmines in county Wexford. Work there was at a standstill, but it was expected that paying quantities of silver could be extracted with the aid of foreign technicians. Negotiations were set on foot in 1545–6, through Garret Harman (? Gerard Hermann), a goldsmith from Antwerp then living in London, with a mining expert from Augsburg, named Joachim Gundelfinger. They went to inspect the mines, and brought back some promising specimens of ore.[22] The project was then held up for a time by the death of Henry VIII, but Edward VI's government took it up again, and Gundelfinger was authorized to recruit a body of German miners.

On 18 October 1550 he wrote to the Council from Antwerp, with a list of 'Master mine workers', whose various skills he proceeded to describe.[23] They included:

One of the most experienced and sworn master mining engineers.

A good metal founder.

Two others for making shafts, tunnels and trenches of mines, called in German *Schirpffer*.

Two carpenters to descend into mines, and prop each side of such shafts and passages, called in German *Steyper*.

One who thoroughly understands the art of draining and carrying off water.

One who understands the assaying of all metals.

Two smiths for making the necessary tools for the pioneers and others.

Two colliers to work the large coal of the mines.

Two who understand the separation of the sulphur before melting.

Twenty pioneers, good, strong and experienced, unmarried if possible.

One who understands the baking of rock alum.

Two with the seed of pine and deal, to sow the same according to the nature of the soil, to increase the forests both of England and Ireland.

All these to be Germans, brought to England from Frankfort the best way he can.

Alum is mentioned more than once as a possible product of the Irish mines, but apparently none was found; at any rate none was worked, and the chief objective was undoubtedly silver.

The government sent the celebrated Oxford mathematician

Robert Record, Fellow of All Souls, as 'surveyor of the mines', but he did not get on with the Germans, and they resented his appointment to supervise their work. In February 1552 Record told the Privy Council that 'the wastes of the Almain miners in their washings, roastings, meltings and finings are excessive. English and Irish men can better skill of that work than the Almains can.' He hoped that when the mines had been sunk deeper there would be 'much greater gains', but 'the King's charges at this hour are above £260 every month, and the gains not above £40, so His Majesty loses £220 monthly'. Harman, on the other hand, reported to the Council that the mines were 'very rich, profitable and commodious', and complained of the 'wilfulness, pride, presumption and covetousness of Doctor Robert Record'.

In face of this conflicting evidence the government sent William Williams as an independent surveyor, with instructions to make a detailed report. It was decidedly unfavourable. Besides £2,000 paid to the Almains 'before they had wrought one day', the King had spent £3,478 15s. 1d., to set against which he had made only £474. A number of the Almains were absent from work, or had to be discharged, and in two years expenditure amounted altogether to £6,665 15s. 3½d.[24] The truth was that the amount of silver in the ore was insufficient to justify the cost of extracting it, and the government decided to close the mines down. Nothing was done there in Mary's reign, and though Elizabeth's government was ready to encourage mining ventures, it prudently decided to give up state management, and leave them to private enterprise.

In spite of the government's losses under Edward VI, there seems to have been no lack of adventurers. The mines in county Wexford were leased to Walter Peppard, who had previously been in government service in Ireland, but he in turn failed to make a success of them. By 1564 he found it impossible to continue working on his own, but still there were entrepreneurs competing to join or succeed him. One was William Humfrey, then in process of forming the group later incorporated as the Mineral and Battery Works, who wished to secure mining rights in the areas not allocated to the Mines Royal. Another applicant was John Chaloner, at one time Mayor of Dublin, supported by Sebastian Speydell and Cornelius de Vos, and by his brother Sir Thomas Chaloner (the elder), of Guisborough in the North Riding of Yorkshire. At one moment it seemed

L

that the competitors might combine, for Humfrey told Cecil that, though he did not know them, he would be prepared to take John Chaloner and Walter Peppard as partners, 'not for any science that I do hear to be in them touching mineral affairs worthy to venture money on', but because he had heard that Chaloner was 'well learned in George Agricola as touching speculation'. This hardly seems a good reason, for he expected that Chaloner would 'talk or write artificially', but lack 'experienced knowledge by daily working'; and Agricola, he added, was 'a present medicine to make a heavy purse light'.[25]

Humfrey had no illusions about the value of the Wexford mines, and did not intend to waste more money there, but there were mines, reputed to yield silver and copper, in the island of Lambay, off the east coast of Ireland.[26] Mines in Cornwall and the Isle of Man, Humfrey pointed out, were as good, if not better; nevertheless, Irish rights might be worth having. Protracted negotiations followed, made longer by the deaths of Walter Peppard and Sir Thomas Chaloner, and Humfrey meanwhile had found a more promising partner in Christopher Schütz. One of the two patents granted to Humfrey and Schütz covered mining rights in Ireland, but the Mineral and Battery company never in fact exercised its rights there, and the Lambay mines fell to John Chaloner. His experiences there were unfortunate. The island was raided by French ships, and the mines proved to be less productive than he had hoped. After his death, in May 1581, his son Thomas continued working there for a while, but he too had little success, and he finally turned for assistance to his namesake and cousin, Sir Thomas Chaloner (the younger). Sir Thomas allowed him a home on his estate at Guisborough; there was no silver to be mined there, but instead he discovered alum.

Another German mining expert who came to England in the middle of the sixteenth century was Burchard Kranich, whom we have already encountered more than once.[27] He is first heard of with his sieve and furnace at Duffield in Derbyshire in the reign of Edward VI. He melted lead there, but what he really wanted was silver, and he left Derbyshire within a year or so when he heard that there were 'better mines' in Cornwall. By a patent from Queen Mary dated 29 May 1554, in which he is described as a 'Hie Almayn', he obtained the right to 'mine, break ground, melt, divide and search for all manner of metals in any place' for 20 years, and for the next six years no one else was to 'melt separate or divide any of the metals Burchard doth melt'.[28] On 28 December 1555 this was followed by a commission 'to digg and followe as well such mynes of golde, sylver and copper as he hath alredie by his industrie and skill searched and tried owte in the countye of Cornwall, as also such other as he shall hereafter happen to discover and finde oute'. Justices of the Peace, mayors, and other authorities were to assist him, and the Receiver of the Duchy was to deliver all such metal to the Queen's use, for which she would pay according to its value. Thomas Treffry of Fowey and John Trethinke were to supervise Kranich's work, making sure 'that there be no melting made by him but that they have knowleage of and be present at'. They were to certify the quantities of metal he had produced, and pay him the sums due to him; they were also 'to procure to learne at his handes the secretes of his arte'.

There was some hitch, however, for six months later Kranich was asking for more time. He was told that 'in consideracion of the benefit that is like to come to this realme by the said mynes' he should be allowed another six months, although the Queen was in great need of silver.[29] Still the expected bullion did not materialize, and in 1557 the government ordered an investigation: John Trelawney, Thomas Treffry, John Tredenick and William Carnsew (the elder) were to take charge of Kranich's mines. One of the mines was Treworthy, which Ulrich Frosse was sent to reopen some 20 years later. William Carnsew the younger then complained that it had been 'by Burchard's frowardness given over', but considering Frosse's difficulties there perhaps Burchard was not really to blame. Soon after this he must have decided to settle in England, for in 1561, having paid 6s. 8d. to be naturalized, he turned to the practice of medicine, in which he spent most of the rest of his life.

He undertook at least one more venture, however, as a mining expert in Cornwall. In 1563 he obtained a patent for the use of 'instruments which he has devised' for 'draining of mines or conveying of water from any place whatsoever from low to high'. The government may have had some misgivings, for the patent included a clause imposing a penalty of £300 should he fail to erect his engines in the counties of Devon and Cornwall within three years. At a subsequent inquiry, held in 1567, it appeared that the Receiver-

General of the Duchy of Cornwall advanced £500 on behalf of the Queen, and that Kranich had spent £220 on opening mines in a number of places, and some £400 on building a melting house 80 feet long and 24 feet wide, with a watercourse 2,000 paces long to supply the necessary power, at 'Laryon' (Lerryn, on a creek of the Fowey estuary). Besides '4 paire of grete bellowes with their geames [? beames] and other necessaries', costing £20, there were also stamps driven by water power ('the whele, exultree and the stampers'), costing £10, but how much silver was produced is not stated. In view of the need for an inquiry one suspects that the results were disappointing.[30]

Cornelius de Vos acquired Kranich's rights under the patent, but what use he made of them we do not know. Kranich returned to London, where in 1576 he bought eight houses and three gardens in the parish of St Clement Danes. In 1577 he was asked to examine some ore, alleged to be gold, which Frobisher had brought back from his first expedition to find the North-west Passage. It had already been tested and declared to contain gold, but Walsingham wanted a second opinion, and called in Kranich. He found a little gold, but not as much as had been claimed.[31] This was his last recorded service for the government. 'Dr Burcot' made his last will on 7 October 1578, and died later in the same month. He had not had much success as a mining entrepreneur, but the reason may be not so much the inadequacy of his skill or of the apparatus he used, as the exhaustion of the silver, or its absence in any profitable quantity, in the terrain he tried to exploit.

Silver mines in the north of England had yielded well in the past, but in the sixteenth century they too were in difficulties. In the early seventeenth century Gerard Malynes, a prolific writer on economic matters, whose father had been at the Mint at the time of the restoration of the currency at the beginning of Elizabeth's reign, published a book in which he wrote in despondent terms of the condition and prospects of the mining industry.[32] He was particularly interested in monetary questions, and wanted to see the country producing its own supplies of the precious metals. He could not, he said, 'without griefe discourse of the Silver Mines of this Monarchie of Great Brittaine, and heartily lament to see them lie dead and buried in oblivion'. About 1608 he had himself brought in 17 workmen from Germany at his own expense, to work at silver mines in the bishopric of Durham, lead mines in Yorkshire, and elsewhere. Lord Eure and some London merchants had 'undertaken to proceed' with him, and the enterprise was 'applauded by a great personage then in authori-tie, and now deceased, who promised all he could do'. Durham people told him that two rich mines in their neighbourhood, though 'fallen in', could 'with a reasonable charge bee brought in working', but 'being in the Wintertime, and the weather very foule', he had had 'not without discontent' to abandon the attempt to revive them.

The most prolific mines in the seventeenth century were the silver-lead mines in Cardiganshire which Customer Smythe had exploited for a time in Queen Elizabeth's reign. After his death they became derelict again until 1617, when they were taken up by Hugh Myddelton, then deeply involved in the most famous of his projects, the New River to supply London with water.[33] Myddelton, who was born probably in 1560, was a younger son of a substantial Denbighshire family, and like many others in his position had gone to London to make a living. He was apprenticed and rose to become prominent in the powerful Goldsmiths' Company, and was a pros-perous business man in the city, not only practising as a goldsmith but participating with an elder brother and other city men in num-erous financial and commercial deals. The need for a better water supply in London has already been mentioned, and by the end of the sixteenth century the city authorities had come to realize that the only effective way to meet the need would be by bringing in fresh water from outside. They obtained statutory powers for this purpose, but they were not prepared themselves to undertake the risk or the necessary financial outlay. Like everyone else in that age, they thought this should be left to private enterprise.

Then a man from Bath named Edmund Colthurst, who had recently served in the Irish wars, offered to dig a channel to bring water to the city from springs in Hertfordshire and Middlesex. His scheme was approved, and he cheerfully started work; but he and his partners had only limited funds, which soon ran out. The scheme hung fire for several years, until in 1609 the city accepted an offer by Hugh Myddelton to undertake the responsibility for it. He got several other business men to become partners with him, and they later held shares in the joint-stock company which was estab-lished to complete and manage the New River; but Myddelton him-self bore a large part of the financial burden, and it was mainly through his fortitude and perseverance in the face of difficulties and opposition that the work was successfully completed.

The source of the New River was at the springs of Chadwell and Amwell, near Ware, whence it ran by a winding course of over 40 miles to 'New River Head' at Islington. Myddelton had no personal training or experience as an engineer; he took on Colthurst, the originator of the scheme, as 'overseer' in charge of operations, and relied on professional mathematical practitioners to survey and plot the course of the river. While great accuracy was required in this, there were no serious physical obstacles to be encountered, but the river had not advanced more than a few miles before construction was held up by the opposition of some landowners on the line of route, who organized a campaign in the House of Commons for the repeal of the Act authorizing the digging of the river. Myddelton had to organize a counter-campaign (he was himself an M.P., representing the borough of Denbigh), and though the immediate crisis was resolved by the dissolution of Parliament in 1611, his anxiety and frustration were not relieved until in 1612 James I himself decided to become a partner. Royal influence could then be used to override objectors, and the financial outlook became brighter, because the King undertook to bear half the cost in return for half the profits. Work was then resumed, rapid progress was made, and on Michaelmas Day, 1613, a kind of pageant was held at New River Head to celebrate the completion of the river.

Mains, consisting of hollowed-out elm-trunks, had still to be laid in the streets to distribute the water; financially, in fact, the completion of the river itself was less than half the whole undertaking. Besides the capital cost, maintenance and repairs involved continual heavy expense, and it was a long time before Londoners in any number could be induced to pay for having New River water brought to their houses. No doubt the King had imagined that he was making a profitable investment, but he was soon disappointed, for though in the long run New River Company shares appreciated enormously in value, in its early years it paid no dividend. In November 1614, when the total outlay amounted to a little over £18,500, the Exchequer authorities decided that the work was complete, and calculated the King's liability as half this sum. Some of it had been paid already, in instalments as the work had progressed, and in the end it was all paid, but only after considerable delays. And it by no means represented the whole outlay. Large outgoings were still being incurred, but the King's share of these was to wait till it could be met out of the profits. Myddelton had exhausted his own resources in the undertaking, and in order to carry on he had to borrow £3,000 at six per cent interest, from the city.

He badly needed a fresh source of income, and given good luck there was no better way of making money quickly than a silver mine, though the risks were notoriously great. Myddelton had the boldness to take the risk, and the energy to add this new undertaking to his other commitments. So in 1617 he obtained a lease from the Mines Royal company of their neglected mines in Wales. According to Pettus his rent to the company was £400 a year, but the venture paid him well, and when the mines were in full production he is said to have 'cleared' £2,000 a month. Thomas Bushell, his successor at the mines, declared that Myddelton sent altogether £50,000 worth of silver to the Mint, but all these figures probably need to be received with caution. Myddelton appears to have opened, or reopened, five mines in north Cardiganshire, the most productive being Cwmsymlog, where he installed pumps to clear the water and reach deeper levels. He rented a house and went with his wife to life in Cardiganshire for a time, while the mines were being developed (one of his daughters married the son of the chief local landowner), but like other entrepreneurs he relied on technical experts to manage operations at the mines themselves and at the smelting and refining mills. Among these was a metallurgist named Walter Basbie, or Barksby, who had previously been employed by Bevis Bulmer, and who years later, in his old age, reappeared in Wales as one of Bushell's advisers.

As so often happened, Myddelton met with hostility and obstruction from some of the local inhabitants; he also had to contend with charlatans who pretended to be able to produce more silver than he could, and tried to have him displaced. Myddelton, however, had the government behind him, including the personal favour of the King, for although James may have regretted his investment in the New River, Myddelton was sending silver to the Mint in gratifying quantities. Orders were given for the produce of the Welsh mines to be coined separately, and to be stamped with the Prince of Wales's feathers as a distinguishing mark; and the

Privy Council issued a proclamation, giving Myddelton special powers to conscript labour, and threatening all who opposed his work with summary punishment by the Council of the Marches. As a further mark of royal favour, Myddelton was made a baronet. This rank, which had recently been invented as a money-raising device, was awarded to knights or esquires who paid £1,000 for it; but Sir Hugh obtained it free of charge, and with a citation of his three notable accomplishments. His fame rests chiefly on two of these, the New River and the Welsh mines; the third, the reclamation of some land in the Isle of Wight, later turned out a failure.

Numerous schemes were promoted in the seventeenth century for reclaiming fens and marshes, and we shall come to these in a later chapter. James I was interested in undertakings of this kind, and Bevis Thelwall, who held a position at Court, used his influence there to obtain approval for a scheme to reclaim some 700 acres of tidal mudflats in Brading Harbour. Like Hugh Myddelton, Thelwall was a junior member of a Welsh family, neighbours of the Myddeltons, who had gone up to London to make his way. He induced Hugh Myddelton to participate in the scheme, and Myddelton in turn brought in several of his fellow-adventurers in the New River. Dutch workmen were engaged, and an embankment was built across the narrow entrance to the haven, near Bembridge. The undertaking cost some £7,000 or £8,000, but the reclaimed land proved poor in quality, and after some unproductive agricultural experiments Myddelton sold out his interest to Thelwall, who meanwhile had become a partner with Myddelton in the Welsh mines. Myddelton was lucky to get out in time, for in 1630 the embankment gave way before a high tide. Thelwall tried to throw the responsibility for the collapse on to Myddelton's shoulders, but Myddelton died in 1631, and Thelwall was left to bear the loss. A few years before this Sir John Wynn of Gwydir had tried to persuade Myddelton to undertake a similar project for reclaiming some inundated land in North Wales, and offered 'to adventure a brace of hundred pounds'. But Myddelton prudently declined to be drawn. The work would cost thousands, not hundreds, he pointed out, 'and first of all his Majesty's interest must be got. As for myself, I am grown into years', he wrote, 'and full of business here at the mynes, the river at London, and other places, my weeklie charge being above £200; which maketh me verie unwilling to undertake

anie other worke : and the least of theis, whether the drowned lands
or mynes, requireth a whole man, with a large purse.'

In some ways an outstanding example of the industrial entrepreneur, Sir Hugh Myddelton differed from the type in that he acted
from other motives besides that of making a fortune for himself;
and if he relied on privileges secured by influence at Court, he
did so not so much for selfish reasons as because in the early seventeenth century this was the best if not the only way in which a
project could be launched. 'I cannot be idle', he once wrote to one
of his Welsh neighbours, explaining why he had undertaken the
New River, and in his letter to Sir John Wynn he wrote of his 'love
to publique works'. He was not only a versatile and tireless entrepreneur, but a public benefactor as well, and as such he deserved his
honour and his reputation. Sir Hugh was not a poor man when he
died, as has sometimes been said. He had a country house near
Edmonton as well as a house in the city; he had lived in style, and
left substantial legacies in his will. But for some years his widow
was encumbered with his business debts, including the £3,000 he
had borrowed from the city, and this she never succeeded in repaying. For several years after her husband's death she could not find
anyone to take over the Welsh mines; work there ceased, and they
soon became flooded again. At last in 1636 she was approached
by Thomas Bushell with an offer to acquire the remainder of
Myddelton's lease, which had been renewed in 1625 for 31 years.
Negotiations were completed by 14 October on the basis that Bushell
should pay a year's rent down, and take over the lease at the existing
rent.

Bushell was a man of very different character from Sir Hugh
Myddelton; in his reckless flamboyance he was more like Sir Bevis
Bulmer.[34] Born about 1594, he came of a landowning family on
the borders of Gloucestershire and Worcestershire, but he was a
prodigal son, and ran away from home at the age of 15. He made
his way to London, not to be apprenticed to a great city company,
but relying on his wits and his good looks, which attracted the attention of Francis Bacon. Bacon took him into his household, where
he became an amanuensis to his master, and was treated with great
indulgence : Bacon three times paid his debts for him, amounting
altogether to £3,000. By his own confession young Bushell lived a
life of extravagance and profligacy punctuated by interludes of

contrition, during which he retreated to self-imposed austerity. On the first of these occasions, which may have been partly prompted by fear lest he be implicated in Bacon's impeachment and disgrace, he retired in disguise to lodge with a fisherman's family in the Isle of Wight. After Bacon's death he spent three years living on a frugal diet in a hut on the Calf of Man.

Meanwhile he had used his position in society to establish useful business connections, and on his return to civilization he engaged in some of the semi-fraudulent commercial concessions which were then such a characteristic feature of 'big business'. With a certain Thomas Carleton as partner he obtained the farm of the imposts on silk, and he had some part, though probably only a minor one, in the famous monopoly of the Westminster soap-boilers. In ways like this he made enough money to acquire a country estate, at Enstone in Oxfordshire, where he imitated the style in which Bacon used to live at Gorhambury. Workmen laying out the grounds at Enstone discovered a rock of curious formation, with orifices and pendants : Bushell had it enclosed in a grotto, installed a piped water-supply, and made it the centrepiece for a display of *jeux d'eau*. These 'waterworks' became one of the sights of the neighbourhood, and in August 1636, when they were visited by the King and Queen, Bushell arranged an elaborate entertainment, which must have cost him a considerable sum.

In his later years Bushell declared that it was Bacon who had urged him to make mining his career, taught him his mining technique, and had devised the schemes he tried to put into practice. He published manifestos to herald his successive projects, and in these he ceaselessly proclaimed his indebtedness to his 'quondam master'. Bushell's technique certainly was not original. It came ultimately from Agricola's *De Re Metallica*, and it may be true that he learned about it from Bacon, for Bacon wished to encourage mining, and knew Agricola's work.[35] But Bushell undoubtedly realized the value of exploiting Bacon's name as an advertisement for the scientific soundness of his projects, and it is noticeable that as the years went by, and he got more deeply into debt, his references to Bacon's behests became progressively more detailed and circumstantial. In the earliest of his mining pamphlets,[36] however, he did not mention Bacon at all. What first suggested to him the idea of reopening the Welsh mines, he then said, was 'a sensible discourse delivered mee by a Portugall ... who had for many yeares beene imployed under the King of Spaine in his West India Mines, purporting that if his Master were Soveraigne Lord of these Brittish hills ... he would not doubt to make them a second Indies'. Accompanying the 'Portugall' on the occasion of this 'discourse' was Sir Francis Godolphin, the youngest son of the famous tin-owner, who on his elder brother's death had inherited his father's tin interests, and himself became a mining expert. He had been called in to adjudicate in a dispute in Cardiganshire while Sir Hugh Myddelton was at work there, and may thus have become acquainted with the value of the Welsh mines; he probably brought the 'Portugall' with him in order to stimulate Bushell's interest. Bushell did not need much persuading, and he and Godolphin accordingly embarked as partners on a plan to reopen Sir Hugh Myddelton's mines. The partnership did not last long, however, for to Bushell's regret Godolphin died in 1640, but he had another partner (whether from the beginning or after Godolphin's death is not clear) in the person of an Oxfordshire neighbour, Edmund Goodyear of Heythrop.

At Bushell's request the Privy Council confirmed the transfer of Lady Myddelton's lease, and the way was clear to start work. Both Sir Hugh and his predecessor Customer Smythe, according to Bushell, had sunk shafts downwards from the heights, and were soon held up by 'damps' from lack of ventilation, and accumulations of water. Bushell proposed to work from below instead of from above, draining the old shafts by driving adits from the bottoms of the valleys. Ventilation was to be provided 'by two men's blowing wind by a pair of bellows on the outside of the adit, into a pipe of lead, daily lengthened as the mine is made longer', thus avoiding 'the tedious and expensive ways of sinking Ayrie shafts at every forty fathoms'. Bushell later claimed that he had learned both these methods from Bacon; nevertheless he now consulted 'the best Mineral masters of our age', among them Joseph Höchstetter, one of Daniel Höchstetter's sons.[37]

According to Bushell's own account, he kept 500 families in employment, cutting adits 'through five severall mountains, at their lowest level'. Work went on, night and day, for four years, and he had spent over £7,000 before he at length achieved success. Cutting an adit to drain a flooded mineshaft was a dangerous operation, and the men at the Tal-y-bont mine narrowly escaped disaster when, on 27 June 1641, the adit which had been driven 1,200 feet into the mountain side finally penetrated 'the chief shaft of the old drowned work, 38 fathoms deep'. Bushell's 'minister resident Preacher to the minerall men' wrote to give him the news.

The foure workemen about one in the night (as their manner was) withdrew to take Tobaco within ten fathome of the Addit's mouth, lest in the forefield it should damp the ayre, which was conveyed to them by your leaden pipe with bellows. Their smoakie banquet was not yet at an end, when they heard a mighty and fearfull noise, which some of them said was thunder. But old Bartholomew Clocker (a well experienced miner) although he left the work without any suspition of so neere an approach, resolved suddenly, the work is holed, come let us away. No sooner had they gotten the free ayre, but out gusheth the torrent of water with an incredible fury, such a breach it made in the solid Rock that it arose fully a yard's height at the Addit's mouth and drove away above 100 Tun of the rockie deads, affrighting the people of Talybont, who heard the noise and felt the water in their houses. . . . About four houres after, the violence of the water being past, Fisher one other of the Miners went in with more curiosity than wit, to see what effect it had wrought there: and being some sixtie fathome in creeping very low, his candle enkindled a vapour, which came on him with three or four flashes, and he suddenly returning had his haire burnt off, and his cloathes scortched, in which conclusion it gave a crack like the report of a peece, and in a fierce gust of wind blew out the candles of three more coming after him.

Rich ore with a high silver content was now at last within reach but, like other 'foreigners' in similar situations, Bushell found local people, including the chief landowner in the district, Sir Richard Price of Gogerddan, hostile and resentful of his presence. Jealous of his success, they stopped up his watercourses, pulled up the pumps and threw rubbish down the shafts, and he had to resort to litigation to defend his rights. With government support behind him he survived these onslaughts, and although we have no figures to show the amounts of lead and silver he obtained, they must have been considerable, for he even secured letters patent authorizing him to establish a mint in Aberystwyth castle, in order to save the risk and expense of transporting all the Welsh silver to be minted in London. As there was a shortage of wood for charcoal, Bushell tried using other fuels for smelting, and claimed to have achieved this with peat, 'by altering the earthy substance of turfe into charkie cynders'; he also experimented with 'sea-coale charked' (i.e. coke) but it is doubtful if he was really as successful as he claimed to be.

For a few years Bushell must have been making a very handsome income. Besides the profit from the mines, he had held since 1637 the farm of the customs on lead. The gross yield was between £10,000 and £14,000 a year, for which he paid a rent of £6,000, and had to bear the cost of collection. He must also presumably have made some money by the silk farm, his tenure of which was renewed in 1638. Unfortunately the Civil War broke out only a short time after the mines had begun to yield, and Bushell was a devoted royalist. At the King's orders he moved the mint from Aberystwyth to Shrewsbury, and thence after a few weeks to Oxford, where with Sir William Parkhurst, from the Tower, he was in charge of melting down the plate requisitioned from the colleges and local gentry. He also became, or made himself, responsible for providing clothes and equipment for several regiments in the King's army, and claimed to have spent £36,000 on this. In the early years of the war he continued to receive the produce of the mines, but later they were seized by the parliamentary forces, and he was soon in debt again. In 1643 he moved from Oxford to Bristol, where he was engaged for a time in striking coins; then, in 1645, when the war seemed likely to end soon in the defeat of the King's cause, he retreated with some 20 of his men to the island of Lundy, at the entrance to the Bristol Channel. He had hopes of reopening the silver mine at Combe Martin, and may have thought that Lundy would be convenient as a safe storage place for the silver from there; also, besides his fondness for islands, and a quixotic determination to hold out to the last for the King, he may well have been afraid of arrest for debt by his creditors. Bushell and his men resisted attempts to storm the island, and rejected terms for surrender long after the royal cause had collapsed everywhere else. It was not until February 1648 that at last he handed over the island to Major Richard Fiennes, son of Lord Saye and Sele, on condition that the mining rights he had possessed before the war should be restored to him.

For the next few years Bushell's men were at work trying to drain the old workings at Combe Martin, but apparently without result, while Bushell himself was busy raising fresh funds. With this end in view he composed and published the second of his self-advertising pamphlets, *The Case of Thomas Bushell ... truly stated, and his Progress in Minerals*. It was published in 1649, and 'tendered to the House of Commons'; but then he was unlucky enough to fall under suspicion of being implicated with Colonel Eusebius Andrews and Sir John Gell in a plot against the Commonwealth government. For a time he had to lie in hiding, in a house at Lambeth, but he finally managed to clear himself of the charge of treason, and in February 1654 the Protector confirmed his rights as a mining entrepreneur. All he needed was more money; but he was now heavily in debt (according to Aubrey his debts at this time amounted to £50,000 or £60,000), and various creditors whom he had ruined were anxious for his blood. He stressed the benefits which would accrue to the public by developing the mines, and it was at this juncture that he seems to have hit on the idea of making capital out of his association with Bacon. He issued a manifesto inviting members of the public to 'repair to the Assurance Office at the Royal Exchange', where they could obtain, from the 'Trustees of the late Lord Chancellor Bacon's mineral design', gold medals worth £5 each. To procure a medal they were to sign a document promising to pay £5 for every pound of the medal's value, i.e. £25, if Bushell should succeed within 18 months in maintaining for a year an output of 'copper, tin, or lead mixed with silver' worth £500 a week. This offer remained open for several years, but it was absurdly optimistic, and financially a failure. Not only was the output anticipated not reached, but there were not enough subscribers for the medals, and Bushell later issued silver and copper medals as well. 'The impressa of Mr. Bushell's golden medal' was printed on the title-page of the next to appear of his publications, in which he described his past endeavours and achievements, and his projects for the future. To this, which was published in 1659, he gave the title *Mr. Bushell's Abridgment of the Lord Chancellor Bacon's Philosophical Theory in Mineral Prosecutions*, and he printed the text of Bacon's *New Atlantis* as an appendix.

'He had the strangest bewitching way', says Aubrey,' to drawe-in people (yea, discreet and wary men) into his projects that ever I

heard of. His tongue was a chaine and drewe in so many to be
bound for him and to be ingaged in his designes that he ruined a
number.' Wherever he went he probably left such a reputation that
it was inadvisable to return. At any rate he never went back to
Wales, nor to Combe Martin. In 1656 he was engaged in a scheme
for driving adits to drain the mines, probably of tin or copper, at
Hingston Down in eastern Cornwall; a year later he was in Somerset, with plans to drain and reopen the rich lead mine, called Broad
Rake, previously worked by Bevis Bulmer, but now flooded once
more. The small local miners lacked the means to drain these workings, and at first welcomed Bushell's proposals. His hopes rose
accordingly to fantastic heights : not only would he 'produce such
store of treasure as to maintain a Mint in your City of Wells', but
he would leave a magnificent monument to Bacon's memory by
'finishing his Solomon's House in all its dimensions'. Bushell's
version of this was a 'select society' of philosophers, engaged in
'vertuous studies' and maintained by the labour of convicted crim-
inals and 'adventurous Voluntiers' working in the mines. Alas for
these fancies. Bushell's plans were upset by 'several misdemeanors
commited against him'. It was the old story. 'By some wicked
persons there was a great Lake of muddy water turned about the
hour of midnight, and upon a great flood' into his mine, 'on purpose
. . . to choak it, and so consequently to drown his men that came
from foreign parts, and were then working twenty fathom deep'.
Some other 'envious person . . . pulled down so much of the under-
timber of his Shaft, that the whole grove of earth fell into Mr.
Bushel's Drift, when his men were at work underneath'.

Apart from dislike at the intrusion of a stranger, some of
the Mendip miners were afraid that Bushell 'did intend to make it a
Mine Royall by his Art and Skill (to the prejudice of us, our Laws
and Liberties)'. These apprehensions are understandable, but were
probably groundless, for Mendip lead held only a small proportion
of silver, and Bushell's talk of a mint at Wells was as chimerical
as Solomon's House. His supporters among the local miners assured
him that if he persevered he would 'make good his Marqus of a
Thousand pounds per week : For there are men yet alive that will
justifie, that the forebreast of Sir Bevis Bulmer's work was nine foot
wide in oar; and we ourselves know that a hundred pounds per

week out of one Grove in the old work is ordinary, when the suffoca-
tion of water doth not hinder them'.

On 5 February 1659 Bushell obtained letters patent from Richard
Cromwell, confirming the privileges and powers granted to him
by 'our late deceased father Oliver Lord Protector of happy
memory', and calling on all Justices of the Peace and other authorities, civil and military, to assist him in his work, and to punish
all who obstructed or molested him. Hitherto Bushell had managed
to elude his creditors, but they chose this moment to launch a
fresh attack, and this time he failed to escape. In April 1659 he
was in Newgate, and was still there a year later. As a result of
renewed protestations of the advantages to the public if he were
released and allowed to resume 'Bacon's' mining plans, he obtained
a brief interlude of liberty in 1660. He had great hopes that the
restored monarch would recognize his devoted services in the
royalist cause, but Charles II had other matters to attend to, and
next year Bushell was back in prison again. He was released in 1663
when, in response to a fresh petition, setting forth how he had
'supplyed and served your Maties late Royall Father during the
Warrs with the utmost of his Estate and Credit', Charles appointed him a 'gentleman of the privy chamber extraordinary', in which
capacity he could only be arrested by the King's special command.
Bushell was thus relieved of anxiety for his personal liberty, and
spent most of his remaining years in repeated efforts to get a renewal
of the farm of the lead customs, and compensation for what he
claimed to have spent on Charles I's behalf during the Civil War.

But Charles II would do no more for him. At some point he
returned to his Mendip mines, for in 1671 the local mineral court
ratified an arrangement he had made to resume work there with a
new partner, Sir Edmund Wyndham, but nothing further was
achieved. Bushell was an old man now, and three years later he
died, at the age of 80. All through his life his debts had continually
piled up, and he never succeeded in repaying more than a fraction
of them. According to Aubrey he died £120,000 in debt, and was
'the greatest arts-master to runne in dept (perhaps) in the world'.
But in spite of the extravagance of his fancies he was not a mere
swindler, promoting fraudulent schemes simply in order to attract
money out of other people's pockets into his own. By all accounts
his work in Wales was successful, but he spent what he had gained

there by his enthusiastic royalism in the war, and afterwards he was never able to recover what he had lost.

He was a genuine 'adventurer', but not in the sense that he was an unscrupulous rogue. He was too sanguine, too wildly hopeful of being able to accomplish schemes which a soberer person would have seen to be obviously fantastic. Anthony Wood sums him up as having 'the Character of one always troubled with a beating and contriving Brain, of an Aimer at great and high things, while he himself was always indigent, and therefore could never accomplish his Mind to his Original Desire'. His manifestos were composed in absurdly rhetorical and magniloquent terms, but nobody expects a mining prospectus to be other than optimistic, and Bushell's pamphlets were frankly propaganda. In his efforts to extricate himself from his financial embarrassments he made exaggerated claims which laid him open to charges of being a liar as well as a cheat. This, however, is to do his memory an injustice. As a mining entrepreneur he was indeed an enthusiast, but I think an honest one, even if he sometimes deceived himself as well as the public.

Pettus concluded some brief comments on Sir Hugh Myddelton with the sententious remark that 'great Wits and Purses seldom know how to give bounds to their Designments, and by undertaking too many things, fail in all': if Myddelton had not wasted his money on the New River, 'certainly he would have been Master of a Mass of Wealth'.[38] This criticism fitted Bulmer or Bushell better than Myddelton; but it would be quite unfair to condemn any of them as having failed in all their undertakings, certainly not Myddelton, who in any case undertook the New River before, not after, his venture in the Welsh mines. Nevertheless, while all three of these entrepreneurs made large sums of money, it is true that all spent it freely, though for different purposes, and all ended their lives in debt. If the success of an entrepreneur is to be measured not by the utility of his undertaking but by the size of the fortune he leaves to his heir, perhaps Pettus's censure was justified after all.

M

8 | Alum

Independence of foreign sources for the supply of necessary raw materials was a constant aim of the government of Elizabethan England, and monopoly rights were often granted to entrepreneurs who professed or seemed likely to be capable of furthering it. A typical example was alum, essential to the cloth industry as a mordant in the process of dyeing, in order to fix the dye insolubly in the fabric. A substance often associated with alum was copperas (ferrous sulphate), otherwise called green vitriol. This has no chemical affinity with alum, but the ores of both were sometimes found together, and copperas was also used in dyeing. Out of copperas there sprang, as a brief excrescence, an alchemical project, not indeed to transmute the base metals into gold, but to make copper out of iron. Through dishonesty and mismanagement, combined with ignorance, inexperience and incompetence, very large sums of money were wasted on these projects, and the alum business in particular exhibited in classical form the notorious defects of early seventeenth-century economic administration.

About the middle of the fifteenth century a rich supply of alum had been discovered at Tolfa, a few miles inland from Civitavecchia, in the Papal States, and this soon became the principal source of all the alum used in Europe. For Elizabethan Protestants there was thus a religious as well as an economic motive for liberating the country from dependence on papal monopoly. The first Englishman to enter the field was a Cornish gentleman from Launceston named William Kendall, who in 1562 was granted for 20 years the sole right of making alum within the southern and south-western counties. What was hoped and planned for his project is expressed in the terms of his patent, according to which he had 'by his great travaile and charges founde out in sundrye partes of this our Realme certaine alum ewer [ore] in great habundance and plentye, and by longe studye and practise devised the waye and feate to make thereof good and perfect alume to the great commodite of us and this our Realme of England, as it is conceaved and hoped'.[1] Kendall began work at Alum Bay in the Isle of Wight, but about six years later he was complaining to Cecil of the vexatious treatment he had received there, and asking for protection from the governor of the island. Apart from the perennial hostility to the intrusion of strangers, something must have gone wrong with Kendall's plans, for in 1564 a fresh patent, with no mention of Kendall's rights, was granted to Cornelius de Vos, described as 'of London, marchaunte and our liege made subjecte'. According to this patent, de Vos had 'founde sondrye mines and owres of allome coperas and other mineralles within certayne partes of this our Realme of England ... and specially within our Isle of Wighte in the County of Southampton, which he entendeth at his own proper costes and charges to work and trye out to the benefit of us our Realme and subjectes'.

De Vos's grant was wider than Kendall's, for it covered the whole realm, and included copperas as well as alum. He does not appear to have done much, if anything, in the Isle of Wight, and directed his attention instead to the coast of the mainland, on the borders of Hampshire and Dorset, where the ore of copperas had been found, and there were hopes of finding alum also. This area was part of the extensive manor of Canford, which belonged to James Blount, Lord Mountjoy. Mountjoy was in financial difficulties, and conceived great hopes of paying off his debts by means of the profits to be made by exploiting the minerals on his estate. De Vos was ready to dabble or speculate in a variety of industrial enterprises, but seems to have done little effective work at any of them. He had difficulty in raising capital for the alum project, whereas Mountjoy was eager to risk all the money he could raise in a venture which, he optimistically declared, would bring in £4,000 a year and 'deliver him from his miseries', besides being 'to the benefit of the realm and annoyance of the Pope'.[2] It was arranged accordingly that Mountjoy should participate in the project, and he entered into it with energy and enthusiasm. In May 1566 he wrote to Cecil from Poole, telling him that copperas was being 'wrought with weekely gayne over and besides all expenses', and was 'like to encrease much rather than diminishe'. A 'small proofe' had shown 'no small likelihood ... of much good to be doonne in the alame as well as in the coperas', and a few months later he even suggested that the Queen might make him an advance of £6,000; he would then undertake within two years to deliver 150 tons of alum and 150 tons of copperas.

In practice, however, the project was in trouble from the start. Local workmen were inexperienced, and de Vos imported labour from Italy, at a cost to Mountjoy of £300, but the Italians proved to be useless. When things went wrong de Vos abandoned his part in the undertaking and returned to the Netherlands, leaving Mountjoy to sustain the burden alone. This he seemed very willing to do. He had moved from his home in Wiltshire and taken up residence at Canford manor house, then occupied by his mother. Here he was close at hand, and took personal charge of the works, though his doing so scandalized his aristocratic friends. 'Some saie', he admitted, 'that I varrye from my vocation to become a myner.'[3] He also obtained an Act of Parliament, confirming the transfer to him of the rights granted by de Vos's patent.[4] The preamble to the Act stated that the Queen was 'desirous that the hidden Riches of the Earthe should by searche and woorke of men skilfull be founde and browght to the use and comoditye' of her realm. Moreover, 'great quantity of Owers apte for the purpose aforesayde' had been 'founde moost aboundauntlye' on Mountjoy's estate, 'by meane whereof and of suche Devyse and Travayle as the sayd Lord Mountjoye hath therein used, he hath growen to such knowledge and perfeccion of the said Woorkes as heretofore hath not been atteyned unto by any within her Maties Realme'. As de Vos 'was otherwyse of no sufficyent welthe and habilitye to bring the said Owers to such effect and perfeccion as was requysite', he had transferred his patent to Lord Mountjoy, who had made good copperas at lower cost than the imported mineral, and was 'in good hope to have lyke successe in woorking of allome, which is a verie necessarye commoditie for the use of Draperye'. Mountjoy therefore was to have a monopoly of the manufacture of alum and copperas for 21 years from 1 April 1567. The Act contained a clause safeguarding Kendall's rights, but nothing more is heard of him, and presumably he ceased to be interested in these minerals.

Mountjoy told Cecil in 1566 that he had given instructions for the 'small proof' of the alum to be followed by a 'proofe in the greate',

but evidently it had failed. Six years later, when Cecil and the Earl
of Leicester had ordered an investigation, he wrote promising that
the 'great proof' should be made shortly, but it is clear that little or
no alum was ever produced on a commercial scale. Copperas, on the
other hand, was being turned out in considerable quantities.
'Houses' for its manufacture, the first of which cost only £5, were
erected at Alum Chine, within what is now the County borough of
Bournemouth, at 'Okeman's' or 'Ockeman's House' near Parkstone,
at Canford Cliffs, and on Brownsea Island in Poole Harbour. The
profits from these, however, were not enough, or came too late, to
save Mountjoy's encumbered estate. His debts were continually
increasing, and in 1567 he had mortgaged Canford to his wife's
uncle; in the following year he leased the alum and copperas works
to George Carleton, a relative of Lady Mountjoy's, and John Hastings, who was distantly related to the third Earl of Huntingdon.
Carleton and Hastings, finding that their resources were inadequate,
applied to Huntingdon for assistance, and the upshot was that in
1570 Huntingdon purchased the manor. It seems that Lady Mountjoy approved of this transaction, but her husband did not, and he
reserved the mineral rights to himself.

Huntingdon, who became President of the Council of the North
in 1572, had neither the time nor the inclination to supervise the
work at the copperas mines himself, in the way Mountjoy had
done, and at first he contented himself with the rents and other
profits from the rest of the estate. Mountjoy meanwhile raised fresh
mortgages on the mineral workings, and borrowed more money on
the security of an undertaking to produce a stated quantity (200
tons a year) of copperas. He had vested the title in the mines in
Lady Mountjoy and her issue, and when she died, in 1577, it passed
to her sons, William and Charles Blount, who resented Huntingdon's having become the owner of the Canford estate. They opened
legal proceedings against him, and Huntingdon found himself involved in six years of litigation in order to maintain his rights. In
the midst of these proceedings Mountjoy himself left Canford and
moved to another house, near Beaminster, where he died in 1581,
but he had fostered rumours that he would establish himself at
Canford again. The tenants of the manor were divided into factions,
some supporting Mountjoy, others Hastings, who was now living

in the manor house, and there were fights and disturbances between the two sides.

In 1585 the dispute was referred to the Privy Council, and in 1586 the ownership of both Canford manor and the mines was at last awarded to Huntingdon, but he was to pay the Blounts £6,000 for renunciation of the Mountjoy claims. The case had also involved heavy legal expenses, but unless he spent even more money to keep the mines working, Huntingdon would have wasted all he had already laid out. He still hoped to make the mines pay and recoup his losses, and as a first step he determined to get rid of Mountjoy's tenants; but the cost of buying out one of the leases came to between £8,000 and £9,000, and besides having to spend money on this scale Huntingdon was also anxious about the monopoly rights confirmed by the Act of 1567. These were to last for 21 years, and he feared that, unless the monopoly were renewed, the works, which he had now re-let to a tenant of his own at a high rent, would be put out of business by competition. In that case he would lose not only the rent but also the capital he had sunk. Huntingdon's tenant, Philip Smith, described as 'citizen and merchant of London', wrote to Burghley stating that 'through his exceeding great travell and industry' he had brought the works 'to such perfection as they are not only able to furnish this realme but other countries with these commodities'. But now other people were intending to set up works, and he would be ruined unless the monopoly were renewed. Huntingdon supported Smith's plea, declaring that he had himself spent £20,000 on the undertaking, and that his tenant would give bond not to raise the price of copperas. No Act of Parliament was passed, however, to confirm the monopoly, and another petition from the earl himself seems also to have met with no response. Huntingdon died in 1595, and soon afterwards the workings were discontinued and allowed to fall into decay.

Alum had never been a success at Canford, but while the monopoly lasted the copperas had become quite a lucrative venture. In 1584 one of the tenants was expected to be able to set aside £100 a month in order to pay off a debt; later the same tenant had some 100 tons of copperas at Poole, for which a buyer in London was offering cash, and the sale of this was expected to pay off a debt amounting to over £1,200. Another tenant claimed that a lease which Mountjoy had granted him in 1579 for £100 a year was worth £1,500 in 1585, and this seems to have been only a slight exaggeration, for in 1588 the rent which Smith offered, and Huntingdon accepted, was £1,300. About 1608 Huntingdon's grandson, the fifth earl, tried to get the mines reopened. His first step was to enclose parts of the Canford waste, to supply peat for fuel, but the people of Poole claimed rights of common and broke down his fences. The earl also had recourse to litigation in Chancery to recover arrears of unpaid rent, and was awarded £800, which the judges estimated would have been the profits had the works been kept in operation, and £1,050 as compensation for his tenant having demolished one of the 'houses' and allowed another to fall into disrepair. Whether or not he succeeded in actually collecting this money, he made no further attempts to revive the industry, and this seems to mark the end of the Canford venture. The copperas works on Brownsea Island, however, apparently went on working, or were later restarted, for about 1685 they were visited and described by Celia Fiennes.[5]

Although, unlike alum, quantities of copperas had been produced, it did not justify the excessive outlay lavished upon it, whether by Mountjoy or Huntingdon. In comparison with alum, the production of copperas was relatively simple. The ore (iron pyrites) was merely piled in layers and dissolved by exposure to rain. The resulting liquor was collected, and copperas was obtained in crystalline form by boiling the liquor with pieces of old iron in iron or lead pans. Over and above the cost of production, however, Huntingdon's liabilities were inflated by expensive litigation, interest on borrowed money, and the high prices he had to pay for the surrender of leases. The enterprise was thus burdened by excessive overheads, and finally any chance of its becoming profitable was ruined by overproduction and a fall in price.

Sir Thomas Smith is chiefly remembered for his work as a lawyer and secretary of state, and for his treatise on the Elizabethan constitution, De Republica Anglorum, but his 'busy active mind' and 'philosophical head' led him to embark, about 1571, 'upon a project of alchymy'.[6] A certain William Medley satisfied him that he had 'by vitriol changed iron into true copper', and though the vitriol, which had to be imported, was too expensive for the process to be commercially profitable, Smith believed that it would pay if the *primum ens vitrioli* (i.e. an 'earth' yielding vitriol) could be found in England. He persuaded Cecil, Leicester, Sir Humphrey Gilbert and others to join him in forming a company to exploit the process under Medley's direction. It is easy nowadays to deride sensible men of the world for being so credulous as to undertake such a project, but on the principles of chemistry as then imperfectly understood it was not so absurd as it appears today. Nevertheless it seems to have rested on a confusion as well as on scientific ignorance. The vitriol used in Medley's first experiments was blue vitriol (copper sulphate); copperas, or green vitriol, is sulphate of iron, but its name suggested some connection with copper.

At any rate, Smith and Gilbert each gave Medley £100 to purchase 'vessels and necessaries', and he proposed to begin operations at Winchelsea, where plenty of wood was available for fuel. The 'earths' there proved unsuitable, however, and hearing that the '*ens* of vitriol' could be dug at Poole, the partners took a lease of one of the copperas 'houses' on the Mountjoy estate, at a rent of £300 a year. Needless to say, for turning iron into copper the 'earth' at Poole was no better than at Winchelsea, and 'the business lay asleep for some time'. When Smith returned after an absence on diplomatic service he found arrears of rent owing to Lady Mountjoy, over £60 for unpaid wages, 'and no copper, nor any crocus of copper made'. ('Crocus' in this sense meant one of various yellow or red powders obtained from metals by calcination.) Paying off these debts and other expenses cost him £200. Medley meanwhile had gone off to Anglesey, where he announced that he had at last found 'fuel, earth, and water proper for his business'. He undertook not only to convert raw iron into good copper 'of the same weight and proportion, abating one part in six; as 600 tons of iron should, by boiling, make 500 tons of perfect copper', but also from 'the liquor wherein the iron was boiled, to make copperas and allum ready for the merchant, which, keeping the price they then bore, should of the liquor of 500 tons of copper be worth £10,000'.

Sir Thomas was convinced that copper could be made by Medley's process, and in January 1574 he obtained a patent of incorporation for his company, with the title 'The Society of the New Art'. The scene of Medley's operations in Anglesey was the Parys mountain, where there was a copper mine. What he did there, as later described in a letter from Sir John Wynn of Gwydir to Lord Eure, President of the Council of the Marches, was to boil up broken pieces of iron in large lead boilers full of the local water. The iron appeared to be converted into copper, but what really must have happened was that copper was deposited on the iron because the water from the mine contained copper sulphate.[7] By 1576 the uselessness of the project was manifest, Medley ended up as a prisoner for debt in the Counter, and the shareholders in the company lost their money.

Early in the seventeenth century, when attempts to produce alum in Dorset had virtually ceased, a more promising supply of ore was discovered in the parish of Skelton, near Guisborough, in north-east Yorkshire, on land belonging to a man named John Atherton. On 15 November 1603 he and his wife made an agreement with Richard Leycolt, a former tenant of one of the alum 'houses' on the Mountjoy estate, by which the Athertons were to bear the cost of furnishing a 'house', which they had already erected, with the necessary equipment of furnaces, pans, cisterns and other appliances, while Leycolt, who was to receive £500, undertook to make 2½ tons of alum a week and to instruct three local men in the art of making alum. Leycolt, however, proved no more capable of making alum in Yorkshire than he had been at Canford, nor did he succeed in imparting the technique to any of the three men. He was on the point of giving up, when in June 1604 there came an offer to take charge of the work from John (later Sir John) Bourchier. Bourchier professed to know London merchants to whom he could sell the alum, and the upshot was that on 10 November 1606 the Athertons granted him a 21-year lease of the alum-bearing parts of their land, and he undertook to enlarge the works and start the production of alum. He was no more successful than Leycolt, however, and a few years later Leycolt, to whom Bouchier had given £30 to clear out and return to the south, alleged that by his skill, intervention and labour he had brought the making of alum to perfection, and claimed that he had been deprived of the opportunity to earn £500 through Atherton granting the lease to Bourchier.

This was a bad start for the Yorkshire alum industry, of which its combination of incompetence with mendacious pretensions was unfortunately to be typical.[8] Meanwhile alum-bearing shales were being discovered in several other places near Guisborough, and also on the coast near Whitby. The landowners on whose estates these discoveries were made wanted to exploit them, and if possible secure a monopoly; three of them combined to use their influence at Court, and on 5 March 1606 they were granted letters patent. They undertook that they would make alum as good in quality as imported alum, and that within two years the quantity they would make would be not less than the average quantity imported yearly during the previous seven years. On these conditions they were to have the sole right to dig and manufacture alum for 21 years and, provided they fulfilled their undertakings, after two years the importation of alum was to be prohibited. The chief of the three patentees was Edmund Lord Sheffield (later the first Earl of Mulgrave), who was Lord Lieutenant of the county and President of the Council of the North. With him was Sir Thomas Chaloner, who had accompanied James I on his journey south at his accession, and had become influential at Court, where he became Governor to Henry, Prince of Wales; the third member of the trio was his brother-in-law Sir David Foulis, a Scottish favourite of the King's. Sir Thomas Chaloner owned land near Guisborough and has been credited with the first discovery of alum in Yorkshire, but this seems to be an error due to confusing him with a cousin of the same name, whose father had earlier been concerned with the search for minerals in the island of Lambay, off the east coast of Ireland.[9] Bourchier's name does not appear in this syndicate, but in December 1606 the patentees surrendered their grant, and Bourchier was included jointly with the other three in a fresh grant issued early in the following January. The duration of the monopoly was then extended from 21 to 31 years, and there was to be a rent of £700 a year, the sum the farmers of the customs were to receive in compensation for loss of duty should the importing of alum be stopped.

These patentees had no intention of incurring the risks of alum manufacture themselves; the capital was to be put up by a group of London business men, to whom a month later they leased their rights. One of these, named William Turner, had a country house near the Mountjoy property in Wiltshire, and married the daughter of a former mayor and M.P. for the borough of Poole, so that he may well have been acquainted with the works at Canford. He and his colleagues, however, had simply taken on the alum business as farmers. As far as they were concerned it was a venture, or speculation, and they engaged contractors for the actual processes of manufacture.

The undertaking was planned on quite a grand scale. To supply fuel Bourchier leased some coal mines at Harraton in county Durham, at a rent of £500 a year, and arranged for the transport of the coal by sea to Yorkshire ports. The incumbents of Guisborough and Lythe were paid additional stipends (80 marks a year in one case, £40 a year in the other) to preach to the alum workers; the vicar of Kirkleatham received the smaller stipend of £12 a year to act as schoolmaster to their children. Some 12 or so skilled foreigners were brought over from Germany or the Netherlands for a year to teach their craft to the English workmen; but while the result was an improvement in the quality of the alum, so that it became more marketable, this was far from sufficient to make the enterprise solvent. Financially it was unsound, indeed extravagant, from the start. Five 'houses' were erected, at Slape Wath, Belman Bank, and Newgate Bank, near Guisborough, and at Sandsend and Assholme, in Mulgrave Woods, near Whitby; thousands of pounds were spent on equipping them, and the losses on working, which in the first year amounted to £20,000, had increased a year later to £30,000. Installation of the complicated apparatus needed for treating the relatively impure English ore undoubtedly accounted for much of the expenditure; labour costs also were high, some 60 workmen being employed at each 'house', apart from the incidental labour of carpenters, coopers, smiths, carriers and so on, but a great deal of money must have been wasted through inexperience.

Chemically alum is a double sulphate of aluminium and potassium, or of aluminium and ammonium. The papal alum contained all three components, sulphur, alumina and potash, but the alum shales found in England contained impurities such as iron pyrites (yielding copperas), and lacked the necessary alkali, without which the alum would not crystallize. Elaborate plant and a complex series of processes were therefore needed to get rid of the impurities and to introduce the alkali at the proper stage. After being quarried the shale had first to be calcined. This was done in the open air, by piling it in heaps with alternate layers of brushwood, which were set on fire. Heaping and calcining went on simultaneously for eight or nine months, and the calcined material was then steeped in pits full of water. The resulting liquor, containing the soluble parts of the shale, was poured into a further set of pits containing more dry calcined material, and the process was repeated until the liquor had acquired the requisite specific gravity. (The test was said to be whether an egg would float in it : this was 'the alum-maker's secret'. Later a specially constructed testing-glass was used for the purpose.) The next stage was to mix the liquor with 'mothers' (see below), and boil it for a time in pans made of lead; the concentrated liquor was then drawn off into cooling-pans. At this point urine was added to provide the requisite alkali, and crystallization then took place; the strong liquid remaining over was known as the 'mothers', and was returned to the boiling pans. After being washed the crystals were dissolved in water and boiled again; finally the solution was poured into casks, to crystallize into the finished product.[10] Seventeenth-century alum-makers had no scientific knowledge of the chemistry underlying these processes; they worked simply by rule of thumb, and though they undoubtedly learned by experience, clearly there were many points at which mistakes could be made, and their alum was often of inferior quality.

By 1608, when the alum patent had run for two years, the adventurers were still losing money, but they asserted that if the importing of foreign alum were stopped there were good prospects that they could make a success of their undertaking. Salisbury, however, who had lately become Lord Treasurer, wished to be sure that they could produce enough alum to meet the needs of the dyers and other consumers, and that its price would not exceed what was usually paid for foreign alum. He therefore sent Arthur Ingram and Sir Nicolas Salter, one of the lessees of the great customs, as commissioners to inspect the works and report. Both seem to have been favourably impressed, and Ingram recommended that the King should take the farm of the works into his own hands. Salter was opposed to this, but Ingram's advice was accepted. Later, when difficulties arose, Ingram was accused of deliberately misleading Salisbury with a view to making dishonest profits for himself. This cannot be proved, and Ingram may have acted in good faith, himself misled by the men at the works in Yorkshire, and the London merchants who had invested in them and now wanted to get out on favourable terms. The whole history of the alum industry is characterized by unwarranted optimism, which led successive speculators and entrepreneurs to sink money in it in the confident expectation of making large profits. Salisbury was assured that nearly 1,000 tons of alum could be sold annually on the home market at a profit of £16 a ton; and another reason why he accepted Ingram's advice may have been to quieten opposition in parliamentary circles to the spread of monopolies in private hands, though consumers might well be expected to complain at having to pay £20 or more a ton for English alum when they had been able to buy superior imported alum for only £15.

Far from making profits, the Crown had to sink more and more money in the industry in order to keep it going, and the only people who made money were the financiers and speculators like Ingram himself. There can indeed hardly have been any period in modern English history when it was more disastrous for the Crown to act as entrepreneur than the early seventeenth century. James's court was surrounded by fortune-seekers; much of his revenue was controlled by farmers and monopolists, with plentiful opportunites for corruption; after Salisbury's death policy-making came into the hands of favourites and adventurers; and administration, whether central or local, was frequently inefficient.

The son of a Yorkshireman who had come to London to make a career, Arthur Ingram had entered the customs service, in which he rose rapidly, and became controller of customs in the port of London. His ability attracted the attention of Robert Cecil, who employed him in a number of business deals, particularly in connection with the letting of customs farms. He had a special talent for acting as an intermediary, a 'contact man', between courtiers who could obtain concessions and city merchants who had capital with which to exploit them, and in this way he established a connection with Lionel Cranfield, which developed into a close partnership and personal friendship. With a larger and more assured income Ingram was in a position to command more credit, and this enabled him to advance from playing the subordinate role of an agent or go-between to becoming a principal in the various enterprises in which he engaged.

In 1608, shortly before Salisbury sent him to Yorkshire to investigate the state of the alum industry, Ingram had had a prominent part in negotiating the sales of Crown lands, and was well-established as one of Salisbury's confidential agents. When the Crown assumed control of the industry in 1609, lavish compensation was provided for the previously interested parties, the landowners who held the patent and the merchants who had combined to provide the finance. The merchants were to get some £6,000 a year, and though the patentees would have nothing at first, after 1616 they were to receive between them annuities of £3,000 for the first year and £6,000 thereafter for the remainder of the term covered by the patent. A proclamation was issued to prohibit the importation of alum,[11] and the works, which were left under the same local management, were expected to produce 2,000 tons of alum a year. With output at this level, and a monopoly of the home market, on which alum would fetch £25 a ton, the rest being exported, it was reckoned that they could not only meet the annuities but pay the Crown £10,000 a year, and still leave a margin of profit for the contractors. It was soon seen that these calculations were wildly exaggerated. In fact the output in any year never exceeded 600 tons, it proved impossible to prevent the smuggling of foreign alum, which was both cheaper and better in quality, and the price of English alum never rose above £23 a ton. By 1612 the accumulated losses had risen to £36,000, or about £19 on every ton sold.

In these circumstances the contractors were unable to carry on, and wanted to be released. Money had somehow to be found for the annuities, and apart from the fact that the numerous employees and their families were dependent on the alum industry for a livelihood (400 men were employed at the works themselves and another 300 in the supply and carriage of raw materials and coal), it would have been a blow to the government's prestige had the whole enterprise been abandoned as a failure. It was decided therefore to take further advice. Three men were consulted: Robert Johnson, an alderman of London who had been financially interested in alum for some time, Sir Walter Cope, a courtier who had acted with Ingram in the sale of Crown lands, and Ingram himself. This time Johnson was sent to Yorkshire to investigate and report. He found the works at a standstill and in disrepair, while the workmen had had no wages for four or five months. To put the plant in order would cost at least £6,000, but if this were done it was estimated that the output of alum should reach 1,000 tons a year, at a cost of about £13 a ton.

Several groups were willing to take over the works, in spite of their past record, but Johnson, Cope and Ingram agreed that instead of letting them out on farm the Crown should now resort to direct administration. The three of them were accordingly appointed as managers on the Crown's behalf. Cope died shortly afterwards, but Johnson and Ingram carried on, paid off the arrears of wages, and got the works going again. To do this they drew £11,500 from the Exchequer, but the terms finally negotiated with the previous contractors were to prove even more expensive. They estimated their liabilities at £44,000; the final figure agreed on in settlement of all outstanding claims, including the annuities, was no less than £77,500.

At the works themselves things continued to go badly; neither costs nor production corresponded with the estimates, and it was evident that they were still losing money. Ingram then became dissatisfied with his position as manager, and began scheming to have the industry converted into a farm again. He was still hopeful that there were profits to be made, and if he could have the farm himself at a fixed rent, he and not the Crown would get them. In 1611, just before this, Ingram's private affairs had been in a critical condition. He had been speculating with borrowed money and had overreached himself, and was being threatened by his creditors; but he was saved by the intervention of Cranfield and other city men, and by his friends at Court, who found him too useful to let him become bankrupt. A kind of testimonial, signed by Ellesmere the Lord Chancellor, Salisbury the Lord Treasurer, and Northampton the Lord Privy Seal, was published as a broadsheet with the title *A formal justification of the character of Arthur Ingram, esquire, citizen of London*, and in it these dignitaries supported Ingram's pose as the innocent victim of a conspiracy, and guaranteed payment in full of all his debts. Thus set on his feet again, and with his credit restored, Ingram was able to resume his career of dealing in Crown lands and other properties, and arranging contracts and similar transactions. Probably through Salisbury's influence he had entered Parliament in 1609; in 1613 he was knighted (so also was Cranfield) and married a wealthy heiress, and in 1614 he became a member of the Council of the North, of which he had previously been made Secretary and Keeper of the Signet.

As Mrs Prestwich remarks, he 'operated in the frontier region between commerce and government finance, and his wealth illustrates how much the Crown lost by collusion between corrupt politicians, rapacious courtiers, and a venal civil service. Ingram pulled in rich and easy hauls from customs farms, monopolies and contracts over Crown land sales, and Cranfield was quick to follow suit.'[12] He was frequently consulted by the government in a wide variety of financial matters, but though he kept within the law he came to acquire an unsavoury reputation. His enemies may have blackened his name through resentment at his rise from comparatively obscure beginnings to a position of wealth and influence, but it can hardly be doubted that ethically his conduct in business often failed to reach even the low standards of his age.

This was nowhere more evident than in his handling of the alum industry, whose shaky prospects were further threatened by the appearance of rival competitors. The first of these, Sir Richard Houghton, had appeared as early as 1609, when he set up an alum 'house' on his estate in Lancashire. It was a small affair at first, costing only £320 to instal, with an output of between five and seven tons, but he had no difficulty in selling his alum to local dyers, who said that 30 shillings would buy what would have cost them 50 shillings if it had had to be brought from a distance. Challenged as violating the monopoly, Houghton replied that not only was he unaware of the letters patent but that he was entitled to work the minerals on his own freehold, as alum was a base mineral and not royal. Apparently this argument was successful, for in 1614 he was granted powers to make alum for 21 years and to export 500 tons a year. How long his enterprise lasted, and whether it ever attained this magnitude, is uncertain, but it was in existence in 1617, when James I visited Houghton Towers and inspected the mines. This was the occasion when the King is said to have knighted the sirloin of beef. Later another alum mine was opened there.

More serious, because he was supported by Ingram's political enemies, was the appearance in Yorkshire of Dr Edward Jordan, Fellow of the Royal College of Physicians of London. After Salisbury's death in 1612 Ingram had cultivated members of the Howard family, who were powerful in Court, in association with the ruling favourite, Robert Carr, Earl of Somerset. Ingram lent them money, and among other services he negotiated the grant to Thomas Howard, later Earl of Suffolk, of the right to licence wine shops and taverns. Dr Jordan, who had studied German technical treatises, claimed that by introducing an improved process he could make alum for £8 a ton. His claim was baseless, but he was backed by the Earl of Southampton and others, and was given a hearing at the Privy Council, which agreed that he should be allowed to demonstrate his methods. Though he subsequently complained that Ingram had hindered and frustrated his work, it appears that Ingram and Johnson agreed to sublet him one of the 'houses', and if his demonstration were successful he was to have an annuity of £1,000 for life and a share of the profits. Thereupon Jordan gave up his house in London and moved with his family to Yorkshire. His improvements consisted in using chalk instead of urine as an alkaline, and peat instead of coal as fuel, and increasing the concentration of the alum liquor before it was boiled. Whether these changes would have been effective was never shown; he claimed to have produced alum at less than £8 a ton, but he underestimated the cost of repairing and renewing the apparatus, which became rapidly corroded, and he never succeeded in making the quantity expected. He was hampered partly by bad weather, but he accused Ingram of bribing his workmen to damage his plant, and of deliberately wrecking his work in other underhand ways.

While Jordan was still in Yorkshire, in April 1615, Ingram obtained approval of his scheme to convert the management of the works into a farm again. In the meantime he had taken in two partners, George Low, an old associate in numerous business deals, and Martin Freeman, and the farm was granted to the three of them, for 21 years. It was stipulated that they were to produce 1,200 tons in the first year, and work this output up to 1,500 tons in the second, and 1,800 tons in the third and subsequent years. The Crown would pay them £10 a ton and make its profit by selling the alum; the farmers' profits would depend on their keeping the cost of production below £10 a ton. Should the stipulated output not be reached, they were to compensate the Crown for loss of revenue by a penalty of £13 for every ton by which production fell short of 1,000 tons; over 1,500 tons the penalty for shortfall was to be £5 per ton.[18] Two years previously, as we saw above, Ingram had obtained £11,500 from the Exchequer to put the works in order; now the farmers were to be given another £10,000 to spend on the works at their discretion, without any obligation to account for it.

N

This seems a remarkable bargain, and what happened to the £10,000, which was paid over to Ingram towards the end of 1615, became a subject of contention between the partners. Low, who was resident manager in Yorkshire, maintained that it should all have gone to him, to be spent on the works. He admitted that he had received £6,400, but he complained that Ingram and Johnson had kept the balance. It is hardly necessary to add that output again fell short; during the first year instead of 1,200 only 740 tons of alum were made. This gave Ingram's opponents a fresh opportunity to launch an attack on him, just at the time when the Howards, with whom he was associated, were under fire from their rivals at Court. Early in 1616 a commission of inquiry was set up, before which Dr Jordan gave evidence of the shabby treatment he had received, and Ingram was charged with dishonesty and mismanagement. Fortunately for him, the storm, which was really political, blew over with the fall from favour of Somerset. The inquiry was dropped, and Jordan, left unsupported, had to abandon his alum-making and moved to Bath, where he took up medical practice again.

Suffolk retained his position for the time being, and in 1617 he connived, as Lord Treasurer, at the cancellation of Ingram's contract, made only two years previously, and the writing off of his unpaid penalties for underproduction, already amounting to £12,340. Ingram then entered into a new contract with the Crown, on a different basis. Conditions regarding output were the same, but now he was to pay the Crown £9,600 a year and have a commission on the alum of £2 a ton. Except for the loss of the money already spent, this arrangement was relatively favourable to the Crown, as it provided a steady income, which was paid regularly while the contract lasted, down to 1624. For the farmers, profit would depend on output, and great efforts were made, mainly by Low, who was in charge at the works, to improve production and cut costs. They did not have much success, and Low complained that Ingram was keeping him short of funds.

Then two men, Thomas Russell and Sir John Brooke, appeared with plans for another new process, by which they claimed that they could make alum at £9 a ton. Low was convinced that their methods would at last solve the industry's problems and put it on a sound footing, and Ingram and he accordingly sublet the works

to Russell and Brooke. The essential features of their new technique
were the substitution of kelp lees for urine and the use of small
shallow pans, in which evaporation would be more rapid, so that
a larger amount of alum could be produced in a given time. In
practice it was a total failure. Not only did production fall, but the
existing lead pans were melted down to make the new ones, and
afterwards they had to be remade, at considerable expense, in the
old pattern. Meanwhile production was interrupted. The immediate
effects of this fiasco were further tension between Ingram and Low,
and a fresh investigation, held in 1618 under the chairmanship of
Sir Edward Coke. There was a demand that this time Ingram should
not escape the penalties for underproduction, but, largely through
Cranfield's influence, he was enabled to compound for a sum of
about half what was due by the terms of the contract. The sub-
lease to Russell and Brooke had next to be terminated, and this was
achieved only after protracted disputes, particularly over the question of who was responsible for paying wages. For some time no
wages were paid, the men were starving and refused to go on working, and once more production was held up.

By 1619 Low had had enough of the alum business, and Ingram
was left as the sole farmer.[14] He got another £1,000 from the
Exchequer, and installed a new group of contractors, William Tappsfield, Richard Wynne and John Turner, to manage the works.
Though the output never reached the target figure of 1,800 tons a
year, it showed an improvement on previous years, and averaged
1,200 tons between 1619 and 1624. Nevertheless the industry was
far from the end of its troubles, and there were to be plenty of new
disputes and recriminations. Tappsfield in particular was blamed for
his rough treatment of some of the workmen, and for swindling
them by paying wages in the form of truck—bad foodstuffs at
high prices. There were also constant complaints of the poor quality
of the alum put on the market.

These grievances culminated in 1623 in fresh attacks on Ingram,
first by Sir John Bourchier, one of the original patentees. This set
off yet another commission of inquiry; next year, with the fall of
Cranfield, on whose support he had long relied, Ingram had to
defend himself against a whole series of charges, which came before
further commissions in January 1625. He was accused of embez-
zling the £10,000 paid him in 1615, and of persistently cheating

the Crown by underproduction and failure to pay the penalties due. Revised figures were quoted, purporting to show that he owed the Crown £65,950, and had made at least £50,000 clear profit for himself. He had been responsible for marketing inferior alum, dyed red with cochineal to make it look like papal alum; and besides these and other frauds in the management of the alum industry he had to face a general assault on his conduct in a number of other business transactions.

This marked the end of Ingram's tenure of the alum farm. He surrendered it in August 1625, but he managed to negotiate terms for a settlement which relieved him of a large part of his liabilities. He undertook to leave the works with a full set of boiling pans, fuel and other equipment for producing an output of 1,800 tons a year. This was estimated to cost £7,000, but against arrears of unpaid penalties and other other past liabilities he was allowed to set off a claim for compensation for loss of his contracts, and when a balance was struck the net amount he owed the Crown was reduced to £4,562. He agreed to pay £1,500 in cash, and to set aside £200 a year from the rent of one of his estates until this amount had been paid off. On the whole he escaped lightly, with his wealth virtually intact.

Ingram's biographer, Mr Anthony Upton, would exonerate him from the worst charges that were brought against him in connection with the alum industry. Possibly he was guilty of large-scale embezzlement, but if so it was only in the early stages, between 1612 and 1615, when large sums of money from the Exchequer came into his hands. After that there was little opportunity for embezzlement, and it cannot be proved that he made any profit out of the industry. He was indeed becoming steadily richer, but most of his wealth probably did not come from alum but from other sources. He may have been guilty of mismanagement, but in the end the industry found its feet, and if he exploited his influence with Cranfield or the Howards to get jobs for himself at the expense of his rivals, it must be remembered that fair and open tendering was virtually unknown in the seventeenth century: the only way in practice to secure a contract was to use influence and provide material inducements for the officials concerned. Ingram did no more than make use of 'all the devious and dubious practices of his age'.[18]

Even when thus whitewashed, Ingram's character remains fairly dusky in hue, but the case for the defence is not entirely without substance. It is true that for some years alum was a source of losses rather than profits; but although his enemies may perhaps have exaggerated the extent of his corrupt practices, there can be little doubt that, whoever lost money, Ingram took care that it should not be himself. The alum farm was the most important single item among his numerous business interests, but it was not therefore necessarily the major source of his wealth. That he became very wealthy, however, is beyond question: Temple Newsam and his other properties in the north were a mark of it, and of the status he had attained in the ranks of the landed gentry. Mrs Prestwich writes of his 'meretricious charm', and says that with 'the mercurial temperament of the gambler ... his fortune represents the parasitical wealth of a brilliant speculator who seized all the opportunities offered by a corrupt political system'. But she also calls him 'perhaps the most unscrupulous tycoon of his age'.[16] The successful entrepreneur must be adaptable and resourceful, and not be afraid of taking risks. Ingram possessed these qualities, but there was also a streak of restlessness and recklessness in his character, which made him find a pleasurable excitement in taking risks, and sometimes led him into serious danger. At the same time he acquired a reputation not only for quickness and astuteness but also for ruthlessness and harsh dealing. This is a combination of qualities which is hardly attractive, and can lead to crime.

After Ingram's departure the alum works were let out on farm again. Sir John Bourchier had a scheme to re-enter the industry, combining it with a soap monopoly. He later obtained a patent for soap, but the alum farm was granted, at a rent of £11,000 a year, to another group, of which the principal member was Sir Paul Pindar, whose previous career had been as a diplomatist in the Near East. Associated with him was William Turner, one of the farmers at the time of the original patent. A fresh proclamation in the name of Charles I forbad the importation of alum, but the industry was still in difficulties, and the farmers found themselves unable to pay their first quarter's rent. In spite of the thousands of pounds which had been spent on them, it seemed unlikely that the works in Yorkshire would ever be made to pay, and in 1627 Pindar and Turner set up new alum-making plant in London, near the Tower. People

9 | Salt and saltpetre

Salt

Common salt (sodium chloride) has always been in demand as a preservative and a seasoner of food, as well as for various industrial purposes, and it was even more essential in times past than it is today. For want of winter feed many farm animals had to be killed off in the autumn, and in the absence of refrigeration and cold storage the only way to preserve their meat was to salt it down: salt was also extensively used for preserving fish. Some of the salt used in England was obtained from inland deposits of rock salt, or by evaporating the brine from saline springs; some also was made by the evaporation of sea water at certain places on the coast. In the sixteenth century, however, these sources supplied only a small proportion of the salt consumed in England, and for the greater part of its needs the country depended on imports from France.[1]

Until about 1555 bay salt (unclarified salt made from sea water, so called from Bourgneuf Bay, near the mouth of the Loire)[2] was sold for about 6d. a bushel, and white salt at about 10d., but after that date prices almost doubled, mainly owing to the debasement of the coinage, and supplies were also threatened by the outbreak of the religious wars and local revolts against the *gabelle* in France. Scotland anticipated England in plans to stimulate the production of salt at home, when in 1562 the exclusive right for 50 years to make salt was granted to an Italian named Angelo Manelio. By December 1564, however, Manelio had gone bankrupt, fought a duel, and disappeared in disgrace. Meanwhile, in March 1563 Cecil invited a German financier from Augsburg, Jasper Selar or Seelar, to come to England and develop the manufacture of white salt. Cecil hoped not only to extend to salt his general policy of making the country independent of foreign supplies, but also to establish the equivalent of an English *gabelle*, by making salt a government monopoly. It was at first proposed that the makers should sell their salt at 7d. a bushel to the government, which would resell it to the public at 1s. 6d., and it was calculated that the proceeds of this, together with a royalty to the Crown of one tenth of the output, would yield an annual revenue equal to that of two tenths and fifteenths (the regular taxes on land and and movables), i.e. about £60,000.

When letters patent were finally issued, on 15 January 1564, these terms had to be modified, but Seelar backed out of his engagement, and on 20 October another contract was made, on similar terms, with an Italian from Florence, a protégé of the Earl of Leicester, named Thomas Baroncelli. This also came to nothing, and finally, on 31 July 1565, the contract was transferred to a Flemish immigrant, Francis Bertye of Antwerp. Bertye claimed to be familiar with improved methods of making salt from sea water then being developed in the Netherlands, but Gresham's secretary was doubtful whether he possessed 'the perfect knowledge by him professed'. It seems that Bertye was already involved in the project, and had had connections with both Seelar and Baroncelli, for his contract was back-dated to the previous 1 December, the date when Baroncelli was to have started manufacture. He was also in financial difficulties, however, and on 5 March he had to be given protection from his creditors for a year. Then on 23 January 1566 new letters patent were issued, in which his name was coupled with those of the Earls of Leicester and Pembroke, Lord Cobham, Sir Francis Knollys, William Cecil himself, and some others, and in December the patent was confirmed by an Act of Parliament.[3] The holders were known as 'Lords of the Salt Privilege', and it is worth noticing, incidentally, that Bertye, as well as Leicester, Pembroke and Cecil, were among the original shareholders in the Society of the Mineral and Battery Works.

These false starts in establishing the production of salt were partly due to practical difficulties. In more southerly latitudes salt could be readily obtained from sea water through evaporation by the sun in open ponds, but this was seldom possible in the English climate, and bay salt so made contained impurities and was rather dirty in appearance. To make white salt the brine was clarified with egg-whites and evaporated by boiling it indoors in shallow metal pans with artificial heat.[4] During the summer of 1565 iron evaporating pans were brought over from the Netherlands and set up at Dover, Southampton and on the coast of Essex, but there was a shortage of timber for fuel, and plans to establish salt-works on the coast of Suffolk encountered the same difficulty. Salt-making on a large scale was scarcely feasible until the makers adapted their furnaces to burn coal, and set up works on the coast of Northumberland and Durham, where coal was available cheaply.

Cecil's agent, a man named Mount, realized this, and after a visit to the north, where salt-boiling for local use had long been practised, suggested Blyth as a suitable locality for the works, but there was difficulty in raising enough capital. Some evaporating pans were shipped to Northumberland but were never erected, and for 20 years lay rusting in Tynemouth castle, until a later patentee found a use for them. The peers associated with Bertye were dubious about Mount's proposals, and were either unable or unwilling to contribute towards them. Mount then suggested that salt merchants might lend £100 each, but they too apparently were suspicious and refused to take the risk. For a few months in 1566 a city merchant named Peter Osborne financed the undertaking, but he withdrew his support in the following year when he found nobody prepared to share the risk with him. In February 1567 Mount was superseded by Edward Goodinge, but the areas he investigated, the coasts of Essex and the south-eastern counties, were too far from a coalfield to be suitable for the purpose.

Seeing no sign of the profits they expected, by August 1567 the projectors wanted to dispose of their interests, and they found a purchaser in a certain Captain Buckholt, who had previously been engaged in producing salt in the Netherlands. The terms agreed on were that Buckholt should be responsible for the tenth payable to the Crown, and should pay the projectors £4,500 out of the profits of his first and £16,000 out of the profits of his next batch of salt. After that he and the projectors were to share the profits equally. It is clear from these figures that an extremely ambitious pro-gramme was envisaged: it was anticipated, in fact, that by 1569 enough salt would be made to supply the needs of the whole of England, and by 1570 those of Ireland as well. Some salt from Northumberland reached the London market, but these plans were wildly unrealistic, particularly in view of the course of events in France, where the chief salt-producing areas, between the Loire and

La Rochelle, came under Huguenot control. In 1568, when the third religious war broke out, the government concluded a contract with the Huguenot leaders for supplying the needs of the English market, and lost interest in the patent for producing salt in England.

With the conclusion of peace in France, attention turned to home production once more, and in 1571 several speculators, among them a Walloon refugee named Francis Franckard, submitted offers to revive the project, but these apparently came to nothing. In the end, however, the dislocation and uncertainty of continental supplies, and the consequent high prices, made conditions more favourable for the production of British salt. As a consequence, the output from the neighbourhood of the coalfields by the Tyne and Forth increased markedly, and salt-making even became profitable in areas such as the coast of Norfolk, to which coal had to be transported by sea.

Though Cecil's scheme for a government monopoly had proved abortive, the industry did not escape monopolistic control, and in the later years of the sixteenth century the salt trade on the east coast was in the hands of Sir Thomas Wilkes, one of the clerks of the Privy Council, much of whose career was spent on diplomatic service abroad. In February 1585 he obtained a patent for 21 years for the sole manufacture and sale of white salt at King's Lynn, Boston and Kingston-upon-Hull, 'and within all the crekes, places and members of the same portes'.[5] The annual rent to the Crown was nominal, only £6 13s. 4d., and the concession was clearly of a quite different type from the previous patents. Wilkes's aim was simply to make money out of his privilege, and he immediately sub-let it for £100 a year to a syndicate consisting of John Smith, or Smyth, searcher of the port of Lynn, Robert Anderson, one of the principal coalowners on the Tyne, who also had salt-pans there, and Robert Bowes, treasurer of the garrison of Berwick-on-Tweed and English ambassador in Scotland. Smyth, who was connected with the prominent merchant family of that name in London, was the most important of the three, and after Wilkes's death he secured the continuance of the patent in his own name.

It seems that the suggestion of this patent had not originated with Wilkes, but had come from Anderson and other salt-makers on the east coast, who wanted to be protected against competition from Scottish salt. By the spring of 1586 people at Boston were complaining that while they could no longer get salt from Scottish shippers, Wilkes and his deputies had failed to produce any. All they did was to buy salt from Scotland and re-sell it at a higher price. The Privy Council directed the Earl of Huntingdon, Lord President of the North, and certain Lincolnshire and Norfolk gentlemen, to call the patentee's deputies before them and examine the causes of the complaints.[6] The upshot was that the monopolists pledged themselves to provide adequate quantities of salt at a reasonable price, but they failed to live up to their promises. Early next year a report from commissioners at Lynn repeated the old complaints. The grant was damaging to a great number of house-holders, and under pretence of making salt the patentees had engrossed the import and 'ruled the price at their pleasure'. Although they subsequently established salt-works (at Sunderland), they were unable to bring their price below 2s. 6d. a bushel, whereas the Scots could sell equally good salt at half that price. Smyth tried to answer these objections. He admitted that his men had taken excessive gains, but they had done so in his absence. He should not be blamed for this, and he would see to it that 'the gaynes from henseforth shalbe ruled by the rate of the Counsell'. He undertook to supply salt 'farr exceeding the Scottish salt' at 18d. a bushel in peace and war, and would lower his price still further if the price of Spanish and bay salt fell, 'as the Counsell will appoint'.

This last phrase apparently won over the Council to his side, and in August 1587 they wrote to the Mayor and Aldermen of Lynn, and the Norfolk county justices, saying that they accepted Smyth's arguments, and ordering the local authorities to enforce the patent and report any further objections.[7] Even if this kept the men of Norfolk quiet, in 1588 objections flared up in Yorkshire, where it appeared that the price being charged for salt was excessive, and in March of that year a conference with the patentees was held at York. Wilkes had recently been imprisoned as a scape-goat for Leicester's activities in the Netherlands; he had now been released, but had not yet been restored to his full clerkship. He and his chief deputy, Smyth, were both present at the conference, and the accomplished diplomat succeeded in turning it into a victory for the patentees. They consented to reduce the price of salt from 16d. to 14d. a bushel, and at that rate to supply sufficient quantities in peace and war, and to employ the shipping of various local ports in fetching the salt from the works. In return the knights and burgesses present 'did on behalf of the whole inhabitauntes undertake and contract to mainteyn and defend the operacion of the pattente among them'. Wilkes declared that so far his licence had brought him 'litel or noe commoditie', and he even suggested that in four years' time it might terminate. The knights and burgesses then promised to 'yielde their best assistance, ayd and furtherance for the due execucon of the said order and agreements'.

Wilkes returned to London 'attending to his restoration', and soon afterwards was sent to the southern Netherlands for negotiations with the Duke of Parma. In his absence Smyth had no scruples about breaking the York agreement, which was intended to cover the whole east coast, and next March Burghley received fresh complaints from people at Lynn of doubled prices and inadequate supplies. The Privy Council had to institute another inquiry, and for a time in 1589 the patentees feared that their privileges might be revoked. They threw the blame on three or four persons at Lynn who, they alleged, resisted and impugned the authority of the Queen's grant. In the end, after much discussion and argument, the influence which Wilkes and Bowes could bring to bear saved the patent, and the Council sent instructions to the Mayor and Recorder of Lynn to enforce it. Council said that Wilkes and his assigns had contracted to serve the country at all times of plenty or scarcity, peace or war, with sufficient quantities of white salt at 14d. the bushel and not above. In comparison with prices elsewhere this was 'greatly beneficiall to her Majestie's subiectes inhabiting within that county'.[8]

Meanwhile there was trouble further north, where Bowes had been using the funds of the Berwick garrison to speculate in mines and salt-pans about Sunderland, and the crash came in 1591. His debts to the garrison amounted to £7,000, and he owed £3,000 more to the town of Berwick, besides £1,500 he had borrowed from Customer Smythe. John Smyth, Wilkes's chief deputy, eventually secured from the Crown the lease of Bowes's mines and salt-pans, but he had to pay a high rent for them—£800 a year—as a condition of getting the reversion of the salt patent after Wilkes's death. Shortly before this more opposition to the patent arose at Lynn, where 'mechanicall persons of no merytt' were said to be smuggling salt. Actually one of these persons was Nicholas Hare, one of the J.P.s to whom the Council's order to enforce the patent had been sent; yet he had freighted four ships with salt in Scotland and brought them to Lynn. For this he was summoned to appear before the Council, but 'upon his submission' he was forgiven. Wilkes's grant had been given him by the Queen, so the Council wrote to the Earl of Huntingdon, 'in some reward of his service, and is a principall parte of his maintenaunce, he being nowe employed in her Majestie's publicke service beyond the seas'. If any persons offered to impugn the grant, then upon information from John Smyth Huntingdon was to summon them before him, examine the matter, and 'take ordre with them, either by comytting them to prison yf you see cause, or otherwise as your Lordship shall thinke fytte, that he [i.e. Wilkes] be not damnified in the tyme of his absence in her Majestie's service'.[9]

After this hardly any complaints against the patent are recorded from the Lynn region until after Wilkes's death, but the fall of Bowes led to a temporary cessation of production by the patentees at Sunderland, and there were fresh complaints from producers on the Tyne, who were disappointed when the licence did not lapse in 1592, in accordance with what Wilkes had suggested at York. Wilkes died early in 1598 at Rouen, on a mission to try to prevent Henry IV making a separate peace with Spain. Smyth obtained a reissue of the grant in the following year, and with Wilkes out of the way he disregarded all pledges. Prices at Scarborough soared from 14d. to 14s. and 15s. the bushel. In the monopolies debate in Parliament in 1601 the salt monopoly came in for severe criticism, and the government had to promise that it should be withdrawn.

There was no patent for salt under James I, but early in Charles I's reign the increasing difficulty of obtaining salt from the region about La Rochelle, where fighting caused the destruction of the salt-works, gave fresh opportunities for entrepreneurs who in return for a grant of monopoly were prepared to contribute handsomely to the royal revenues. Early in 1636, accordingly, the Company of Saltmakers of South and North Shields received a charter of incorporation. The immediate result was that the price of salt on the east coast rose from £4 15s. to £6 per London 'weigh' (40 bushels), at a time when even on the south coast salt could be bought for £3. East coast fishermen were aggrieved, and objections to the

company's monopoly were also raised by Nicolas Murford, who
had previously been granted a patent for an improvement he
claimed to have introduced in the process of manufacture. On the
appearance of dissension within the company, some members of
which were prepared to relinquish their privileges, it was proposed
to transfer the monopoly to Murford, but the other members, led by
one Thomas Horth, resisted this and asked for a fresh patent in their
own names. In January 1639 they obtained it, and Murford and his
supporters were sent to prison for 'animating others with their
refractoriness and obstinacy'. The victors' triumph was brief, however, for their patent, along with others, was revoked by the Long
Parliament: but by this time the manufacture of salt was firmly
established.[10]

The increase in population had led to a rapid growth in the
demand for salt, particularly in urban areas such as London, where
it was needed for the preservation of perishable foodstuffs. Continental production had fallen off so much that British salt not only
served the needs of a considerable part of the home market but
was even being exported to Holland and the Baltic countries. It
has been estimaged that the annual output of salt at the mouth of
the Tyne had risen from 'a few score or at most a few hundred
tons' in Henry VIII's reign to some 15,000 tons a century later, while
the output from the whole country was probably 'at least 50,000
tons'.[11]

Saltpetre

Saltpetre, or nitre (potassium nitrate), has nothing in common with
salt except part of its name. It was the chief ingredient in gunpowder, to make which six parts of saltpetre were mixed with one
each of sulphur and charcoal. Saltpetre was found in abundance in
a natural state in India and several other countries in Asia, but
there was none in Europe. At first, therefore, it had to be imported
from the East, but the difficulty of getting it in sufficient quantities
impelled men to find out ways of making it artificially. Like various
other industrial processes, the art was unknown in England until the
reign of Elizabeth I, when the arrival of foreign immigrants gave the
government the opportunity of discovering a number of hitherto
well-guarded secrets. In March 1561 an agreement was made with a

German captain named Gerrard Honrick, who undertook for £300 to instruct English subjects in the art of making saltpetre, of which he claimed to have 'perfect knowledge'.[12]

He must have kept his word, for though we hear no more of him Honrick's description of the process was still being used by gunpowder-makers 80 years later, and within a year Brian Hogge, Robert Thomas and Francis Lee, who stated that they had at great cost erected five new powder-mills, were undertaking to supply the Queen yearly with 100 lasts of fine 'cornpowder' (the best quality of gunpowder, well 'corned' or granulated, and so most resistant to damp) at £3 5s. a cwt, and another 100 lasts of 'serpentine' powder at £2 16s. 8d. a cwt. (A last, the usual measure for gunpowder in large amounts, was 24 cwt, a cwt of gunpowder being actually 100 lb, whereas a cwt of saltpetre was 112 lb, the difference being the margin allowed to the makers for wastage in manufacture.) In November 1566 Lee was appointed a gunner at the Tower, and with his mill at Rotherhithe he was still gunpowder-maker to the Queen in 1578.

'The trew and perfecte arte of the making of saltpetre to grow in cellars, barnes, or in lyme or stone quarrees', consisted essentially of making a 'lye' by mixing earth saturated with animal excrement ('the blacker the better') with lime and ashes. Heaps of this were exposed to the air, wetted at intervals with urine, and continually turned over until the saltpetre crystallized. It was hard to find enough suitable earth to supply the needs of the gunpowder-makers without interfering with the rights of property-owners, and the country was divided into districts, each of which was required to furnish a stated amount. Commissioners of Saltpetre were appointed, who allocated a number of saltpetremen to each district. The saltpetremen were licensed to enter and dig in such places as dovehouses, barns, stables, outhouses, cellars, vaults and warehouses. They were supposed to re-erect any buildings they had undermined or demolished, to level the earth where they had dug, and not to dig again in the same place within so many (usually four) years. Owners of pigeonhouses (described in one patent as 'the chiefest nurses of saltpetre of the kingdom'), stables and similar places were not allowed to pave them with stone or brick, or to lay boards on the floor, and though some restrictions were imposed on the saltpetremen (by a proclamation of 1625, for example, saltpetremen were forbidden to dig in dovehouses or pigeonhouses for more than two hours a day) it is not surprising that their demands aroused widespread resistance. In 1606, in response to complaints in Parliament, the King undertook to revoke the saltpetremen's commissions,[13] but in the following year their right to enter private property was upheld in a famous case by Chief Justice Coke.[14]

The manufacture of gunpowder was well-established in England by the middle of Elizabeth's reign, but Lee and his colleagues did not produce enough for the country's needs, and although some continued to be imported from abroad, in the year of the Armada there was a shortage. At a shilling a pound imported gunpowder cost half as much again as the home-made product, and in 1589 the Council decided that all the gunpowder required should be made within the country. Letters patent were then issued to George Evelyn and his son John, and Richard Hill (or Hills), licensing them for 11 years to dig and get saltpetre anywhere in the realms of England and Ireland, except in or within two miles of London and in the five northern English counties, and to make it into gunpowder for the Queen's use. Their first mills were near Kingston-on-Thames (John Evelyn later moved to Godstone), but the three patentees did not operate jointly. Hill, who later took George Constable, of the Minories, into partnership, worked independently of the Evelyns, and the saltpetre supplied by the saltpetremen was shared. Thus in the months from March to September 1589 the Evelyns took 45,585 lb of saltpetre, Hill 19,754 lb. It seems that still not enough gunpowder was being made, for it was being bought abroad at 1s. a lb as late as 1595, when the English makers' price was 7½d. or 8d.

George Evelyn and Richard Hill retired from the business when the first patent expired in 1599, but John Evelyn, with his brother Robert and three other partners, obtained a new patent, and the Evelyn brothers remained the chief entrepreneurs for the manufacture of gunpowder for many years. As the size of armies and the scale of warlike operations were continually expanding, there was an ever-increasing demand for gunpowder, and the family made a great deal of money. With it they bought landed property, notably Wotton, near Dorking, where the diarist John Evelyn was born in 1620. By the terms of the 1599 patent the partners undertook to supply 100 lasts, or if required 120 lasts, of gunpowder yearly at

7d. a lb, and it was reckoned that this would save the government £5,000 a year. Any powder over and above government requirements could be sold privately at 10d. a lb, and they evidently succeeded in stepping up production, for two years later they were allowed to export 30 lasts of powder and 10 of saltpetre to the Dutch. They also agreed to 'renew' all the powder that had become unserviceable in the Queen's stores, and between September 1595 and January 1604 they received 117 lasts, 21 cwt, 53 lb of 'decayed' powder from the stores in the Tower, and returned 96 lasts, 3 cwt, 93 lb of reconditioned powder.

In reply to complaints against the patents, the law officers of the Crown drew up arguments to show that they were useful and did not constitute a monopoly, and that the patentees were not in fact the only gunpowder-makers in the realm. A man named Richard Neede was at work at Rotherhithe in 1600, and in 1607 the Earl of Worcester was granted a 21-year patent for saltpetre and gunpowder. By this time the country was producing more than enough for its needs, and in 1610 the earl obtained a licence to export 1,200 barrels to friendly nations. He relinquished his patent in 1617, but John Evelyn remained at work, and accounts show that in 1620 he was again 'renewing' decayed powder and saltpetre from the government stores. In the course of the 1620s the government apparently got into arrears in its payments, and by 1628 he was in serious financial difficulties, with the result that the quantity of powder he could supply fell off. Meanwhile the East India Company had set up powder mills, using imported saltpetre, at Chilworth, near Guildford, and Evelyn had to face not only competition from them and other gunpowder-makers in different parts of the country, some of them unlicensed, but also accusations by his rivals of having made a fortune by deceitful methods. By 1635 he had such difficulty in securing payment from the government that he asked to be relieved of his contract, and the Chilworth mills then became the only authorized gunpowder mills in the country. They were worked for a time under contract by two men named Samuel Cordwell and George Collins, but in 1641 the Long Parliament abolished the monopoly by an Act 'for the free bringing in of gunpowder and saltpetre from foreign parts for the free making of gunpowder in this realm'.[15]

o

The manufacture of glass, by fusing together silica and an alkali, had been carried on at various places on the borders of Surrey and Sussex, particularly about Chiddingfold, since the thirteenth century. Silica was obtained from the coarse local sand, vegetable alkali (potash) from the ashes of wood or 'fern' (i.e. bracken), or sometimes of beancods or seaweed. The resulting glass varied in quality, owing to the presence of impurities, and was generally coarse and rough. Casting molten glass on a flat stone surface produced a crude form of window-pane, smooth on one side and irregular on the other; blown glass bottles and other vessels for domestic use, of a coarse green type, were also made. By the middle of the sixteenth century this industry was facing extinction, partly because the iron industry was competing with it for limited supplies of timber for fuel, partly because of a growing taste for the finer kinds of glass, imported first of all as expensive luxuries, but later in increasing quantities, from Venice and other places abroad.[1]

Various attempts were made to establish the manufacture of fine glass in England. In 1549 eight Venetian glass-makers left Murano, owing to unemployment there, and moved to Antwerp, then an important glass-making centre. Edward VI's government offered to set them up in England, and they came to London, where they were given a place to work in in the hall of the Crutched Friars, in Hart Street, Aldgate. Within a couple of years, however, seven of them had obeyed an edict of the Council at Venice, ordering all truant craftsmen to return home. The eighth, named Josepo Casselari, remained at work in London, with another Italian who had come from Antwerp, until 1569, but he then left England for Liège, where an expanding industry offered better prospects. This first effort to attract foreign glass-makers to England thus ended in failure, and a second venture was no more successful. In 1564 Connelius de Lannoy, an alchemist from the Netherlands, arrived in England, and received a subsidy from the government on condition of introducing improvements in glass-making, and giving instruction to English craftsmen. De Lannoy, however, was dissatisfied with the materials available to him in England, as well as with the ability of the pupils he was supposed to teach, and within three years he too disappeared from the English scene.[2]

Then in August 1567 Cecil received an application from Jean Carré, a merchant of Antwerp, and Pierre Briet, a glass-maker from Lorraine, backed by a recommendation from the Vidame of Chartres (the officer who managed the temporalities of the see).[3] They asked for an exclusive licence for 21 years to erect a furnace in London for the manufacture of crystal glass (i.e. fine quality glass, of high transparency), for drinking vessels, façon de Venise, and within three years they hoped to adorn London with an art as famous as that of Venice or Antwerp. All the necessary materials existed in the country, except only soda, and they expected to find the proper herbs for this in time. Meanwhile they asked permission to buy some of the necessary soda from an Italian merchant. (Crystal glass could not be made with any kind of alkali, and the best for the purpose was soda made from a plant grown in Spain, called barilla). Fuel could be brought by sea from Arundel, and no more would be needed than was used in a brewery. At the same time they asked that the importation of similar glass vessels from abroad should be prohibited, save only those from Venice itself. It would thus seem that the intention of the applicants was not to compete with genuine Venetian glass, which was a luxury, but only to secure the trade in the imitations of it imported from Antwerp and elsewhere in northern Europe.

Carré was a business man who saw an opportunity for profit if he could capture the growing market for fine glass in England. Previous attempts to attract Venetian workmen had proved abortive, but there were better prospects of success with the so-called gentilshommes verriers of Lorraine and Normandy. Though their workmanship was inferior to that of the Venetians, the Frenchmen were proficient craftsmen, who could turn out products greatly superior to the native English glass. Some French glass-makers who were Protestants had already come to England as refugees from religious intolerance, and settled in the Weald. Carré's hope was, protected by a grant of monopoly from the government, to attract more immigrants with the prospects of secure employment, organize their work under his control, and secure a slice of the profits for himself. Besides crystal glass he also hoped to capture the sheet-glass industry, and together with his application for a license for crystal glass he submitted a petition from some Frenchmen already in Sussex, for a monopoly for 30 years of the manufacture of glass for windows.

The government was hesitant at first, in case the scheme might injure the native industry in the Weald, but it appeared that the making of window-glass there had ceased, for in reply to an inquiry one of the Chiddingfold glass-workers declared that he and his fellows did not make anything except bottles, 'urinals' (orinaux: vessels used for inspecting liquids), and similar small articles. The Frenchmen proposed to erect 12 furnaces in England and six in Ireland, and offered to pay a royalty of 2s. on each case of glass, containing 45 or 48 bundles, and valued at 40s. Each furnace could be expected to turn out 480 bundles weekly, and would yield the Queen a yearly income of £40 or £50. They also offered Cecil himself the same royalty, which, to their surprise, he refused to accept; but on behalf of the Queen the glass-makers received a favourable reply. Two furnaces were then erected; one in London for crystal glass, employing workmen from Lorraine, whom Carré specially brought over, as he later protested, at his own 'great cost'; the other for window-glass, at 'Fernfol' (Fernfold Wood, near Loxwood) in Sussex.[4]

Unfortunately for Carré's plans, a rival appeared in the person of another projector, Anthony Becku, alias Dolyn, who like Carré himself came originally from Antwerp, though he had been resident for 12 years in England. Carré was afraid that Becku would get a concession, and finding he could not prevent this he decided to invite Becku to join him as a partner. The result was that on 8 September 1567 a patent for 21 years was issued to Carré and Becku jointly. They undertook to practise the 'arte, feate and mysterie of glas for glazinge, such as is made in Fraunce, Lorrayne and Burgundy', in sufficient quantities to supply the realm, and to teach 'English men our subjectes the same scyence or arte'. Two days before this patent was issued, they applied for leave to cut wood and make charcoal in Windsor Great Park, and convey it thence, possibly to Carré's crystal glass furnace in London.[5]

Before long the success of the partnership was undermined by disagreements. Carré introduced a third party, named John Chevallier, as a counterweight to Becku, while Briet, the chief of the Lorraine workers, was reduced to a subordinate position. Carré and Chevallier made a contract, dated 22 April 1568, with 'Thomas and Balthazar de Hamezel esquires, dwelling at the glashouses of Vosges in the countrie of Lorrayne', who undertook to come to England, bringing with them four 'gentlemen glaziers', and 'there cause to be builded and edified two Ovens to make great glas'. They would make 'every daye in eche of the sayd Ovens the quantitie of thirtie bundells of glas, whyts or coullers, good lawfull and merchauntable, of good height and largenes well proporcioned, so that we be not deteyned by sicknes or urgent lettes'.

Becku complained to Cecil that Carré and Chevallier, 'who hath no privilege in the glass-making', were usurping control of the whole undertaking, and accused Carré of double dealing. Unwisely he tried to enlist the support of Briet, but Briet saw no reason to help Becku, who had virtually displaced him, and he was equally disgusted with Carré's proceedings. Instead Briet decided to quit, and he set up a glass furnace 'on the other side of the sea by Bullen' (i.e. Boulogne). He made no secret of his intention to cut out his late partners: the site was conveniently near England, yet no privilege was required for working there, and he would 'kepe the science out of the Realme'.[6] Becku meanwhile had found an ally in an Englishman, Ferdinand Poyntz, described as citizen of London but probably of Sussex origins. It seems that they planned to set up their own glass works, and Becku sent his son to Germany to recruit more workmen in place of the Normans who had gone off with Briet, but it is doubtful if anything came of this scheme.

Carré had hoped to establish a monopoly which, if it had been realized, might have anticipated the empire acquired by Sir Robert Mansell in the seventeenth century. Although these hopes were wrecked, Carré nevertheless has quite an important place in the history of the glass industry. Apart from the furnace in London, he erected at least four furnaces for window-glass, worked by French immigrants, in the Weald, where his sphere of operations lay east and south-east of the old-established works at Chiddingfold. He settled in Sussex, where he had a house at Wisborough, and was buried at Alfold, under the name 'John Garry, master of the glasshouse'. Schism between the partners, however, led to open affrays between sections of the Frenchmen in Sussex. In July 1658 Peter and John Bongar (or Bungar; the latter apparently an ancestor of Isaac Bongar, whom Mansell was to find troublesome) made an assault, one with a great staff, the other with a hot iron having heated glass on it, on James Arnold, Becku's son-in-law and deputy, so that Arnold was 'sore wounded and burnt'. The Bongars also refused to instruct Englishmen (probably meaning Arnold) in the art of glassmaking, saying they were not bound by Carré's contract with the Queen. In the following year this and other questions in dispute were referred to arbitration, and the decision went against Carré's side. Becku and his employees were declared to be sober and honest men, and the Bongars were made to pay 40s. damages to Arnold.[7]

Apart from these quarrels, the French immigrants were not popular in Sussex, and the rapid expansion of the iron industry in the later sixteenth century made it difficult for them to obtain fuel. In 1581 the mayor and jurats of Rye complained that the woods near Rye, Winchelsea and Hastings were being wasted by the iron and glass works, and local dissatisfaction at the presence of foreign workmen culminated in plots 'to rob and murder the French glassmakers and burn their houses'. When the government placed restrictions on the cutting of timber the French had no alternative but to move. By the occurrence of their names (Hennezels, Tyzacks and others) in parish registers their peregrinations have been traced, in a generally westerly direction, halting briefly at a series of places until the local supplies of wood were exhausted. From Sussex they migrated *via* Petersfield, and Buckholt Wood near Winchester, to Newnham-on-Severn and Newent, on the borders of the Forest of Dean. By the seventeenth century they had moved to Stourbridge in Worcestershire, where a number of them remained. As they moved on, the window-glass making which had originally been their speciality was apparently displaced by the manufacture of glass vessels of relatively crude workmanship, sold about the countryside by pedlars; and the workers also declined from their original status of 'gentlemen' to become undistinguished and uneducated artisans.

The other side of Carré's project, the making of crystal glass in London, ultimately achieved success, but the real credit for this belongs not so much to him as to Giacomo Verzelini. Carré brought over six Venetians from the Netherlands in 1571, in order to re-establish the glass works at the Crutched Friars. One of them,

Domenico Casselari, was a relative, probably brother, of Josepo Casselari, the last to remain in England of the immigrants who had come in 1549, and it may have been his influence that led them to accept Carré's invitation. Verzelini came to England with this party. Born in Venice in 1522, like others of his countrymen he disliked the rigid control imposed on the glass-workers by the Venetian government, and migrated to Antwerp, where in 1555 he married a Dutch lady of good family. When Carré died, in 1572, Verzelini was left in charge of the workmen at the Crutched Friars. The manufacture of Venetian glass in England aroused the resentment of the Glaziers, or glass merchants, whose business was the importing of glass ware from abroad, and they protested to the Privy Council that Verzelini's work would mean the overthrow of 50 households living by the glass trade. They evidently thought that protests would be more effective if backed up by direct action, for on 4 September 1572 the glass-house at the Crutched Friars was destroyed by a great fire, which there seems reason to suppose was not an accident.

For Verzelini, aged 53 and with a wife and nine young children, this sudden loss of his livelihood was a serious disaster, and he applied to the Privy Council for protection. The government, which had wished all along to see the art of making fine glass established in England, responded favourably, and on 15 December 1575 Verzelini obtained a monopoly for 25 years of the manufacture of drinking glasses like those of Murano, on condition of his teaching the art to 'Englishmen our natural subjects'. He set up a glass-house on a new site, in Broad Street, and the works at the Crutched Friars were repaired, work being resumed there under the management of Casselari, while Verzelini, who took out letters of denization in November 1576, was in general control of the whole concern. Briet and Pierre Appell, another Netherlander, who had succeeded to Carré's patent, then applied for its confirmation and renewal, but their application was disregarded, and that is the last we hear of the projectors from the Netherlands. The French glass-makers, soon to start on their wanderings from Sussex, were now independent (the de Hennezels' agreement with Carré, dated 22 April 1568, had been for nine years), and in any case they did not compete with Verzelini's monopoly of the manufacture of Venetian glass. Verzelini differed as a monopolist from his predecessors and successors in the glass industry, in that he alone was a professional glass-maker, and not simply a capitalist entrepreneur. After 17 years in practice he retired from business in 1592, and went to live at Downe, near Orpington in Kent, where he died, aged 84, in 1606. His descendants fell out after his death, and control of the glass industry then passed into the hands of a series of English monopolists, but it is evident that his business had prospered, and surviving specimens of his workmanship show his success in establishing in England the manufacture of articles of artistic as well as purely utilitarian value.[8]

As fine glass vessels became more plentiful, the demand for them increased, and at the same time rising standards of comfort created an expanding market for window glass. English capitalists began to realize the potentialities of glass-making as an investment for their money, and the industry came to acquire a solid economic foundation. At first, however, English would-be entrepreneurs had an eye on the market for utilitarian articles rather than the fine-quality products of Verzelini's furnaces. In 1589 Hugh Miller and Acton Scott, described as 'footmen of the Queen', asked for a licence to make 'all manner of glasses whatsoever which are usually made within your Hygnes Realme of England', viz. 'urynals, bottles, bowles, cupps to drink in and such like except those that is already granted to one Jacob a stranger [i.e. Verzelini] dwelling in the Crutched Friars ... for the makinge of all manner of counterfayt Venyse drinkinge glasses, and except all manner of glasses for glazing windows'. They added that strangers were depriving Englishmen of work, although Englishmen were 'as well able to exercise that trade and with as moch scyll as any others are'.

Their request, apparently aimed at the French glassmakers, seems to have met with no response, nor did anything come of a petition with a similar objective, submitted to Burghley in the same year by a man named George Longe. He pointed out that owing to the dissension between the foreigners (meaning Carré and Becku) their project had collapsed, and meanwhile glass was being made by divers unlicensed persons with great loss of timber. According to Longe there were 15 glass-houses in England; these he proposed to reduce to four, and re-erect the others in Ireland, where there was superfluous wood, and every glass-house would be as good as a garrison of 20 men. He undertook to employ all the workmen thrown out of work in England, declaring that he had spent his whole time in the glass industry, and that after two years of trials he had brought to perfection the manufacture of glass in Ireland, where he had found the proper materials. Burghley seems to have been attracted by this project, and suggested that Longe should consult Becku, but apparently it was dropped, for no more is heard of it, though it appears that later Longe erected 10 glass furnaces in Ireland, with the assistance of a Captain Wodehouse.

As happened in other industries, a number of the entrepreneurs who succeeded Verzelini in the glass monopoly were courtiers or speculative noblemen. They often had other financial interests as well—colonizing or piracy, for example—and had no special artistic or technical qualifications for control of the art of glass-making. The first of them, Sir Jerome Bowes, was a member of the Court circle, who in 1583 had been sent as ambassador to Russia, where his rude behaviour had led to his dismissal. When Verzelini retired, Bowes obtained a licence, dated 5 February 1592, entitling him, at an annual rent of 100 marks, to the sole right for 12 years to make drinking vessels in the Venetian fashion.[9] His licence expired in 1604, but was renewed, and on 8 October 1607 Sir Percival Hart, another courtier, in partnership with Edward Forcett (probably a subordinate figure), obtained a patent for 21 years. These patents were for glasses in the Venetian style, which represented only a small fraction of the whole market for glass ware. Ordinary glass vessels were being made by the wandering Frenchmen and others, and the old English Wealden industry still survived, though on a diminishing scale. The next phase was an attempt to bring the manufacture of ordinary glass under monopoly control, and so in 1608 a licence was granted to Edward Salter, to make 'all manner of drinking glasses and other glasses and glasse works not prohibited by the former letters patent'. Who Salter was is unknown, but he does not seem to have made a success of his monopoly. The attempts of Simon Sturtevant and John Rovenson to use coal for smelting iron have already been mentioned,[10] and although they failed, it was not long before means were found to use coal for various industrial processes, including glass-blowing. The use of wood fuel was then prohibited, and Salter was probably put out of business because he did not know how to use coal.

On 28 July 1610 a special licence for 21 years was granted to Sir William Slingsby, Andrew Palmer, Edward Wolverstone, and

Robert Clayton, to erect furnaces, ovens and engines for brewing, dyeing, baking, roasting, brick, tile and pot-making, as well as for melting glass, ordnance, bell-metal, latten, copper and other metals with sea-coal or pit-coal. Palmer was a younger son of the Andrew Palmer who was employed at the Mint and had been a shareholder and the first secretary of the Mineral and Battery company.[11] The younger Palmer also had an appointment at the Mint, and probably was the member of the group with some technical knowledge of furnaces, whereas Slingsby, 'one of the Carvers of the most excellent Princess Queen Anne', was simply an ignorant, if influential courtier, and the other two partners seem to have been unimportant. The patent was a barefaced attempt to monopolize the use of coal in a dozen different industries at once, and was hardly likely to succeed. As Mr Thorne put it, 'the combine in its headlong opportunism failed to understand that there is no large manner of imposing improvements; every industry, by feeling its needs and answering them, grows its own innovations. If Slingsby had been content to confine himself to one industry . . . he might have succeeded; he failed because he tried to encompass all.'[12]

What Slingsby and his associates actually achieved was to draw the attention of other entrepreneurs to the possibility of using coal, and very soon Sir Edward Zouche collected a more effective group of partners. Zouche was an active man of affairs who, among other positions in the public service, had been deputy-governor of Guernsey and president of the Council of Wales. He also had colonial interests, and served at different times on the councils of Virginia and of New England. His chief partner in the glass monopoly was Bevis Thelwall, a member of a prominent Welsh family who had acquired an influential position at the court of James I and among other interests had shares in some of Sir Hugh Myddelton's enterprises. Associated with Zouche and Thelwall, though in a subordinate position, were Thomas Percivall and Thomas Mefflyn. Percivall was the partner with technical knowledge of coal furnaces, while Mefflyn was a 'glasier', i.e. not a glassmaker but a dealer in glass, and he thus formed a link between the manufacturing and the marketing sides of the business.

When Slingsby became aware that a rival combine was being formed, he wrote to Salisbury, on 26 February 1611 urging him to refuse the application for a patent from Zouche and his partners, on the ground that it would be an infringement of Slingsby's own patent. Slingsby also claimed that he and his partners had invented the coal furnace, but at the same time he admitted that 'our busynes hathe had as yet but slow progression', and the truth was that they had not done or invented anything. A month later, on 25 March 1611, Zouche's combine obtained a patent for making 'all manner of glasses' for 21 years, and though special provisions were included to protect Slingsby's group, and Sir Jerome Bowes as well, these reservations were virtually meaningless. Slingsby's patent included all sorts of other industries, so that he and his friends had plenty to occupy them, and they made no further moves to substantiate their claims to be glass-makers. Bowes's patent had been for glass-making with wood fuel, and as long as Zouche and his partners used coal they would not be infringing any previous patents. The Zouche enterprise was on a substantial scale, for the partners spent £5,000 on developing the coal furnace. Glass was traditionally melted with wood fuel in open pots, and when coal was used the sulphur in it injuriously affected the glass, particularly when fine, clear glass was being made, with flint instead of sand. For a time this baffled the glass-makers, but the difficulty was overcome by using closed pots, which kept out the coal fumes. Although Percivall was later described as the inventor of the new process, it seems doubtful whether he could claim personal credit for the discovery. According to one account coal was first used in glass-making on Lord Dudley's Staffordshire estate, by Paul Tissac.[18] This may well be true, for Tissac (also spelt Tyzack) was the name of one of the migrant French families who had settled at Stourbridge, where coal was available, and the local clay was particularly suitable for glass-making pots, as it would stand great heat without cracking. There is no doubt, however, that the Zouche company's glass-house, which was set up at Lambeth, soon became highly successful, and aroused envy and opposition from the owners of existing wood-fired glass-houses.

In 1613 Sir Jerome Bowes reappeared at the head of a fresh group of partners and asked for a patent for glass-making with the newly-invented coal furnaces. Presumably he was hoping to oust Zouche, for two rival sets of entrepreneurs were hardly likely to be licensed to operate simultaneously. The government appointed Sir George More and Sir Edmund Bowyer as commissioners to make inquiries, and they reported that the glass-house lately erected at Lambeth

by Zouche and Thelwall was using coal from Scotland and producing glass which was clear and good, and satisfactory to the glaziers,
although it was 'in some places uneven and full of spots by reason
of the negligence of the workmen'.

On 11 February 1614 Zouche and his partners surrendered the
patent they had obtained in 1611, but it was they and not Bowes
who won the contest, for on 4 March a fresh patent for 21 years
was issued to Zouche, Thelwall and Percivall, with Robert
Kellaway in place of Mefflyn, who had recently died. The now
elderly Bowes was offered as compensation an annuity of £1,000
a year; he refused it, but did not trouble the new patentees for long,
for he died in 1616.[14] The prosperity of the enterprise may be
gauged by the rent the partners had to pay. Under the patent of
1611 it had been £30 a year; now it was raised to £1,000, and the
prospects of large profits were so enticing that several titled persons
soon wanted to participate. The result was the issue, on 19 January
1615, of yet another patent, in which the names of Philip Earl of
Montgomery, Thomas Viscount Andover, Sir Thomas Howard, Sir
Robert Mansell, Sir Thomas Tracy and Thomas Hayes were
included, as well as those of Zouche, Thelwall, Percivall and Kellaway. These 10 were to have the sole right for 21 years of making
all kinds of glass with sea-coal, pit-coal or any other fuel not being
timber or wood, at a rent of £1,000 a year, and the sole right to
import glasses from abroad. A bill to preserve the woodlands had
been promoted, but like other bills in the Addled Parliament it met
with opposition and failed to get through. Instead, on 23 May 1615
a Proclamation touching Glasses was issued, prohibiting the use of
timber as fuel for glass-making.[15]

The combined effect of the latest patent and the proclamation was
to create an oligarchy which dominated the whole industry. It soon
became a complete monopoly, for Sir Robert Mansell bought out his
nine partners with an annual payment of £1,800, and undertook sole
responsibility for the rent of £1,000 a year to the Crown. This was
not a sudden decision, for it seems that Mansell had been interested
in glass manufacture since about 1606. By 1618 he had the whole
business in his hands, and remained in control for nearly 40 years.

Born in 1573 into a prominent Glamorganshire family, owners of
Margam Abbey, Sir Robert Mansell was a professional sailor, who
became Treasurer of the Navy in 1604, and Vice-Admiral of England

in 1618. He was knighted for his exploits in the Cadiz expedition
in 1596, and saw active service on a number of occasions after
that. He was also a capitalist, with shares in the Muscovy and East
India Companies, besides sitting in the House of Commons, mostly
for constituencies in South Wales, in nearly all the parliaments of
the early seventeenth century. Above all, he was a man of action,
and stories about him show that on occasion he did not hesitate
to act boldly and decisively. When he accompanied Lord Howard on
a mission to Corunna in 1605, a grand entertainment was arranged in
honour of the English visitors. Detecting one of the Spaniards in the
act of hiding some silver under his clothes, Mansell 'rose, took the
Spaniard to where sat the grandees of his nation, and there and then
shook him till the plate tumbled out'. From Corunna the mission
went on to Valladolid, and there 'he pursued a thief of some rank
. . . and by force recovered a jewel stolen from his person'.[16]

Such was the man into whose hands the control of glass-making
now fell, and he soon made his control into a despotism. First of
all he took steps to suppress or absorb the numerous small glass-
houses which were producing inferior ware in various parts of the
country. This was not difficult, for their consumption of wood not
only made them unpopular locally but was an infringement of the
proclamation. Thus early in 1618 he procured the arrest of Peter
Comley and a Fleming named Paul Vinion, for making glass with
wood, contrary to the proclamation; on 4 May, with a gesture of
magnanimity, he wrote to the Privy Council, requesting that they
might be released on giving bond not to repeat the offence.[17] But
when in January 1619 Vinion petitioned the King for leave to use
up the stock of materials he had laid in for glass-making before
the issue of the proclamation, Mansell interposed with the objection
that he would be greatly prejudiced in his patent for the sole manufacture of glass if Vinion were allowed to go on making green glass
drinking vessels.[18] He might, he hinted, be unable to pay the King
his £1,000 a year. It was on this occasion that James 1 made one of
his often-quoted joking remarks : 'I marvel that Robert Mansell, who
has won so much honour on the water, should meddle with fire.'

Though Mansell was given power to stop unauthorized glass-
makers, in many cases he allowed them to continue under licence.
This seems to have been his policy towards the French glass-makers
at Stourbridge, who hitherto had been independent craftsmen. Some

of them put up a determined resistance, but in the end, as the only alternative to abandoning their craft, they fell under Mansell's domination; some migrated to Newcastle, and accepted employment in the glass-works he established there. In 1619 Mansell resisted a proposed grant to Sir Ralph and Dame Ann Bingley of a licence to manufacture looking-glasses.[19] This, he said, was a department of the industry which he had been at great charge in perfecting. It was true that Mansell's interest in glass-making was not purely financial, in that he had taken some pains to become conversant with the processes involved; but the manufacture of looking-glasses employed a different class of workmen, and was quite distinct from the manufacture of drinking glasses, which at first formed the most important side of Mansell's business. He was determined, however, to monopolize the manufacture of every kind of glass, and his empire came to embrace glass for windows and mirrors as well as for all kinds of bottles and other vessels.

An objectionable feature of the system of monopoly is illustrated by the petition of an hour-glass maker, Ralph Colbourne, in March 1620, to be relieved from oppression by Sir Robert Mansell, who made him buy his glasses in London. These were bad and highly priced, and he begged to be allowed to buy them at any of Mansell's works.[20] Shortly before this Peter Howgill and John Greene had been committed to the Marshalsea for importing foreign glass, contrary to the patent, on the pretext that it was for the King's use, and on 4 February they petitioned the Council for release. Next month another petition about the importation of foreign glass queried Mansell's ability to supply enough glass, and a number of glaziers complained that his glass was scarce, bad and brittle. Mansell replied that the scarcity of glass was not his fault. He had incurred great expense in order to improve its quality, and the high price was due to a rise in the cost of coal. Even so, glass was cheaper than it had been before his patent. The glaziers were not satisfied with Mansell's excuses, and while admitting that some of his glass was serviceable they still complained that much of it was bad. This verdict was confirmed by a report to the King from the architect Inigo Jones, then engaged on the Banqueting House in Whitehall, that Mansell's glass was mixed, good and bad together, and very thin in the middle.[21]

Though Mansell had no claim to be an artist or a connoisseur of fine glass, he was not unappreciative of the need for high standards of workmanship and materials, and he made some effort to maintain them. In this he was assisted by a fellow-countryman from Wales, James Howell, best known as a literary man, author of *Epistolae Ho-Elianae*. Mansell employed Howell as a kind of travelling agent and adviser, and between 1618 and 1621 he visited Holland, Flanders, France, Spain and Italy, studying continental methods of glass-making and sending frequent reports to Sir Robert. In one letter he described the Venetian glass-works at Murano, and among other things he reported on the Spanish soda-plant, *barilla*, which he saw growing at Alicante—'a strange kind of vegetable, and it grows nowhere upon the surface of the earth in that perfection as here. The Venetians have it hence.' According to Howell, soda made from its berries fetched 100 crowns a tun, but he got some for less. Mansell placed an order for £2,000 worth with a Genoese merchant, and this seems to be the first instance of its regular or extensive use in England, for there is no evidence that it was used by Verzelini or Bowes.

Through Howell Mansell also secured the services of Antonio Miotti, an accomplished member of a glass-making family from Murano, who brought three other experienced glass-makers with him. But Italians who emigrated seldom stayed long in one place. Miotti left Mansell after four years and moved to Brussels; another Venetian named dell' Acqua stayed only two years and then left to become master of a glass-house in Scotland. He explained that he left Mansell because he found that his work increased but not his wages, but he seems to have been dissatisfied in Scotland too, for he only stayed there a short time, and later re-entered Mansell's service.[22] The Italians undoubtedly effected an improvement, if only a temporary one, in Mansell's glass, for on 4 April 1621 the Glaziers' Company certified that it was cheap, plentiful, and of good quality, superior to the glass made in Scotland.[23] Later, in the middle 1630s, when there were fresh complaints of the poor quality of his glass, Mansell, at considerable expense, imported a whole company of glass-makers from Mantua.

Besides the London glass-works in Broad Street, which dated from Verzelini's time, Mansell had works, some of which failed, in various other places, including the Isle of Purbeck and Milford Haven, where he tried using Welsh anthracite, which was less sulphurous than ordinary coal. He also made an agreement with Sir Percival

Willoughby for glass-making with coal on the Wollaton estate,[24] but the cost of transporting the finished glass to London was too great. Finally Mansell set up works for window-glass at Newcastle-on-Tyne, where cheap coal and suitable clay were both available. Later he also acquired control of glass-works in Scotland. In 1610 James VI had granted the exclusive right for 31 years to make glass at Wemyss, in Fife, to Lord George Hay. Works were also set up at Glasgow and elsewhere, and in 1627 the right was acquired from Hay by Thomas Robinson, a merchant tailor of London, and he in turn conveyed it to Mansell for a rent of £250 a year.

Meanwhile Mansell was sent to sea again, in command of a fleet against the pirates of Algiers. He left Plymouth on 12 October 1620, and during his absence various troubles came to a head. His monopoly was adversely criticized in Parliament, and a number of previously independent glass-makers made a determined attempt to break it. One group, headed by John Worrall, declaring that they had learned the art under Sir Jerome Bowes, but were prevented by Mansell's patent from pursuing their calling, asked for a licence and offered to pay the Crown £1,000 a year for it. About the same time Isaac Bongar, one of the glass-makers of French descent, and spokesman for another body of malcontents, offered the King £1,500 a year if he would revoke Mansell's patent and allow free manufacture, and undertook to sell glass at 2s. a lb below Mansell's price. Bongar, however, carried his opposition to Mansell too far, for he aroused the hostility of the Glaziers' Company, which accused him of seeking to engross the whole glass trade himself, and Bongar found himself committed to prison. He apologized for the expressions he had used against Mansell, and Dame Mansell, who was looking after her husband's interests during his absence at sea, was willing to procure his release if he would promise not to infringe Mansell's patent nor to disturb his works.[25] Bongar, however, was unwilling to bind himself by pledges which might subsequently be 'strained' to his disadvantage, and maintained his opposition.

In consequence of objections raised in Parliament in 1621, the patent granted in January 1615, from which Mansell had bought out his partners, was declared to be prejudicial and hurtful, and to have become void. On 22 May 1623, however, in consideration of his faithful service, the expenditure of his whole fortune, and the success of his labours in making glass with sea-coal and pit-coal, the patent was renewed to him alone for 15 years, free of rent. It empowered him to make all kinds of glass whatsoever; besides his, there were to be no glass-houses in England save those working under licence from him, and he was to have power to search and demolish all unlicensed ones. On the other hand there was to be no restraint on the importation of foreign glass.

Mansell's enemies refused to acquiesce in this renewal of his monopoly, and in 1624 there was a protracted dispute, in which Bongar and Worrall joined forces against Mansell, and both sides argued their case in a series of pleadings and replies submitted to the House of Commons.[26] Mansell's opponents pointed out the evils arising from a monopoly. 'Artists' and poor glass-makers were restricted, prices were raised (examples they quoted were coarse drinking glasses which used to cost 8d. but now cost 12d. or more; window-glass formerly sold at 16s. a case, now 22s. 6d.), and consumers also suffered by no longer being able to buy on the open market what suited them best. Mansell, the complainants alleged, was unskilful and incapable, and they further dilated on the injustice of prohibiting the use of wood by glass-makers, who only burnt the 'lops' of trees, while the iron men, who used much more wood, were allowed to work unhindered.

If the statements in Mansell's reply may be accepted, his enemies had gone to criminal lengths to injure him. When he tried to get clay from Staffordshire for his melting-pots, Bongar and his friends 'corrupted' it so that the pots broke. He then sent for clay from beyond Rouen, but that too was spoilt, probably, he suspected, by Bongar's kinsmen there. Then he was driven to procuring clay from 'Spawe' in Germany (i.e. Spa, now in Belgium), but his enemies ruined a whole shipload. In the end a satisfactory clay was found at Newcastle, but Bongar bribed the workmen at the furnaces there to turn out inferior glass, and Mansell had been obliged to introduce expert strangers from abroad. These, he declared, not only made 'all sorts and kinds of right Christalline Morana-glasses . . . never made or attempted here before', but also instructed English workmen in their art. During his absence at sea Bongar had also persuaded the Scottish shipmasters to raise their charge for the coal they carried to London from 14s. to 24s. a ton. This was a prohibitive increase, and brought Mansell's London glass-house to a standstill. The situation was saved by the energy and good sense of Dame

P

Mansell, who had succeeded in organizing a supply of coal from Newcastle. By 1624 the use of Scottish coal in London had practically ceased, and a fleet of 40 vessels was engaged in conveying coal and window-glass from the Tyne.

Bongar and Worrall returned to the charge, categorically denying Mansell's statements, and declaring that they did not want a patent for themselves, but only leave to pursue their calling freely. Now they blamed unrestricted importation, which they said was injurious to the poor glass-makers, while Bongar claimed that his ancestors were 'the men who brought the trade of window-glass into England, which had been lost many years before'. In the end the dispute was referred to the Privy Council, which decided in Mansell's favour. His patent was exempted from the Act against Monopolies, and on 6 December 1626 Bongar was ordered not to presume to trouble His Majesty further, on pain of punishment.[27]

After this there was an interlude of peace, but within a few years Bongar was stirring up trouble again. On 28 January 1635 Mansell addressed a further statement to the Privy Council, enlarging on the costs, charges, losses and difficulties he had sustained in the glass business. Much of it recapitulated the sad story he had already put before Parliament in 1624. He had had to spend £30,000, he declared, before the manufacture of glass could be 'perfected'; yet, although so far he had not reaped any profit, he had neither relaxed his efforts nor raised his prices. Although he was paying £250 a year for the Scottish patent, his men were again being enticed into Scotland (presumably to a rival concern there), and now attempts were on foot to produce glasses in Ireland.[28]

On 14 October a proclamation was issued prohibiting the importation of foreign glass during the continuance of his privilege,[29] but before long the quality of Mansell's glass must have declined again, for in December 1637 the Glaziers' Company once more complained of its badness, dearness, scarcity, and want of full size. Mansell replied that the dearness was due to the rise in the cost of materials, and the scarcity partly to mortality among the workmen at Newcastle and partly to lack of shipping: he agreed that bad glass ought not to be sold but should be broken at the furnace. The Council found Mansell's answer 'reasonable', but they went on to say that they themselves had found by experience that glass was 'not so fair, so clear, nor so strong as the same was wont to be', and they ordered him to 'take effectual care in those particulars', and to make sure that the glaziers received a proper supply of window-glass at a reasonable price.[30] A fresh complaint also came from the hour-glass makers: the vials they were accustomed to buy were now so bad that one in every four was useless. But they were told that their complaints were frivolous and they would be committed to prison if they repeated them.

After this Mansell enjoyed another brief respite, but when the Scottish army appeared before Newcastle in 1640 he was in serious difficulties, as he explained in a letter to Secretary Windebank. Work stopped at his three furnaces, at which window-glass was made, and all his workmen with their wives and families, to the number of 60 persons, fled. He had 1,200 cases of glass, worth £1,500, packed ready for shipment to London, and had laid out over £4,000 on the buildings and equipment needed for supplying the whole kingdom with window-glass. Now he was likely to lose all this, as well as the work of 20 years and the £30,000 he had spent in the past. He wanted to get his men back at work, but could not maintain them, nor pay his rent, unless he could sell his glass. He therefore begged for two, three or four ships to take his glass to London, and also to carry coal in order to keep his London factory at work.[31] It seems doubtful whether this appeal had any effect, for in May 1641 Mansell was appealing to the Lords for protection against persons importing glass in contravention of his rights. An order was granted in his favour, but two months later he complained that in spite of this Richard Batson and others had imported large quantities of glass, and violently resisted officers seeking to enforce the House's order. In the same year Jeremy Bago, who had married Suzanna Henzey (de Hennezel, one of the French glass-making families), was charged, along with his partner Francis Bristow, of actually running an illicit glass-house at Greenwich, where Mansell lived. At Mansell's instance the House of Lords served an order on them, but they defied it, and even had the temerity to complain of the grievous wrongs and insults they had suffered at his hands.

On the outbreak of the Civil War, when the political leanings of the Navy seemed doubtful, it was suggested that Mansell might resume his nautical career and take command of the fleet, but he was then about 70, and though there was no question of his experience and loyalty it was decided that he was too old. The fleet passed under parliamentary control; and in war conditions Mansell found his monopoly virtually impossible to enforce. He assigned his right to make sheet glass to a man named Hercy Pate, but Pate's workmen took advantage of the war to combine with some London glaziers and others who sympathized with the parliamentary side. An order in the King's name from 'our Court at Oxford', dated 1 December 1643, charged the men to perform their covenant with Pate, and instructed sheriffs, colonels and others to seize and dispose of any glass sent to London or other places in rebellion;[32] but such orders cannot have been effectively observed. There seems to be some doubt as to the date of Mansell's death. According to his biographer G. T. Clark, he died on 12 August 1653, aged over 80. Hartshorne, however, says that the exact date is uncertain, but must have been a few years before 1660. In the *Dictionary of National Biography* the date is given as 1656.[33]

Historians of the glass industry have varied in their judgments on Mansell and his monopoly. Hartshorne, while admitting that he was disliked and attacked, thought on the whole that the concentration of the industry under his control had advantages which may even have outweighed its drawbacks. If glass-making had remained in small scattered country glass-houses, owned and worked by men out of touch with the progress being achieved elsewhere, the development of the artistic quality of English glass might have been delayed for perhaps a century.[34] W. A. Thorne, on the other hand, is less favourable. He admits Mansell's capability as an organizer, and describes his despotism as 'if not beneficent . . . certainly beneficial', agreeing with Hartshorne that but for the stimulus provided by Mansell's combination of all sorts of glass-making—'window glass, medical and scientific glass, rough peasant glass, mirror glass, as well as the common and finer sorts of domestic glass'—under one management, the 'wayward and individual glassmakers in various parts of England . . . might never have gone beyond their crude peasantries'. Yet Mansell relied too much on his foreign experts, and never succeeded in encouraging native English talent to develop. Hartshorne dismissed Bongar as 'assuredly a vindictive, untruthful, and unscrupulous knave', but Thorne saw in his enmity to Mansell a 'declaration of independence', and concluded that it was not from Mansell's monopoly but from the opposition to it that the 'real English tradition' in the glassmakers' art eventually grew.[35]

Entrepreneurs in some miscellaneous industries

Tapestries

As standards of domestic comfort rose, a demand sprang up among the wealthy for tapestries to hang on the walls of their castles and mansions. The art of tapestry-weaving, well-established in France in the Middle Ages, spread into Flanders, and much of the tapestry used in England was imported thence. Some kinds were known in consequence as arras, from the town of their origin. There was no native English tapestry-making industry, and attempts to naturalize the art in this country necessitated the introduction of designers and artisans from abroad. The most successful of these ventures was the well-known factory at Mortlake, set up in 1619 in pursuit of a deliberate policy of establishing foreign industries in England. The Mortlake factory became justly famous, for it produced work of the highest quality, rivalled only by the Gobelins in France, but the Mortlake tapestries were not the first tapestries to be made in England.

The credit for this must be given to a rich Worcestershire squire, William Sheldon, of Beoley near Redditch, who developed a plan to introduce tapestry-making into England at the beginning of Elizabeth's reign.[1] Sheldon, whose family came originally from Warwickshire, had been employed by Thomas Cromwell to supervise the dissolution of the monasteries in his locality. He 'acquired many large properties' when Pershore Abbey was suppressed, and at the sale of the contents of the Cistercian house at Bordesley, near Beoley, he 'made several large purchases of stuff'. In 1546–7 he held the post of receiver of all the monastic estates in Warwickshire, and he added further to his possessions by his marriage to Mary Willington, the daughter of a wealthy wool-merchant and landowner from Barcheston, near Shipston-on-Stour. Sheldon acquired the manor of Weston, a few miles from Barcheston, and he also bought another estate to form a park around his mansion at Beoley. Established thus as a county magnate, he was one of the members for Worcestershire in the parliaments of 1547, 1554 and 1555. In spite of having profited so much from the sale of monastic lands he remained a Roman Catholic, as also did his son Ralph. Ralph Sheldon was suspected of complicity in some of the treasonable activities of the time,[2] but unlike some of his friends and relatives he cleared himself and escaped disaster.

How exactly William Sheldon conceived the idea of introducing tapestry-making into England is uncertain, but it seems possible that the project originated with a certain Richard Hyckes, or Hicks, whom he engaged to act as a companion to his son on a journey abroad after coming down from Oxford. While they were in Flanders Hicks became interested in weaving and arras-making and set himself to learn the art, and when he returned to England he may have brought some Flemish weavers with him.[3] Sheldon meanwhile, in May 1561, had acquired the manor of Barcheston, and he settled Hicks and his weavers there, with their looms for making tapestry. Sheldon died on 23 December 1570, and in his will, which he had made in the previous January, he paid tribute to Hicks as 'the only author and beginner of this Art within this Realm'.

He declared that his 'will and mind' was that all the profits arising from a lease which he had bought of 'all the toll or custom as well of fairs as of market days every week', at Bishop's Castle in Shropshire, 'with all customs, fees, profits, tolls, commodities and other things whatsoever to the same fairs and markets appertaining or belonging', were to be 'lent freely' by his executors 'from time to time upon good securities to such person and persons as shall occupy and use the art of making tapestry and arras or either of them within the counties of Worcester and Warwick and in the cities of Worcester and Coventry'.

'William Dowler, now servant to Richard Heekes', was to have the first call on a loan, repaying £26 13s. 4d. after 10 years; 'Thomas Chaunce' was also mentioned by name, with the wish that if possible loans should be made to English workers, preferably from Worcestershire or Warwickshire, or failing that from some neighbouring counties. At the same time Sheldon acknowledged the indebtedness of the project to foreign workmen, for he went on to provide that 'every stranger born that shall work with the said Richard Heeks, Thomas Chaunce and William Dowler in the said Art at the time of my death' should also be eligible for a loan. In a codicil, dated 28 September 1570, Sheldon stated that he had established Hicks 'in the mansion house at Barcheston, with the myll, orchards and gardens and pastures, without paying any rent in money', and that Hicks and he had agreed that 'certayn money shall be yerely disbursed and laid out by me and my heyres towards the makyng the said tapestry'. He believed that the trade would be 'greatly beneficiall to the Commonwelthe to train youth in, and a means to secure great somes of money within this Realme'. Trusting therefore that his 'well beloved son Rauf' would 'have the same consideration to the Commonwelthe as I now have or more', he urged him to 'permit and suffer the said Richard Heeks to have and enjoye the said howse and all other things specifyed in the said wrytings made betweene me and the said Richard Heeks'. In conclusion he expressed the hope that 'Richard Heeks will contyneue the exercysing of the same trade to so good purpose as he hath begun'.

It would seem that various other textiles were being made at Barcheston besides tapestry or arras, for Sheldon mentions 'moccadoes, carolles, plomets, grograynes, sayes, and sarges'. It also appears that weaving had been set up not only at Barcheston but also at Bordesley, close to Sheldon's own residence at Beoley, and it seems probable that it was at Bordesley that Thomas Chaunce was employed, very possibly in the former conventual buildings. The reputation of the Sheldon enterprise was evidently well established by the time of William's death, for an entry in the Black Book of Warwick, dated 27 November 1571, records that when the borough sent their town clerk to Greenwich Palace for an interview with Robert Dudley, Earl of Leicester, soliciting his help in relieving the poverty of the town, the earl replied. 'I marvaile you do not devise some ways amongst you, to have some speciall trade to kepe your poore on woork as such as Sheldon of Beolye wch mythinkith should not only be very profittable, but also a meanes to kepe your poore from Idelnes.'[4]

Ralph Sheldon, who was aged 33 when his father died, married Anne Throckmorton, daughter of Sir Robert Throckmorton of Coughton in Warwickshire. He did not fail to carry out the intentions expressed in his father's will, and Hicks also remained in charge of the looms at Barcheston. In 1584–5 Richard Hicks's name, together with that of his son Francis, appears among those of arras-workers employed by the Great Wardrobe. For a time they were engaged in repairing arras and tapestry at the Tower of London, Westminster, Hampton Court, Richmond, Windsor Castle and other royal palaces. The materials they used came from Barcheston, where there must by now have been enough skilled craftsmen to continue working the looms in their absence. By about 1588 Richard Hicks was back at Barcheston, and as it was about this time that Ralph Sheldon began building a mansion on his estate at Weston close by, we may perhaps assume that Hicks had returned to supervise the making of tapestry for the new house.

Richard Hicks survived Ralph Sheldon, who died at the age of 76 on 30 March 1613, for he reached the great age of 97, and did not die until 21 October 1621. His son Francis succeeded him in charge of the looms, and tapestry-making seems to have continued until nearly the middle of the seventeenth century. Among the best-known products of the factory are the tapestry maps of a number of English counties, based on the maps published by Christopher Saxton in 1579; another set of tapestries from Barcheston, where they were woven in 1611, is the series of the Seasons, at Hatfield House. Sheldon tapestries no doubt adorned a number of houses in the west Midlands, and examples have been found at Chastleton House, at Sudeley Castle and elsewhere. The Sheldon enterprise has been credited with the creation of a school of English tapestry-workers which had an important and far-reaching influence on the development of the art in England.[5] Whether it was financially successful is another question, and one which we cannot answer. William Sheldon's will made provision for repayable loans to workers in his factory, but references to money 'yerely disbursed and laid out by me and my heyres' suggest that the enterprise depended for its continuance as well as its inception on subsidies from the Sheldon estate.

In any case tapestry-making was a luxury trade, catering for a limited market among the wealthy, and the Mortlake tapestries were dependent on royal patronage and subvention. Here the entrepreneur was Sir Francis Crane, who in 1606 was appointed Clerk of the Parliament, and later became secretary to Prince Charles. Crane's family came from East Anglia, but he established connections with

Cornwall; his two sisters married Cornish husbands, and through the influence of the Prince of Wales as Duke of Cornwall Crane himself entered the House of Commons as a member, first for Penryn and later for Launceston. It was in 1619 that James I, who had become interested in tapestry-making, decided to promote it in England, and on the King's promising to support him Crane undertook to start a factory. To launch the enterprise he was to be allowed the making of three baronets (that is, he could keep the fees, about £1,000 a head, paid by those wishing to have this title), and a subsidy of £2,000 a year.[6] He built his factory on the north side of the High Street at Mortlake, on a site formerly occupied by the laboratory of the famous mathematician John Dee, and in the following year (1620) he had 50 skilled Flemish workmen brought over from Bruges and Oudenarde. By about 1622, according to a letter he wrote to the King, Crane needed more money. He had spent £3,200, he said, on orders for the Marquis (later Duke) of Buckingham; he also owed £300 for designs made by Raphael for Pope Leo X, which the Prince of Wales had given him orders to procure, apart from the cost of bringing them to England. Altogether, he told the King, 'I am out already above £16,000 in the busynes, and never made returns of more than £2,500'; as a result, his estate was 'wholly exhausted' and his credit 'so spent, besides the debts that lye upon me', that he could not carry on for a month longer without assistance.

Within a few years, however, the outlook was much rosier: indeed, according to the report of an inquiry in 1630, on four copies of a tapestry of Vulcan and Venus, woven on the King's orders, together with other allowances, Crane had made no less than £12,255, besides his profits on other works sold at home and abroad. Whether or not this figure was accurate, there can be no doubt that under the patronage of the King and the Prince of Wales, who continued to buy tapestries after coming to the throne, and whose example was followed by the Duke of Buckingham and other members of the nobility, the works rapidly became highly prosperous. At any rate Crane himself did well out of the business, and before long the King was borrowing money from him. In 1628 he lent Charles I £7,500, as security for which the King gave him possession of the manor of Grafton in Northamptonshire; later he lent the King another £5,000, receiving grants of several more Northamptonshire manors, at one of which, Stoke Park, he built himself a mansion. At one time Crane thought of establishing a second factory in the manor house at Grafton, and training a succession of apprentices there, but this scheme seems to have been dropped.[7]

The high standard of excellence attained by the Mortlake tapestries was largely due to the skill of their designers. Crane got famous artists such as Rubens and Van Dyck to make cartoons (i.e. designs) for him; he also had a permanent designer, at a salary of £100 a year, in Francis Cleyn, or Klein, a native of Rostock in Mecklenburg, who had previously been in the service of the King of Denmark, and came to Mortlake in 1623.

In the spring of 1636 Crane, who was suffering from the stone, travelled to Paris and underwent an operation, which at first was thought to be successful, but the wound became gangrenous and on 26 June he died.[8] At the time of his death Charles I owed him some £5,800 for eight pieces of tapestry then on the looms, besides which he had previously undertaken to pay an annuity of £1,000 for three suits of gold tapestry, valued at £6,000, in addition to a subsidy of £2,000 a year for 10 years 'for the better maintenance' of the factory. The undertaking passed to Sir Francis's brother, Captain Richard Crane, but he apparently lacked the resources to keep it going. The workmen, 140 in number, petitioned the King to help them get the sum of £545 3s. 8d., which they said was owing to them from Captain Crane. It was nine months, they declared, since they had received any wages, and then only £200 between them. All the money paid by the King had been spent on buying materials.[9]

The upshot was that Crane sold the works to the King, who entered into an agreement with the five chief workmen, all Netherlanders. They undertook to produce 600 ells of tapestry yearly, and to take on either their own children or boys from the Foundling Hospital as apprentices. The King promised an annual subsidy of £2,000, while the salary of Cleyn, the artist, was to be raised to £250 a year, and he was to engage an assistant.[10] For the rest of Charles's reign the factory was at the height of its fame, but after his execution the works of art he had collected, including his tapestries, were sold. On 15 August 1649 the Council of State directed the Surveyor of Works to inspect the now disused factory and estimate the cost of repairs, 'so that it may be kept from ruin and be fit for habitation and the use of the work'. Production of tapestries was resumed after the Restoration, but later in the seventeenth century the factory had fallen into disrepair again, and it seems probable that tapestry-making did not continue after 1688.

Paper

Paper plays such an important part in modern life that it is hard to imagine a time when it did not exist. Paper was being made in southern Europe in the Middle Ages, and began to displace vellum and parchment as writing materials; some was imported into England, but in a largely illiterate age the demand must have been small. The invention of printing in the late fifteenth century created a new and expanding market for paper, but even 100 years or more later, when a quire (24 sheets) of white writing paper cost 4d. or 5d., almost the equivalent of a labourer's daily wage, it is unlikely that much was bought except by the educated and well-to-do, or by those engaged in business or administration. Besides writing paper there was (and is) a demand for brown paper as a wrapping material. The use of this must have increased with the expansion of trade, but for much of the sixteenth century England was dependent for both kinds of paper, as for many other necessary commodities, on supplies from abroad. There were a few spasmodic attempts to start the manufacture of paper in England, but none seems to have survived more than a few years. In the seventeenth century some brown paper was being made in England, but most of the white paper still had to be imported, largely from France and the Netherlands.

The first recorded attempt to make paper in England was that of John Tate, Citizen and Mercer of London, who set up a mill at Hertford towards the end of the fifteenth century. It seems to have had only a brief existence, for there is no evidence that it was at work before 1495, when it supplied paper for a book printed by Wynkyn de Worde, or after 1498, when it was visited by Henry VII. Tate died in 1507, and his will shows that the mill then contained a stock of white and other paper, and was still equipped for paper-making; but as, instead of leaving it to his son, he directed that the mill with its contents should be sold, a probable inference is that it had failed and ceased working.[11] The reason for the failure is indicated in a passage in the *Discourse of the Common Weal*, whose probable author was either William Stafford or John Hales, or possibly Sir Thomas Smith. In the second dialogue the 'Doctor' remarks that he once asked a bookbinder 'why we had no white and browne paper made within the Realme as well as they had made beyond the Sea'. The reply was that 'there was a paper made a whyle within the Realme', but the maker found that he could not make paper 'as good cheape' as imported paper, and was therefore obliged to abandon the enterprise. The reference must be to Tate and his mill, for no other paper-mill is known to have been in existence before the date of this book (c. 1549). The writer goes on to say that he wishes foreign paper were either 'staied from cumming in, or els so burdined with custome' that English paper could compete with it. As things were, foreigners bought up 'our broken linnen cloth and ragges' and resold them to us as 'paper both whit and browne'.[12]

Nothing seems to have been done to remedy this state of affairs, after the failure of John Tate's mill, until the 1550s, when according to Thomas Churchyard, the author of a poem about paper, another attempt was made by Thomas Thirlby.[13] Thirlby was the first and only bishop of Henry VIII's short-lived see of Westminster; later he became bishop of Norwich, and from 1554 to 1559 he was bishop of Ely. A paper-mill was in existence at Fen Ditton in 1557, and it seems likely that this was Thirlby's mill, as Fen Ditton was a manor belonging to the Ely bishopric. Thirlby had been employed in a diplomatic capacity in the Netherlands, and according to Churchyard he brought back with him 'a learned man, Remegius by name' (or Remigius), who no doubt possessed the necessary technical knowledge of paper-making. Like Tate's, this venture also had only a brief existence. In 1559, when the mill was leased to Corpus Christi College, Cambridge, it had already become a corn-mill.

In his Brief Lives Aubrey refers to a paper-mill at Bemerton, near Salisbury, which he implies was erected in 1569,[14] though in his Natural History of Wiltshire he makes out that its date was about 1554.[15] He says that it was the first erected in the county, and that he was told by the workmen that it was the 'second paper mill in England'. If this is correct, 1554 would seem a more appropriate date than 1569, but nothing more is known about it. Churchyard refers to yet another brief paper-making venture in the later sixteenth century. This was undertaken by Sir Thomas Gresham, on his estate at Osterley in Middlesex. According to Churchyard, Gresham built the mill before the Royal Exchange, that is, before

1566; but this is questionable, for some years later, when an Exchequer inquiry was being held, it appeared that the mill had been built between 1574 and 1576. Even Gresham could not make a success of his venture, for when Norden wrote his *Description of Middlesex* in 1593 he noticed that the mill was 'decayed'.

In 1585 the well-known London stationer and publisher Richard Tottel, or Tottyl, wrote to Burghley asking for the grant of a monopoly of paper-making for 31 years, coupled with a prohibition of the export of rags. In his petition Tottel stated that 'almost 12 years' previously he and other members of the Stationers' Company, seeing 'the want and dearth of good paper in this Realme, and also the disceite that is used Dailye in makinge thereof', had agreed to 'bestowe some labour and cost for the ereccion of a paper mill' in England. But his 'companions in this travaile', reflecting that two or three previous attempts to establish the manufacture of paper had been failures, and fearing that 'it wolde so fall out in this our attempte', had 'thought good to surcease and not goe forwardes therein'.[16] What exactly Tottel meant by 'deceit' in the manufacture of paper is not clear. Apparently some paper was being made in England, but not enough to meet the demand; probably what was made was not as good as its makers pretended. Tottel was more hopeful of success, by trying to discover the weak points in his predecessors' plans and guarding against them beforehand. The government, however, was disinclined to grant Tottel the privileges he sought. Arguments were adduced against the grant of monopolies to private persons, and it was pointed out that previous monopolies, such as those granted to Mountjoy for alum or Remigius for paper, had failed, though it was suggested that the same objections would not apply to a monopoly held by a corporate body.[17] Tottel had asked for 'a conveyent plott for the ereccion of this mill', but his petition met with no response, and his project never got beyond the planning stage.

The main reasons why such of these early ventures as were launched soon afterwards broke down are clear enough. They simply were not economic, nor could they procure an adequate supply of linen rags. In his petition to Burghley Tottel complained that French manufacturers tried to impede the making of paper in England by buying up all the English rags,[18] and early paper-making entrepreneurs were obliged to ask for an embargo on the export of rags as well as a manufacturing monopoly. Even so the supply was apt to be insufficient, owing to the widespread use of wool in the six-teenth century, and the absence of a native linen industry of any size.

Paper-making required special apparatus and skilled labour, which in the early days had to be foreign. This meant that it could only be carried on in a mill or factory; it could not operate, like cloth-making, on the domestic or putting-out system. It also needed abundant clear water, so that the mill must be on the banks of a suitable river. Dependence on a supply of rags further restricted the location of the mill, and meant that in practice it must be near a town, and preferably not too far from London, where rags were most plentiful. While paper-making was thus essentially a factory process, it did not involve an outlay of capital on anything like the scale of alum-making, or the extractive industries for coal or metals. A building was needed to house the plant and work-people, but a Tudor or early Stuart paper-mill was generally quite a small affair. An existing corn-mill or fulling-mill might be adap-ted for the purpose, and revert to its old use when the paper-making venture ceased. Such a venture might be within the capacity of an individual entrepreneur, or of a small partnership: there was no need to raise large sums or float a joint-stock company. The mill might be rented, perhaps for £25 a year or less; in some cases the tenant would undertake the costs of conversion and maintenance, but sometimes they might be borne by an enterprising landlord, who could then charge a higher rent by way of return on the capital he had invested.[19]

What appears to have been the most successful, or at any rate the most lasting, of these early paper-making enterprises was started in 1588 by a German from Lindau on Lake Constance, named John Spilman, or Spielmann; it also became the best-known, through being made the centrepiece of Churchyard's poem. Spilman held an appointment as goldsmith or jeweller to the Queen, an office which he retained under James 1. No doubt he made money by execut-ing orders for the Court, but also, like other goldsmiths, he had opportunities for money-lending and financial deals, as well as carrying on a trade in gold and precious stones. He thus had resources at his disposal, and was willing to risk some of them in a paper-making project. As a German immigrant he may have been in a position to arrange for the introduction of the skilled workmen needed to launch the enterprise, but there is no reason to suppose that he personally possessed any technical expertise. His role was that of the entrepreneur who organized and financed the venture, and used his position at Court to secure the privileges without which it could not succeed.

In 1588 he obtained from the Crown a lease of two existing mills on the River Darenth, in the royal manor of Bignours, or Bignores, near Dartford in Kent.[20] The mills, or buildings attached to them, had previously been an ironworks; the repairs or alterations necessary to adapt them for paper-making cost Spilman some £1,400 or £1,500, but in consideration of this outlay the rent to the Crown, which had been £10, was reduced to £4 per annum. He was then granted a monopoly for 10 years, covering both the manufacture of paper and the collection of rags and other materials. The objective of the enterprise was stated to be the manufacture of 'whyte writing paper', and the patent prohibited the use of existing mills as well as the erection of new ones by anybody other than the patentee. Existing mills were presumably making brown paper, in which Spilman was not interested, but he was anxious to prevent them attempting to make white paper, and a warrant he obtained in October 1588, ordering Justices of the Peace 'to make stay of all High Germans' working for him,[21] suggests that the owners of other mills were trying to entice his workmen to leave him and work for them instead.

Churchyard's doggerel verses have neither merit as poetry nor technical value as a description of the processes of manufacture, but a couple of stanzas may be quoted, to show the impression the mill made on an unsophisticated visitor.

> The mill itself is sure right rare to see,
>> The framing is so queint and finely done
> Built all of wood, and hollowe trunkes of tree,
>> That makes the streames at point device to runne,
> Nowe up, nowe downe, now sideward by a sleight,
> Nowe forward fast, then spouting up on height,
> As conduits colde could force so great a heate
> That fire should flame where thumping hammers beat.

> The hammers thump, and make as lowde a noise
>> As fuller doth that beates his wollen cloth,

In open shewe, then sundry secrete toyes,
  Make rotten ragges to yealde a thickened froth:
Then is it stampt, and washed as white as snowe,
The flong on frame, and hang'd to dry, I trow:
Thus paper streight it is, to write upon,
As it were rubde and smoothde with slicking-stone.

In an earlier stanza Churchyard declares that

Six hundred men are set at worke by him
  That else might starve, or seeke abroad their bread.

This figure may well be an exaggeration, and even if it is accurate it need not necessarily mean that they all worked at the mill. It might include people employed in collecting rags, washing and sorting them, and so on.

Notwithstanding his patent, within a few years Spilman found that his monopoly was being threatened, and he sought protection from the Privy Council, which issued a 'warrant to all public officers', enjoining them to assist in the enforcing of the patent. 'Divers and sundry persons', it was stated, had not only gathered and bought up linen rags and other materials and 'converted yt to the makeing of browne paper, whereas yt would have made good wrightinge paper, but have erected divers milles for the makeinge of paper', so that materials had become scarce.[22] John Turner, Edward Marshall and George Frend, it appeared, had set up a paper-mill in Buckinghamshire and collected rags in defiance of Spilman's privilege; he had obtained a warrant from the county magistrates, summoning the offenders and ordering them to cease making paper, but they had 'with unseemly gesture and words contemptuously declined to obey'. As a result Spilman was 'forced to make brown paper, when otherwise he would make wryting paper', and so got 'smale benefit of her Majestie's graunt'. There may have been other reasons why he had not succeeded as well as he had hoped in the manufacture of white paper. To make writing paper of good quality, better materials and more skill were required than to make coarse brown paper; certainly some of the materials mentioned in his patent (not only 'all manner of lynnen ragges' but also 'Scrolles or Scrappes of parchment peeces of lyme leather shredds and clyppings of Cardes and old fyshing nettes') hardly suggest a high-grade paper.

Be that as it may, in July 1597 Spilman obtained fresh letters patent for 14 years, covering all sorts of paper besides white paper, and it seems that his competitors later came to terms, and made paper under licence from him. All did not go smoothly, however, for in 1601 Edward Marshall, together with a man named Robert Style, both of whom appear to have had paper-mills, brought an action in Chancery against Spilman, the outcome being that Style was obliged to surrender his licence and cease making paper, but Marshall was allowed to continue, on condition that he bought his rags and other stuff from Spilman. Spilman's new patent gave him more extensive powers to monopolize the collection of materials for paper-making. Customs officers were to stop the export of rags, and authority was given to search in all sorts of places, including outgoing ships. These powers soon brought Spilman into conflict with the City of London, which was jealous of its own jurisdiction, and tried to prevent him exercising his powers of search. Once more he invoked the assistance of the Privy Council.

On 21 May 1601 the Council wrote to the Lord Mayor and aldermen, pointing out that Spilman was protected by letters patent and that they must not hinder but help him. In reply they declared that 'he began to offer wrong to the charters of this city, by authorizing great numbers of poor people, especially girls and vagrant women, to collect rags within the city and liberties, who, under pretence of that service, ranged abroad in every street, begging at men's doors'. The result was trouble and disorder, 'the said poor people sometimes assaying to steal small things from houses and stalls'. The Common Council thought it 'more convenient for the city in the gathering of such refuse stuff to employ our own poor, otherwise idle', and had therefore forbidden such collecting except by persons licensed by the Governors of Bridewell. They went on to point out that Spilman had no grounds for his contention that he had always enjoyed his privilege without hindrance. There had been other paper-mills, at Osterley, Cambridge, in Worcestershire and elsewhere, but they agreed not to hinder Spilman in the exercise of his powers provided he did so outside the city and its liberties.[23]

Just now, when a campaign against monopolies was coming to a head in the House of Commons, was hardly the best moment for enforcing respect for such privileges, and knowledge of popular sentiment on the subject may have encouraged

Q

the resistance of the city authorities. But although the Queen promised to withdraw the more objectionable monopolies, Spilman's does not seem to have been affected. He was knighted in 1605 by James I, when the King visited his mill, and in the same year he received a grant in fee farm of the manor of Bicknores, in which his mill was situated: in other words, instead of holding it on a lease he now had the freehold. He also remained in business as jeweller and goldsmith until his death in 1626, and in 1617 he obtained a patent for making 'a new and more pleasant kind of playing cards'. There seems to be no direct evidence whether the paper-mill was a paying concern. He may have maintained it out of the proceeds of his other businesses, but the fact that one of his sons succeeded him at the mill and kept it going until he died, in 1641, suggests that it was not actually losing money. Such profits as it made, however, probably came from the manufacture of brown rather than white paper. There were paper-mills elsewhere in the seventeenth century, such as one at Cannock Chase in Staffordshire, and in 1638 a mill 'called Lowd Water Mill, new built', near High Wycombe, was let for £50. Aubrey tells us that he remembered a paper-mill at Yatton Keynell in Wiltshire, built in 1635 by a Bristol merchant named Wyld, and he adds: 'It serves Bristow with brown paper. There is no white paper made in Wiltshire.'[24] He also refers to 'coarse paper, commonly called whitebrowne paper', which he says was first made in England in James I's reign. Genuine white paper may have been made occasionally here and there, but it is unlikely to have been of good quality; practically all the paper for writing and printing still had to be imported. It was not until late in the seventeenth century that, partly through improved technique, England began to produce white paper in significant amounts.

Pins

Pin-making was another industry which, like the manufacture of paper, became the subject of a monopoly, and attracted capital from entrepreneurs.[25] Some pins were made in England, by small masters organized in the Pinners' Company, but as with numerous other commodities in daily use England relied largely on supplies from abroad. In an attempt to foster English manufacture, legislation had been enacted in Edward IV's reign to prohibit the importation of pins, but the supply of English pins was quite insufficient to meet the demand. In any case the pinners were incapable of enforcing the prohibition, and as consumers favoured free trade in pins, all through the sixteenth century they continued to be imported in large quantities from Holland. Meanwhile the pinners were absorbed by the Girdlers' Company, and in the early seventeenth century, feeling that their interests were inadequately protected, they were anxious to regain their independence. Lacking the resources to pay for a new charter of incorporation for themselves, they obtained one through the influence of a courtier, and in 1605 were incorporated as the Pinmakers' Company, promising in return to pay him a levy for the next 40 years of 4d. on every 12,000 pins they made.

Meanwhile their cause was taken up by Sir Thomas Bartlett, 'carver in ordinary' to the Queen, who had amassed a fortune of £40,000 and was looking for an investment for his money. He brought an action against an English merchant named Ellis, who had imported pins, and this led to a protracted dispute in which the pinmakers and their friends at Court were ranged against the consumers' interests, represented by the Haberdashers' Company and the City of London, together with the Dutch exporters. The pinmakers declared that Dutch pins were being dumped in England at a price kept artificially low by subsidies and the use of pauper labour, with the deliberate intention of destroying the English industry, which, they alleged, provided employment for '20,000 impotent people, some even without legs'. The merchants in reply argued that English makers could supply only a third of the demand, so that importation of pins was unavoidable; moreover, if Dutch pins were excluded the result would be retaliation in Holland and a corresponding fall in exports from England. If the facts were as stated by both sides, a fair solution would have been a compromise, whereby the market would be shared between English and foreign pins, and in 1608 the Privy Council promoted a temporary settlement on these lines. The importation of foreign pins was to be allowed, at a duty of 6d. per 12,000, while the pin merchants agreed to find a market for the English pins.

This arrangement, however, satisfied neither the pinmakers, who wanted to build up their trade and create a monopoly, nor Sir Thomas Bartlett, who was prepared to back them financially, with the expectation of a handsome profit for himself. At the end of 1614 he wrote to Sir Ralph Winwood, one of the secretaries of state, offering him £4,000 as an inducement to use his influence to obtain a royal grant, incorporating the pinmakers as a joint-stock company in which he could invest his capital: he then reopened the previous dispute by launching a fresh prosecution against Ellis. In April 1616 the Privy Council again tried to effect a compromise settlement: both importation and domestic manufacture were to continue, and the merchants were to take the whole output of English pins as long as they were of satisfactory pattern and material and were sold at a price comparable to that of imported pins, while any disputes were to be referred to a panel composed of two Haberdashers appointed by the merchants and two Girdlers appointed by the pinmakers. Within a few months the pinmakers were complaining that the Haberdashers had not fulfilled their part of the agreement, and the Privy Council had to admit that the settlement had broken down again. Sir Thomas Bartlett then renewed his efforts to secure a monopoly in the interests of himself and the pinmakers, undertaking to supply them with wire and to take their whole output at an agreed rate.

This was only one part of his plans, however; to complete the monopoly he must also be able to control the importation of foreign pins. They could not be excluded entirely because of the pinmakers' admitted inability to make enough to meet the whole demand, so he aimed instead at getting into his hands the sole right of importation. In March 1618 he succeeded in obtaining a grant of this privilege, but the merchants and other interested parties maintained a determined opposition, and in October the monopoly was restricted to London and its suburbs, with a proviso that the pinmakers were not to raise the price of English pins above its level two years previously. In practice this limited monopoly proved impossible to maintain. Sir Thomas could not prevent the traders importing pins, and although he was successful in an action against them for infringing his patent, the government felt obliged, in the interests of good commercial relations with Holland, to forbid execution of the judgment. The effect was that the pinmakers, faced with unrestricted competition, were unable to fulfil their part of the bargain, and in the effort to uphold his privileges Sir Thomas found himself involved in a contest with the government. The government proved the stronger party, and finally Sir Thomas was committed to the Tower, and soon afterwards died.

The monopoly remained in abeyance for a few years, but about 1630, as we saw in an earlier chapter, the Mineral and Battery company leased its calamine and brass works to James Lydsey.[26] As Lydsey had interests in the pin trade, the company hoped that the market for brass wire would be enlarged, while Lydsey no doubt saw advantages in securing control of the production as well as of the sale of wire. Lydsey also undertook, on behalf of Bartlett's heirs, to try to recover some of the money he had sunk in the pin-making business, and in 1635 he took steps to obtain for himself an even wider monopoly than Bartlett's. Charles I's government at this time was increasingly dependent on the grant of monopolies, along with other unpopular methods of raising revenue, and renewed the pin-makers' charter in return for an undertaking by Lydsey to pay an annual rent of £500. In spite of complaints from the pinmakers that the wire supplied by Lydsey was both poor in quality and dear in price, Lydsey pressed on with his plans. Bartlett had aimed at controlling the importation of foreign pins, but he had not tried to prevent the pinmakers using foreign wire. Lydsey, on 19 August 1638, obtained a proclamation prohibiting the importation of brass wire, raised the price of wire produced at his works from £6 to £8 a cwt, and extracted from the pinmakers an agreement to buy 200 tons annually of his brass wire.

He was not left very long in enjoyment of this commanding position. He became involved in a lawsuit with Bartlett's heirs, who charged him with a breach of trust; the pinmakers also brought proceedings against him, and were supported by the Merchant Adventurers. Lydsey stood to lose the £7,000 which he claimed to have invested in the enterprise, and in these circumstances it was decided that the King himself should intervene as an entrepreneur. Lydsey had tried to benefit from two monopolies which were really conflicting, but though he had failed the King might succeed. As Professor Unwin put it: 'The possibility of maintaining a steady market for unsatisfactory English wire was dependent on the possibility of guaranteeing a regular demand for unsatisfactory English pins. It seemed a natural inference from this that the King, who alone had the power to exclude competition in each of these industries, should assume the function of regulating their mutual relations, and, in return for the protection thus afforded, should enjoy some of the profit due to the middleman and entrepreneur'.[27]

Sir Thomas Bartlett had had a fortune to sink in the business, but the King was in financial straits, and in any case he had no intention of personally carrying out the responsibilities of an entrepreneur. In the usual fashion of the time, these were to be farmed, by a capitalist named Lawrence Halstead. The terms agreed on were that the Pinmakers' Company should be provided with a hall, and Halstead, as the King's agent, should put up £10,000 on their behalf. The King undertook to supply the pinmakers with 'merchantable' wire at £8 a cwt, and covenanted with Lydsey to take so much of his wire, at £6 13s. a cwt, as should be required to supply the needs of the kingdom. The pinmakers, for their part, were to be obliged to use only the wire supplied by the King, unless they received permission from the King's agent. Should imported wire be seized and supplied to the pinmakers, Lydsey was to have 10s. a cwt in compensation. Besides the capital outlay, Halstead was to defray the costs of management and pay £1,000 a year to the Exchequer. He was to be allowed a dividend of eight per cent on his capital; out of any remaining profits Lydsey's £7,000 was to be repaid, with interest, and if any money were still left over it was to go to the King.

Owing to the outbreak of the Civil War the financial soundness of this arrangement was never tested, but a similar arrangement with Charles II after the Restoration encountered difficulties and opposition. On the face of it the scheme sacrificed the interests not only of the consumers but also of the producers—the craftsmen and workers in the industry—to the capitalist entrepreneur; and even he was as likely to lose money as to make it. Some monopolies may have helped nascent industries to find their feet, but this kind of monopoly benefited nobody except possibly the King, and even he lost much good will by it.

Gold and silver thread

Pin-making was by no means the only trade in which the King acted, directly or indirectly, as entrepreneur; we have already seen, for example, how James I took over the alum monopoly. In 1628 Charles I granted a charter to the playing-card makers, and in 1637, by way of protecting them against foreign competition, he agreed to buy from them 'a constant weekly proportion of good cards', at specified rates, while they in return would allow him 36s. on every gross of cards made and sold in the kingdom. This, it was estimated, would provide the Crown in perpetuity with an annual revenue of £5,000 or £6,000.[28] Another example of a monopoly in which the Crown took part, and which ended in disaster, was the manufacture of gold and silver thread.[29] The process consisted of winding fine strips of silver gilt round a core of silk thread, and was introduced into England in the reign of Queen Elizabeth. Later, when a monopoly had been established, Lady Bedford drew £1,000 a year from the patentees on the strength of her contention that it had first been made by a Frenchwoman whom she had brought over to England. However introduced, the process was taken up by English embroiderers and silkworkers, who presently began to desire protection against imports from abroad. In 1611 a body of silkmen submitted a petition to the King for a charter of incorporation, so that they might be enabled to check 'falsity' in the dyeing of silk and in the working of gold and silver thread. Under pressure from Lady Bedford and Lord Harrington, however, James granted a monopoly of the production and distribution of gold and silver thread to four patentees, Matthias Fowle, Richard Dike, Humphrey Phipps and John Dade. The silkmen, backed by the goldsmiths, protested that the process was not a new invention but part of their own established 'mystery', and it was in fact difficult, if not impossible, to distinguish the thread made by the patentees from thread made by interlopers, or to prevent the smuggling of thread from abroad. Though they were imprisoned and had their tools confiscated, interlopers defied the patentees, and went on practising their trade. In 1616 the situation came before the Privy Council, which had doubts about the validity of the patent; but Sir Edward Villiers, brother of the royal favourite, Buckingham, invested £4,000 in the undertaking, and then after long deliberation new letters patent, granting exclusive privileges, were issued to Fowle and Dike, together with a man named Francis Dorrington.

The silkmen and goldsmiths persisted in their opposition, and the upshot of more arrests, protests, and petitions to the Council was that in 1618 the patentees surrendered their privileges, and it was decided that the process should be taken over by the King. Actually it was farmed by one of the original monopolists, Matthias Fowle; meanwhile Sir Edward Villiers was granted an annuity of £500 (representing a return of over 12 per cent on his investment of £4,000), and his brother Christopher, who had also taken an interest in the business, got even more (£800 a year). Offences against the patent were to be investigated by a high-powered commission, among whose members were the Lord Chancellor, the Lord Treasurer, the Secretaries of State, the Lord Chief Justice and the Attorney-General. The goldsmiths and silkmen were required to sign bonds undertaking not to sell their materials to anyone but the owner of the monopoly, but despite continued arrests they maintained their resistance. The interlopers engaged a solicitor named Henry Wood, who by bringing to bear the influence of the Goldsmiths' Company secured their release, and illicit production was organized on such a scale that Fowle and Villiers were faced with ruin. In 1618 Fowle sent the King a detailed account of the interlopers' misdeeds, and Bacon was asked to investigate. Wood was examined and given a warning, and a few women workers were arrested; then, as the monopoly still seemed insecure, Sir Giles Mompesson and Sir Francis Michell were added to the commission.

Mompesson, who had married Sir Edward Villier's sister-in-law, had risen rapidly in the entourage of the Court; among other appointments he held the patent for the licensing of alehouses and inns, and together with Michell had the reputation of a ruthless and unscrupulous 'projector'. When he joined the commission, renewed and more energetic action against the interlopers was to be expected, and he is reported to have threatened that 'thousands should rot in prison' if they failed to enter into substantial bonds not to practise any branch of the gold and silver thread business. But though their solicitor Wood was persuaded to desert the interlopers' cause, resistance continued. When six leading mercers were committed to the Fleet prison there was indignation in the City, and four aldermen offered to stand bail in the sum of £100,000. The King gave way and released the mercers, but he confirmed the monopoly. Next year, however, a different note was sounded, and it was admitted that the monopoly product was inferior to thread imported from Venice and Cologne.

Richard Dike (one of the original patentees) then obtained a licence, together with Sir Nicholas Salter, to import gold and silver thread, and in return for this favour the licensees agreed to pay Michell an annuity of £100 for five years. In the face of the open importation of superior gold thread, and continued illicit production at home, it proved impossible to sustain the monopoly, and in April 1620 it had to be abandoned. The King then granted the right to all the profits from importing, producing, and sealing gold and silver thread to Dike, Salter, and a man named William Bennett, for an annual rent of £200. Meanwhile the Merchant Adventurers' company, which had been restored after the collapse of the Cockayne project, wished to participate in the trade, and obtained the right to import, on payment of 6s. 8d. on every paper of thread imported by them. They pressed, however, for the complete removal of all restrictions on the importation of thread, and when Parliament met in January 1621 the long pent-up indignation against monopolists could no longer be resisted. Mompesson was impeached, but escaped to France; Michell, together with Dike and Fowle, was imprisoned and fined, and both the manufacture and importation of gold and silver thread became open to private enterprise. Mompesson was sentenced in absence to degradation from the order of knighthood, forfeiture of his property, and a fine of £10,000, besides disqualification from holding any office under the King, and other penalties and disabilities. Although Parliament ordered 'that he be ever held an infamous person', and that 26 March should always be observed as a holiday to commemorate the country's deliverance from his oppressions, Mompesson was allowed to return to England in 1623, and spent his remaining years in retirement in Wiltshire, apparently as a reformed character.

Mompesson and Michell were really secondary figures in comparison with men like Buckingham and his brothers, but the revival of the process of impeachment put into the hands of Parliament a weapon which acquired far-reaching political significance. Much of the ill-feeling against Bacon, whose impeachment soon followed, was due to the favour he had shown to monopolists; before long an impeachment, albeit an abortive one, was to be directed against Buckingham himself, and thereafter impeachment was regularly used to destroy a whole series of royal advisers. Not all monopolists were entrepreneurs, nor were all entrepreneurs monopolists, but in the early seventeenth century there were powerful forces tending to make industrial and commercial enterprise conform with this pattern. Some industries lent themselves more readily than others to the intervention of the monopolist entrepreneur; others survived, in spite of rather than because of their subjection to monopoly control. And there were some which could never be made viable, despite all the money poured into them, and all the resources marshalled in their defence.

Leather

An instructive contrast to these monopolies is presented by the manufacture of leather.[30] Leather had a great variety of uses in the sixteenth and seventeenth centuries, as indeed it had had in the past, for boots and shoes and gloves, for breeches and belts and other articles of clothing, as well as for saddles, reins, collars, and all manner of trappings for horses. Buckets were often made of leather, as were the bellows used for industrial as well as domestic purposes. The English leather industry was second only to cloth, and outdistanced the metal industries in the number of workpeople employed in it. It escaped the attention of the monopolist entrepreneur, and consequently its history had been relatively neglected.

Two processes were involved in the conversion of hides into leather: 'tanning', to produce heavy, stout leather, and 'dressing', for the lighter kinds used for gloves and clothing. Tanning was usually done with oak-bark, and hence tanneries were often to be found in woodland areas, alongside the iron industry, or in London, where the consumption of meat provided a ready supply of hides; but wherever they were, they seem generally to have been quite small. Occasionally we hear of a tanner who operated on a more ambitious scale: such was John Neall, of Horncastle in Lincolnshire, who had nearly £800 invested in his business and when he died, in 1567, left property worth over £1,300. Another tanner, John Tatam, who was three times mayor of Leicester towards the end of the sixteenth century, was probably a capitalist on a similar scale, but such men seem to have been exceptional. In the light leather industry, in which the skins were 'dressed' with oil or alum, capitalism made its appearance in a form similar to that of the clothiers in the textile industry. Besides the glovers who carried on their trade as master craftsmen, there were leather merchants who were also employers, supplying materials to working artisans on the putting-out system; but none seems to have attained an outstanding position.

12 | Draining the fens

The Dovegang lead mine[1] was only a small item among Cornelius Vermuyden's numerous and varied enterprises, and his principal claim to be remembered rests on his achievements in draining the Fens. Some reclamation of marshland and fen, principally near the coast, had been accomplished in the Middle Ages by the erection of embankments to keep out the sea, but the fens farther inland presented a more difficult problem. Here the land was swamped by the overflowing of the sluggish meandering rivers, the outfalls of which became choked with silt, and it was not until the seventeenth century that the reclamation of these areas was achieved.

In 1563 the Italian Protestant Acontius (Giacopo Aconcio), who had taken refuge in England and been granted an annuity of £60 by the Queen, undertook to drain the Erith and Plumstead marshes, on the Thames estuary below Greenwich, in return for half the reclaimed land, and eventually some 2,000 acres there were recovered and enclosed.[2] Projects like this, however, were no more than continuations of what had been begun in earlier times, and in contrast with both previous and subsequent periods land reclamation in the sixteenth century seems to have been on a relatively small scale. Several reasons have been suggested for this. It may be, for instance, that expanding trade, or the new manufacturing and mining industries, seemed more attractive investments for capital. Questions of drainage were the concern of the Commissioners of Sewers, usually local landowners, whose duty it was to maintain existing embankments and keep watercourses clear; but they often neglected these tasks, until forced to take action when flooding led to complaints or orders from the courts. New undertakings were generally beyond the means of individual landlords, the impoverished government had no money to spare, and it was hard to secure agreement to undertake concerted schemes.

Another obstacle to action in many places was the existence of rights of common over much of the land offering the most scope for improvement. By the medieval Statute of Merton, re-enacted in 1549, lords of the manor were entitled to enclose for their own purposes parts of the common or waste land, provided that they left enough for the use of the commoners. To reclaim a whole area, however, legally required agreement with the commoners, and in fenland districts agreement was often hard to secure. Many of the poorer inhabitants lived by fishing and wildfowling in the flooded marshes, and resisted suggestions that they should change their way of life, and accept an allotment of reclaimed land, on which they would have to labour, and which might be insufficient for a living, in exchange for their customary rights over the unreclaimed waste. In later years landowners sometimes entered into contracts for reclamation without previous agreement with the commoners, but this was apt to lead to trouble.

About the middle of Elizabeth I's reign there seems to have been more widespread interest in fen reclamation. In 1576 the Queen granted powers to Sir Thomas Cecil and a group of associates to undertake a drainage project in the Fens, towards the cost of which the inhabitants of towns and villages in the neighbourhood were to contribute. A survey was made of the ground, but nothing effective seems to have been carried out.[3] In 1585 a General Drainage Bill for the Fens, to facilitate procedure, was introduced in the Commons, but it encountered objections, and did not finally become law until 1600.[4] Meanwhile, in 1593 a man of English descent who lived at Bergen-op-Zoom, named Humphrey Bradley, submitted to Burghley a grand scheme for draining the fens in all the eastern counties. He estimated that 700 or 800 labourers could finish the job in six months for an outlay of only £5,000, and that the revenue would benefit by some £40,000 a year. If neither Burghley nor the Queen were in favour of the scheme, he could name 'certain gentlemen of wealth' who were prepared to undertake it. Burghley had more sense than to be taken in by Bradley's absurd figures, and his proposal was not accepted.[5]

Though comparatively little progress was made in the sixteenth century, in the seventeenth land reclamation began to be undertaken more energetically. Monetary inflation was putting increasing pressure on landowners to raise the rentals on their estates, and an

obvious way to achieve this was by the improvement or reclamation of waste land. At the same time London business men were
looking out for ways to invest their capital, and some were willing
to speculate in drainage schemes. The type of arrangement envisaged in the Drainage Act was that in return for 'draining and keeping perpetually dry' an area of fen, entrepreneurs should receive
an agreed proportion, usually a third, of the reclaimed land, whose
value would be increased sufficiently to make the enterprise a profitable investment.

Surveys were made accordingly, and a number of projects were
suggested, yet for some years little was actually accomplished.
There were disputes over such questions as whether the Commissioners of Sewers had powers to cut new drains besides maintaining
existing ones, and even if agreement had been reached on a project,
local opposition often prevented its being carried out. In these
circumstances little could be effected until the Crown used its
influence to enforce the execution of a major scheme.

Towards the end of Elizabeth's reign the local Commissioners of
Sewers gave their approval to the suggestion of Thomas Lovell, 'a
man skilful in like works, wherein he had been beyond the seas
much used and imployed', to drain Deeping Fen, near Spalding. In
return for a grant of a third of the reclaimed land he undertook
to drain the fen at his own expense, and to complete the work in
five years. He set to work, but later complained that though he had
spent his whole estate, to the value of some £12,000, he could not
obtain possession of his third share because of disputes 'wilfully stir-
red' about the boundaries of the land. Inquiries and conferences were
held, but in the end it seems that Lovell had to abandon the project.[6]

This sort of experience was hardly encouraging to enterprising individuals, and projects promoted by groups of London capitalists also ended in failure. In 1605 Sir John Popham, the Lord Chief
Justice, headed a syndicate which embarked on an ambitious
scheme to reclaim some 300,000 acres of land peculiarly liable to
flooding, about Upwell on the River Nene. As compensation they
were to receive 130,000 acres 'to be taken out of the worst sort of
every fen proportionably', and inhabitants who did not actually
surrender land were to be rated by the Commissioners of Sewers
for money contributions towards the cost of the scheme. An anony-
mous writer warned the King that 'covetous bloody Popham' would

ruin many poor men,[7] but in fact he and his partners did not
achieve much. A watercourse running into the Ouse, called
'Popham's Eau', marks the scene of their operations, but they had
started work without sufficient practical knowledge or experience
of the problems to be faced. Popham, who was about 75 when he
undertook this project, died in 1607; the undertakers then abandoned their original plan and transferred their efforts to improving
the outfall of the Nene at Wisbech.[8] This was a sensible move,
although by itself it was relatively ineffectual.

The celebrated financier Alderman Cockayne was one of those
who became interested in fen-draining about this time, and he
joined with several other Londoners in a smaller scheme to drain
some 3,000 acres near Upwell, in agreement with the inhabitants.
Cockayne's undertaking was apparently completed, but after a few
years the waters broke in again and the area reverted to fen, until
it was once more reclaimed, along with other parts of the Great
Level, by the Earl of Bedford.[9] Other groups of Londoners were
also engaged about this time in similar schemes in various parts
of the Fens, but although a number of projects were put forward,
owing to disputes and opposition, as well as natural difficulties, for
some years little progress was made. Among applications submitted in 1606, but rejected, perhaps because Popham had more
influence, was one from two men, Cornelius Liens and Cornelius
Verneuil, referred to as 'the French contractors'. Verneuil, of
whom nothing seems to be known, may have been a Frenchman,
but Liens was a Netherlander, from the same town (St Maartensdijk
in Zeeland) as Vermuyden. Liens was probably backed by a group
of associates in Zeeland, in a combined undertaking such as had
long been common in land reclamation in the Netherlands. The
scheme came to nothing, and Vermuyden was then only 16, but
what he heard of Liens's plans may perhaps have helped to engage
his own interests later on in English projects.[10]

On his journey south at his accession James I had been met near
Stamford by a company of fenmen on stilts, and he took a lively
personal interest in drainage schemes.[11] Financial stringency necessitated the sale of much Crown land, but surveys of what was
retained suggested that the King's income could be increased
considerably if the marshes and waste land on royal property were
reclaimed and made agriculturally more productive.[12] In view of

the failure of earlier schemes, and continued opposition to new ones, for some years little more was done to reclaim the Fens, and in course of time it came to be realized that in such a large area as the Great Level digging drains or ditches here and there was useless: to achieve success there must be a comprehensive plan for the whole region. An important step in the right direction was taken in 1618, when the Commissioners of Sewers for all the Fenland counties agreed on the necessity first of all to improve the outfalls of the chief rivers, the Ouse, Nene and Welland.

In the following year Sir William Ayloffe and Anthony Thomas, after inspecting the area, asked the Privy Council to grant them powers to undertake to drain it, which they said they could do in three years; but although the King supported them the Council hesitated to do so until it had fuller details of their plans, which quite possibly they had not worked out. The Bishop of Peterborough and other local personages were hostile, and by November 1620, when nothing had been settled, the projectors were complaining that they had spent £2,400 and ridden 10,000 miles in vain.[13] In February 1621 James declared that he himself would be the undertaker, taking in compensation 120,000 acres of the land to be reclaimed, for he would not 'any longer suffer these countries to be abandoned to the will of the waters'. Again nothing was actually done, for however good the King's intentions he lacked the resources to implement them.[14]

It was in this year that Vermuyden came to England. At whose invitation he came seems to be uncertain, but it is possible that he, or Dutch associates of his, had been in negotiation with the King for the use of Dutch resources. For the time being no more progress was made in the Fens, but Vermuyden obtained a contract to repair a breach which had recently occurred in the bank of the Thames at Dagenham in Essex. This was his first engagement in this country, and he does not seem to have been altogether successful in carrying it out. At any rate the local Commissioners of Sewers were dissatisfied, and complained that 'by his delays and the want of durability in the work he has accomplished the land is in worse condition than it was before'.[15] It also appeared that he had failed to pay his workmen their wages, while the men employed by another contractor, named John Foster, who was also engaged in repairing embankments at Dagenham, were similarly unpaid. They alleged that Foster had had to abandon his part of the work 'owing to the decay of Mr. Vermuyden's portion'; Vermuyden for his part complained that while his contract was for £2,000 he had received nothing from the Commissioners, though he had actually spent £3,600, and he would gladly pay his workmen when the Commissioners paid him.[16]

These recriminations may have been partly due to jealousy of a foreigner, but it looks as if Vermuyden had underestimated the extent and the difficulty of the undertaking. The King, however, did not lose confidence in him, and not only employed him on the (admittedly minor) task of draining some land in Windsor Great Park, but confirmed the grant of certain lands at Dagenham to him as a reward for what he had done there. Through Crown favour Vermuyden also obtained his first major engagement, the reclamation of Hatfield Chase, where there were some 70,000 acres of swamp and marsh, on the borders of Lincolnshire and Yorkshire. Possibly beginning to despair of achieving anything in the Great Level of the Fens, James may have decided that there would be better prospects of success if a start were made on a rather smaller scheme. A further advantage lay in the fact that the land was Crown property, and in Hatfield Chase itself there were no common rights to be considered.

In 1622 the King appointed a group of landowners in the neighbourhood as commissioners to investigate conditions there. They told him that he was being 'encroached upon' by tenants who had usurped various rights and privileges; they also stated that in their opinion, 'considering how great the Levels were, and how continually deep with water, how many rivers run thereunto, and such like, they did humbly conceive that it was impossible to drain and improve them'.[17] James, however, refused to be discouraged by this report, which may well have reflected the commissioners' own unwillingness to lose their current opportunities of illicit hunting, and he sent Vermuyden to make an independent investigation. Vermuyden had no doubts about the feasibility of draining the marshes, and was prepared to organize a syndicate of his fellow-countrymen to undertake the work.

James I died in March 1625, but Vermuyden had a friend at Court in the Attorney-General, Sir Robert Heath, who was ready to support a project likely to improve the King's revenue. Charles I proceeded with his father's plan, and on 26 May 1626 concluded an agreement with Vermuyden for the drainage of Hatfield Chase and the neighbouring 'surrounded (i.e. flooded) grounds'. Vermuyden was the principal entrepreneur, and was to direct the work, but most of the capital was subscribed in the Netherlands. Altogether there were 35 Dutch participants, entitled to share in the proceeds of the enterprise: one of them, Philibert Vernatti, was later to become a close associate of Vermuyden's in his work in the Great Level. One third of the reclaimed land, estimated to amount to 24,405 acres, was to be distributed among the participants, Vermuyden himself taking 4,554 acres. Another third was to be divided among the tenants, and the remaining third was reserved for the Crown.

With the aid of a number of foreign workmen whom Vermuyden brought in, Walloons and French Huguenots as well as Dutch,[18] the work of reclamation went rapidly ahead, and within not much more than a year he declared it to be complete, and asked that commissioners should be appointed to survey the ground and allot their portions to the various claimants. When the commissioners began doing so, however, in the course of 1628, they soon found evidence of strong local dissatisfaction with Vermuyden's proceedings, and it seems clear that he had made two serious mistakes.[19] It was true that the Crown's tenants in Hatfield Chase had no legal rights of common, except that of cutting turf, but in adjacent areas included in the project, such as the manor of Epworth (John Wesley's birthplace) in the Isle of Axholme, there were commoners with a definite legal status. Their agreement was necessary before the Crown could assign or allot the common land, but possibly unaware, or even reckless, of the trouble this would cause, Vermuyden had started work without having secured the commoners' consent. The result was concerted obstruction, backed by some of the landowners in the neighbourhood who disliked the project and resented the intrusion of Vermuyden and the foreigners associated with him. The adventurers found themselves involved in costly litigation to defend their claims, and the reclamation work was threatened by organized violence. Embankments were thrown down, and when Vermuyden met opposition with force of arms, an Englishman was killed. After continued rioting and disturbances the government issued a proclamation (28 September 1628) which

R

for the time being cowed the villagers into acquiescence;[20] the allocation of land went ahead, and on 6 January 1629 Vermuyden was rewarded with a knighthood. More troubles ensued, however, and there were fresh complaints that the allocation of land at Epworth had been unfairly carried out, and eventually it had to be adjusted in the commoners' favour. Meanwhile the effects of Vermuyden's other mistake began to appear.

The area to be drained was intersected by several rivers, chief of which was the Don. This split into two branches, one to the north flowing into the Aire, while the southern branch, joined by the Rivers Torne and Idle, pursued a tortuous course through the marshes, ultimately reaching the Trent near its mouth, at Adlingfleet. Vermuyden's plan was to confine the Don to its northern branch, and to replace the meandering channels of the other rivers by straight cuts, running into the Trent farther south, at a tidal sluice near Althorp. The general principle, to carry off the water more rapidly by straightening the rivers, was sound, but the new channels proved insufficient for the volume of water they had to carry. The northern branch of the Don could not take the whole river, and the inhabitants of Fishlake, Sykehouse and Snaith complained that in order to drain useless marshes Vermuyden had subjected their land, hitherto dry and fertile, to repeated flooding. Vermuyden replied that they were themselves to blame, by neglecting to keep their banks in repair, but after a time it became clear that this was not the real cause of the trouble. They continued to protest vigorously, and eventually their case came before Thomas Wentworth, later to become famous as the Earl of Strafford, and then President of the Council of the North. As a result of his judgment, the adventurers were obliged to cut a new channel, still called the Dutch River, to carry the Don straight into the Ouse at Goole. They bought the land for this from Sir Arthur Ingram, who no doubt knew how to charge for it, and altogether the additional works cost them £20,000. Coming on top of their other expenses it finally extinguished their hopes of making a profit.

Vermuyden's New Idle and New Torne also proved inadequate in time of flood, and the inhabitants of Epworth and Haxey similarly suffered from the waters that descended upon them from regions outside their own area. Already dissatisfied with the allocation of land they had received in lieu of their lost common rights, the people of Epworth later took advantage of the Civil War to rise up in arms and destroy the drainage works made in their neighbourhood.[21] The whole enterprise cost some £200,000, but although it was financially disastrous for the adventurers, and in spite of the setbacks and defects encountered in its execution, as a piece of land reclamation it was by no means a failure. In the end the disturbances died down, and what had previously been a swamp worth less than 6d. an acre became fertile land valued at 10s. The participants, it is true, lost their money, and disheartened by continual litigation and expense they parted with their shares in the enterprise. For the King, on the other hand, it turned out a good bargain. By disposing of Hatfield and four adjacent manors to Vermuyden he obtained a capital payment of £16,000 and an annual rent of some £195, rising when the improvement had been completed to £425, while from his third share in the reclaimed ground he obtained a rent of £1,228.[22]

Vermuyden himself was blamed, not unjustly, for many of the troubles in which the enterprise became involved, and made himself greatly disliked, but in the end he emerged remarkably unscathed. He had borrowed £25,000 by mortgaging the land to be drained,[23] and had also raised capital at the outset by selling blocks of land to his Dutch fellow-entrepreneurs in anticipation of the project being completed. These involved him in quarrels and lawsuits with his disappointed partners, and for a time he appeared to be in difficulties. He was imprisoned in 1633, when he refused to contribute to the cost of making the Dutch River, but later gave way and paid up. His refusal seems to have been due to stubbornness and pride rather than inability to pay, for while he disposed of most of his interests at Hatfield he seems to have done so on terms very favourable to himself. At any rate he did not lack the means to speculate in various other enterprises. In 1630 he bought 4,000 acres of Sedgemoor, in Somerset, for £12,000, presumably with a view to future reclamation; he also paid £5,000 for Malvern Chase. It was about the same time that he and Heath took shares in the Dovegang mine, and soon he was to be occupied in the project of draining the Great Level.

Plans to drain this area, which had hung fire for some years, received a stimulus from the enterprise at Hatfield Chase, though at the same time it was a warning of the risks involved. Conditions in the Fens were deteriorating, and landowners were not only becoming convinced of the necessity for action, but also wanted to participate in the gains to be expected from it. Meanwhile the King's advisers invented an ingenious method of overcoming the opposition of recalcitrant commoners. The Commissioners of Sewers would meet and impose an impossibly high tax on the land (generally common land) they adjudged to be 'hurtfully surrounded' —possibly as much as £1 an acre on land worth only 6d. The Commissioners had power to sell land on which sewer rates remained unpaid, and they would proceed to 'sell' part of the fens to entrepreneurs, not for cash, but in return for their undertaking to drain the whole. When the work had been completed the Commissioners would meet again, and sanction the allocation to the entrepreneurs of the portion they had 'bought'. As the consent of the Crown was required at the initiation and conclusion of these transactions, influence at Court became the key to success in bidding for a drainage project.[24]

Vermuyden was hoping for an engagement in this field, but many people looked on him with disfavour, and he had a rival in the person of Anthony (now Sir Anthony) Thomas, who had made an unsuccessful bid for a contract, in partnership with Sir William Ayloffe, in 1619. Thomas now had fresh associates, and once more approached the Crown. Charles I was willing to nominate him as undertaker, and instructed the Commissioners of Sewers to meet and come to terms with him. Prominent among them, however, was the Earl of Bedford, who wished to participate in the project, and when the Commissioners met at Cambridge on 1 October 1629, they asked Sir Anthony to show them his plans. Whether because the plans were not yet ready, or because he wanted first to make sure of his profit, Sir Anthony declined to produce his plans unless the Commissioners agreed in advance to levy a tax of 10s. an acre on all the 300,000 acres to be reclaimed. The Commissioners refused, on the ground that £150,000 was an unreasonably large sum. Thomas and his partners produced their 'propositions' for drainage in the following January, offering to carry out the work in return for an allocation of 80,000 acres. They also undertook to set 'a rent of 4d. an acre out of the whole 80,000 acres, amounting to £1,333 per annum, for the maintenance of the work, and will give to every cottager whose house shall happen to stand upon any part of the lands allotted to us, the summe of four pounds towards the erecting of a new house, in some other part of the Common'.

Meanwhile the government was negotiating with Vermuyden, on the basis of an allocation of 90,000 acres, 30,000 of which should be taken by the King. Vermuyden may have been hoping to raise more capital in the Netherlands, but after their experiences in the Hatfield scheme his Dutch friends were probably in no mood to incur fresh risks. There may also have been opposition to the award of the undertaking to a foreigner, although in 1624 Vermuyden had taken English nationality; at any rate, these negotiations broke down, and in the end the contract was given to the Earl of Bedford. Bedford has been credited with highly patriotic motives in sponsoring the undertaking, but as the owner of extensive tracts of fen he clearly stood to gain by its reclamation, and like other landlords who improved their estates he no doubt regarded his outlay as likely to be a profitable investment. The terms he obtained represented a setback for the King, however, for instead of 30,000 acres the royal share was to be only 12,000.[25] Sir Anthony Thomas felt that both Charles and his father had treated him badly. On the occasion of the abortive project of 10 years previously, he alleged, James I had bidden the Privy Council come to terms with Ayloffe and himself, and the Council had told them to promote a Bill in Parliament. This they had done, but soon afterwards Parliament was dissolved and the Bill had lapsed. Then, when the King declared himself to be the undertaker, he had promised Thomas a 'reward' of £10,000 'for his great travell and charge therein'. Needless to say, Sir Anthony had never seen this money, and now Charles I whom he regarded as under an obligation to him, was guilty of bad faith.[26] Be that as it may, it was clear that in fen drainage, as in other schemes, much depended on influence at Court.

Francis, fourth Earl of Bedford, was the owner of 20,000 acres of fen near Thorney and Whittlesey, and his family had long had in mind the possibility of reclamation. His father, Sir William Russell, who had served at Flushing, had been approached in 1589 by the Commissioners of Sewers, and agreed to bring over three Dutch drainage experts to advise on how to proceed. He then submitted a proposal to the Privy Council, stating that he was 'seized of . . . a great quantity of Marsh and drowned grounds, late parcels of the possessions of the Monastery of Thorney', which now in-

volved him in more charge than profit. The Dutchmen were willing
to leave their own country and 'endeavour the recovery thereof', on
condition that they should be free to transport any produce of the
reclaimed land, should not be pressed to serve in the wars for 40
years, and should be exempt from assessment to taxation for 10
years. The Privy Council replied favourably, but a scheme of this
kind required larger resources than an individual could command,
and there is no evidence that Russell proceeded with it.[27]

The agreement made with the Earl of Bedford in January 1630,
which became known as the Lynn Law, from the place where the
Commissioners who sanctioned it met, provided that the earl and
his partners were to have 95,000 acres, of which 40,000 were to be
earmarked for bearing the cost of maintaining the works, and
12,000 were to be allotted to the Crown, leaving 43,000 acres for
the benefit of the undertakers themselves. In the following year, in
the 'Indenture of Fourteen Parts', 13 fellow-adventurers were associated with the earl, the whole undertaking being divided into 20
transferable shares, each of which bound the holder or his assigns
to find one-twentieth of the expenses, with a minimum of £500.[28]
Bedford himself took three shares and was the principal shareholder;
among others who held shares, besides several peers and other substantial landlords,[29] were Sir Robert Heath, Vermuyden himself,
and one of his Hatfield partners, Philibert Vernatti. In 1634 the
adventurers obtained a charter of incorporation as a joint-stock
company, undertaking that the work should be completed within
six years from 1631, the date of the Indenture of Fourteen Parts.
As was usual with early joint-stock companies, shareholders were
liable to a series of 'calls' as more capital was needed, and by 1637,
when their undertaking was declared to have been fulfilled, £93,000
had been called up, or £4,650 per share, roughly £1 for every acre
allotted to the company.[30]

Although Vermuyden had not secured the contract for himself, Bedford engaged him to plan and manage the work of reclamation, but there was considerable mistrust of him, and a number of
fenmen disagreed with his plans. What he proposed was similar in
principle to his scheme at Hatfield Chase—to shorten the courses of
the chief rivers, replacing their winding channels by straight cuts.
Their gradient would thus be increased, and Vermuyden believed
that the water would then run out with sufficient force to keep the

outfalls scoured clear of silt. Another Dutchman, Jan Barents Westerdyke, was called in to give advice, and maintained that all that was needed was to clean out and deepen the existing channels and build embankments along them to prevent overflowing. Vermuyden insisted that this would be both ineffective and more expensive, and finally got his own plans accepted. Westerdyke returned to Holland in a resentful frame of mind, to reappear 20 years later, when the fifth earl was engaged in further reclamation work.[31]

Vermuyden's chief cut was the Bedford River (now called the Old Bedford River), 70 feet wide, running in a straight line for 21 miles, from Earith, near St Ives, to Salter's Load, near Downham Market, with sluices at both ends. This relieved the old course of the Ouse, flowing by Ely, of most of its water, leaving it to take only the Cam, and the small rivers Lark, Little Ouse and Wissey, flowing in from the east. A number of other cuts similarly shortened and straightened the River Nene, and sluices were erected at various points, some to keep back the tides at the river mouths. Work proceeded vigorously, in spite of widespread and sometimes violent opposition. A detailed survey was made in 1635–6; then, on 12 October 1637 the Commissioners of Sewers met at St Ives and declared that the work had been completed according to the 'true intent' of the Lynn Law, and proceeded to allot their 95,000 acres to Bedford and his colleagues. Some of them contended, however, that the work had not been properly carried out; they also disputed the distribution of the land, and were supported in their objections by a number of local inhabitants, including the Dean and Chapter of Ely.

The main point in dispute concerned precisely what Bedford had undertaken to do. The Lynn Law merely stated that he would 'do his best endeavour at his own charge to drain the said marsh, waste . . . etc. . . . in such manner as that they shall be fit for meadow, or pasture, or arable', and provided that 'overflowings by sudden water which shall not lie longer upon the lands than in convenient time the same may fall away again, shall not be esteemed a not draining thereof.' Much of the fen country used to be under water in the winter, and at other times too in wet years, but though the land could not be used for arable farming, the drier parts were available for grazing in the summer. Drainers generally aimed to make the better parts suitable for tillage, and to improve the worse land to a condition equal to that in which the better had been previously. Vermuyden contended that this was what he had undertaken to do —to make the fens 'summer grounds'—and the Commissioners had made their award on this basis;[32] but the complainants were not satisfied with this, and argued that they should have been made 'winter grounds'. The St Ives award may perhaps have been premature, but some such relief was probably essential, since repeated calls had reduced some of the shareholders nearly to bankruptcy. On the other hand, it was argued that the only way to justify the heavy outlay was to make the whole area fit for ploughing, and the objectors got their way.

A new body of Commissioners met at Huntingdon on 12 April 1638, and while they were sitting a letter arrived from the King, 'in which, with his accustomed indiscretion, he announced that he had formed a decided opinion that the works were incomplete, and then added that he was prepared to take them into his own hands'.[33] After inquiries and surveys the Commissioners declared that the work so far done was defective—in view of the King's letter they could hardly have said anything else—and the St Ives award was set aside. Sitting at Wisbech, on 23 May the Commissioners decided that taxes, varying from 10s. to 40s. an acre, should be levied on the land; finally, at a meeting at Huntingdon on 18 July it was announced that the King himself would become the undertaker and make the fens 'winter grounds'. According to Sir John Maynard Charles had heard privately of 'all the Cheats of the Undertakers', and his motives may in part have been an honest desire to see justice done. Considering the state of his finances, however, it seems likely that the hope or expectation of gain played a considerable part,[34] for instead of the 12,000 acres assigned to him by the Lynn Law, under the new arrangement he was to get 57,000, nearly twice the 30,000 he missed getting in 1630 when Bedford secured the contract.

S. R. Gardiner thought that the King's sudden intervention revealed in 'clear relief both the merits and the defects of Charles's character. It is evident that he was anxious to carry out a work of real importance.... It is evident, too, that he desired both that the rich should be benefited and the poor should not be wronged. Yet he gained no credit for his good intentions. He took his decision in private before any inquiry had been held, and he stultified his Commissioners by announcing his decision just as they were starting to make the inquiry upon which it was ostensibly to be based. When all this parade of investigation ended in the assignment of a large number of acres to himself, it was easy to leap to the conclusion that the sole object of the whole proceeding was to fill the Exchequer at the expense of a popular nobleman.'[35]

Bedford indeed felt himself unjustly treated, but Gardiner's view was that he and his partners had no reasonable cause for dissatisfaction, at any rate on financial grounds. Out of the 95,000 acres originally allotted by the Lynn Law, only 43,000 were to be theirs absolutely; now they were offered 40,000, with no further obligation to complete the work. The reclaimed land was said to have an annual value of 30s. an acre, and if this estimate were correct 'they would get a yearly income of £60,000 by a capital expenditure of £100,000. They had no reason to complain.'[36] These profits would not accrue at once, however, and for some time the fortunes of the Russell family were adversely affected by their part in the fen-draining enterprise. The fourth earl died of smallpox in 1641, and his son William, who succeeded him as fifth earl, found himself in difficulties which were not made easier by the devious part he played in the Civil War.

The King retained Vermuyden as the engineer in charge, and wanted work to proceed without delay, but violent opposition and disorder were renewed, and crowds gathered to break down the partition ditches which were being dug to mark off the adventurers' portions of the ground. Oliver Cromwell is commonly credited with having lent his support to the objecting commoners but, as Gardiner pointed out, while there is no reason to doubt his sympathy with the poorer inhabitants of the Fens, he was not at this date taking political sides against the King. Nor was he opposed in principle to draining the Fens; as Protector he in fact encouraged it.[37]

One of the intentions of the royal entrepreneur was to build 'an eminent town in the midst of the Level ... and to have it called Charlemont ... the design wherof he drew himself, intending to have made a navigable stream from thence to the river of Ouse'.[38] Little progress had been made, however, when operations were interrupted by the outbreak of the Civil War. Many of the drainage works either fell into decay or were deliberately destroyed, and when in 1646 Parliament decided that reclamation should be resumed, in many areas a fresh start had to be made.

The King's participation in the project, and the arrangements made at Huntingdon in July 1638, were now ignored, and the fifth Earl of Bedford was recognized as the inheritor of his father's interest in the undertaking. Local inhabitants continued to protest and petition against the scheme, but the national advantage of converting 300,000 acres of swamp into fertile agricultural land was so obvious that the most the objectors could do was to cause more delay, and on 29 May 1649 an 'Act for the Draining of the Great Level of the Fens' passed the Commons. In view of his experience, the undertakers could hardly avoid putting Vermuyden once more in charge of the work, but some of them still questioned his plans, and consulted Westerdyke again. They were in fact short of funds, and were hoping to find a cheaper method than Vermuyden's; but Vermuyden stood firm, and in the end, after more controversy, his plans were accepted. A number of additional embankments, drains, and cuts were made, notably the New Bedford River, close to and parallel with the Old Bedford River, the strip of land between them being left as a receptacle for the water in time of flood. More sluices were erected at various places, including Denver Sluice on the Ouse, which later became the subject of acute controversy. Its object was to stop the tide flowing up the river, but it was said to prevent the fresh water in the old course of the Ouse from getting away until it reached a higher level than the water in the Bedford River; the southern fens were then flooded and the old Ouse became silted up.[39]

The drainage work was finally adjudged to be complete on 23 March 1653, and the Earl of Bedford and his associates at length obtained possession of their 95,000 acres. Vermuyden's part in the enterprise came to an end in 1655, but it appears to be uncertain whether this was the result of a quarrel with Bedford, or because Westerdyke had been consulted again and pronounced an unfavourable verdict, or simply because Vermuyden believed that he had no more to do in the Great Level, and wished to devote his time to other enterprises. He meant to drain the 4,000 acres of Sedgemoor which he had bought in James I's reign, but as usual there were objections from the commoners there, and in 1656 a Bill enabling him to undertake this was rejected.

Unfortunately for Vermuyden's reputation, in the course of the later years of the seventeenth century the fens he had drained became once more subject to flooding, and by the eighteenth century the level of some areas had sunk so much that, like the polders in Holland, they could only be kept dry by pumping. It was then said, and the charge was often repeated, that Vermuyden's faulty methods were responsible for the renewed inundation,[40] and that he had not paid enough attention to the outfalls of the rivers; but more recent writers have exonerated him. Admittedly he made some mistakes, but the real cause for the sinking of the land was that the underlying peat shrank as it dried; Vermuyden can hardly be blamed for not anticipating this, and really it was a testimony to the effectiveness of his work.[41]

Accounts of Vermuyden's later years vary considerably. Samuel Smiles said that he had to sell off his share of all the lands he had helped to reclaim, in order to pay his debts. Bedford's company preferred heavy claims on him, which he had no means of meeting, and shortly afterwards he went abroad and died 'a poor, broken down old man'. His latest biographer, however, tells us that he remained in England and lived until 1677, and that, judging by the size of his house, he was very comfortably off.[42] No doubt he had owed much, especially in his earlier years, to royal favour, and Sir Robert Heath had certainly been a useful ally; but his success in life was largely due to his own ability and character. He had many of the qualities—energy, adaptability, ruthlessness when necessary—that go to make the successful entrepreneur, and he did not care if his masterfulness made enemies, provided he achieved what he set out to do.

While Bedford's company and Vermuyden reclaimed the central and southern parts of the Great Level, other parts were being reclaimed by neighbouring landlords. In Lincolnshire as long ago as 1553 a scheme was on foot for draining parts of Kesteven and Holland, under the direction of a Mr Ogle. Several landowners subscribed towards it, including Sir William Cecil.[43] In January 1631 the Earl of Lindsey obtaining approval for a project to drain some 70,000 acres of fen in the same district. The formulation and execution of the scheme owed much to Lindsey's own initiative and energy, but, like the Earl of Bedford, he himself put up only part of the capital. The project was financed by eight partners, who though not formally incorporated as a company, between them held 18 shares. Their total outlay is stated to have been £45,000, equivalent to £2,500 per share, the area allotted for division among the shareholders being 24,000 acres. Lindsey himself and his son held five shares, and another five were taken by a courtier, the Cornishman Sir Robert Killigrew, through whose influence the scheme obtained royal support. Lord Willoughby and the Earl of Dorset had two each, the remaining four being divided between three substantial knights from the neighbourhood. Part of the money was subscribed in the usual manner by a series of calls on the shareholders, but part was raised as the work went on by selling off the drained land at £4 an acre. Some was sold in this way in sizeable lots (for example, 300 acres were bought by the Earl of Lincoln, 145 by Lord Cottington), but most of the purchases were on a smaller scale, and were taken up by members of the gentry, sometimes from as far away as Somerset or Worcestershire.[44]

The principal drainage operation of Lindsey's group was the cutting of the channel known as the South Forty Foot Drain which, it was said, would provide 'a navigable river from Bourne to Boston, a distance of 24 miles'. Houses and farmsteads were built, and the former fens brought into cultivation; but, as so often happened, the commoners and fenmen were up in arms. When the local Justices of the Peace failed to restore order, in 1640 Lindsey submitted a petition to Parliament against 'ill-affected persons' who 'have not only excited the meaner sort of people, but have themselves likewise in a tumultuous and illegal manner' invaded parts of the land reclaimed, 'thrusting their cattle into the same and keeping them there with force and violence, and have likewise cut the banks and works in several places', and prevented the earl's agents and workmen from effecting repairs.[45]

In the end the project was completed, and in the meantime the same group of partners undertook to drain an additional 22,000 acres, adjacent to the area comprised in their original scheme. In the first six months this is said to have cost them £12,000. This was in 1638; a few years previously, in 1635, Lindsey had also appeared as 'sole undertaker' of another project in the same county.[46] In the early years of Charles I's reign there were a number of other drainage undertakings, mostly financed, like Lindsey's, by unincorporated partnerships, on the usual basis of the partners receiving a portion of the drained land. One of these, a project for draining the fens near Witham, was started in 1631 by the group headed by Sir Anthony Thomas, who had recently been disappointed in his bid for the contract to drain the Great Level. They completed their task by 1634, and the land was then described as 'fitt for arable, or meadowe, or pasture'. They did not long enjoy the fruits of their labours, however, for the outbreak of the Civil War gave the resentful fenmen the chance to reassert themselves, and in 1642, 'a little before Edgehill fight', they 'took arms, and in a riotous manner they fell upon the Adventurers', broke the sluices, laid waste their lands, threw down their fences, destroyed all the drainage works, together with the houses built on the reclaimed land, and forcibly resumed possession of their old haunts.[47] More successful was the undertaking in the Ancholme Level in Lincolnshire, possibly because it was of relatively small size. One of the landowners there, Sir John Monson, secured the cooperation of his neighbours; of the eight local Commissioners of Sewers seven took shares in the enterprise, and for an outlay of £14,500 they obtained 5,827 acres of reclaimed land.[48]

In the long run the reclamation of the Fens became highly profitable to all concerned, but at first it must have seemed to many a costly undertaking, in which the prospects of gain continually receded. The fourth Earl of Bedford had had to borrow money to sustain his share in the enterprise, and was heavily in debt at the time of his death; in 1653, on the completion of the second stage of the work, the fifth earl said that the profits were inconsiderable in proportion to the charge and hazard. He estimated the total outlay to date at some £300,000, with an annual charge of £10,000, and declared that most of the partners had ruined themselves by the enterprise.[49] He may have exaggerated. At any rate, later generations of his family had no reason for regret; they drew substantial rents from what had previously been almost worthless land, as also did other landlords who had taken part in reclamation, such as the Earl of Exeter. From the national point of view the advantage of these enterprises was beyond question, for the whole Great Level has become the most intensively cultivated land in the country, 'unsurpassed in productivity anywhere in these isles'.[50]

13 | Land and water

Draining the Fens was the most conspicuous, but by no means the only way of profiting by the exploitation of landed property. Another way, as we saw in earlier chapters, was by working the minerals under the soil. Landlords not fortunate enough to own estates in the coal-fields, or in metal-mining regions, could still play the entrepreneur by becoming commercial farmers, and in the Elizabethan age a number did so on a substantial scale. Marxist historians have interpreted the contrast between the Tudor and the medieval economy, in which a military aristocracy was supported by the labour of their agricultural tenants, in terms of the displacement of feudalism by capitalism. Apart from the exaggeration and over-simplification that such an interpretation involves, Professor Lawrence Stone has pointed out that it does not fit the situation actually existing in the sixteenth century. Some Elizabethan aristocrats, though no longer feudal barons, found a full occupation at Court or in politics, and became rentiers, letting out their estates on lease: it was those actually living on their estates who exploited them as entrepreneurs. When they did so it was not usually as arable farmers but as the owners of extensive flocks of sheep, or in some areas, particularly in the north of England, of herds of cattle. The displacement of tillage by sheep-farming became a familiar topic of complaint in Tudor times, but the government's efforts to check it proved largely abortive, for it was far too profitable, even though the price of corn rose faster than the price of wool. It is a mistake, however, to regard the intensive sheep-breeding of Elizabethan times as primarily aimed at supplying the demand for wool: in the later sixteenth century sheep were being reared just as much, if not more, for sale as mutton, especially in the area round London.[1]

These trends may be illustrated by a study of the fortunes of some landowning families in one of the midland counties. John Isham was born in 1525 into a gentry family, but as a younger son he was sent up to London at the age of 16 to make his way as a city merchant. After serving his apprenticeship he became a freeman of the Mercers' Company, and acquired the capital needed to set up in business on his own by marrying a wealthy fellow-mercer's widow. He traded in wool and cloth, and bought property in and near London, letting it out for rent; he also made money by financial transactions of various kinds, lending on mortgages and other security, and dealing in annuities and rentcharges. By 1560 he was rich enough to buy the manor of Lamport in his native county of Northamptonshire (still the Ishams' family seat), and set up as a country gentleman. He then proceeded, by enclosure and the purchase of adjacent pieces of land, to consolidate his estate and convert it into a business concern, concentrating on the rearing of sheep, partly for wool, but mainly for sale as meat, at first supplying local butchers, but later the London market as well. After John Isham's death, in 1596, the business was carried on by his son and grandson, and by 1634 the annual value of the property at Lamport was over £1,000, twice what it had been in the 1580s. Some income came from rents, but it was still mainly derived from the sale of meat and wool,[2] though no doubt the increase was partly a question of inflation.

Another Northamptonshire family which made its money, and actually rose into the ranks of the peerage on the profits of sheep-breeding, was that of the Spencers of Althorp.[3] They maintained a permanent flock of about 13,000 sheep, to which some 4,000 or 5,000 lambs were added every spring. This was business on a larger scale than most landowning entrepreneurs attained to, though not so large as that of Thomas Howard, Duke of Norfolk, the senior English peer, whose permanent flocks in East Anglia alone, not counting the lambs which were sold off each year, amounted in 1571 to nearly 17,000 beasts.

George Talbot, Earl of Shrewsbury, besides his numerous industrial and commercial interests, exploited the agricultural as well as the mineral products of his vast estates. His wife, Bess of Hardwick, claimed to be the owner of 8,000 sheep, and in 1591 the sales from only one of Shrewsbury's many demesnes came to over

£3,000. Exact figures of the whole extent of his wealth do not seem to be available, but Professor Stone thinks that his profits from farming his own land 'must have amounted to many thousands of pounds'. In 1607 the seventh earl's steward accounted for receipts of over £45,000 in a period of nine months.[4]

Of course the agricultural entrepreneur was by no means assured of lasting success; that folly and extravagance could lead the big farmer to ruin as easily as other men is shown by the decline and fall of another Northamptonshire family, the Treshams of Rushton. Sir Thomas Tresham was an improving landlord, and was regarded by Tawney as a typical specimen of the enterprising gentry who rose by working their land as a commercial undertaking. Professor Trevor-Roper, on the other hand, cited him as an example of 'mere gentry', though his estate brought him in an income of £3,500 a year, which should ordinarily have sufficed to maintain a knight and his family. But Tresham was a Catholic, and though in 1588 he estimated that in the previous eight years he had paid £2,800 in recusancy fines, besides other expenses, he persisted in lavishing money on elaborate building operations, on his great house and elsewhere. By the time of his death, in 1605, his debts outdistanced his resources, and his reckless son Francis, who after participating in Essex's rebellion first joined and then betrayed the conspirators in the Gunpowder Plot, died in that same year.[5] This was the end of the Treshams as country gentlemen.

Successful Elizabethan sheep-farming entrepreneurs, like the Spencers of Althorp, were men who lived mainly in the country and devoted much personal attention to the management of their estates.[6] In the course of the seventeenth century the number of landlords, or at any rate of the greater landlords, prepared to do so diminished markedly. This was partly because the levelling-off of prices in the 1620s reduced the profits to be made by the sale of meat or wool, and instead of keeping their demesnes in hand landlords tended to lease them out to tenant farmers. Some landlords, like another Northamptonshire family, the Brudenells of Deane (later Earls of Cardigan), had begun much earlier to abandon the personal direction of agricultural work:[7] by 1640 many prominent landlords 'had reduced their demesne husbandry . . . to the narrow limits of a home farm to supply the needs of the household'. Most of them had become 'little more than rentiers, and often absentee rentiers at that'.[8]

Though landowners had less incentive in the early seventeenth century to act as agricultural entrepreneurs, the growth of London offered opportunities to those fortunate enough to own land which could be developed for building.[9] At the end of the sixteenth century the city of London still contained the homes of its wealthy merchants, as well as its hordes of poorer inhabitants; farther up the Thames lay Westminster, which was the centre of government, with the law courts and the royal court itself. Bordering the river frontage between them, along the Strand, lay a series of noblemen's palaces, but the area west of the city and north of this was still largely unbuilt on. It was mostly in noble ownership, and was obviously well situated to supply the growing demand for good-class houses and shops. Although there were exceptions, the usual practice, then as in modern times, was for a landlord not to develop a site with his own capital but to divide it into lots and let them to tenants, who undertook to build houses of a specified size and value; sometimes a speculative builder might take a whole block, and build houses for sale or subletting. At first leases were for only 31 years, which seems a short period for a building lease: perhaps the reason was that houses were still mostly built of wood, in spite of efforts by the government to check the use of timber for buildings in London. The landlord thus avoided financial outlay, while retaining control over the development, and though during the currency of the lease he drew only a small ground rent, usually between £1 and £5 per plot, at the end of the 31 years the property reverted to him, and he could then let it for short terms, at rack rents and with fines for renewal.

In the early seventeenth century quite a number of landlords were engaged in building projects on these lines. Shakespeare's patron, the third Earl of Southampton, owned the Bloomsbury estate, and had his town house on the north side of the present Great Russell Street, east of the site of the British Museum. As early as 1594 he had begun developing some of his land between this and Lincoln's Inn Fields, and in the course of the next 20 years the frontages to Holborn became filled with houses, built on the usual 31-year leases. Although the earl did not himself supply the capital, which was put up by the lessees, the initiative was his, and he also

s

planned the layout and laid down architectural standards to which
the builders had to conform.

Government policy was to prevent the growth of London, but
proclamations and legislation designed to effect this were largely
evaded. There were occasions, however, when the regulations
against new building were enforced. In 1636 the fourth Earl of
Southampton wished to launch a further scheme of development
by pulling down Southampton House and building a number of
smaller houses on the site. His plans had the backing of the King,
but they were vetoed by the Council, and he had to wait till 1652
before permission was granted.[10]

It was not until 1669 that the Bloomsbury estate passed to the
Russell family, by marriage with the fourth Earl of Southampton's
heiress,[11] but they had begun developing their other London property some years before this. Houses were built along Long Acre in
1612, and by 1618 the third Earl of Bedford's rental from his
property in London exceeded £500 a year. Then in 1631 the fourth
earl, already committed to his fen-draining enterprise, embarked
upon a considerable building venture, the Covent Garden piazza.
Houses and a church (St Paul's), designed by Inigo Jones, formed
three sides of a square, and the place became one of the sights of the
town. The scheme was unlike the usual type of building development, in that the earl financed it himself, and it has been calculated
that it cost him over £28,000. Expense on this scale, partly due to
the King's insistence that the piazza should be planned as a single
architectural feature, must have contributed greatly to the earl's
monetary embarrassment, but in the long run the venture became
moderately remunerative. The fifth earl drew an annual income of
over £1,300 in rents, apart from renewal fines; after the Restoration
his London rental, from Covent Garden and the houses in Long
Acre, had risen to well over £2,000 a year.

Another peer who invested some of his own, or borrowed, capital
in a building project was Robert Cecil, the first Earl of Salisbury,
and he also let plots for building houses, on land he had bought
for the purpose. In 1608–10, for less than £500, he acquired a strip
of about nine acres up the west side of St Martin's Lane, and
let it out on 31-year leases at ground rents of a shilling per foot
frontage. No restrictions were placed on the type of houses the
tenants built, except that they were not to use them for commer-

cial purposes, or as inns or alehouses. This was the fashionable side of a fashionable street, and by 1642, when the leases expired, these houses brought in rents of £750 a year, as well as heavy fines for the renewal of tenancies.

In 1606–7, shortly before starting the development of St Martin's Lane, Salisbury had embarked at his own expense on a novel venture, the erection of a 'New Exchange', planned as a rival to Gresham's famous institution in the City.[12] For this purpose he acquired a piece of the Strand frontage, and a slice of land down the east side of Durham House, formerly the London palace of the Bishops of Durham. Shopkeepers in the Royal Exchange were indignant, and their protests were backed by the Lord Mayor, fearing that the City would suffer if business developed in the West End. Salisbury ignored them, however, for this was just what he intended. The New Exchange was to become the Bond Street of its day—a shopping centre selling expensive articles of clothing and fancy goods to the wealthy clientèle who passed along the Strand between Westminster and the City.

Several architects were consulted, including Inigo Jones, who made a design, though it was not accepted, and we do not know whose plans were finally chosen. In spite of the difficulty of collecting enough masons and other labourers, building proceeded with great speed, and on 11 April 1609 the New Exchange was formally opened by the King himself, who named it 'Britain's Burse'. It was an expensive undertaking: the site had cost £1,200, and the outlay for the building came to £10,760. Salisbury, who was engaged at the same time in building Hatfield House, as well as enlarging Salisbury House in the Strand, and was getting deeply in debt in consequence, hoped that the shops in the Exchange would bring in rents of £1,200 a year, but he never achieved this. For the first few years, from 1611 to 1617, the management was let at £1,000 a year to a syndicate of merchants, but shopkeepers were slow to take up leases, and the syndicate declined to continue the arrangement. Salisbury (the second earl, that is—the first earl died in 1612) then had to take over the management of the letting himself. The shops had been sublet on 11-year leases, and it was unfortunate that the expiry of the leases coincided with the trade depression of 1620–1. As a result half the shops were empty, in 1621 the rental fell to £361, and by 1627 it had only risen to £415.

Next year it was decided, in spite of difficulties over sanitation, to convert the upper story into 16 flats, which were offered for occupation on 21-year leases at rents of £12 to £15. This operation was reasonably successful. So great was the demand for living accommodation in the district that, in spite of their inconvenience, within three years all 16 flats were let, and by 1631 they were bringing in rents of £205, while the rental from the shops on the ground floor was £387. By 1638 the development of the neighbourhood had led to a revival of trade, and the flats were then converted back into shops. They were rapidly occupied, and by the time of the Civil War the rental for the building recovered to £987; but the conversion, together with some other structural alterations, had cost over £1,000, and from a financial point of view the New Exchange can hardly be called an unqualified success.

Salisbury no doubt had hoped that his New Exchange would be a profitable investment, but in reality it was largely a prestige project, like Bedford's Covent Garden piazza, designed to enhance its promoter's reputation. It was financially safer, if less spectacular, to stick to development by house-building. This was the course followed by John Holles, created Earl of Clare, who has been called 'perhaps the greatest London entrepreneur of all'. Inheriting Clement's Inn and part of Drury Lane from his great-grandfather, who had been a successful City merchant, in 1623 he bought a further part of Drury Lane and half Prince's Street from William Drury for £1,500. He then developed the whole of this area, and by the middle of the 1630s was drawing rents from it of over £1,200 a year. Unlike peers who granted leases to speculative builders, Clare himself planned and financed these operations, ploughing back part of his profits into new building. In 1639 he acquired Reindeer Yard, which then consisted of a mixture of stables and tenements, and had become filthy and impassable. He proposed to demolish the existing tenements, which, as he said, were 'inhabited by poor, mean people ... likely to bring a charge to the parish and endanger the neighbourhood by sickness', and to put up 'greater and fewer houses' in their place. Inigo Jones, Surveyor of His Majesty's Works, reported in favour of Clare's plans, and what had been a slum was converted, not of course into better housing for its existing inhabitants, but into dwellings 'fit for persons of some good quality'.[13] In 1641 Clare went on to develop St Clement's Fields, and by 1648 he owned more than 200 dwellings, bringing him in a rental of over £2,000, in addition to which the fines on renewal of tenancies amounted on average to £800 a year.[14]

It was not only the land itself which offered opportunities to entrepreneurs. Developing trade, and above all the increasing use of coal, created the need for better means of transport, but in the seventeenth century nearly all the roads were no better than unmetalled tracks, virtually impassable in winter, and the only way an individual traveller could cover any distance was on horseback. Some goods were conveyed by packhorse, but the easiest and cheapest, if not the only method of transport from one part of England to another was by water, either coastwise by sea, or by river. Rivers such as the Thames and the Severn, the Trent, and the Bedfordshire and the Yorkshire Ouse, had been used as highways for centuries, but few English rivers in their natural state could carry boats or barges of any size. Acts of Parliament were passed in Henry VIII's reign to stimulate the dredging and clearing of obstacles from rivers, but locks and weirs were needed to make them navigable far inland. In this field of engineering, as in many others, England was relatively backward in comparison with continental countries.

Locks had been known in Italy since the fifteenth century, but it was not until about 1566 that the first lock was built in England, on the Exeter canal. In early times ships had been able to sail up to Exeter on the River Exe, but in 1284 Isabella de Fortibus, Countess of Devon, offended by some affront the citizens had offered her, revenged herself by building a weir a couple of miles downstream, so preventing ships from reaching the city. Cargoes then had to be loaded and discharged at Topsham, and the trade of Exeter suffered severely. The citizens endured this until Henry VIII's reign, when powers were granted to by-pass Countess Weir by cutting an artificial channel, some three miles long, parallel to the Exe. This was undertaken by an enterprising man from South Wales, named John Trew, but his work somehow failed to satisfy the mayor and corporation, who alleged that he had not carried out his part of the agreement they had made with him. They disputed his claims, and instead of a reward for his labour the resulting litigation brought him penury and mortification.

In despair he appealed to Burghley for help. 'The varyablenes of men', he wrote, 'and the great injury done unto me, brought me in such case that I wyshed my credetours sattisfyd and I away from

earth: what becom may of my poor wyf and children, who lye in
great mysery, for that I have spent all.' According to his own
acount 'of the things wherein God hath given [him] exsperyance',
Trew was a skilled practitioner in several branches of civil and military engineering, including mining. At length, in 1573, he reached
a settlement of his claims on the Exeter corporation, which agreed
to pay him a lump sum of £224, and an annuity of £30 for life. In
1581 he was engaged, at a salary of 10s. a day, as the engineer in
charge of improvements to Dover harbour; but we must note that
again he failed to satisfy his employers, who accused him of unduly
protracting the work, and summarily dismissed him.[15] After that no
more is heard of him, but whatever his shortcomings as an engineering contractor, Trew at any rate deserves credit for having been
the first to introduce into England the foreign invention of the pound
lock. It is true that his lock on the Exeter canal had only a vertical
sluice above and a single gate at the lower end, but within less than
10 years a lock of the modern type, with double mitre-gates at
both ends, was built on the River Lea, at Waltham Abbey.[16]

From then onwards a number of schemes were suggested
for improving inland navigation, including a 'new cut' to avoid
some of the windings of the Lea. It was not until the middle of
the eighteenth century, however, that James Brindley and others
began digging canals all over England. Before that inland navigation depended on improving the rivers, and there were legal as well
as financial and practical obstacles to be overcome before improvement schemes could be put into effect. Tidal rivers were regarded
as the property of the Crown, and were open to all as highways,
but above the tide a river was the private property of the riparian
owners. On some rivers a right of navigation had become established by usage, like a right of way by land; otherwise, however,
access to the river, or the right to use its banks as a towing-path,
could only be obtained by agreement with the landowners
concerned, or by Act of Parliament. The local Commissioners of
Sewers were the authorities responsible for looking after the condition of rivers and other watercourses, and could levy rates for their
upkeep, but they were mainly concerned with drainage and the
prevention of floods, and were incapable of promoting effective projects for the improvement of navigation.

When a scheme was put forward in 1624 for making the Thames

navigable for barges and lighters as far as Oxford, commissioners were appointed for the purpose under the provisions of a special Act of Parliament.[17] The preamble enlarged on the convenience of being able to convey 'freestone commonly called Oxford or Headington stone' to London and other parts, and supplying Oxford with 'coals, fuel and other necessaries'. The Act then provided that the Lord Chancellor should choose four commissioners for the University and four for the City of Oxford, from panels nominated respectively by the Chancellor or Vice-Chancellor and the Mayor and Corporation. Although the commissioners seem to have been chosen for their general eminence rather than knowledge of or interest in navigation—the university representatives were a Prebendary of Christ Church and three heads of colleges—some useful works were carried out under their authority, including some of the first locks on the Thames, at Iffley, Sandford and elsewhere. The commissioners were given powers, like the Commissioners of Sewers, to levy contributions to finance the scheme, on the assumption that all the inhabitants of the district would benefit from it; but more usually both the inauguration and financing of a project to improve a river depended on the energy and resources of private entrepreneurs.

Local landowners sometimes combined to sponsor a scheme, but their attitude was more often hostile, and the initiative generally came from merchants in the towns. After the Commonwealth it became usual to authorize river improvements by Act of Parliament, but in the early seventeenth century a private entrepreneur usually sought letters patent. These were drawn up on lines similar to those granted to monopolists, and entitled him to recoup his outlay by charging tolls. Thus on 3 January 1627 Arnold Spencer, who had already carried out works to improve navigation on the Great Ouse, in return for which he was allowed to charge users of the river 3d. a ton, obtained a patent 'to make other rivers, streams, and waters navigable and passable for boats, keeles and other vessels to passe from place to place'. For 11 years he was to have the sole right to use 'his own methods and engines' for this purpose, and for 80 years to take all the profits from the rivers he had made navigable, paying £5 to the Exchequer for every river. Later he obtained an extension of time from 11 years to 21, and worked on several East Anglian rivers, including the Essex Stour, but he subsequently assigned his rights to others.[18]

The grant of a patent might enable an entrepreneur to come to terms with landowners, but, unlike an Act of Parliament, its capacity to override rights of property was open to challenge. When disputes occurred the government, while generally favourable to improvements, seems to have done its best to safeguard the public interest. In 1635 Henry Lambe obtained approval for a proposal to make the River Lark navigable for lighters and similar vessels between Bury St Edmunds and the River Ouse, but he had not proceeded more than a mile when he was held up by Sir Roger North and Thomas Steward, on the ground that the work would damage Sir Roger's mill. In February 1636 the case was brought before the Star Chamber, which appointed a commission of inquiry and ordered Lambe to suspend operations until the commission had reported. In April five of the commissioners found that 'generally the work is much distasted and feared, and not desired of any, either of the county or of the town of Bury'. The corporation of Thetford also opposed it, and there were objections from various owners and occupiers of land and mills. Three of the commissioners, on the other hand, reported that, apart from the rent the King was to get, the Commonwealth would benefit by the scheme, so long as Lambe charged less for water-carriage than the cost of land-carriage.

This was a sensible criterion, and in view of the difference of opinion the commissioners, with some changes of personnel, were asked to reconsider the case, and Lambe was told to state his proposed charges for carriage and to give particulars of the works he intended to carry out. On 9 September 1636 he submitted his rates—2s. 8d. per ton for carriage and 4s. per ton for carriage and delivery, as against rates by land of 4s. and 10s. respectively. He also agreed to pay for land used as a towing path and for trees cut down, to preserve existing fords, or to erect bridges where necessary. Further objections were then brought forward, to which Lambe replied, saying he had already spent £2,000 on the work, and expressing the hope that the King would be present in person at the council-board when his case was heard. The King agreed, and in December 1637 appointed the first Sunday in the coming Hilary Term for the business to be heard in his presence. Resistance at length ceased, even on the part of Lambe's original opponents, and finally, on 23 March 1638, he obtained a licence to proceed. He was to pay the Crown a rent of £6 13s. 4d. a year, and to have the benefit of all water-carriage on the river, except that navigation between Mildenhall and the Ouse was to be free for all.[19]

Lambe's experience reminds us of the resistance encountered by Sir Hugh Myddelton when he was making the New River. Another entrepreneur who had to face persistent opposition before achieving success was William Sandys, of Fladbury in Worcestershire, who undertook to make the Warwickshire Avon navigable from its junction with the Severn at Tewkesbury to a point near Coventry. Sandys, who was of gentry origin, also proposed improvements to another tributary of the Severn, the River Teme, making it passable for boats up to Ludlow. No more is heard of the latter scheme, but when in 1636 Sandys applied for letters patent, he told the Privy Council that he had already been 'at great charge' on the Avon. All sorts of miscellaneous objections were put forward, some of which sound highly unreasonable. One would have expected the project to benefit trade, but on the contrary it was alleged that it would cause 'very great damage to this country in carrying away coles and other fewell and butter and cheese which is the life and chiefe supportation of the same'. Somehow also it would 'hinder bringinge up of the low country malt', and 'cause corn to be dearer in our Marketts, hinder the common commerce and traffique which wee have with other Countrys, and be divers other ways very prejudiciable to this Country'.[20]

Sandys' most determined individual opponent was the Sheriff of Worcestershire, Sir William Russell. Russell's servants seized a boat which Sandys sent to 'view' the river, and when Sandys protested, Russell declared that he had no desire to hinder the work, but frankly admitted that he wanted to make sure that he got satisfactory compensation. The council, 'desirous that so public a work may receive no interruption', bade the Lord Privy Seal call the parties before him and try to bring about an amicable agreement. A few months later, however, Richard Hollington and Peter Noxon, Sandys' deputies, were complaining that they had been committed to gaol by Sir William, 'without cause, and of purpose to affront Mr. Sandys, out of a disaffection conceived against the matter of the navigation of the Avon'. In January 1637 Russell alleged that his miller had been assaulted and he himself abused in his house by some of Sandys' servants; Sandys replied, and brought counter-charges of 'wrongs and assaults' against Russell. Both parties were then ordered 'to forbear to use any violence on either side', and to appear before the council in the following month.

Sandys declared that his undertaking not only had the approval of King and council but was desired by 'most of the principal persons upon the river' : the King said that he had taken Sandys' undertaking 'especially into his consideration', and, as in the case of Henry Lambe's project on the River Lark, he announced that he would be present in person at the hearing of the matters in dispute.[21] Another landowner who caused trouble was Sir Edward Alford, and it subsequently appeared that he was dissatisfied with the price Sandys was to pay for the land needed for one of his sluices. In spite of these setbacks, within three years Sandys had opened the river for navigation as far as Stratford-on-Avon, some 20 miles distant, and nearly 40 miles by the course of the river. He erected sluices at 12 places, besides a number of locks, and 'placed many wires in the quickest streams'; altogether the undertaking was said to have cost £20,000. He never succeeded in reaching Coventry, but by 1641 the river was navigable to within four miles of Warwick, and was soon found to be particularly useful for the carriage of coal. Previously it had been difficult 'in these exceeding foul wayes to fetch coles from remote places', but now people could have coal delivered to their doors.[22]

Tudor governments showed considerable interest in maritime affairs, partly for naval reasons. Henry VIII granted a charter to Trinity House, which later became responsible for the maintenance of beacons and other aids to safety in navigation, and money was spent on improvements to harbours, but for many years English shipping ranked a long way below that not only of the Dutch but of many other countries as well. In the course of Elizabeth's reign the number of English ships began to increase, partly owing to the development of the fishing industry, fostered by legislation and the demands of a rapidly growing population, partly also to the expansion of the coal trade, particularly on the east coast. Shipbuilding and ship repairing therefore became a flourishing industry, but it does not seem to have provided openings for entrepreneurs. Ships were built to order, and payment, as for house-building, was made in instalments, as work proceeded, so that little working capital was needed. Many shipwrights were not the owners of their yards, but leased them; they were relatively heavily concentrated in certain areas, on the Thames for example, or the creeks of the Essex coast or of the west country, but individual shipyards were usually small, as were the ships built at them. They were owned and managed not by great capitalists but by practical master shipwrights who worked with their own hands, and only a few turned out as much as a single ship in a year.[23]

On the other hand, entrepreneurs often invested their money in the ships themselves, and in the trading, fishing, exploring, and sometimes piratical voyages in which they were engaged. Among his multifarious activities George Talbot, sixth Earl of Shrewbury, was a shipowner as well as a great industrial capitalist and commercial farmer. He had at least two ships of his own, the *Phoenix* and the *Anne Galante*, engaged in transporting the lead from his Derbyshire mines to London and the continent, bringing return cargoes of wine and barley from France and arms from Germany.[24] He also owned a ship called the *Talbot*, which undertook two fishing voyages to Newfoundland. In Elizabethan times merchant and fishing vessels were freely used for naval purposes, and the *Talbot* subsequently sailed in warlike expeditions against Spain, including Drake's raid on the West Indies in 1585, and she was in action against the Armada in 1588. It was not uncommon in those days for great aristocrats and other wealthy men not only to invest money in maritime adventures but also to own the ships participating in them. Thus the 400-ton galleon *Leicester* belonged to Robert Dudley, Earl of Leicester. She became Edward Fenton's flagship on his abortive expedition to the East Indies in 1582 : subsequently, like the *Talbot*, she sailed with Drake to the West Indies and took part in the fight against the Armada. At her owner's death in the year of the Armada she was valued at £1,500.[25]

The outbreak of open war with Spain made privateering a tempting field for speculative investment. Merchants in London and other ports, and sometimes the Queen herself, took shares in privateering expeditions, which were organized by syndicates on a regular commercial basis. At first they aimed at relatively modest returns— £200 or so to be gained by a short trip with a medium-sized vessel of some 100 or 200 tons. Later their expeditions became much more ambitious, and a group of some 20 or 30 London merchants made large profits by mingling privateering and trade. Between 1589 and 1591 they captured sugar valued at £100,000, whereas previously the annual import was worth only £18,000.[26] One of these privateering merchants was Sir Hugh Myddelton's elder brother Thomas, later Lord Mayor of London;[27] perhaps the most prominent was Alderman Sir John Watts. Besides fitting out a number of privateering expeditions, he served in one of his own ships against the Armada, and was also an active member of the Virginia Company, as well as becoming a Governor of the East India Company.

The exploits of merchants were outdone, however, by noblemen such as George Clifford, third Earl of Cumberland (1558–1605), or in the next century Robert Rich, second Earl of Warwick (1587–1658). Cumberland,[28] who was in command of one of the Queen's ships in the Armada campaign, was a favourite at Court, a star performer at jousts and tournaments, and regarded himself as one of the Queen's champions. He once picked up a glove the Queen had dropped, and from then on wore it on his hat, mounted with jewels. His lavishness and showmanship were equally displayed in his life as a privateer. Between 1586 and 1598 he fitted out 11 privateering ventures, in six of which he went to sea himself. His first ship, the *Clifford*, which he acquired in 1586 for a voyage to Brazil, was a vessel of 130 tons. In the course of the next few years he built up a private fleet of some five or six vessels of varying sizes, ranging from a 12-ton pinnace to the *Sampson* of nearly 300 tons, which took part in all his expeditions for the next ten years. At first his fleet sailed under the protection of one of the Queen's ships, which he borrowed; the Queen herself took shares, and some prizes were captured.

Cumberland's most successful voyage was his fifth, in 1592, undertaken in conjunction with Sir Walter Raleigh and others. A great Spanish carrack, the *Madre de Dios*, was captured off the Azores with a miscellaneous cargo worth £150,000, out of which Cumberland, who had ventured £19,000, got £36,000; but he never had such good luck again. Spanish resistance stiffened; the *Cinco Llagas* (Five Wounds) and *San Felipe*, which were attacked on the next voyage, in 1594, refused to surrender, and the expedition returned with nothing but losses to show. The Queen would not allow her own ships to be laid alongside the Spaniards, for fear that they should catch fire, so in 1595, in order to be free of this restriction, Cumberland had the *Malice Scourge* built to his own order, a great armed ship of 600, or according to other accounts of 800 or even 900 tons, as large as a first-rate man-of-war. But size did not guarantee success, and after three more voyages, which failed to win the hoped-for prizes, Cumberland came to the end of his resources. At last he had to admit defeat, and finally he sold his great vessel to the East India Company for £3,700.

Fuller's comment on him was that 'his fleet may be said to be bound for no other harbour but the port of honour, though touching at the port of profit in passage thereunto'.[29] His thirst for adventure and glory tempted him to gamble with his fortune, but profit eluded him. He persevered undeterred by repeated disappointments, and in the end he had dissipated his wealth on voyages which, for all the damage they inflicted on the national enemy, were costly failures, practically as well as financially. According to his own account, he had spent £100,000 on his ships and privateering ventures. He had to sell up part of his estate and mortgage the rest; as he put it, he had 'thrown his land into the sea'.[30]

When peace was made with Spain in 1604 privateering was no longer allowable, and many who had previously indulged in it were obliged to seek other outlets, such as colonization, for their patriotism and their capital. In practice, however, there was little difference between legitimate privateering and sheer piracy, and the colonies themselves sometimes served as bases for piratical raids as well as lawful trade. Robert Rich's career[31] opened with a commission from the Duke of Savoy to prey on Spanish shipping. Two ships sailed for the West Indies and two to the Red Sea, where they gave chase to a ship belonging to the Great Mogul, and aroused the indignation of the East India Company. Rich, who became Earl of Warwick on his father's death in 1619, was an experienced sailor, and in spite of the King's disapproval went on plundering throughout James' reign. He was not alone in these ventures, but was backed in what had become the customary manner by a group of London merchants, for whom piracy was a form of business.

The renewal of war with Spain in 1625 opened a fresh period of privateering, and Warwick and his merchant backers were soon operating on a scale comparable with that of the Earl of Cumberland and his fellow adventurers. Fleets were sent to the Mediterranean as well as the West Indies, and in spite of heavy losses in the previous year, in 1628 and 1629 some of their ships took part in the settlement of Providence Island in the Caribbean. Warwick, who had previously been associated in the foundation of the colonies of Massachusetts and Connecticut, on the North American mainland, then became a leading member of the Providence Island Company, and used the island as a convenient base for the piratical operations against Spanish trade and shipping which continued after the conclusion of peace. Like other members of the company, he became an active supporter of the parliamentary cause, and at the same time widened the scope of his maritime ventures, not only using his own ships but lending money for voyages undertaken by others. His return on a privateering voyage in which he invested in 1643 was to be 20 per cent of all his captures, and about the same time he financed the raiding expedition under Captain William Jackson which temporarily captured Jamaica. In the following year he took part in founding the colony of Rhode Island.

Cumberland and Warwick were exceptional in the scale of their personal commitments, but numbers of sixteenth- and seventeenth-century entrepreneurs found outlets for their energies in similar combinations of piracy and colonization. It may be thought questionable whether so unconstructive an occupation as piracy entitles them to be regarded as entrepreneurs, but they were like other entrepreneurs in exploiting the opportunities that were open to them. The difference was that in their case the opportunities were political and social rather than physical or material; we may recall, too, that Aristotle (and a number of other writers after him) included piracy in his list of ways of making a living.[32]

Nearer home, the plantations in Ulster, like the settlements in parts of central and southern Ireland in Elizabethan times, may also be regarded as the work of entrepreneurs: indeed, the men responsible for them were known as 'undertakers'.[33] So also with the voyages of discovery and the beginnings of settlement overseas, for which the Elizabethan age is famous. Entrepreneurs like Sir Thomas Smythe, whose share in the development of industries we have already seen, were also much concerned in these activities. But whole books have been written about exploration and the foundation of colonies, and it is impossible to do more than mention them here.[34]

14 | Conclusion

Unlike political revolutions, industrial revolutions do not come to an end. Perhaps this is a reason why 'revolution' is an inappropriate word to apply to changes in industrial organization and the production of goods, whether they occurred in the sixteenth and seventeenth or in the eighteenth and nineteenth centuries. 'Tawney's century', the century between the Dissolution of the Monasteries and the Great Rebellion, to which we have confined our main attention in this book, is not an entirely self-contained period: the processes of development, already at work at its opening, were still continuing at its close. It is true that these processes were not evenly spread. While some branches of trade or industry were developing in 1540, others were yet unknown; in the years after 1640 developments were more extensive and more rapid in some directions than in others; but the economic situation as a whole was never static.

If we move forward another century, to the eve of the Industrial Revolution as usually understood, the same generalizations remain true. Some of the earliest changes resulted from a series of mechanical inventions in the textile industries. These industries continued to expand, but in the meantime experiment, research and scientific discovery were to introduce new sources of power, and lead in time to the creation of entirely new processes and industries. Not only have these developments never ceased to proliferate in the country where they originated, but they have spread far and wide, and are still in process of transforming the whole world. These more recent changes have moreover been accompanied by a social revolution.[1] To point to only a few aspects of this, there have been great and continuing increases in population, great concentrations of population in the form of urban proletariats, great increases in the mobility of the population through the creation of new means of transport, a marked increase in the average expectation of life, and a considerable rise in standards of living (in spite of the continuance of widespread poverty, and even destitution in some places), as a result of increased productivity and the greater abundance and availability of all kinds of consumer goods.

In these respects the industrial revolution which has continued ever since the mid-eighteenth century differs from the industrial developments in the sixteenth and seventeenth centuries which we have been studying in this book. Some historians have suggested that the political revolution in seventeenth-century England, which S. R. Gardiner called the Puritan Revolution, was due fundamentally to social and economic causes; others again have discussed the existence of a 'general crisis' in seventeenth-century Europe. But surely nobody comparing the material conditions or standards of life (housing, clothing, diet and so on), or the generally accepted attitudes to the structure of society, at the beginning and the end of the seventeenth century (Locke's view about property and the social position of the property-less labourer, for example, do not differ in any essential way from those expressed in Elizabeth's reign by Sir Thomas Smith) could plausibly maintain that the industrial developments of this period had produced, or amounted to, a social revolution. The rise of the entrepreneur, important as it was, can hardly be called that.

The men whose careers have been sketched, in more or less detail, in the preceding chapters are indeed only a selection of those whose names might have been mentioned, and whose achievements might, with more research, have been described. But though it would be impossible to fix a rigid criterion by which to decide, among those engaged in industry, who were and who were not eligible for admission to the category of entrepreneur, and equally impossible to hazard even a guess at the total number who would obtain admission, I doubt if they were at all numerous in comparison with the total population. What marked them out was their individuality—their inventiveness, their enterprise and determination, and their administrative capacity. The motives that inspired many of them were not particularly admirable; some in fact were frankly scoundrels, who took advantage of the low standards then prevailing in political and commercial ethics. We saw reason to query whether these early entrepreneurs constituted what in an economic sense could be called a class, not simply because they were important as individuals, or because they were insufficiently numerous, but because they were drawn from more than one class, and not least from the titled aristocracy. This perhaps was truer of the earlier than of the later stages of the process we have called 'the rise of the entrepreneur'. Having appeared, and 'risen', entrepreneurs had come to stay; they became more numerous, and exercised an ever widening influence. Then perhaps entrepreneurs could indeed be called a class, but if so this was because they became merged in a wider class with every kind of capitalist and business man.

Professor N. S. B. Gras went so far as to suggest that nowadays the concept of entrepreneur 'largely is a figment of the imagination'. The word 'suggests risk-taking', but 'many business men today, notably executives, are in no special sense risk-takers'. He would prefer to use 'the ineuphonious term "business man" as the most general and useful for historical and current purposes. This term embraces risk-taking, policy-formulation, management, and control.'[2] It does indeed, but surely it also embraces a great deal more, at subordinate levels of commerce, which form no part of the concept of the entrepreneur, as we have understood it. Even if the word were dropped from the modern economic vocabulary, it would still be useful for historians of the sixteenth and seventeenth centuries, as the equivalent of the 'adventurers', or 'undertakers', or 'projectors' of that age, since all these words have since then acquired different meanings.

Professor Gras regarded the 'sedentary merchant' as the key figure of economic progress in the early modern period. The preceding age of what he called 'petty capitalism' was characterized by 'the traveling merchant—a kind of glorified pedlar—who never got far because too much adventure was mixed with business'. But 'the big shot of the new regime' was the merchant 'who stayed at home', who 'left to others the various jobs of business operation, while he himself kept control of all his agents and partners, strung the keys of his strong boxes to his belt, and saw that his clerks made the proper entries in his account books. . . . Concentrating on policy-formulation, he left operation to others. Control of operations, far and near, came through knowledge of the men whom he chose as agents or accepted as partners, together with the detailed accounts

T

he kept and required others to keep. This sedentary merchant was the master spider of his race.'[3]

Some of the men who in the sixteenth and seventeenth centuries would have been called 'adventurers' because they put their money into enterprises of various kinds, some even of those whom we have admitted to our gallery of entrepreneurs, answer the description of the sedentary merchant. But by themselves such men would never have launched the industrial projects of that age, even though it may be true that projects could not have been launched, and when launched kept afloat, without their capital resources and business acumen. Their successors are modern industrial and commercial capitalists, notwithstanding the fact that these are far from stationary, though they are just as sedentary as their predecessors, travelling as they do in air-liners from one end of the earth to the other.

In emphasizing the role of the sedentary merchant Professor Gras's point was that 'the essential element in the system of capitalism is administration'. In capitalist production 'the owner of capital enters into partnership with the administrator to produce an income for all concerned—themselves chiefly, but also for workers and the owners of land and other natural resources as well as the owners of trained abilities. Of course', he continues, 'the owner of the capital and the administrator of production might be the same person, and in fact the two were commonly identical in early times'.[4] The fact is that, in order to prosper, industry and commerce need both sedentary and more active men—not only administrators but also men who go out to find new markets and develop new processes. In different epochs one may for a time be more important than the other, but in the age when new industries were being created and old ones expanded, the sedentary administrator was hardly the typical entrepreneur.

Professor Gras avoided the word 'entrepreneur' because modern businessmen often do not take risks in any 'special sense'. The amount of risk in business no doubt varies, and in many established businesses it may be relatively slight, but it must always be present in some degree, and to launch a new industry involves a high degree of risk. Because of this the industrial pioneers of the sixteenth and seventeenth centuries were in the fullest sense entrepreneurs, and we have seen that many of them not only faced risks but incurred

heavy losses and financial disaster. To emphasize the importance
of the administrator in business, it has been suggested, does not
necessarily mean neglecting the element of risk-taking, nor on the
other hand is it simply an interpretation of history 'in terms of
great leaders'. The 'administrator concept' recognizes that administration is more than a 'mere routine job': it is 'a series of efforts
driving towards an end. This involves taking risks, assuming responsibilities, making decisions, and effecting countless adjustments, in
individual and larger relationships, within the business unit and in
its external relations, but always with the object of getting something done. Business administration is creative....'[5]

Put in this way, the description seems a more recognizable like-
ness of our entrepreneur, whatever we may call him. Indeed,
whether we call him 'entrepreneur' or 'administrator' is perhaps
largely a question of words; but, at any rate during the century of
his rise, I prefer to go on calling him 'entrepreneur', if only because
this word lays stress, as stress should be laid, on the innovating and
risk-taking aspects of his function, rather than on that of controlling an organization already established.

How far were our rising entrepreneurs aware of the role they
were fulfilling? According to Professor Stone, 'Elizabethan peers
would have been both astonished and disgusted to hear themselves
described as men of business. Though they needed money, some
of them desperately, the lives of few social groups have ever been
less dominated by the profit motive. It was the various ways of
conspicuous consumption, the maintenance of "port" and hospit-
ality, that was their main economic concern.'[6] The profit motive,
however, has never been more than part of the incentive of the
entrepreneur. Professor Stone himself admits that noblemen who
took up industrial leadership did not simply aim at acquiring a
larger income; they also wanted an occupation to enable them 'to
pass the time without suffering the torments of boredom'. He suggests, for example, that one reason why the Earl of Shrewsbury
became the leading industrialist of his age was that he was 'exiled
on his estates in charge of Mary, Queen of Scots'.[7]

This may be part of the explanation of Shrewsbury's work as an
entrepreneur, but even a landed aristocrat may be credited with
more positive ambitions, and we should remember that active
politicians, like Burghley and Leicester, also found time for indus-

trial interests. And by no means all entrepreneurs came from a leisured class in search of relief from boredom. Some, like Sir Hugh Myddelton, were merchants in the City, with plenty of business to keep them occupied. Some, like Sir Bevis Bulmer, were 'hasserd adventurers'; others, like Thomas Bushell, were inspired by the invincible optimism of the gambler. It would, of course, be foolish to query Sombart's 'spirit of capitalism' and simply substitute for it a spirit of entrepreneurship.[8] But the fact remains that, apart from economic incentives, or the profit motive, all these men were possessed, in varying degrees, by a restlessness and energy which made it impossible for them to be content with a life either of idleness or of mere routine. Some may have been principally administrators, some, like Customer Smythe, were sedentary; but they did not just want an occupation. Some entrepreneurs were fortunate and became rich men; some were primarily speculators, or greedy monopolists. But it would be a grave misunderstanding if we rated either the historical importance or the social value of all their enterprises simply in terms of the profits obtained by the entrepreneurs themselves. Judged on this basis some of their work must seem fantastic and much of it unfruitful—certainly unremunerative regarded merely as an investment of capital. But even though their plans sometimes went astray through rashness or ignorance and inexperience, they taught their successors a lesson, and the life of the community as a whole was enriched.[9] Industrial pioneering, and exploiting the natural resources of the land, was only one, though an important one, of the outlets for the urge to activity which was characteristic of the entrepreneur. It found expression in all the ways that marked the Elizabethan age as an age of expansion and adventure.

Notes

List of Abbreviations

D.N.B.: Dictionary of National Biography
E.H.R.: English Historical Review
H.M.C.: Historical Manuscripts Commission
L.&P.: Letters and Papers
L.Q.R.: Law Quarterly Review
N.&Q.: Notes and Queries
N.S.: New Series
P.C.: Privy Council
S.P.D.: State Papers Domestic
V.C.H.: Victoria County History

I THE MAKING OF THE ENTREPRENEUR (pages 9–29)

1 F. A. Walker, *A Brief Text-Book of Political Economy*, 1885, p. 60
2 R. T. Ely, *An Introduction to Political Economy*, 1891, p. 170
3 J. A. Schumpeter. *The Theory of Economic Development* (*Harvard Economic Studies*, xlvi, 1949), p. 74
4 Papers presented at the annual conference of the Economic History Society in Cambridge (England), April 1957 (published by the Research Center in Entrepreneurial History, Harvard University)
5 H. R. Trevor-Roper, *The Gentry 1540-1640* (*Economic History Review Supplement*), p. 1; cf F. J. Fisher (ed.), *Essays in the Economic and Social History of Tudor and Stuart England in honour of R. H. Tawney*, 1961, p. 1
6 In *The Devil is an Ass*
7 J. U. Nef, 'The Progress of Technology and the Growth of Large-Scale Industry in Great Britain, 1540-1640', *Econ. Hist. Rev.*, 5, 1934-5, p. 3ff; 'A Comparison of Industrial Growth in England and France from 1540 to 1640', *Jnl. of Pol. Econ.*, 44, 1936, pp. 289ff, 505ff, 643ff. See also his *Rise of the British Coal Industry*, 1932
8 On the other hand, in his inaugural lecture at the London School of Economics, Professor F. J. Fisher lamented the dearth of statistics

for the sixteenth and seventeenth as compared with the eighteenth and nineteenth centuries, while the historian of the early modern period is 'almost equally deficient in those more esoteric methods by which the truth about the Middle Ages is discovered' ('The Sixteenth and Seventeenth Centuries: the Dark Ages in English Economic History?', *Economics*, N.S. 24, 1957, p. 5)

9 J. U. Nef, *Cultural Foundations of Industrial Civilization*, 1958, p. 36
10 E. J. Hobsbawm, 'The Crisis of the Seventeenth Century', in *Crisis in Europe* (ed. Trevor Aston, 1965; reprinted from *Past and Present*), pp. 16-8
11 G. Unwin, *Studies in Economic History*, 1927, p. 324
12 J. K. Galbraith, *The New Industrial State*, 1967
13 Review by W. H. B. Court, in *History*, 52, 1967, p. 97, of S. Pollard, *The Genesis of Modern Management: A Study of the Industrial Revolution in Great Britain*, 1965
14 F. A. Walker, *A Brief Text-Book of Political Economy*, p. 61
15 *Ibid*
16 W. Holdsworth, *History of English Law*, iv, p. 343ff. The introduction was due to Acontius (Aconcio), of whom we shall hear again (page 249, below)
17 W. H. Price, *The English Patents of Monopoly* (*Harvard Economic Studies*, 1906), p. 8ff; G. Unwin, *The Gilds and Companies of London*, 1908, p. 293ff
18 G. N. Clark, *Science and Social Welfare in the Age of Newton*, 1937, p. 104ff (from 'Early Capitalism and Invention', *Econ. Hist. Rev.*, 6, 1935-6, p. 150ff)
19 G. Unwin, *The Gilds and Companies of London*, p. 312
20 L. Stone, 'The Nobility in Business', in *The Entrepreneur*, pp. 19, 21. See also his *The Crisis of the Aristocracy*, 1965, p. 375
21 M. L. Campbell, *The English Yeoman under Elizabeth and the Early Stuarts*, 1942, p. 160ff
22 *The Commonwealth of England*, in G. W. Prothero, *Statutes and Constitutional Documents*, p. 177
23 E. Lipson, *Economic History of England*, 1931, ii, 6; F. J. Fisher, 'Some Experiments in Company Organization in the early Seventeenth Century', *Econ. Hist. Rev.*, 4, 1932-4, p. 177ff; M. Dobb, *Studies in the Development of Capitalism*, 1946, pp. 5ff, 18, 25. On the stages in economic development from the medieval gild see G. Unwin, *Industrial Organization in the Sixteenth and Seventeenth Centuries*, 1904, esp. pp. 10ff, 69, 79, 97, 103
24 W. Sombart, *Der Moderne Kapitalismus*, i, 2nd ed., 1916, pp. 836ff, 896ff ('Die Geburt des kapitalistischen Unternehmers')

25 E. J. Hobsbawm, 'The Crisis of the Seventeenth Century', in *Crisis in Europe* (ed. Trevor Aston, 1965), p. 16

26 A. G. Dickens, *The English Reformation*, 1964, p. 355. On this whole subject, which has given rise to a considerable body of controversial writing, see, e.g., M. Weber (tr. Talcott Parsons), *The Protestant Ethic and the Spirit of Protestantism*, 1930 (original work published in German in 1904-5); E. Troeltsch (tr. O. Wyon), *The Social Teaching of the Christian Churches*, 1931; R. H. Tawney, *Religion and the Rise of Capitalism*, 1926, and his Introduction to Thomas Wilson's *Discourse upon Usury*. See also C. Hill's essay, 'Protestantism and the Rise of Capitalism', in *Essays in the Economic and Social History of Tudor and Stuart England in honour of R. H. Tawney* (ed. F J. Fisher, 1961). A paperback in the series 'Problems of European Civilization', *Protestantism and Capitalism: the Weber Thesis and its Critics* (ed. R. W. Green, 1959) contains excerpts from the writings of some of the leading contributors to this controversy

27 J. U. Nef, *Cultural Foundations of Industrial Civilization*, pp. 47, 48

28 Earl J. Hamilton, 'American Treasure and the Rise of Capitalism', *Economica*, 9, 1929, p. 338ff. On p. 356 he quotes figures to suggest that the lag of wages behind prices might have quadrupled a capitalist's profits. See also his *American Treasure and the Price Revolution in Spain* (Harvard Economic Studies, xliii, 1934); G. N. Clark, *Science and Social Welfare in the Age of Newton*, p. 54; A. L. Rowse, *The England of Elizabeth*, 1950, p. 108ff

29 J. U. Nef, 'Prices and Industrial Capitalism in France and England, 1540-1640', *Econ. Hist. Rev.*, 7, 1936-7, p. 155ff, reprinted in E. M. Carus-Wilson (ed.), *Essays in Economic History*, i, 1954, p. 108ff

30 See J. U. Nef, 'War and Economic Progress, 1540-1640', *Econ. Hist. Rev.*, 12, 1942, p. 13ff

31 A. L. Rowse, *The England of Elizabeth*, pp. 109, 111, 114. See W. R. Scott, *The Constitution and Finance of . . . Joint Stock Companies to 1700*, 1910-12

32 R. H. Tawney, Introduction to Wilson's *Discourse upon Usury*, pp. 17ff, 50. Tawney also thought that the new types of capitalist enterprise were more important than the 'casual and intermittent transactions occasioned by aristocratic extravagance' (*ibid.*, p. 43)

33 P. J. Bowden, *The Wool Trade in Tudor and Stuart England*, 1962, pp. 77–9, 83

34 E. Lipson, *Economic History of England*, i, 5th ed. 1929, p. 416

2 THE CLOTH INDUSTRY (pages 30–52)

1 Figures from P. Ramsey, *Tudor Economic Problems*, 1963, p. 48. The standard size of a 'cloth', laid down in the Middle Ages, was 1½ ells in width and 26 ells in length (an ell was 45 inches), but in practice sizes varied with different kinds of cloth

2 For further details about the different kinds of cloth and the regions where they were made see P. J. Bowden, *The Wool Trade in Tudor and Stuart England*, 1962, pp. 45–56

3 *ibid.*, p. 6. cf p. 268, below

4 G. Unwin, *Studies in Economic History*, pp. 186–9, 318–9. The restrictions were finally abolished altogether in 1624

5 G. D. Ramsay, *The Wiltshire Woollen Industry*, 2nd ed. 1965, pp. 16–7. Cf also E. Lipson, *Economic History of England*, ii, 1931, pp. 8–9

6 G. D. Ramsay, *op cit.*, pp. 11, 12, 15, 19; *V.C.H. Glos.*, ii, p. 158; J. Leland, *Itinerary* (ed. Toumin Smith), i, p. 129. On the relative economic stability of clothiers and merchants see B. E. Supple, *Commercial Crisis and Change in England*, 1959, pp. 11–3

7 G. N. Clark, *The Wealth of England*, 1946, p. 31

8 G. D. Ramsay, *op. cit.*, p. 17

9 T. Fuller, *History of the Worthies of England* (ed. Nuttall, 1840), i, p. 137

10 'The Pleasant History of Iohn Winchcomb . . .', in F. O. Mann (ed.), *The Works of Thomas Deloney*, 1912, pp. 1–68

11 E. Lipson, *Economic History of England*, i, p. 419

12 G. Unwin, *Studies in Economic History*, p. 195

13 P. Laslett, *The World We Have Lost*, 1965, pp. 153–4

14 E. Lipson, *Economic History of England*, i, pp. 419–21

15 T. Fuller, *Worthies*, iii, p. 337. Fuller calls him 'T. Stumps'. The following account of Stumpe is drawn mainly from G. D. Ramsay, *op. cit.*, pp. 31–7, and articles by Canon F. H. Manley in *Wiltshire Notes and Queries*, 8, 1916, pp. 385ff, 444ff. Further articles on pp. 481ff and 531 trace the later history of other descendants and collateral relatives of the clothier

16 J. Leland, *Itinerary*, i, p. 132

17 T. Fuller, *Worthies*, iii, p. 337

18 G. D. Ramsay, *op. cit.*, p. 37

19 P Laslett, *op. cit.*, p. 153

20 *L. & P. Henry VIII*, 13, part 1, 1538, nos. 332, 415

21 T. Fuller, *Worthies*, i, pp. 136–7

22 E. Lipson, *Economic History of England*, i, pp. 413, 422

23 H. Heaton, *The Yorkshire Woollen and Worsted Industries*, 2nd ed.

1965, p. 90; A. P. Wadsworth and J. de L. Mann, *The Cotton Trade and Industrial Lancashire*, 1931, pp. 6–7

24 G. D. Ramsay, *op. cit.*, p. 40
25 J. Leland, *Itinerary*, i, pp. 127, 135, 143
26 G. D. Ramsay, *op. cit.*, p. 42
27 J. Prince, *The Worthies of Devon* (1810 ed.), p. 89
28 G. Unwin, 'The History of the Cloth Industry in Suffolk', *V.C.H. Suffolk*, ii, pp. 254-61 (reprinted in *Studies in Economic History*, p. 262ff)
29 G. D. Ramsay, *op. cit.*, pp. 43-7, 65, 71. John Methuen, M.P. for Devizes at the end of the seventeenth century, was the son of a clothier, but not a clothier himself
30 H. Heaton, *op. cit.*, pp. 100-1; H.M.C. Middleton, p. 498
31 The following account is based on the article by Esther Moir, 'Benedict Webb, Clothier', *Econ. Hist. Rev.*, 2nd ser. 10, 1957-8, pp. 256-64. Webb wrote a short autobiography, now preserved in Gloucester City Library
32 E. Wyndham Hulme, 'A History of the Patent System...', *L.Q.R.*, 12, 1896, p. 147; *Cal. S.P.D.* 1547-80, pp. 421, 438, 443
33 A. Friis, *Alderman Cockayne's Project and the Cloth Trade*, 1927. See also P. J. Bowden, *op. cit.*, pp. 187-9; C. Hill, *The Century of Revolution*, 1961, pp. 35-7; B. E. Supple, *Commercial Crisis and Change in England*, 1959, ch. II
34 F J. Fisher, 'Some Experiments in Company Organization in the Early Seventeenth Century', *Econ. Hist. Rev.*, 4, 1932-4, pp. 191-3

3 COAL (pages 53-72)

1 J. U. Nef, *The Rise of the British Coal Industry*, 1932, i, p. 135; *id.*, *Cultural Foundations of Industrial Civilization*, 1958, p. 46ff
2 L. Stone, *The Crisis of the Aristocracy*, 1965, p. 340
3 J. U. Nef, 'A Comparison of Industrial Growth in England and France from 1540 to 1640', *J. Pol. Econ.*, 44, 1936, pp. 506, 507; P. Ramsey, *Tudor Economic Problems*, 1963, p. 93
4 R. L. Galloway, *History of Coal-Mining in Great Britain*, 1882, p. 55; cf G. R. Lewis, *The Stannaries*, 1924, pp. 10-1
5 J. U. Nef, 'Dominance of the Trader in the English Coal Industry in the Seventeenth Century', *Journal of Economic and Business History*, 1, 1928-9, p. 423; *Rise of the British Coal Industry*, i, pp. 350ff, 378
6 *Rise of the British Coal Industry*, i, pp. 423, 427-8; ii, pp. 30, 33-34, 56
7 J. U. Nef, *J. Econ. and Business History*, 1, pp. 423-4, 427-31
8 The following paragraphs are based on the introduction by F. W.

Dendy to *Extracts from the Records of the Company of Hostmen of Newcastle-upon-Tyne*, Surtees Soc., vol. cv, 1901, pp. xiii, xxx-xxxix, xliii

9 Presumably the London chaldron of approximately 26½ cwt. A Newcastle chaldron, about half as big again as a London chaldron in 1600, increased in size during the seventeenth century, and was fixed in the eighteenth century as twice a London chaldron. See J. U. Nef, *Rise of the British Coal Industry*, ii, p. 367 (appendix c), corrected by T S. Willan, *The English Coasting Trade*, 1938, appendix 3

10 J. U. Nef, *op. cit.*, i, p. 150ff; *D.N.B.*

11 *ibid.*, i, pp. 38, 417, 421; ii, pp. 21-2

12 L. Stone, *The Crisis of the Aristocracy*, p. 341

13 R. L. Galloway, *History of Coal-Mining in Great Britain*, p. 56; J. U. Nef, *op. cit.*, i, p. 43; J. Nichols, *The Progresses ... of King James the First*, 1828, iii, p. 327; *D.N.B.* s.v. 'Taylor'

14 J. U. Nef, *op. cit.*, ii, pp. 3-11

15 There are numerous references to the Willoughbys' industrial activities in H.M.C. Middleton. Besides these, I am indebted in the following pages to J. U. Nef, *op. cit.*, i, p. 59; ii, pp. 3, 14ff; and R. S. Smith, 'Huntingdon Beaumont, Adventurer in Coal-Mines', *Renaissance and Modern Studies*, 1, Nottingham, 1957, p. 115ff. This article is based on correspondence among the Middleton MSS now in Nottingham University Library

16 R. A. Pelham, 'The Establishment of the Willoughby Ironworks in North Warwickshire in the sixteenth century', *Univ. of Birmingham Hist. Jnl.*, 4, 1953-4, pp. 18-29. This enterprise is described more fully in the next chapter

17 T. S. Ashton, *Iron and Steel in the Industrial Revolution*, 3rd ed. 1963, p. 6; H.M.C. Middleton, p. 496

18 R. H. Tawney, Introduction to Wilson's *Discourse upon Usury*, p. 52; B. G. Awty, 'Charcoal Ironmasters of Cheshire and Lancashire', *Lancs. & Cheshire Hist. Soc. Transactions*, 109, for 1957, 1958, p. 72

19 H.M.C. Middleton, pp. 182, 497, 500, 538, 589, 619; cf H. R. Trevor-Roper, *The Gentry 1540-1640* (*Econ. Hist. Rev. Supplement*), p. 16

20 H.M.C. Middleton, pp. 148-9.

21 J. U. Nef, *op. cit.*, ii, pp. 12-4

22 R. S. Smith, *Renaissance and Modern Studies*, 1, p. 125

23 J. U. Nef *op. cit.*, i, p. 384

24 Mr Smith shows that the date 1598 given in a reference to the rails in H.M.C. Middleton, p. 169, is an error for 1608

25 H.M.C. Middleton, pp. 172, 177

26 *Renaissance and Modern Studies*, 1, p. 147

27 H.M.C. Middleton, p. 183. The letter is dated 'c. 1615' in the H.M.C. Report, but its references to 'Mr Bate' and 'Lenton', of whose inactivity Beaumont is complaining, point to a date some years earlier

28 H.M.C. Middleton, p. 176

29 *Renaissance and Modern Studies*, i, p. 151

30 J. U. Nef, *op. cit.*, ii, pp. 16–7; L. Stone, *The Crisis of the Aristocracy*, p. 340

4 IRON AND STEEL (pages 73–105)

1 H. R. Schubert, *History of the British Iron and Steel Industry*, 1957, p. 162ff; id. ,'The First Cast-Iron Cannon made in England', *Jnl. of the Iron and Steel Institute*, 146, 1942, p. 131ff; E. Straker, *Wealden Iron*, 1931, pp. vi, 16; Rhys Jenkins, 'The Rise and Fall of the Sussex Iron Industry', *Transactions of the Newcomen Soc.*, i, for 1920-1, 1922, p. 16ff

2 In Edward VI's reign Norfolk's ironworks came into the hands of Lord Seymour of Sudeley, Somerset's younger brother. He too was attainted and executed soon afterwards. Cf M. S. Giuseppi, 'The Accounts of the Iron-Works at Sheffield and Worth in Sussex, 1546-49', *Archaeological Jnl.*, 69, 1912, p. 276ff. The double furnace and the forge at Worth together employed 33 workmen: H. Ellis, 'Inventories of Goods &c. . . . with the Iron Works belonging to the Lord Admiral Seymour . . .', *Sussex Archaeol. Collns*, 13, 1891, p. 120

3 T. S. Ashton, *Iron and Steel in the Industrial Revolution*, 3rd ed. 1963, p. 6; M. A. Lower, 'Iron Works of the County of Sussex', *Sussex Archaeol. Collns*, 2, 1849, p. 186

4 L. Stone, *The Crisis of the Aristocracy*, pp. 315–6; E. Straker, *Wealden Iron*, pp. 109, 117, 122ff; D. and G. Mathew, 'Iron Furnaces in South-Eastern England and English Ports and Landing-Places, 1578', *E.H.R.*, 48, 1933, p. 91; Lord Leconfield, *Petworth Manor in the Seventeenth Century*, 1954, pp. 93–103. An exception to the usual waste was the careful preservation and coppicing of the woodland at Newdigate in Surrey, belonging to Christopher Darrell, who had ironworks there and at Abinger (*V.C.H. Surrey*, ii, p. 269)

5 *Jnl of the Iron and Steel Institute*, 146, p. 139

6 Numerous accounts and other papers connected with the Sidney ironworks have been preserved (H.M.C. De l'Isle and Dudley, i, p. 305ff), and form the basis of descriptions by several historians. The fullest is by D. W. Crossley, 'The Management of a Sixteenth-Century Ironworks', *Econ. Hist. Rev.*, 2nd ser. 19, 1966, p. 273ff.

One of the account books has found lodgment in the Huntington Library in California, and is discussed by E. Straker, 'Westall's Book of Panningridge', *Sussex Archaeol. Collns*, 72, 1931, pp. 253–60. See also his *Wealden Iron*, pp. 49, 310ff

7   In 1574 the lease of Panningridge was obtained by the Ashburnham family, who were already working furnaces and forges, one dating from 1549, on their own estate close by. Sir John Ashburnham, as we saw in the last chapter, became entangled in Huntingdon Beaumont's coal-mining ventures, and had to alienate his ancestral property. The wife of his eldest son, who was a prominent royalist in the Civil War, sold her own property in order to buy back the Ashburnham estate. The family continued to be important ironmasters for many years, and the last furnace working in the county, which did not close down till 1812, belonged to them

8   E. Straker, *Wealden Iron*, pp. 192, vii

9   There had been some previous attempts at steel-making, earlier in the century, in Ashdown Forest, but they apparently did not long survive. My account of the steelworks is based on Rhys Jenkins, 'Notes on the Early History of Steel Making in England', *Transactions of the Newcomen Soc.*, 3, for 1922-3, 1924, p. 16ff; H. R. Schubert, 'The Economic Aspect of Sir Henry Sidney's Steelworks at Robertsbridge in Sussex and Boxhurst in Kent', *Jnl of the Iron and Steel Institute*, 164, 1950, pp. 278–80; id., *History of the British Iron and Steel Industry*, p. 314ff; E. Straker, *Wealden Iron*, p. 312ff

10   W. Llewellin, 'Sussex Ironmasters in Glamorganshire', *Archaeologia Cambrensis*, 3rd ser. 9, 1863, pp. 83ff, 95ff

11   H.M.C. De l'Isle and Dudley, i, p. 29

12   T. Bevan, 'Sussex Ironmasters in Glamorgan', *Cardiff Naturalists' Soc. Reports and Transactions*, 86, 1956-7, pp. 5–12

13   The following pages are based on M. B. Donald, *Elizabethan Monopolies*, 1961, pp. 3–4, 61, 109–35; H. R. Schubert, *History of the British Iron and Steel Industry*, pp. 117–9, 293–9

14   M. B. Donald, *Elizabethan Monopolies*, pp. 121, 136, 137, 160, 162

15   H. G. Nicholls, *Iron Making in the Olden Times in the Forest of Dean*, 1866, p. 27. The following account is based mainly on Rhys Jenkins, 'Iron-making in the Forest of Dean', *Trans. Newcomen Soc.*, 6, for 1925-6, 1927, p. 47ff; H. R. Schubert, *op. cit.*, p. 195ff

16   T. Fuller, *Worthies* (ed. Nuttall, 1840), i, p. 547; Rhys Jenkins, *Trans. Newcomen Soc.*, 3, 1924, pp. 18–23; H. R. Schubert, *op. cit.*, pp. 323–5. The Meyseys were a family with estates in Wiltshire and Gloucestershire, but there seems to be no direct evidence of any previous connection with Brooke. On Fludd see *D.N.B.* and Sir

George Clark, *History of the Royal College of Physicians of London*, i, 1964, p. 200

17 Rhys Jenkins, *Trans. Newcomen Soc.*, 6, pp. 49–52

18 B. G. Awty, 'Charcoal Ironmasters of Cheshire and Lancashire', *Lancs. and Cheshire Hist Soc.*, 109, for 1957, 1958, p. 74

19 H. C. B. Mynors, 'Iron Manufacture under Charles I', *Transactions of the Woolhope Naturalists' Field Club*, 34, 1952, p. 3ff. Further details of costs are given on p. 5

20 W. H. B. Court, *The Rise of the Midland Industries*, 1938, pp. 36, 71ff

21 R. A. Pelham, 'The Migration of the Iron Industry towards Birmingham during the Sixteenth Century', *Trans. Birmingham Archaeol. Soc.*, 66, 1950, pp. 143–8; *id.*, 'The Establishment of the Willoughby Ironworks in North Warwickshire in the Sixteenth Century', *Univ. of Birmingham Hist. Jnl*, 4, 1953-4, p. 19; L. Stone, *The Crisis of the Aristocracy*, pp. 348, 350

22 H. R. Schubert, 'Shrewsbury Letters, a Contribution to the History of Ironmaking', *Jnl. of the Iron and Steel Institute*, 155, 1947, p. 521ff. In the following account I am indebted to this article, based on a collection of letters in Sheffield Central Library

23 H.M.C. Cal. Shrewsbury and Talbot Papers, i, p. 92

24 L. Stone, *The Crisis of the Aristocracy*, pp. 351, 352, 375. Details of the working of a coalpit belonging to Shrewsbury may be found in Prof. Stone's article 'An Elizabethan Coalmine', *Econ. Hist. Rev.*, 2nd ser. 3, 1950, pp. 97–106

25 H.M.C. Middleton, p. 494

26 R A. Pelham, *Univ. of Birmingham Hist. Jnl*, 4, pp. 18–29

27 L. Stone, *The Crisis of the Aristocracy*, p. 347

28 A. Fell, *The Early Iron Industry of Furness and District*, 1908, pp. 24–9, 76, 179, 256–7

29 W. I. Macadam, 'Notes on the Ancient Iron Industry of Scotland', *Proc. Soc. Antiquaries of Scotland*, N.S. 9, 1887, p. 89ff

30 Rhys Jenkins, 'The Slitting Mill', in *Collected Papers*, 1936, pp. 9–23; W. H. B. Court, *The Rise of the Midland Industries*, pp. 105–8; J Nicholls, *Some Account of the Worshipful Company of Ironmongers*, 2nd ed. 1866, p. 164ff. According to Schubert (*History of the British Iron and Steel Industry*, p. 306) Foley set up his slitting mill about 1625

31 *Cal. S.P.D.* 1635-6, pp. 400, 435; L. Stone, *op. cit.*, p. 348

32 Dud Dudley, *Mettallum Martis*, reprinted 1855; R. L. Galloway, *History of Coal-Mining in Great Britain*, pp. 42–50; W. H. Price, *The English Patents of Monopoly* (Harvard Economic Studies, 1906), p. 107ff; R. A. Mott, 'Dud Dudley and the Early Iron Industry',

Trans. Newcomen Soc., 15, for 1934-5, 1936, p. 17ff; T. S. Ashton, *Iron and Steel in the Industrial Revolution*, pp. 10–2

33 J. U. Nef, 'Notes on the Progress of Iron Production in England, 1540-1640', *Jnl of Pol. Econ.*, 44, 1936, pp. 400–3

34 L. Stone, *op. cit.*, pp. 345, 348, 351

5 COPPER AND BRASS (pages 106–126)

1 *L. & P. Henry VIII*, 4, part 2, no. 5110; *ibid.*, 14, part 1, no. 946

2 The following account is based mainly on the information contained in M. B. Donald, *Elizabethan Copper*, 1955; also on H. Hamilton, *The English Brass and Copper Industries to 1800*, 1926; W. R. Scott, *The Constitution and Finance of . . . Joint-Stock Companies to 1720*, 1912, ii, p. 383ff; W. H. Price, *The English Patents of Monopoly* (*Harvard Economic Studies*, 1906), p. 49ff. On Gundelfinger and Kranich see below, pp. 138, 158, 16off. W. G. Collingwood, *Elizabethan Keswick* (Cumberland and Westmorland Antiq. and Archaeol. Soc., Tract Series, viii, 1912), based on the journals of the German miners preserved at Augsburg, is full of domestic and other details about their life and work. The *Calendars of State Papers Domestic*, 1547-80 and 1581-90, contain numerous references to the subjects described in this chapter

3 Printed in R. H. Tawney and E. Power, *Tudor Economic Documents*, 1924, i, pp. 240–1

4 *ibid.*, i, pp. 247-50

5 *Cal. S.P.D., Addenda* 1566-79, pp. 17, 19

6 The mine had been known since the thirteenth century, and it seems strange that the Germans did not start work there at once (W. G. Collingwood, *Elizabethan Keswick*, p. 10)

7 *The Case of the Mines* is reported in 1 Plowden, 310–40; the judgments are at p. 336

8 1 William & Mary c. 30; 5 William & Mary c. 6

9 M. B. Donald, *Elizabethan Copper*, p. 242. The charter is printed in Tawney and Power, *op. cit.*, pp. 250–62

10 H. Hamilton, *The English Brass and Copper Industries*, p. 12

11 M. B Donald, *Elizabethan Copper*, p. 216ff

12 In the following pages I am indebted to the information about the history of this company in M. B. Donald, *Elizabethan Monopolies*, 1961

13 R. H. Tawney and E. Power, *Tudor Economic Documents*, i, pp. 242–3

14 *ibid.*, i, pp. 243–5

15 Latten (French *laiton*) meant an alloy of copper and zinc, or rather

calamine (zinc carbonate), for metallic zinc was unknown, in certain proportions; but it was often used to denote any kind of brass. Brass was also sometimes used loosely to include bronze (an alloy of copper and tin)

16 R. H. Tawney and E. Power, *op. cit.*, i, pp. 245–6

17 M. B. Donald, *Elizabethan Monopolies*, p. 87ff; *Cal. S.P.D.* 1547-80, pp. 259, 261, 278, 311; J. W. Gough, *The Mines of Mendip*, 1930, p. 206ff; H. Hamilton, *The English Brass and Copper Industries*, p. 14ff; J. Pettus, *Fodinae Regales*, 1670, p. 20ff; Moses Stringer, *Opera Mineralia Explicata*, 1713, p. 34ff

18 Acts P.C., N.S. xxvii, p. 235 (1597)

19 On Brode see M. B. Donald, *Elizabethan Monopolies*, pp. 179-94; H. Hamilton, *op. cit.*, pp. 32–6; J. W. Gough, *op. cit.*, pp. 209–13

20 *Cal. S.P.D.* 1634-5, p. 579

21 It has generally been said that the two companies were amalgamated in 1668, but this seems doubtful: see D. Seaborne Davies, 'The Records of the Mines Royal and the Mineral and Battery Works', *Econ. Hist. Rev.*, 6, 1935-6, p. 212

22 H. Hamilton, *op. cit.*, p. 31

23 M. B. Donald, *Elizabethan Monopolies*, p. viii. Weston's identity has puzzled previous writers on this subject

24 T. Fuller, *Worthies* (ed. Nuttall, 1840), iii, p. 482; J. W. Gough, *Sir Hugh Myddelton*, 1964, p. 102

25 See M. B. Donald, *Elizabethan Copper*, p. 299ff; W. R. Scott, *Joint-Stock Companies*, ii, p. 396ff; A. L. Rowse, *Tudor Cornwall*, 1941, pp. 56-8, and for Carnsew's life as a country squire, pp. 426-33

26 *Cal. S.P.D.* 1581-90, pp. 172–3

27 *ibid.*, pp. 153, 164

28 *ibid.*, p. 194

29 *ibid.*, p. 176. One of Frosse's letters to Carnsew, reporting on conditions at Treworthy and Illogan, is printed in Tawney and Power, *Tudor Economic Documents*, i, pp. 264–6

30 *Cal. S.P.D.* 1581-90, p. 201

31 H.M.C. Salisbury, v, pp. 14–5, 198–9, 206; vii, p. 233

6 TIN AND LEAD (pages 127–146)

1 On the early history of the tin industry see G. R. Lewis, *The Stannaries* (Harvard Economic Studies, iii, 1907); A. K. Hamilton Jenkin, *The Cornish Miner*, 1927, ch. 1–4; L. F. Salzman, *English Industries of the Middle Ages*, 2nd ed. 1923, ch. 4; A. L. Rowse, *Tudor Cornwall*, ch. 3

2 R. Carew, *Survey of Cornwall*, 1602, f. 15ᵛ. The passage quoted is

printed in Tawney and Power, *Tudor Economic Documents*, pp. 290–1

3 *Cf* R. H. Tawney's Introduction to Wilson's *Discourse upon Usury*, pp. 54–7; H. Levy, *Monopoly and Competition*, 1911, pp. 54-5

4 R. Carew, *Survey of Cornwall*, f. 14ᵛ; Tawney and Power, pp. 289–90

5 Symonds's Diary, quoted by A. L. Rowse, *Tudor Cornwall*, p. 217

6 G. R. Lewis, *The Stannaries*, pp. 128–9, 189

7 *ibid.*, p. 223

8 R. Carew, *Survey of Cornwall*, f. 10ʳ

9 *ibid.*, f. 13ʳ

10 H. R. Coulthard, *The Story of an Ancient Parish, Breage with Germoe*, 1913, pp. 95–6, 105. This suggestion is based on the occurrence of the name Erasmus in the Breage parish registers. It seems unlikely that the man was related to the great Dutch humanist of the same name

11 G. R. Lewis, *The Stannaries*, pp. 144ff, 217ff; A. L. Rowse, *Tudor Cornwall*, p. 63ff; *Cal. S.P.D.* 1598-1601, pp. 202, 330; H.M.C. Salisbury, x, pp. 375, 426–7

12 A L. Rowse, *op. cit.*, p. 62; M. Coate, *Cornwall in the Great Civil War*, 1933, pp. 6–8

13 G. R. Lewis, *The Stannaries*, pp. 18–9, and appendix J

14 L. F. Salzman, *English Industries of the Middle Ages*, p. 66

15 *V.C.H. Derbyshire*, ii, p. 331; L. Stone, *The Crisis of the Aristocracy*, pp. 343–4

16 M. B. Donald, *Elizabethan Monopolies*, p. 148ff; L. Stone, *op. cit.*, p. 343, attributes the ownership of Beauchief and support of Humfrey to the Earl of Shrewsbury, but see C. Kerry, 'Notes on the Pedigree of the Strelleys . . .', *Derbyshire Arch. & Nat. Hist. Soc. Jnl*, 14, 1892, p. 95; S. Glover, *History of the County of Derby*, ed. T. Noble, 1929, ii, p. 94

17 The depositions in these disputes are summarized in M. B. Donald, *Elizabethan Monopolies*, pp. 142-75, and my account is based on this source unless otherwise stated

18 A. Raistrick and B. Jennings, *History of Lead-Mining in the Pennines*, 1965, p. 74; M. B. Donald, *op. cit.*, pp. 155–6

19 *V.C.H. Derbyshire*, ii, p. 331; H.M.C. Rutland, i, p. 116; H.M.C. Cal. Shrewsbury and Talbot Papers, i, p. 43

20 Shrewsbury may have agreed with Humfrey on the same terms, but in 1578, when with Humfrey's consent he erected smelting works at Crich Chase, he refused to pay more than 2s. 6d. a fother, or a lump sum of 100 marks (M. B. Donald, *op. cit.*, p. 170). *Cf* also H.M.C. Cal. Shrewsbury and Talbot Papers, i, p. 42

21 H.M.C. Cal. Shrewsbury and Talbot Papers, i, p. 176

22 J. W. Gough, *The Mines of Mendip*, pp. 140, 144–9

23 e.g. in L. F. Salzman, *English Industries of the Middle Ages*, p. 27;
    A. L. Rowse, *The England of Elizabeth*, p. 128; M. B. Donald, *Eliza-bethan Monopolies*, p. 160; and in his article on Burchard Kranich
    in *The Annals of Science*, 6, 1950

24 Above, chapter 4

25 M. B. Donald, *Elizabethan Monopolies*, p. 175; A. Raistrick and
    B. Jennings, *History of Lead-Mining in the Pennines*, pp. 73–81; E.
    Wyndham Hulme, 'A History of the Patent System under the Pre-rogative and at Common Law', *L.Q.R.*, 12, 1896, p. 148, reprinted
    in *Early History of the English Patent System*, 1909, p. 126

26 A. Raistrick and B. Jennings, *op. cit.*, p. 72; N. Kirkham, 'The
    Tumultuous Course of Dovegang', *Derbyshire Arch. & Nat. Hist.
    Soc. Jnl*, 73, (N.S. 26), 1953, pp. 6–7

27 Henry Carey, Viscount Rochford, who became Earl of Dover in
    1628, was a landowner in the neighbourhood

28 N. Kirkham, *Derbyshire Arch. & Nat. Hist. Soc. Jnl*, *loc. cit.*; F. N.
    Fisher, 'Sir Cornelius Vermuyden and the Dovegang Lead Mine',
    ibid., 72 (N.S. 25), pp. 74–118

29 R. S. France, 'The Thieveley Lead Mines, 1629-35', *Lancs. & Cheshire
    Record Soc.*, 102, for 1947, 1951, pp. iv, 1ff. The mine was reopened
    in the eighteenth century, but again made losses and was abandoned
    once more within a few years

30 A. Raistrick and B. Jennings, *History of Lead-Mining in the Pennines*,
    p. 56

31 *ibid.*, pp. 59–60, 110–3

32 Some details of the bishops' income from lead are given in P. M.
    Hembry, *The Bishops of Bath and Wells, 1540-1640*, 1967, pp. 187–92, 263. The lot-lead received in the seventeenth century by the
    Waldegrave family at Chewton is given in J. W. Gough, *The Mines
    of Mendip*, pp. 152–6. In Derbyshire the 'thirteenth dish' was pay-able as a royalty to the Crown

7 GOLD AND SILVER (pages 147–175)

1 R. W. Cochran-Patrick (ed.), *Early Records relating to Mining in
   Scotland*, 1878, pp. xiv, xv

2 *ibid.*, p. xvi

3 S. Atkinson, *The Discoverie and Historie of the Gold Mynes in
   Scotland*, 1825; written in 1619, p. 18ff. See also R. W. Cochran-Patrick, *op. cit.*, p. xviff; J. Calvert, *The Gold Rocks of Great Britain
   and Ireland*, 1853, p. 131ff; A.B.G[rosart], 'A Trip to the Gold
   Regions of Scotland', *Gentleman's Magazine*, N.S. 39, 1853, p. 462ff

4 S. Atkinson, *op. cit.*, pp. 21–2

5 H. M. Robertson, 'Sir Bevis Bulmer', *Jnl of Economic and Business History*, 4, 1931-2, p. 99ff. I am much indebted to this article in the following account of Bulmer's career; also to Rhys Jenkins's note on him in *Collected Papers*, 1936, pp. 24–7 (reprinted from *N. & Q.*, 11th ser., iv, 1911)

6 Acts P.C., N.S. xiv, 353ff; J. W. Gough, *The Mines of Mendip*, pp. 126–9

7 S. Atkinson, *op. cit.*, p. 51ff

8 H. M. Robertson, *op. cit.*, p. 104

9 S. Atkinson, *op. cit.*, pp. 53–4

10 *Cal. S.P.D.* 1603-10, pp. 51, 68, 196, 221, 298

11 J. Calvert, *op. cit.*, p. 160; H. M. Robertson, *op. cit.*, p. 107

12 S. Atkinson, *op. cit.*, p. 42

13 *ibid.*, pp. 44–7

14 According to Atkinson, *op. cit.*, pp. 30–1, but his chronology must be wrong. He makes Bowes go to England to report to 'the Queen', and says that when the accident happened Daniel Höchstetter was with him and was hurt, but escaped alive. But Daniel Höchstetter died in 1581, and even if Atkinson meant one of his sons, the reference to the Queen must be an error, for Bowes was still working at Wanlockhead in 1604 (R. W. Cochran-Patrick, *op. cit.*, pp. xixff, 103ff)

15 Extracts of the accounts of the Hilderstone mine, with lists of workmen ('pickmen, draueris up of watter, cuttaris of wode, caryaris of wode, smythis, wrichtis, quarriours', etc.) may be found in R. W. Cochran-Patrick, *op. cit.*, p. 141ff, and in appendix v of S. Atkinson, *Discoverie and Historie*, p. 92ff

16 H. M. Robertson, *op. cit.*, p. 118; S. Atkinson, *op. cit.*, p. 40

17 J. Webster, *Metallographia, or an History of Metals*, pp. 20–1, 24. This book was published in 1671, and the writer says that Bulmer was at work 'betwixt 50 and 70 years since'

18 S. Atkinson, *op. cit.*, p. 43; H. M. Robertson, *op. cit.*, p. 119. But cf the reference in J. Calvert, *The Gold Rocks*, p. 134, to a paper, damaged by fire and fragmentary, among the Cottonian MSS (Otho E.x)

19 S. Atkinson, *op. cit.*, pp. 40–1

20 *ibid.*, p. 40

21 L. F. Salzman, *English Industries of the Middle Ages*, p. 41ff

22 Acts P.C. 1542-7, p. 501

23 *Cal. S.P. Foreign*, 1547-53, p. 57

24 *Cal. S.P. Ireland*, 1509-73, pp. 123, 124, 128

25 M. B. Donald, *Elizabethan Monopolies*, p. 12; R. B. Turton, *The Alum Farm*, 1938, p. 12
26 *Cal S.P. Ireland*, 1509-73, pp. 218–9, 236
27 See M. B. Donald, 'Burchard Kranich (c. 1515-1578), Miner and Queen's Physician', *Annals of Science*, 6, 1948-50, pp. 308–22
28 Acts P.C. 1554-6, pp. 211–3. The reference to separating and dividing points to the refining of silver as the primary objective
29 *ibid.*, p. 294
30 Part of the list of items of expenditure in connection with the melting-house was printed by L. F. Salzman, *op. cit.*, p. 75. But its purpose was to produce silver, not tin as he stated
31 He seems nevertheless to have recommended the ore as worth pursuing, and further tests were made; but it turned out to be valueless, and a number of people, including the Queen, lost the money they invested in subsequent expeditions which brought tons of it back to England. See A. L. Rowse, *The Expansion of Elizabethan England*, pp. 193–4
32 Gerard Malynes, *Consuetudo, vel Lex Mercatoria*, 1622, pp. 262–3. The book continues with accounts of the work of Bevis Bulmer and other mining entrepreneurs in Scotland, at Combe Martin, and elsewhere
33 The following pages are based on my account of Myddelton's career, *Sir Hugh Myddelton, Entrepreneur and Engineer*, 1964, in which references to sources will be found
34 The following account of Bushell is based on my biography of him, *The Superlative Prodigall*, 1932, q.v. for a fuller account, with references. The title was taken from his own description of himself in 1628, when he published *The First Part of Youth's Errors*, by 'Thomas Bushel, the Superlative Prodigall'
35 Cf B. Farrington, *Francis Bacon, Philosopher of Industrial Science*, 1951, pp. 10, 12
36 *A Just and True Remonstrance of His Majesty's Mines Royal in the Principality of Wales*, 1642
37 Fuller accepted Bushell's claim to be putting Bacon's ideas into effect, and referred to the 'rarest invention' of ventilating mines by pipe and bellows as 'the master-piece of Sir Francis Bacon, Lord Verulam' (*Worthies*, ed. Nuttall, ii, 482–3). But, like the use of adits, it had really been invented by the Germans and was illustrated in Agricola
38 J. Pettus, *Fodinae Regales*, 1670, p. 33

8 ALUM (pages 176–196)

1 Rhys Jenkins, *Collected Papers*, 1936, p. 198. In the following pages I rely largely on his paper, 'The Alum Trade in the Fifteenth and Sixteenth Centuries, and the Beginnings of the Alum Industry in England, *ibid.*, pp. 193-203; also on Claire Cross, *The Puritan Earl: Henry Hastings, Third Earl of Huntingdon*, 1966, p. 87ff

2 *Cal. S.P.D. Addenda*, 1566-79, p. 24

3 L. Stone, *The Crisis of the Aristocracy*, p. 336

4 8 Eliz. I, c. 21

5 *The Journeys of Celia Fiennes*, ed. C. Morris, 1949, p. 10. The process used in 1634 at a copperas works at Queensborough in the Isle of Sheppey, though differing in details, was essentially similar: see W. Brereton, *Travels in Holland, the United Provinces, England, Scotland, and Ireland*, ed. E. Hawkins, Chetham Soc., i, 1844, pp. 2-3

6 J. Strype, *Life of Sir Thomas Smith*, 1820, p. 100ff

7 Sir John Wynne, *History of the Gwydir Family*, 1878, p. ix; Rhys Jenkins, *Collected Papers*, p. 203

8 The fullest account of the alum industry in Yorkshire is in R. B. Turton, *The Alum Farm*, 1938, p. 59ff, and in the following pages I am greatly indebted to this. I have also used W. H. Price, *The English Patents of Monopoly*, 1906, p. 83ff. There is a brief account of the early stages of the alum ventures in G. Malynes, *Consuetudo, vel Lex Mercatoria*, pp. 270-1

9 The confusion (e.g. in *D.N.B.*) has been cleared up by R. B. Turton. On Lambay cf above, chapter 5, p. 116; chapter 7, p. 160

10 For descriptions of the processes of alum manufacture see Rhys Jenkins, *Collected Papers*, pp. 198, 201-2; R. B. Turton, *The Alum Farm*, p. 102ff. Cf also J. Beckmann, *A History of Inventions, Discoveries and Origins*, trans. W. Johnston, 4th ed., revised by W. Francis and J. W. Griffith, 1846, p. 197

11 R. Steele, *Tudor and Stuart Proclamations*, i, 1081

12 Menna Prestwich, *Cranfield: Politics and Profits under the Early Stuarts*, 1966, p. 59

13 'Star Chamber Proceedings against the Earl of Suffolk and others' (1619), *E.H.R.*, 13, 1898, pp. 718-9

14 A vivid impression of the state of affairs at the works about this time is given in letters to Ingram from George Low and Thomas Russell, printed in H.M.C. *Various Collections*, viii, pp. 11, 14-19

15 A. F. Upton, *Sir Arthur Ingram*, 1961, p. 145. I am much indebted to this work for my discussion in the preceding pages of Ingram's career and his part in the alum business

16 Menna Prestwich, *op. cit.*, pp. 59, 64ff
17 Acts P.C. Jan.-Aug. 1627, pp. 434, 444–5; *ibid.*, Sept. 1627-June 1628, p. 20. Cf Sir George Clark, *History of the Royal College of Physicians*, i, 1964, p 255

9 SALT AND SALTPETRE (pages 197–207)

1 In the following account I am indebted to E. Hughes, 'The English Monopoly of Salt in the years 1563-71', *E.H.R.*, 40, 1925, p. 334ff, and his essay 'The Elizabethan Salt Patents', in *Studies in Administration and Finance*, 1934, pp. 31–66; also, for some information about Francis Bertye, to M. B. Donald, *Elizabethan Monopolies*, pp. 54–7. On the numerous uses of salt about this time, and the chief European centres of production, see A. R. Bridbury, *England and the Salt Trade in the Later Middle Ages*, 1955
2 J. A. Twemlow, *E.H.R.*, 36, 1921, pp. 214–8
3 8 Eliz. c. 22
4 The processes at Lymington in Hampshire in the later seventeenth century were described by Celia Fiennes (*Journeys*, ed. C. Morris, pp. 49–50). She also refers to the salt-works at Nantwich and Northwich in Cheshire (pp. 177, 224–5) and Droitwich in Worcestershire (p. 231)
5 R. H. Tawney and E. Power, *Tudor Economic Documents*, ii, pp. 254–7
6 *ibid*, ii, pp. 257–62; Acts P.C. 1586-7, p. 395
7 Acts P.C. 1587-8, p. 216
8 Acts P.C. 1588-9, pp. 384–5
9 Acts P.C. 1590, p. 186
10 W. H. Price, *The English Patents of Monopoly*, pp. 112-6
11 J. U. Nef, 'A Comparison of Industrial Growth in England and France from 1540 to 1640', *Jnl Pol. Econ.*, 44, 1936, pp. 296-7
12 *V. C. H. Surrey*, ii, pp. 307ff, on which the following account is based
13 J. P. Kenyon, *The Stuart Constitution*, 1966, p. 69
14 *The Case of Saltpetre*, 12 Co. Rep. 12. For some examples of the activities of the saltpetremen in Dorset in 1635 see the article by J. P. Ferris in *Proc. Dorset Natural History and Archaeol. Soc.*, 85, for 1963, 1964
15 16 Charles I, c. 21

10 GLASS (pages 208–226)

1 C. Dawson, 'Old Sussex Glass: its Origin and Decline', *The Anti-*

quary, N.S. I, 1905, p. 8ff; S. E. Winbolt, *Wealden Glass*, 1933, p. 7ff; *V.C.H. Surrey*, ii, p. 297ff; W. H. Price, *The English Patents of Monopoly*, 1906, p. 67ff

2 A. Hartshorne, *Old English Glasses*, 1897, pp. 148–51; W. A. Thorne, *A History of English and Irish Glass*, 1929, pp. 61–2

3 For the following account I am indebted, besides the works mentioned in the last note, to three articles by E. Wyndham Hulme, entitled 'English Glass-Making in the Sixteenth and Seventeenth Centuries', *The Antiquary*, 30, 1894, pp. 210–4; 31, 1895, pp. 68–72, 102–5. The same author's 'The French Glass-makers in England in 1567', *ibid.*, 34, 1898, pp. 142–5, contains transcripts of their applications for grants. A number of original documents are also printed in the appendix to Hartshorne's work. Sir Robert Mansell's patents are printed in appendixes Y and z in W. H. Price, *The English Patents of Monopoly*. The fullest account of the early English industry, and of the work of Carré and the French glass makers he introduced, is in G. H. Kenyon, *The Glass Industry of the Weald*, 1967

4 *Cal. S.P.D. Addenda*, 1566-79, p. 34

5 *ibid.*, p. 315

6 R. H. Tawney and E. Power, *Tudor Economic Documents*, i, pp. 302–7

7 S. E. Winbolt, *Wealden Glass*, p. 17

8 The four surviving glasses then attributed to Verzelini were described by W. A. Thorne, *op. cit.*, p. 78. Two others have since come to light

9 *Cal. S.P.D.* 1591-4, p. 179

10 Above, p. 103

11 Above, p. 119, M. B. Donald, *Elizabethan Monopolies*, p. 58

12 W. A. Thorne, *op. cit.*, p. 90

13 L. Stone, *The Crisis of the Aristocracy*, p. 353; G. H. Kenyon, *op. cit.*, p. 125

14 *Cal. S.P.D.* 1611-8, p. 207

15 R. Steele, *Tudor and Stuart Proclamations*, i, no. 1164; *Cal. S.P.D.* 1611-8, p. 287

16 For Mansell's career, besides the works already mentioned, I have used G. T. Clark, *Some Account of Sir Robert Mansel Kt.*, 1883. These exploits are referred to on p. 12

17 *Cal. S.P.D.* 1611-18, p. 538

18 *Cal. S.P.D.* 1619-23, p. 3

19 *ibid.*, p. 138

20 *ibid.*, p. 129

21 *ibid.*, pp. 121, 134

22 *ibid.*, p. 114
23 *ibid.*, p. 243
24 Above, p. 65
25 *Cal. S.P.D.* 1619-23, p. 330
26 *Cal S.P.D.* 1623-5, p. 215. The documents in the dispute are cited in A. Hartshorne, *op, cit.*, pp. 195-8. Numerous references to Mansell's monopoly, and the objections and disputes to which it gave rise, will be found in the Acts P.C.
27 Acts P.C. June-Dec. 1626, pp. 394-5
28 *Cal. S.P.D.* 1634-5, p. 476
29 *Cal. S.P.D.* 1635, p. 429
30 *Cal. S.P.D.* 1637-8, pp. 153-4
31 *Cal. S.P.D.* 1640-1, p. 65
32 H.M.C. Leeds, p. 91
33 G. T. Clark, *op. cit.*, p. 52; A. Hartshorne, *op. cit.*, p. 203
34 A. Hartshorne, *op. cit.*, p. 202
35 W. A. Thorne, *op. cit.*, p. 98

II ENTREPRENEURS IN SOME MISCELLANEOUS INDUSTRIES
(pages 227-248)

1 J. Humphreys, 'Elizabethan Sheldon Tapestries', *Archaeologia*, 74, 1923-4, p. 181ff; E. A. B. Barnard and A. J. B. Wace, 'The Sheldon Tapestry Weavers', *Archaeologia*, 78, 1928, p. 255ff. My account is based largely on these articles
2 See *Cal. S.P.D.* 1591-4, pp. 531, 541-7, 552, 554, 555; 1603-10, p. 479
3 J. Humphreys, *op. cit.*, p. 183; but according to Lord Crawford (*ibid.*, p. 201) the Sheldon tapestries had nothing in common with contemporary Flemish work, and he believed that tapestry-making must have been already in existence in England before the Sheldon enterprise. A. J. B. Wace (*Archaeologia*, 78, p. 287) argued that Sheldon's wish for his workers to be Englishmen meant that 'no foreigners need have been brought over'; but this does not seem to follow. Many Elizabethan entrepreneurs wanted to establish industries which should employ English workmen, but they often needed foreigners to get their enterprises started
4 Quoted in their articles by both Humphreys and Barnard
5 E. A. B. Barnard, *Archaeologia*, 78, p. 272. Yet Flemings were imported to start and run the factory at Mortlake
6 J. E. Anderson, *A Short Account of the Tapestry Works, Mortlake*, 1894, p. 4; *Cal. S.P.D.* 1619-23, p. 72; 1623-25, p. 445. The following account is based largely on Anderson; see also *V.C.H. Surrey*, ii,

p. 354ff, and E. Müntz (tr. L. J. Davis), *A Short History of Tapestry*, 1885, pp. 295–306

7 J. E. Anderson, *op. cit.*, pp. 8–9; *Cal. S.P.D.* 1629-31, p. 442; 1631-3, p. 110; 1633-4, p. 474

8 *Cal. S.P.D.* 1635-6, pp. 274, 321, 372; 1636-7, p. 25

9 *Cal. S.P.D.* 1636-7, p. 278

10 *ibid.*, p. 567; J. E. Anderson, *op. cit.*, p. 12

11 Rhys Jenkins, 'Early Attempts at Paper-making in England, 1495-1586', in *Collected Papers*, pp. 155–8: D. C. Coleman, *The British Paper Industry*, 1958, pp. 4, 40

12 *A Discourse of the Common Weal* (ed. E. Lamond, 1929), pp. 63, 65

13 Thomas Churchyard, 'A Description and playne Discourse of Paper, and the whole benefits that Paper brings, with rehearsall, and setting foorth in Verse a Paper-Myll built near Darthford, by an High Germaine, called Master Spilman, Jeweller to the Queen's Majestie', in J. Nichols, *The Progresses and Public Processions of Queen Elizabeth*, ii, 1823, pp. 592–602

14 J. Aubrey, *Brief Lives* (ed. A. Clark, 1898), ii, p. 323

15 J. Aubrey, *Natural History of Wiltshire*, 1847 ed., p. 95. He says that it 'is now, 1684, about 130 yeares standing'

16 Rhys Jenkins, *loc. cit.*, pp. 160–1

17 *Cal. S.P.D.* 1581-90, p. 378; R. H. Tawney and E. Power, *Tudor Economic Documents*, ii, 251–4

18 *Cal. S.P.D.* 1581-90, p. 296

19 D. C. Coleman, *op. cit.*, pp. 34–9, 53, 80–3

20 For the following pages I have used the accounts of Spilman's enterprise in Rhys Jenkins, *op. cit.*, p. 162ff, and D. C. Coleman, *op. cit.*, pp. 43–54; also G. H. Overend, 'Notes upon the Earlier History of the Manufacture of Paper in England', *Proc. Huguenot Society of London*, 8, 1909, pp. 177–95

21 *Cal. S.P.D.* 1581-90, p. 556

22 Acts P.C. 1598-99, pp. 106–7

23 Acts P.C. 1600-1, p. 274; *Cal. S.P.D.* 1601-3, pp. 43–4

24 J. Aubrey, *Natural History of Wiltshire*, p. 95

25 In the following pages I am indebted to Professor George Unwin's account of the pin-making monopoly in his *Industrial Organization in the Sixteenth and Seventeenth Centuries*, 1904, p. 164ff; also to the discussion of the relationship between pin-making and the market for wire manufactured by the Mineral and Battery Works, in H. Hamilton, *The English Brass and Copper Industries to 1800*, p. 46ff. Cf also G. Unwin, *The Gilds and Companies of London*, 1938 ed., pp. 306, 316–7

26 Above, p. 121
27 G. Unwin, *Industrial Organization*, p. 168
28 *ibid.*, pp. 144–5
29 My account follows M. A. Abrams, 'The English Gold- and Silver-Thread Monopolies, 1611-21', *Jnl of Economic and Business History*, 3, 1930–1, p. 382ff; also G. Unwin, *The Gilds and Companies of London*, pp. 316–7
30 L. A. Clarkson, 'The Organization of the English Leather Industry in the Late Sixteenth and Seventeenth Centuries', *Econ. Hist. Rev.*, 2nd ser. 13, 1960-1, p. 245ff

12 DRAINING THE FENS (pages 249–267)

1 Above, p. 142
2 *Cal. S.P.D. Addenda 1547-65*, pp. 538–9; G. N. Clark, *The Wealth of England*, 1946, p. 44. Plumstead Marsh seems to have been harder to reclaim than Erith, and a whole series of Acts of Parliament were required, authorizing additional works, the last enacted as late as the 27th year of the Queen's reign: A. L. Rowse, *The England of Elizabeth*, p. 68
3 W. Dugdale, *The History of Imbanking and Draining of Divers Fens and Marshes ...*, 1662, p. 375ff
4 43 Eliz. I, c. 11
5 L. E. Harris, *Vermuyden and the Fens*, 1953, p. 23. Bradley had some experience as an engineer. He drained marshes in France, improved the navigation of the River Neckar in Germany, and made siege-works in various places: see G. N. Clark, *The Seventeenth Century*, 1929, p. 18 and footnote
6 W. Dugdale, *op cit.*, p. 205
7 *Cal. S.P.D. 1603-10*, p. 300
8 W. Dugdale, *op. cit.*, pp. 383–4; W. Elstobb, *An Historical Account of the Great Level of the Fens called Bedford Level ...*, 1793, pp. 164–7
9 H. C. Darby, *The Draining of the Fens*, 2nd ed. 1956, p. 32
10 L. E. Harris, *op. cit.*, p. 27
11 J. Nichols, *The Progresses, Processions and Magnificent Festivities of King James the First*, 1828, p. 94
12 C. Wilson, *England's Apprenticeship*, 1965, pp. 30, 103
13 Acts P.C. July 1619-June 1621, pp. 15, 27, 84, 250; *Cal. S.P.D. 1619-23*, pp. 80, 120, 141, 193
14 L. E. Harris, *op. cit.*, pp. 28–32
15 *Cal. S.P.D. 1619-23*, p. 486
16 *ibid.*, p. 475; Acts P.C. July 1621-May 1623, p. 377

x

17 L. E. Harris, op. cit., pp. 41–2
18 Some of them formed a settlement of their own, at Santoft in the parish of Belton, where they had their own church and minister, much to the scandal of the Archbishop of York: G. Stovin, 'A Brief Account of the Drainage of the Levells of Hatfield Chase...' (1752), Yorks. Archaeol. Jnl, 37, 1948–51, p. 385ff; W. Dugdale, op. cit., p. 145; S. R. Gardiner, History of England 1603-1642, viii, p. 294
19 J. Korthals-Altes, Sir Cornelius Vermuyden, 1925, is almost entirely concerned with the Hatfield Chase enterprise, and in its appendixes reproduces a number of original documents
20 Cal. S.P.D. 1628-9, pp. 262, 338, 366
21 W. Dugdale, op. cit., pp. 146–9
22 Cal. S.P.D. 1638-9, p. 499; 1639-40, p. 427; G. Stovin, op. cit., p. 386; L. E. Harris, op. cit., p. 51
23 L. Stone, The Crisis of the Aristocracy, p. 355
24 M. Albright, 'The Entrepreneurs of Fen Draining in England under James I and Charles I...', Explorations in Entrepreneurial History, 8, 1955, p. 56
25 ibid., p. 60
26 L. E. Harris, op. cit., pp. 60–3
27 For details see Gladys Scott Thomson, Family Background, 1949, pp. 161–71
28 H. C. Darby, op. cit., p. 40. Details of the Lynn Law and the Indenture may also be found in most of the other works on draining the Fens
29 L. Stone, op. cit., p. 355
30 W. R. Scott, The Constitution and Finance of ... Joint Stock Companies, 1912, ii, pp. 354-5. Scott pointed out that the actual cost to the shareholders would be more than £1, for 12,000 acres were to be given to the King. He calculated that the shareholders would have to pay nearly 22s. 6d. an acre, but he seems to have forgotten that 40,000 acres were to be earmarked for future maintenance, and only 43,000 acres were left for the shareholders' own profit. The real cost to them must therefore have been considerably more
31 L. E. Harris, op. cit., p. 66
32 Vermuyden adhered to this view in the Discourse he composed to explain and justify his plans. This was published in 1642, and was reprinted in S. Wells, The History of the Drainage of the Great Level of the Fens, called Bedford Level, 1830, appendix
33 S. R. Gardiner, History of England 1603-1642, viii, p. 296
34 H. C. Darby, op. cit., p. 59; L. E. Harris, op. cit., p. 69
35 S. R. Gardiner, op. cit., viii, p. 299

36 *ibid.*, p. 298
37 *ibid.*, p. 297 and footnote. For the disturbances near Ely in June 1638, see the report sent by local J.P.s to the Privy Council, *Cal. S.P.D.* 1637-8, p. 503
38 W. Dugdale, *op. cit.*, p. 415
39 W. Elstobb, *op. cit.*, p. 203
40 e.g. by S. Wells, *op. cit.*, p. 161. The charge was repeated by Samuel Smiles in his account of Vermuyden in *Lives of the Engineers*, and by other writers in the nineteenth century, including S. R. Gardiner
41 L. E. Harris, *op. cit.*, p. 125; C. Singer *et al.* (ed.), *A History of Technology*, iii, 1957, pp. 315-21
42 L. E. Harris, *op. cit.*, p. 151. The date 1683 given in the *D.N.B.* appears to be an error due to a mistake in identity
43 H.M.C. Salisbury, i, 119
44 W. R. Scott, *op. cit.*, ii, p. 357; L. Stone, *op. cit.*, p. 356; M. Albright, *op. cit.*, p. 59, C. Wilson, *England's Apprenticeship*, p. 105
45 H. C. Darby, *op. cit.*, pp. 48, 62
46 *Cal. S.P.D.* 1635, p. 50
47 H. C. Darby, *op. cit.*, p. 46; W. Cunningham, *The Growth of English Industry and Commerce*, 3rd ed. 1903, II, i, p. 116
48 M. Albright, *op. cit.*, p. 58. On p. 62 a table gives details of acreage and expenditure for the principal drainage enterprises up to 1640
49 W. R. Scott, *op. cit.*, ii, p. 356
50 L. E. Harris, *op. cit.*, p. 16; C. Wilson, *op. cit.*, p. 31

13 LAND AND WATER (pages 268-284)

1 L. Stone, *The Crisis of the Aristocracy*, pp. 297-8; P. J. Bowden, *The Wool Trade in Tudor and Stuart England*, p. 6
2 M. E. Finch, *The Wealth of Five Northamptonshire Families, 1540-1640* (Northants Record Soc., 1956), pp. 4-31. Two of John Isham's account books have been published (ed. G. D. Ramsay, Northants Record Soc., 1962)
3 *ibid.*, p. 40ff
4 L. Stone, *op. cit.*, p. 299; H.M.C. Cal. Shrewsbury and Talbot Papers, i, p. x.
5 M. E. Finch, *op. cit.*, p. 66ff; A. L. Rowse, *The England of Elizabeth*, pp. 457-60
6 L. Stone, *op. cit.*, pp. 299, 332
7 M. E. Finch, *op. cit.*, p. 135ff
8 L. Stone, *op. cit.*, pp. 300, 303. As Professor Stone remarks, 'Given the prevailing economic conditions this change may well have pro-

duced the optimum financial return, but it certainly had important social consequences'

9   In the following paragraphs I am indebted to L. Stone, *op. cit.*, p. 357ff

10 N. G. Brett-James, *The Growth of Stuart London*, 1935, pp. 115, 400

11 G. Scott Thomson, *The Russells in Bloomsbury*, 1940, pp. 13–18; also pp. 24–33 for the Earl of Southampton's building there

12 L. Stone, 'Inigo Jones and the New Exchange', *Archaeol. Jnl*, 114, for 1957, 1959, pp. 106–21

13 *Cal. S.P.D.* 1639, pp. 110, 347

14 L. Stone, *The Crisis of the Aristocracy*, p. 361. He also cites other noblemen who followed the example of these 'giants' among London entrepreneurs

15 S. Smiles, *Lives of the Engineers*, 2nd ed. 1874, i, pp. 120-1

16 C. Singer *et al.*, *History of Technology*, iii, p. 451

17 21 James I, c. 32

18 T. S. Willan, *River Navigation in England, 1600-1750*, 1936, pp. 25–6

19 *Cal. S.P.D.* 1635, p. 524; 1635-6, pp. 209, 255, 270, 386, 434; 1636-7, pp. 119, 323; 1637-8, pp. 26, 323; T. S. Willan, *op. cit.*, pp. 27–8

20 T. S. Willan, 'The River Navigation and Trade of the Severn Valley, 1600-1750', *Econ. Hist. Rev.*, 8 ,1937-8, p. 70

21 *Cal. S.P.D.* 1635-6, pp. 280, 522–3; 1636-7, pp. 203, 351, 357, 372, 377; Rymer, *Foedera*, xx, p. 6

22 T. Habington, *A Survey of Worcestershire*, ii, (ed. J. Amphlett, Worcs. Hist. Soc., 1899), pp. 468–9

23 R. Davis, *The Rise of the English Shipping Industry*, 1962, pp. 1–3, 54–6

24 H.M.C. Cal. Shrewsbury and Talbot Papers, i, pp. x, 45, 55, 56

25 L. Stone, *The Crisis of the Aristocracy*, p. 364. As Professor Stone points out (p. 357), aristocratic investment in shipping was not a new phenomenon. In the late fifteenth century Warwick the Kingmaker owned about 10 ships, and several other medieval noblemen were ship-owners

26 A. L. Rowse, *The Expansion of Elizabethan England*, 1955, p. 296

27 See the essay on him by A. H. Dodd in *Elizabethan Government and Society* (ed. S. T. Bindoff *et al.*, 1961)

28 G. C. Willliamson, *George, Third Earl of Cumberland*, 1920

29 Quoted *ibid.*, p. 282

30 *ibid.*, p. 274; L. Stone, *op. cit.*, pp. 364–5; A. L. Rowse, *The Expansion of Elizabethan England*, pp. 292–3, 295–6

31 W. F. Craven, 'The Earl of Warwick, a Speculator in Piracy',

Hispanic-American Hist. Review, 10, 1930, pp. 457–79; L. Stone, *op. cit.*, p. 367

32 Aristotle, *Politics*, I, viii, 1256a

33 See A. L. Rowse, *The Expansion of Elizabethan England*, pp. 86–7 and ch. iv

34 *ibid.*, ch. v and vi, and references there given. See also T. K. Rabb, *Enterprise and Empire*, 1968

14 CONCLUSION (pages 285–290)

1 Cf H. J. Perkin, 'The Social Causes of the British Industrial Revolution', *Trans. Royal Hist. Soc.*, 5th ser. 18, 1968, p. 123ff

2 N. S. B. Gras, 'What is Capitalism in the Light of History?', *Bulletin of the Business Historical Soc.*, 21, 1947, pp. 79–120, at p. 118

3 *ibid.*, pp. 95–6; also 'Capitalism—Concepts and History', *Bulletin of the Business Hist. Soc.*, 16, 1942, pp. 21–52, at p. 28ff

4 *ibid*, pp. 22–3

5 *ibid.*, pp. 39–40 (discussion by Henrietta M. Larson)

6 L. Stone, 'The Nobility in Business', *The Entrepreneur*, p. 14

7 *ibid.*, p. 20

8 Cf above, p. 23

9 I quote some of C. S. Orwin's comments on the value of the work, frequently criticized if not ridiculed, of John and Frederic Knight, who created a thriving agricultural community out of an area of waste land: *The Reclamation of Exmoor Forest*, 1929, pp. 14–15, 163

Index of persons

Abergavenny (Bergavenny), Lord,
 see Neville
Abraham the Tinner, 129
Acontius (Aconcio), 249, 292
Agricola (Bauer), G., 14, 15, 116,
 139–40, 160, 168, 305
Anderson, Sir F., 72
Anderson, H., 60, 63
Anderson, R., 200
Appell, P., 213
Arnold, J., 212
Ashburnham, Sir J., 70–1, 76, 298
Atherton, J., 183
Atkinson, S., 151, 153, 156
Aubrey, J., 172, 174, 234, 240
Aylotte, Sir W., 253, 258–9

Babington family, 134
Bacon, Sir F., Lord Verulam, 52,
 98, 167–9, 172–4, 246–7, 305
Bago, J., 225
Bainbridge, R., 97
Ballentine, R., 148
Balmerino, Lord, see Elphinstone
Barnes, Bp. R., 60
Baroncelli, T., 198
Bartholomew, J., 141–2
Bartlett, Sir T., 241–4
Basbie (Barksby), W., 165
Baynton, Sir E., 39, 42
Beaumont, F., 67
Beaumont, Sir H., 71
Beaumont, Huntingdon, 67–72
Beaumont, N., 64, 67
Beaumont, Sir T., 67, 71
Becku (Dolyn), A., 210–1, 214
Bedford, Earls of, see Russell
Bennett, W., 247
Bertie, R., 1st Earl of Lindsey, 265–7

Bertye, F., 198–9
'Bess of Hardwick', Countess of
 Shrewsbury, 134, 136
Bingley, Sir R., 220
Blanket, T., 43
Blount, J., 6th Lord Mountjoy, 112,
 177–81, 235
Bludder, Sir T., 132
Blundell, P., 44
Bongar, I., 212, 222–4, 226
Bongar, J. and P., 212
Bourchier, Sir J., 183–5, 193, 195
Bowde (Budde), J., 80–2
Bowes, G., 154–5, 304
Bowes, Sir J., 215, 217–8, 221–2
Bowes, R., 200, 202–3
Box, G., 101
Bradley, H., 250, 311
Bridges, G., 90
Briet, P., 209, 211, 213
Bristow, F., 225
Brocklesby, P., 121
Brode, J., 119–21
Bronkhorst, N., 149
Brooke, Sir B., 90–2
Brooke, Sir J., 192–3
Brudenell family, 270
Buckholt, Capt., 199
Buckhurst, Lord, see Sackville
Buckingham, Duke of, see Villiers
Bulmer, Sir B., 101–2, 132, 146,
 149–57, 165, 167, 175
Burchard, see Kranich
Burghley, Lord, see Cecil
Bushell, T., 146, 165, 167–75, 305
Byron, Sir J., 66–8

Caesar, Sir J., 121, 150
Carew, R., 124–6, 161

316

Index of places